MODES OF FAITH

MODES OF FAITH

Secular Surrogates for Lost Religious Belief

THEODORE ZIOLKOWSKI

THE UNIVERSITY OF CHICAGO PRESS

CHICAGO AND LONDON

THEODORE ZIOLKOWSKI is the Class of 1900 Professor of Modern Languages and professor of German and comparative literature emeritus at Princeton University.

The University of Chicago Press, Chicago 60637
The University of Chicago Press, Ltd., London
© 2007 by The University of Chicago
All rights reserved. Published 2007
Printed in the United States of America

16 15 14 13 12 11 10 09 08 07   1 2 3 4 5

ISBN-13: 978-0-226-98363-9 (cloth)
ISBN-10: 0-226-98363-3 (cloth)

Library of Congress Cataloging-in-Publication Data

Ziolkowski, Theodore.
    Modes of faith : secular surrogates for lost religious belief / Theodore Ziolkowski.
        p. cm.
    Includes bibliographical references and index.
    ISBN-13: 978-0-226-98363-9 (cloth : alk. paper)
    ISBN-10: 0-226-98363-3 (cloth : alk. paper)
        1. Implicit religion—Europe—History—20th century.   2. Religion and literature—Europe—History—20th century.   3. Secularism—Europe—History—20th century. 4. Secularism in literature.   5. European literature—20th century—History and criticism.   6. Europe—Religion—20th century.   I. Title.
    BL98.7.Z55 2007
    306.6—dc22

                                                                            2006039645

⊗ The paper used in this publication meets the minimum requirements of the American National Standard for Information Sciences—Permanence of Paper for Printed Library Materials, ANSI Z39.48-1992.

TO MY COUSINS IN KRUSZWICA, POLAND

Anna and Malgorzata Konik

WHOSE FAITH SUSTAINED THEM

For Modes of Faith let graceless zealots fight;
His can't be wrong whose life is in the right.

ALEXANDER POPE, *An Essay on Man*

CONTENTS

Can any thoughtful person at the beginning of the twenty-first century, believer or not, doubt that religious faith constitutes a powerful and often fateful force in the affairs of our modern, widely secularized world? As I draft these lines, the news carries reports of violent conflicts between Shiites and Sunnis in Iraq, between Hindus and Muslims in India, between Coptic Christians and Muslims in Egypt, and between Palestinians and Israelis in Gaza. Recent weeks saw huge demonstrations in the Middle East protesting cartoons published in a Danish newspaper that were believed to denigrate Mohammed and Islamic faith. Less publicity accompanied the case reported a year earlier in the *New York Times* (29 March 2005) of a museum curator in Moscow convicted and fined for inciting religious hatred with an exhibition of paintings and sculptures that allegedly ridiculed the Russian Orthodox Church. At the same time the Vatican and the governments of several Catholic countries have expressed their dismay because the new constitution of the European Union omits any mention of the Christian heritage of their cultures.

The controversy is of course not restricted to Europe and the Middle East. The U.S. Supreme Court recently turned down an atheist's challenge to the words "under God" in the Pledge of Allegiance. Frequent protests mark the national debates over abortion, homosexuality, euthanasia, polygamy, the teaching of evolution, and other issues that bring religious beliefs into conflict with constitutional law. A computer game called "Civilization IV" (and hailed by *Time* in 2005 as a Top Pick) challenges the players to convert their neighbors or to destroy them in crusading wars. According to the *New York Times* (21 June 2004), religion is a more accurate predictor of voting preferences in the United States than income, education, gender, or any other social or demographic factor except race.

The phenomenon has not failed to catch the eye of scholars here and abroad. In May 2005 the American Institute for Contemporary German Studies in Washington, D.C., sponsored a conference on the "God Gap" separating the United States and Germany. In the summer of that same year the Humboldt University in Berlin created an interdisciplinary research center on "Religion und Politik" charged with investigating the newly labile relationships between church and state in a globalized world. Religious faith matters, whether we like it or not. In a provocative book entitled *The God Gene* (2004) the geneticist Dean Hamer even argued that faith is hardwired into our genes.

Faith is of course not limited to religion. To believe in something—a deity, a nation, a race, art, sex, money, sports teams—appears to be a fundamental human need. Forty years ago, in his essay "Wells, Hitler, and the World State," George Orwell argued that "the energy that actually shapes the world springs from emotions—racial pride, leader-worship, religious belief, love of war—which liberal intellectuals mechanically write off as anachronisms." The emotions that Orwell cites do not necessarily coexist with religious belief. In what Pope Benedict XVI recently labeled the "aggressive secularism" of our age they often function as surrogates when religious faith has been lost—surrogates to which individuals transfer the psychic energy formerly reserved for religion and in which they seek the same gratifications, and often the same forms and rituals, as previously afforded by religion.

Conflicts of faith have occupied my thoughts and imagination for many years and provided a significant theme in several of my books since *Fictional Transfigurations of Jesus* (1972). *The Mirror of Justice* (1997) focused on legal crises arising specifically from the conflict between systems of belief as reflected in literary works from antiquity to the present. *The Sin of Knowledge* (2000) considered three archetypal myths—Adam, Prometheus, Faust—in which religious faith is challenged by knowledge. *Hesitant Heroes* (2004) traced literary heroes from Orestes and Aeneas by way of the medieval Parzival to Hamlet and beyond, whose crucial moment of hesitation exposes a clash between the existing value system and an emerging one.

Issues and interests of this sort prompted me, finally and almost inevitably, to explore the crisis of faith that shook Europe in the decades before and after World War I and the responses that crisis elicited as individuals sought surrogates to fill the spiritual emptiness in their minds and souls. This modern crisis differed appreciably from earlier ones inasmuch as the prevailing religious faith was threatened not by a single new one—monotheism in antiquity, the Reformation in the late Middle Ages,

the Enlightenment in early modern centuries—but by a congeries of possibilities: Marxism, modern science, Nietzschean ideas, and critical theology
among others. These reflections gained relevance and poignancy for me from
the fact that, according to many reports and surveys, society in the United
States at the turn of the millennium is experiencing a crisis of faith remarkably similar to the one that tormented European minds a century ago—and
often responding to it in astonishingly similar ways.

I have singled out five "modes of faith" that were particularly conspicuous in the first third of the twentieth century: art for art's sake, the flight
to India, socialism, myth, and utopian vision. These five surrogates are not
exhaustive, but they are representative to the extent that they attracted to
their ranks many of the most thoughtful minds of the twentieth century. I
have emphasized the literary reflections of these crises because poets and
writers have dealt sensitively, articulately, and vividly with individual cases
rather than with sociological or theoretical generalities.

Since "faith" and its loss or recovery are essentially individual and private matters, the biographical documentation demanded my attention in
every case. A pattern emerged showing that the loss of faith was triggered in
most cases by a trivial childhood incident, and that initial doubt was then
broadened and channeled by subsequent intellectual experiences. I have focused on late nineteenth-century childhoods, but the pattern is a timeless
one, extending back to Augustine's *Confessions*. Most of the chapters required historical contextualization because the "modes of faith" did not
always spring into existence for the first time in the twentieth century but
were adapted by individuals to suit their circumstances. In some cases—
notably "myth" and "utopia"—it seemed useful to explore the intellectual
background informing the literary responses because those surrogates have
often engaged some of the most provocative and imaginative minds of our
century, philosophical as well as literary. Because these "modes of faith" are
perennial and not time-bound I also sought, whenever it seemed relevant,
to trace their survival into our own time. Since my primary interest in this
book revolves around intellectual and cultural history, I have emphasized
those substantive aspects of the works covered, and not their purely literary
value.

Needless to say, I have made grateful use of the vast secondary literature surrounding the thirty-odd writers here discussed as well as the major
rubrics under which I have included them. To emphasize the fact that the
loss of religious faith and the turn to surrogates was a general European
phenomenon, and not limited to a single national culture, I have chosen

examples from several literatures—principally English, German, and French, but also Italian and Russian. In most cases I chose to make my own translations in order to bring out most clearly the thematic connections evident in the language. Elsewhere I have used existing translations, taking the liberty, as indicated from case to case, of modifying them for consistency.

⦿

I am enormously indebted to the Andrew W. Mellon Foundation for its generous support of this project since its inception. Thanks to a Mellon Emeritus Fellowship I have been able to carry out my research extensively in Europe as well as in libraries here in the United States. The Princeton University Library with its resourceful staff—in Reference, in Rare Books, in Interlibrary Loan, and elsewhere—has afforded me for some forty years ideal circumstances for scholarly research. For several years I have also spent many pleasant and profitable weeks annually in the majestic premises of the Staatsbibliothek zu Berlin, Unter den Linden.

Alan G. Thomas of the University of Chicago Press shepherded my manuscript through the editorial process with professional skill and personal encouragement. I am especially grateful to him for his initiative in finding two readers whose thoughtful responses and insightful comments contributed significantly to the sharpening of my argument at several points. My manuscript benefited especially from Susan Tarcov's meticulous and sensitive editorial eye.

On this occasion I would like to remember with affection and admiration Alfred Owen Aldridge, a distinguished scholar of comparative literature, in whose stimulating seminar on eighteenth-century English poetry over fifty years ago at Duke University I first read the great poem from which I have borrowed my title.

Finally, I want once again to thank my family—my wife, Yetta; my daughter, my two sons, and their spouses; and my seven grandchildren: a truly ecumenical family in which several religions are practiced and *all* faiths are respected and studied—for their constant inspiration, help, and support.

Theodore Ziolkowski
Princeton, New Jersey

PART ONE

The Decline of Faith

The sea of faith
Was once, too, at the full, and round earth's shore
Lay like the folds of a bright girdle furl'd.
But now I only hear
Its melancholy, long, withdrawing roar,
Retreating to the breath
Of the night-wind down the vast edges drear
And naked shingles of the world.
—Matthew Arnold, "Dover Beach"

CHAPTER ONE

Introduction

A lexander Pope, that sly skeptic, understood that "graceless zealots" have always fought over the modes of faith. The history of Western civilization amounts in a significant sense to a catalog of epochs in which the breakdown of traditional systems of belief opened the way for more or less violent conflicts among competing value systems—conflicts that in an inevitable dialectic generated the emergence of a new dominant faith and, often, the concomitant production of cultural monuments commemorating these epochs. Several of the most notable texts of Greek literature—for instance, Aeschylus's *Oresteia* and Sophocles' *Antigone*—document the crucial moment in preclassical Greece when cultic religion began to give way to civil law.[1] Orestes is torn between the primitive culture of blood vengeance and the emerging polity of law and justice, while Antigone upholds the values of an archaic matriarchal cult of the dead against the injunctions of Creon's progressive secular state.

In the first centuries of the Common Era until the establishment of the New Testament canon and the Christianization of the Roman Empire, one appeal of Christianity was the novelty of its simple faith. Before the late first century CE, the terms *pistis* and *fides* had for the Roman mind no association with belief in gods and conveyed no meaning beyond the legalistic notion of reliability in keeping oaths.[2] Romans had long been accustomed to a religion of ritual without doctrine, of knowledge rather than faith, of orthopraxy instead of orthodoxy.[3] Their polytheistic religion invoked the principle known as *evocatio* to incorporate ever more new gods as the empire's borders expanded, thereby accelerating the diffusion of any primal religious sense. Conversely, their satisfaction with polytheism inspired substantial Roman opposition to the Judeo-Christian idea of monotheism, as in the anti-Jewish critiques of Juvenal and the anti-Christian polemics of

Celsus.[4] Meanwhile considerable dispute arose among the early Christian sects before something resembling a unified church emerged following the Council of Nicaea in 325.[5] Moreover, it is increasingly recognized by scholars that there were many continuities as well as a notable reciprocity of influence between paganism and Christianity on various points of ideology, such as resurrection.[6] Yet the desire for faith ultimately prevailed, laying the spiritual foundation for the works of Saint Augustine and other documents of early Christianity that established the doctrines of the new belief. This is the situation and the process outlined by Hegel in the penultimate chapter of his *Phenomenology of Spirit* ("Revealed Religion"), which posits the exhaustion of Roman Stoicism as the necessary precondition for the rise of Christianity.

The High Middle Ages witnessed an ongoing struggle for power between popes and emperors, a struggle epitomized in the spiritual turmoil of the eponymous hero in Wolfram von Eschenbach's verse epic *Parzival*, who as a naive youth is confused by the conflicting values of religion and knighthood.[7] The friction between the church and secular culture in the late Middle Ages generated much of the intellectual and cultural energy that precipitated the Reformation and informed the Renaissance. In the eighteenth century a bland orthodox Christianity, challenged by the extremes of rationalist skepticism and Pietism's spiritual intensity, brought forth Voltaire and Kant on the one hand and German Romanticism on the other.

The erosion of Christian faith accelerated in the course of the nineteenth century as the Creation narrative was undermined by spectacular findings in geology and by Darwin's biological reordering of the descent of man, as the Higher Criticism of the Bible and its startling historical and anthropological discoveries qualified the understanding of Jesus and early Christianity, and as the social criticism of such radically different thinkers as Karl Marx and Friedrich Nietzsche tore at the ideological roots of Christianity.[8] The resulting growth of secularism—a term coined in 1851 by the English atheist George Holyoke as a designation for the belief that religion should play no role in the temporal affairs of the state—reached a peak in 1914.[9] By 1922 the perceptive social critic Siegfried Kracauer was able to identify what he termed a generation in waiting: "They are suffering to the core from their expulsion from the religious sphere, from the enormous alienation prevailing between their spirit and the absolute. They have lost faith, indeed almost the capacity for faith, and the religious truths have become for them colorless thoughts which they are capable only of thinking."[10]

The tensions that these issues raised, most bitterly perhaps within families, produced a conspicuous surge of autobiographies and autobiographical novels revolving around the crisis of faith as experienced by thoughtful individuals from England across Europe to Russia. Successive waves of literary works in the years up to and following World War I recorded the responses, the modes of secular faith, that individuals sought to replace the religious faith that had been challenged and often destroyed by the nineteenth century.

The first wave bore individuals inward, to aesthetic realms they discovered within themselves, and outward, on a flight to find new faiths in exotic places. But the cataclysm of 1914 forced many thoughtful people to the realization that the leisure and liberty that supported or tolerated their aesthetic realms and exotic flights had depended heavily on the traditional forms and values that had been destroyed by World War I. They therefore turned from individual to sociopolitical collective modes of faith, such as socialism, myth, and utopia—initiatives that produced yet another wave of literary responses.

At the same time traditional Christianity, whose inability to prevent the ravages of politics and war had been exposed anew, came under fresh attack from other quarters. Among the most obvious examples of the new threat to faith were the Russian Revolution, which disestablished the Orthodox Church and campaigned zealously against religion; the pronounced secularist tendency among many Zionists; the movement toward modernization in Turkey and other Muslim lands; explicit programs of radical secularization in most European socialist parties; and the Scopes trial in the United States, in which the traditional biblical version of Creation was publicly challenged.

⋅⊱⊰⋅

The dilemma of the decade was persuasively analyzed by Sigmund Freud in his book with the provocative title *The Future of an Illusion* (*Die Zukunft einer Illusion*, 1927). It is Freud's argument (chap. 3) that religion traditionally had a threefold task: to exorcize the terrors of nature; to reconcile men to the cruelty of fate; and to compensate humankind for the sufferings imposed by civilization—tasks more than adequately appropriated in the twentieth century by science and human reason. Religion's claim to belief is based on tradition, on proofs handed down from antiquity, and on the prohibition of questioning their validity (chap. 5). Freud maintains that these beliefs are illusions, grounded on teachings and not on experience or thought; they represent no more than fulfillments of humankind's own desires (chap. 6). It would be nice, Freud concedes, if there were a God who created the world and a moral order governing the universe; but this belief is only a consolatory wish-dream. It is time to replace religious faith with convictions stemming

from the operation of the intellect and to find rational grounds for the pre-
cepts of civilization (chap. 8). Freud's rhetorical antagonist objects that if
religion is expelled from European civilization, it will simply be replaced
by another system of doctrines, which would take on all the psychological
characteristics of religion: sanctimoniousness, rigidity of form and belief,
and intolerance of free thought (chap. 10). Freud agrees that it is difficult
to avoid illusions: humankind requires faith in some form. But unlike religious *delusions*, the illusions produced by reason and intellect are capable
of constant correction. If the delusions of religion are discredited, the world
of the believer collapses and nothing is left but despair. But science, being
modified by ever new understanding, is not a delusion and provides a firmer
basis for modern civilization than does religion.

   Freud and the very real challenges he defined and exemplified provoked
a powerful counterreaction: a worldwide upsurge of fundamentalism in the
1920s, when the term "fundamentalism" in its current sense was coined by
conservative Protestants in the United States.[11] A wave of conversions to
Catholicism among European intellectuals engulfed England and the continent. Others were attracted to the radically antidemocratic and antimodern
Traditionalism proposed by the charismatic René Guénon, who argued in
several influential works that "the crisis of the modern world" could be
averted, at least in the Occident, only by an "élite intellectuelle" recovering the "traditional spirit" and true "universality" of the pre-Reformation
Catholic Church.[12] About the same time such conservative groups as
the Muslim Brotherhood in Egypt were formed, along with the Rashtriya
Savayamsevak Sangh in India and similar movements elsewhere. The literature of the 1920s again fulfilled its traditional role by incorporating and
reflecting the spirit of the times, its turn to mysticism, its (re)conversions,
and its search for new modes of religious faith.

〜∞〜

Many observers would say that our society today in the United States is
undergoing a spiritual crisis and transition similar to that of the 1920s, as
the growing interest in Islam, Buddhism, Zen, Kabbala, Gnosticism, Scien-
tology, Wicca, and a well-nigh unsurveyable congeries of neopagan and New
Age fads challenges traditional Christian beliefs and calls forth in response
a new fundamentalism. The recent revival of interest in the apocryphal
gospels of early Christianity can in no small measure be attributed to the
search for faith or, at least, a reaffirmation of faith.[13]
   The situation in the United States differs conspicuously from that in

Western Europe. According to a Gallup survey of spirituality in the early twenty-first century, 96 percent of Americans believe in God or a universal spirit. The authors of the survey conclude that "the United States is unique in that it has one of the highest levels of formal education in the world, and at the same time, one of the highest levels of religious faith."[14] The statistical generalization is borne out by the spectacular attraction of Mel Gibson's 2004 film *The Passion of the Christ* or the apocalyptic novels of Tim LaHaye and Jerry Jenkins in their series "Left Behind," which sell rampantly in the Bible Belt and elsewhere.

The U.S. figures contrast sharply with those of a Gallup Millennium Survey of religious attitudes around the world, according to which a growing secularism prevails among contemporary Europeans. Roughly half of the Scandinavians surveyed said that God did not matter to them.[15] In 2003, a scandal was aroused in Denmark by a popular Lutheran minister who asserted that he did not believe in a physical God, in the afterlife, in the resurrection, or in the Virgin Mary.[16] In June of that same year, at the convention to draft a constitution for the European Union, the most hotly debated topic dividing its members concerned religion. Should God or Christianity be cited among the sources of the values constituting the common European culture and heritage?[17] The preamble approved by the majority contented itself with vague and inoffensive references to "the cultural, religious, and humanist inheritance of Europe," prompting a prominent constitutional lawyer to speak of a current European "Christophobia."[18] In 2004 a cover story in the *New Statesman* opened with the assertion that "Europe is a godless quarter of the globe and Britain the most atheistic part of it," even though "the government is anxious to keep God onside" and "religion is also a baleful presence in education."[19]

In France, according to recent polls, only 13 percent of the population considers a belief in God necessary to morality.[20] The official government policy of a self-consciously secular state antagonized many citizens by prohibiting the wearing of any explicitly religious apparel in public schools— Muslim veils, Jewish yarmulkes, or conspicuous Catholic crosses. "Religion is frightening," began a front-page article on the 2003 Church Congress in the German newspaper *Die Zeit*, "—at least to nonbelievers and those of other beliefs, to the TV viewers, to enlightened Europe." In a country where Muslim head scarves arouse nervousness, the piece continues, "religion has again raised its head in the midst of modernity, and the visage that it displays is grim and threatening." A land where Christianity is little more than "a museum with associated charitable functions" lacks all understanding for such spiritual phenomena as American piety, Turkish fundamentalism, and militant Israeli policies.[21] When the newly elected Pope Benedict XVI visited his native Germany in the summer of 2005 the newsweekly *Spiegel* headed its cover story "Return to an Unchristian Land."[22] And yet, as the story in the *New Statesman* observed, "In one of the world's most secular societies, ministers tremble at an archbishop's words and give clergy a hand in forming policy" (18), and the leaders of secular states flock to Rome to confer with the pope, to receive his benediction, and to be photographed with him for the newspapers back home.

If issues of faith are once again à la mode—the debate in the United States over school prayer and abortion, or in Muslim countries the rise of radical movements such as Al Qaeda and the Taliban—the roots of the debate can be traced back at least for a century, and its offshoots have sprouted again at the beginning of the twenty-first century. Freud recognized that humankind requires some sort of sustaining faith or "illusions." The same fundamental human need has been acknowledged by thinkers across the centuries. The generations that lived prior to Christianity, when religion was based on ritual and not belief, had their own modes of "faith." Believers in the various non-Christian religions around the contemporary world share different "faiths" that may or may not have anything in common with Christian values. Max Weber observed in 1915 that there are many possibilities of faith, but inevitably they constitute "a response to something in the real world that is felt to be specifically 'meaningless'" and hence implicitly a demand "that the world order [*Weltgefüge*] in its totality be somehow a meaningful 'cosmos.'"[23] As T. S. Eliot phrased it more cogently in *Four Quartets* (1943), "human kind / Cannot bear very much reality."[24]

If the preceding analysis is valid, then our contemporary age of spiritual crisis—of conflict between faith and unbelief, of strife between fundamentalism and secularism, of the search for nontraditional sustaining values—would do well to contemplate the period that marked the starting point for our situation today, to analyze the various modes through which those predecessors responded to their loss of faith, and to ponder the shift through which some of them regained some sort of faith that could be called religious. As was the case in Greek antiquity, in early Christianity, in the Middle Ages, the Renaissance, and the Age of Enlightenment, the situation of decline and loss followed by the search for a new faith produced as testimony and reflection of the process a wave of often outstanding and always revealing literary documents. Whether we look back as believers seeking to counter nonreligious modes of faith or as skeptics considering alternatives to religious belief, the comparison can be illuminating. What will turn out to be the "modes of faith" in the twenty-first century?

CHAPTER TWO

The Melancholy, Long, Withdrawing Roar

Matthew Arnold heard the signals. Writing "Dover Beach" (from *New Poems*, 1867) in the decade following the publication of *On the Origin of Species* (1859), he lamented the ebbing of the tide of Christian faith by which, for all his reverence of Greek antiquity and his affection for such great nonbelievers as Goethe and Heine, he remained consoled until his death in 1888. But some of his younger contemporaries reacted differently.

The bleak vision of James Thomson's masterpiece *The City of Dreadful Night* (1874), which according to Edmund Blunden "after fifty years retains its dark splendour" and may be "the most anticipative poem of his time," amounts to a cry of despair in twenty-one cantos for faith lost.[1] It may be true that Thomson, despite the alcoholism that finally destroyed him, was by temperament a genial, charming, and often merry man.[2] Certainly his religious doubts emerged in stages, graduating from a traditional Christian upbringing through theism to atheism and the furious war on Christianity that he waged in a series of biting essays published principally in Charles Bradlaugh's *National Reformer*.[3] By 1870, when he wrote the first sections of *The City of Dreadful Night*, his loss of faith was absolute and militant. Why does he "evoke the spectres of black night" and "disinter dead faith from mouldering hidden?" he asks in the proem.

> Because a cold rage seizes one at whiles
> To show the bitter old and wrinkled truth
> Stripped naked of all vesture that beguiles,
> False dreams, false hopes, false masks and modes of youth;
> Because it gives some sense of power and passion
> In helpless impotence to try to fashion
> Our woe in living words howe'er uncouth.

9

Thomson's City is dominated by the image of Dürer's Melencholia, who sits "stupendous, superhuman," gazing forth "in bronze sublimity" over subjects ruled by "renewed assurance / And confirmation of the old despair" (section 21). "There is no God," he exclaims (section 16).

> I find no hint throughout the Universe
> Of good or ill, of blessing or of curse;
> I find alone Necessity Supreme.
> (section 14)

As is often the case, the poets were among the first to sense the mood of the age. The nineteenth-century loss of faith finds its earliest literary expression, whether elegiacally or mordantly, in such poems of the late 1860s and 1870s as those by Arnold and Thomson. A decade later the same spirit shows up on the stage, where cassocks and collars fall to the right and the left as clergymen come to feel that intellectual responsibility and social reform and all the other grand ideals of humanity are unattainable within conventional ecclesiastical structures. Henrik Ibsen's Johannes Rosmer (*Rosmersholm*, 1886), the scion of two centuries of Norwegian ministers, shocks his brother-in-law by proclaiming grandly toward the end of act 1 that he has "given up his faith." Turning to the "great world of truth and freedom" that has been revealed to him in a grand epiphany, he resolves to devote his life to "the creation of a true democracy." Similarly, Gerhart Hauptmann's Johannes Vockerat (*Lonely Lives*, 1891) dismays his pious parents by renouncing his promising career as a theologian in order to dedicate himself to his "philosophical" work. In these dramas the loss of faith is already a fait accompli. As in the earlier poems, we do not witness or experience the process of disenchantment by which the various speakers or protagonists are led from faith through doubt to disbelief. That task is left for the more analytical fictions that began to appear in the first years of the new century.

The Contest of Faith and Reason

The intellectual history of the nineteenth century is in one sense a chronicle of the steadily intensifying contest of faith and reason—a process registered in such contemporary accounts as John W. Draper's *The Conflict between Science and Religion* (1874) and Andrew Dickson White's classic *History of the Warfare of Science with Theology in Christendom* (1896). At the fin de siècle Ernst Haeckel, in his enormously popular theory of a world unified by a "monistic" philosophy based on Darwin, proclaimed that "one of the most distinctive features of the expiring century is the increasing vehemence of the opposition between science and Christianity"⁴—a view seconded by his English translator, who added that later ages will probably regard the conflict of theology with philosophy and science as "the most salient feature of the nineteenth century" (xi).

The assault on traditional Christian beliefs came in waves and from various quarters. The Old Testament version of the Creation, which Archbishop James Ussher had confidently and authoritatively dated to the year 4004 BCE, was undermined by a series of geological findings beginning in the late eighteenth century with the dispute between the Neptunists and the Vulcanists—that is, whether the formation of the earth's crust was aqueous or igneous, whether it was gradual or cataclysmic.⁵ By the mid-nineteenth century, responsible scientists had almost without exception abandoned their belief in the Mosaic account of Creation, including notably the biblical flood. The conspicuous exception was Philip Gosse (the father of Edmund Gosse, to whom we shall return), an otherwise distinguished zoologist who with his book *Omphalos* (1857) left the solid terrain of his discipline in the futile attempt to reconcile science with his fundamentalist Christian beliefs.

While the biblical story of the Creation was being challenged by geology, scholars in the new field of comparative philology undermined the theologically based theories of language: that Hebrew was the original language in which God spoke to man, that the names of all created things (except fishes) were bestowed by Adam, that the divergence of languages stems from the Tower of Babel. August Wilhelm Schlegel and Friedrich Schlegel's recognition of the antiquity of Sanskrit, Franz Bopp's establishment of the relationship among the Indo-European languages, Jacob Grimm's laws concerning the evolution of language, Wilhelm von Humboldt's fascination with such non-Indo-European languages as Basque and Malayan-Polynesian—these studies effectively put an end to the theory of language implicit in the Old Testament.⁶

At the same time, the more relaxed attitude toward religion and the Bible engendered by the Enlightenment produced a liberal view of Jesus among such thinkers as Voltaire and Thomas Paine, who regarded him as a great ethical teacher rather than as the divine Son of God.⁷ The first systematic criticism of the Gospels was the work of a professor of Oriental languages, Hermann Samuel Reimarus, who argued in daring studies (published posthumously, 1774–78) that Jesus was a Jewish nationalist who was executed for political reasons and whose death was redefined after the fact by his admirers as an act of spiritual self-sacrifice. Fictionalizing works by more adventuresome writers such as Karl Friedrich Bahrdt and Karl Heinrich

Venturini—works more akin to Gothic romances than to scholarly biographies—depicted Jesus as a member of a secret society resembling such
eighteenth-century associations as the Freemasons and Illuminati, which
trained him to carry out its mission. Meanwhile, scholars of the more academic school of "thoroughgoing rationalism" sought to find rational expla-
nations for the miracles reported in the New Testament. The Heidelberg
professor H. E. G. Paulus wrote a two-volume life of Jesus "as the basis of
a pure history of early Christianity" (*Das Leben Jesu als Grundlage einer
reinen Geschichte des Urchristentums*, 1828) which succeeded in explaining away every wonder in the Gospels except the Virgin birth.

These developments preluded one of the most brilliant intellectual accomplishments of the nineteenth century, David Friedrich Strauss's *Life of
Jesus* (*Das Leben Jesu*, 1835). Strauss, a lecturer at Tübingen and a Hegelian
by temperament and training, sought to synthesize the supernatural and the
rational approaches through a mythic interpretation of the Gospels. Rather
than accepting the miracles on faith or explaining them away by reason,
he argued that these elements were literary conventions added to accounts
of the life of Jesus by the authors of the Gospels, who wanted to make of
the historical individual a figure corresponding in every respect to the pre-
dictions of the prophets.

It is difficult to overemphasize the impact of Strauss's two volumes,
which George Eliot, at the suggestion of her freethinking friends, translated
into English (1846) and which the contributors to *Essays and Reviews* (1860)
incorporated into their controversial discussion of problems aroused by the
Higher Criticism. Strauss was the first scholar to distinguish systematically
between the Christ of faith and the Jesus of history, who can be reached only
by stripping away the "mythic" additives from the recorded life. Yet it was
not Strauss's work, exciting but intellectually demanding, that commanded
broad public attention, but Ernest Renan's *Life of Jesus* (*Vie de Jésus*, 1863),
a volume whose critical inadequacies are matched by its literary charm.

Destined for the priesthood, Renan left the seminary of St. Sulpice in
Paris in 1845, his faith corroded by German critical theology and by the
ideas of Paulus and Strauss to which he had been exposed. Following a
decade of further studies, in 1862 he assumed the professorship of Semitic
languages at the Collège de France, from which he was promptly removed
because of the unorthodox views advanced in his *Life of Jesus*. Based not
so much on rigorous scholarship as on his personal experiences in Syria,
Renan's work portrays an amiable young carpenter wandering through the
lovely Galilean countryside in the company of gentle fisherfolk and urging
upon his listeners a "délicieuse théologie d'amour." For all its theological

inadequacies, Renan's readable *Life* determined more than any other work of the nineteenth century the public image of Jesus as a man rather than a god—a Jesus of reason and history rather than a Christ of faith. In harmony with Renan, Matthew Arnold introduced the notion of the "sweet reasonableness" of a very human Jesus in a series of works beginning with *St. Paul and Protestantism* (1870).[8]

Already at mid-century, Arthur Schopenhauer observed in one of his *Parerga and Paralipomena* devoted to religion ("Über Religion," 1851) that "[i]n the nineteenth century we see Christianity significantly weakened, almost wholly deserted by serious faith, yes, already struggling for its very existence." "All in all," he concludes, "and undermined constantly by the sciences, Christianity is gradually moving toward its end."[9] In the second half of the century many fields of intellectual endeavor made advances that contributed directly or indirectly to undermine further any literal understanding of the Bible and that relativized the tenets of Christian faith. Charles Darwin's *On the Origin of Species* (1859), which flatly contradicted the biblical teachings on the creation of man, became a cause célèbre and ignited a controversy that has lasted into the twenty-first century. The field of anthropology produced results which, as summarized and elaborated by James George Frazer in *The Golden Bough* (1890), exposed many of the beliefs and practices of traditional Christianity as superstitions. "It is indeed a melancholy and in some respects thankless task," Frazer confessed in the author's introduction to the second edition (1900),

> to strike at the foundations of beliefs in which, as in a strong tower, the hopes and aspiration of humanity through long ages have sought a refuge from the storm and stress of life. Yet sooner or later it is inevitable that the battery of the comparative method should breach these venerable walls, mantled over with the ivy and mosses and wild flowers of a thousand tender and sacred associations.[10]

In *The Varieties of Religious Experience* (1902) William James analyzed the "faith-state" as a biological as well as a psychological condition and surveyed the various forms of its manifestations, which when carried to an extreme can even become pathological.[11] Max Weber concluded in his *Protestant Ethic and the Spirit of Capitalism* (*Die Protestantische Ethik und der Geist des Kapitalismus*, 1904) that the rationalized capitalism of 1900, especially in the United States, had been stripped of all religious and ethical meaning.[12] As capitalism grows increasingly rational and pragmatic, religious faith wanes in an inverse proportion.

There is no need to rehearse in detail the manifold reasons for "the melancholy, long, withdrawing roar" of religious faith, which include findings from fields ranging from astronomy and archaeology to world history and the history of medicine, and which have been thoroughly explored.[13] Not all believers lost their faith as a result of these various intellectual challenges from every direction: witness the case of Philip Gosse. Such representative documents as the perennially popular *Diary* of Robert Francis Kilvert (1840–79), a country curate, display not the slightest trace of spiritual doubt or, indeed, of the fierce religious controversies raging elsewhere in England.[14] Many devout believers simply ignored, and continue to ignore, the findings of science: witness the laws in certain of the United States which still require the biblical account of the Creation to be taught alongside the "unproved theory" of Darwinism.

Others, in contrast, found their faith purified and enhanced by the elimination of superstition and myth. It was Andrew Dickson White's conviction, as he expressed it in the introduction to his *History of the Warfare of Science with Theology*,

> that Science, though it has evidently conquered Dogmatic Theology based on biblical texts and ancient modes of thought, will go hand in hand with Religion; and that, although theological control will continue to diminish, Religion, as seen in the recognition of "a Power in the universe, not ourselves, which makes for righteousness," and in the love of God and of our neighbor, will steadily grow stronger and stronger, not only in the American institutions of learning but in the world at large. (1: xii)

William James, while perhaps not so sanguine about "the Divine Power in the Universe" as was White (2: 395), nevertheless ended the postscript to his book with the confession that "the practical needs and experiences of religion seem to me sufficiently met by the belief that beyond each man and in a fashion continuous with him there exists a larger power which is friendly to him and to his ideas. All that the facts require is that the power should be both other and larger than our conscious selves" (396). In everyday life, he concludes in his essay "The Will to Believe," "the *chance* of salvation is enough. No fact in human nature is more characteristic than its willingness to live on a chance"—a thought consistent with his defense of Pascal's wager (the notion that, other things being equal, it is better to cover one's bets by believing: after all, what have you got to lose?).[15] Indeed, the essays in *The Will to Believe* (1897), as James states in his preface, "are largely concerned with defending the legitimacy of religious faith" for the members of a Harvard student club, in whom "paralysis of their naive capacity for faith" represents a special form of mental weakness in academic audiences (x). "I do not think that any one can accuse me of preaching reckless faith. I have preached the right of the individual to indulge his personal faith at his personal risk" (xi).

Albert Schweitzer emerged from his magisterial survey of eighteenth- and nineteenth-century studies of the historical Jesus (*Von Reimarus zu Wrede*, 1906) convinced that "it is not Jesus as historically known, but Jesus as spiritually arisen within men, who is significant for our time and can help it. Not the historical Jesus, but the spirit which goes forth from Him and in the spirits of men strives for new influence and rule, is that which overcomes the world."[16] Similarly Frazer, despite his introductory admonition that "whatever comes of it, wherever it leads us, we must follow truth alone" (xxvii), ends his epoch-making work with "the sound of the church bells of Rome ringing the Angelus" across the marshes of the Campagna to the sacred grove of Nemi, where his account of ancient myth began. "*Le roi est mort, vive le roi! Ave Maria!*" (11: 309).

Yet despite the protestations of lingering faith among these authors, the mood of doubt pervading the turn of the century is evident from the titles of their celebrated works: *History of the Warfare of Science with Theology, The Golden Bough: A Study in Magic and Religion, The Varieties of Religious Experience,* or *The Quest for the Historical Jesus.* Indeed, cultural historians now understand that "doubt is ubiquitous in the discourse of the Victorians."[17]

Historians do well to remind us that intellectuals and scientists constituted only a minority among freethinkers of the late nineteenth century. The loss of faith among working-class agnostics and atheists was based less on intellectual conclusions than on moral and social concerns.[18] At the same time, the assaults on conventional faith by rationalism and science produced often violent counterattacks from religious authorities. The papacy responded with its dogma on the immaculate conception (1854), with the encyclical of 1864 condemning modern culture and anathematizing the rationalistic principles of science, and with the pronouncement on papal infallibility (1870). The so-called *Kulturkampf* was mounted from 1872 to 1878 by Bismarck in an attempt to reduce the power of the Catholic Church in Germany where the "liturgical movement" sought to respond to the increasing alienation of Catholics by combining social, cultural, and religious aspects in liturgy as a *Gesamtkunstwerk.*[19] These various controversies were almost immediately reflected in the literature of the age.

Religion in Nineteenth-Century Literature

Earlier European literature, to the extent that it was not simply devotional, did not often feature religion centrally. In the novels of personal cultivation (*Bildungsromane*) that became increasingly popular in nineteenth-century Germany and England, religion rarely plays a role in the young protagonist's experience. Goethe's *Wilhelm Meister's Apprenticeship* (1795–96), which provided the master pattern for the genre, deals with religion and faith only in its subtle case study of religious hysteria in book 6, the "Confessions of a Beautiful Soul."[20] In Stendhal's *Le Rouge et le noir* (1830), whose hero is a seminarian, Julien Sorel chooses the church over a military career not for reasons of faith but because he shrewdly concludes that, in the post-Napoleonic world, greater power and glory could be achieved in the cloth than in the uniform (chap. 5). The situation was slightly different in Victorian England; but even there J. Hillis Miller had to isolate for his purposes five writers who, unlike most of their contemporaries, belonged to a "romantic" tradition that still believed in God (De Quincey, Arnold, Browning, Hopkins, and Emily Brontë).[21]

The pattern at mid-century was sometimes a return to faith through doubt, for which Tennyson's *In Memoriam* (1850) provides the archetypical model in England. "There lives more faith in honest doubt, / Believe me, than in half the creeds" (section 96), we read. Yet ultimately "We have but faith: we cannot know; / For knowledge is of things we see" (prologue). A year later Melville's Ishmael calls himself "a good Christian; born and bred in the bosom of the infallible Presbyterian Church" (52); yet he learns from the "wild idolator" Queequeg that "even Christians could be both miserable and wicked; infinitely more so, than all his father's heathens."[22] By the end of his voyage on the *Pequod*, Ishmael has discovered that "there is no steady unretracing progress in life" with a fixed conclusion. Instead, after passing through certain "fixed gradation"—"infancy's unconscious spell, boyhood's thoughtless faith, adolescence' doubt (the common doom), then scepticism, then disbelief, resting at last in manhood's pondering repose of If"—we are destined to begin the eternal round all over again (486). Similarly Raskolnikov, in Dostoevsky's *Crime and Punishment* (1866), asserts before Nietzsche that "There is no God" (in his theological conversation with Sonia in book 4, chapter 4). He later tells his saddened mother that, like so many other young men of the period, he is "not a believer" (bk. 6, chap. 7). In the Siberian prison camp he is attacked by fellow inmates as an atheist (epilogue). Yet despite the Napoleonic theory that motivates his murder of the old pawnshop owner—his hope of using the money to undertake a grand work for humanity—he is reconverted on the last page of the novel by his love for the devout Sonia.

⟨∞⟩

But for most of the major nineteenth-century novelists, many of whom had lost—or never gained—their faith, religion was simply one among many aspects of the societies that they were depicting. For Flaubert's Emma Bovary (1857), religion is little more than an occasional transitory infatuation. As a thirteen-year-old girl, she initially experiences a romantic pleasure in the exaltations of her convent but, soon tiring of the routine, "continued from habit first, then out of vanity." The nuns, "who had been so sure of her vocation, perceived with great astonishment that Mademoiselle Rouault seemed to be slipping from them."[23] Later, in the course of a prolonged illness, she undergoes a temporary relapse into religiosity with a mystical vision in which she fancies "she heard in space the music of seraphic harps, and perceived in an azure sky, on a golden throne in the midst of saints holding green palms, God the Father, resplendent with majesty, who ordered to earth angels with wings of fire to carry her away in their arms" (154). Generally, in Flaubert's fictional world, religious faith is restricted to the delusions of emotional adolescents and hysterical patients (or, as later in Flaubert's story *A Simple Heart*, to such simpleminded folk as the servant woman Félicité).

In the rich social fabric of George Eliot's *Middlemarch* (1872)—even though it is set in the rural England of 1829–32, well before the mid-century challenges to faith—religion provides at most a single strand, which is treated with a delicious irony.[24] Casaubon, the unimaginative scholar pursuing the "Key to All Mythologies," is used as the model for the painted head of Saint Thomas Aquinas; the banker Bulstrode is generally disliked and distrusted for his "religious tone," which is ultimately exposed as being no more than a hypocritical mask for his disreputable past; the young Dorothea Brooke is characterized by an "excessive religiousness" that she wastes upon the false idol Casaubon. Altogether, religion concerns the community of Middlemarch only to the extent that it becomes a political issue—either national (the "Catholic Question") or local (the dispute over the hospital chaplaincy). Faith never enters the discussion. Looking back at English society as it existed some fifty years earlier, George Eliot perceives what U. C. Knoepflmacher has called "a 'middle' march between religious despair and religious affirmation," a compromise based on her essential humanism.[25]

Tolstoy's *Anna Karenina* (1878) is only seemingly at odds with the general pattern. For most of the novel, an essentially ritualized religion constitutes only one facet in the glittering life of upper-class Russians in Moscow, St. Petersburg, and on country estates. We hear about Kitty's exposure to spiritual life through her acquaintance with the Pietist Madame Stahl (pt. 2, chap. 33). Indeed, Kitty is the single genuinely Christian spirit in the vast cast of characters although even her spirituality is implicit rather than explicit. Anna, in contrast, is a thoroughly secularized figure. As the misery of her circumstances as a "fallen woman" becomes apparent, "[t]he idea of seeking help in her difficulty in religion was as remote from her as seeking help from Aleksey Aleksandrovich himself, although she had never had doubts of the faith in which she had been brought up. She knew that the support of religion was possible only upon condition of renouncing what made up for her the whole meaning of life" (pt. 3, chap. 15).[26] Her lover, Vronsky, is mindlessly areligious. The more thoughtful Levin, "an unbeliever who respected the beliefs of others," finds it "exceedingly disagreeable to be present at and take part in church ceremonies" (pt. 5, chap. 1)—and, accordingly, no such ceremonies are depicted in the novel's hundreds of pages. Levin's brother, a skeptic, experiences a deathbed reconversion; yet Levin understands that "his present return to faith was not a legitimate one, . . . but simply a temporary, selfish return to faith in desperate hope of recovery" (pt. 5, chap. 20). Generally speaking, most of the figures in the novel are freethinkers—either like the true freethinker of former days, "who had been brought up in ideas of religion, law, and morality, and only through conflict and struggle became a freethinker"; or like the uncouth modern breed, described contemptuously, "who are reared *d'emblée* in theories of atheism, skepticism, and materialism" and negate everything (pt. 5, chap. 9).

Tolstoy originally meant to conclude the novel with Anna's suicide beneath the wheels of the freight train. He added the last section, which portrays Levin's return to faith, in response to his own spiritual crisis, which he was soon to describe in greater detail in his autobiographical account *A Confession*.[27] In the two years after his brother's death, the freethinking Levin begins to reconsider questions of life and death "in the light of these new convictions, as he called them, which had during the period from his twentieth to his thirty-fourth year imperceptibly replaced his childish and youthful beliefs." His thinking is further jolted by the extraordinary circumstance that, during his wife Kitty's labor of childbirth, "he, an unbeliever, had fallen into praying" (pt. 8, chap. 8). In the effort to resolve his doubts, he studies philosophical and theological works, but can "find no answer to the questions and [is] reduced to despair" (pt. 8, chap. 10). A chance conversation about a peasant who "lives for his soul" and "remembers God" triggers an epiphany (pt. 8, chap. 11). Levin considers his own life and comes to the realization that "that joyful knowledge, shared with the peasant, that alone gives peace to my soul" has always come, wittingly or not, from his "faith in God, in goodness, as the one goal of man's destiny" (pt. 8, chap. 13). Levin realizes that his character will not change—that he will continue to lose his temper, quarrel with his wife, and fail to understand with his reason why he prays. "But my life now, my whole life apart from anything that can happen to me, every minute of it is no longer meaningless, as it was before, but it has an unquestionable meaning of the goodness which I have the power to put into it." With this insight, which has been anticipated by nothing in its first seven parts, the novel ends.

If we turn to Theodor Fontane's *Effi Briest* (1895), a masterpiece of German nineteenth-century realism and the last of the three great novels of adultery, we encounter a similar indifference toward religion and questions of faith. The heroine of the novel, often known as the German Madame Bovary, has been much affected by her father, a freethinking Prussian landowner "to whom nothing is sacred."[28] Accordingly, when the newly married girl of eighteen years first arrives in the Baltic coastal town with her much older husband, her "rationalistic" tendencies cause the local aristocrats with their "Christian-Germanic rigor of faith" (253) to regard her as an "atheist" (159). Effi displays no religious beliefs whatsoever—only an adolescent tendency toward superstition (her fear of the ghostly Chinaman reputed to haunt the attic). The late nineteenth-century society of the novel, rejecting divine judgment as "nonsense," accepts as its idolatry an "honor cult" (322) which first necessitates the duel in which Effi's husband kills her lover and then forces her through divorce into a life of disgrace and an early death. It is an utterly mundane world in which "Bible jokes" are the latest rage (281) and in which "churchly questions" are treated with the utmost irony. Characteristically, the church is invoked only for marriages and baptisms—ritual occasions which are disposed of almost en passant in a single sentence. The only figure demonstrating Christian humility and love is Effi's faithful maidservant, Roswitha, who calls herself "a bad Catholic" (203).

A conspicuous variant is evident in the well-known Christian socialist novels of the period—for instance, Eliza Lynn Linton's appallingly bad but sensationally successful *True History of Joshua Davidson* (1872) and Mrs. Humphry Ward's controversial but highly literary bestseller *Robert Elsmere* (1888), which is based on an acquaintance with Renan as well as Strauss and the German Higher Criticism. These works are not expressions of doubt, much less loss of faith, but attacks on the sterile theology and self-centered clericalism of the times. The response of Joshua Davidson and Robert Elsmere is a turn to a primitive Christian faith outside the framework of the traditional church.[29] Such modern "imitations of Christ," featuring heroes who try to lead an authentic Christian life outside their respective churches, were written not just in England but all over Europe, Protestant and Catholic alike: Benito Pérez Galdós's *Nazarín*, Hans von Kahlenberg's (pseud. for Helene Kessler) *Der Fremde* (1901; The stranger), Antonio Fogazzaro's *The Saint* (*Il santo*, 1905), and other less popular examples.

꘡

It is a curious fact of German literary history that many of its writers since 1750 have been trained theologians or the sons of Lutheran ministers—a fact that inspired Robert Minder to write a classic essay on "the image of the vicarage in German literature from Jean Paul to Gottfried Benn."[30] As a result, Minder concluded, "Germany has produced no anticlerical Protestant writers of universal reputation" (58). Rather the contrary, since at times of threat to the nation the vicarage has often constituted the cell of intellectual resistance, as evidenced most recently in the opposition movement to the communist government in 1989 in the German Democratic Republic. Even those few who broke with the Christian faith—the pastors' sons Gotthold Ephraim Lessing and Friedrich Nietzsche and the intended theologian Friedrich Hölderlin—continued to appreciate the discipline and warmth experienced in their childhood. Thus in 1881 Nietzsche reminisced in a letter to Peter Gast about his childhood in the vicarage: "It is the best example of ideal life that I have ever known; from childhood on I have pursued it, into many corners, and I believe that I have never in my heart opposed it."[31]

Yet if the traditional attitude toward Christianity, in contrast to the coziness of the vicarage, was radically modified among many intellectuals at the end of the nineteenth century, it was due in no small measure to the growing influence of Nietzsche's ideas. Only a year after his letter to Peter Gast, Nietzsche published *The Gay Science* (*Die fröhliche Wissenschaft*, 1882) where for the first time, and fifteen years after Dostoevsky, he proclaimed that "God is dead." "The greatest modern event—that 'God is dead,' that the belief in the Christian God has become untenable—is already beginning to cast its first shadows across Europe."[32] In his posthumously published notes from that period he joked that "nowadays we would treat any tendency toward religious raptures with laxatives." The *religion nouvelle* he envisaged would have "no God, no Beyond, no reward and punishment."[33] And in his notes on religion he observed that "[e]very church is the stone on the grave of a god-man: it wants at any cost to prevent him from being resurrected.

God suffocated from theology."[34] Inevitably, these tensions between faith and doubt began to surface in a broad spectrum of autobiographical accounts of the later nineteenth century.

Two Lives

The conflict of faith and reason was resolved in the case of Leo Tolstoy into a renewal of faith. Tolstoy was baptized and raised in the Orthodox Christian faith, he informs us in the opening paragraph of *A Confession* (1879), and instructed in that faith throughout his childhood and youth. "But when I abandoned the second course of the university at the age of eighteen I no longer believed any of the things I had been taught." Tolstoy presents his lapse from faith as typical among his intellectual peers—as represented, as we have seen, by Levin in *Anna Karenina.* That is to say, he never seriously thought about the things he was taught but simply repeated the catechism by rote and received his certificate of communion. But

> religious doctrine, accepted on trust and supported by external pressure, thaws away gradually under the influence of knowledge and experience of life which conflict with it, and a man very often lives on, imagining that he still holds intact the religious doctrine imparted to him in childhood whereas in fact not a trace of it remains.[35]

By the time he was sixteen Tolstoy had stopped praying and going to church, and his rejection of religious doctrine was a conscious one reinforced by his reading of philosophical works.

In *A Confession,* however, Tolstoy does not analyze the process of rejection. Apart from a glancing reference to Immanuel Kant's arguments against the possibility of proving the existence of a deity (62), he does not discuss the intellectual sources for his loss of faith. He passes quickly over his ten years of passion (ambition, love of power, covetousness, lasciviousness, pride, anger, violence), another six years during which his "religion" amounted to no more than faith in poetry and a Goethean personal cultivation, and fifteen years of family life.

Then about the age of fifty something strange happened: he began to experience "moments of perplexity and arrest of life" (15), moments that gradually occurred more frequently and with greater intensity. Although he rotely maintained the basic acts of living, he came to the conclusion that, despite his success and good fortune, life is meaningless (17). "I knew

I could find nothing along the path of reasonable knowledge except a denial of life; and there—in faith—was nothing but a denial of reason, which was yet more impossible for me than a denial of life" (47). Following these brief preliminaries, the remaining pages of A Confession deal with Tolstoy's return to a faith that offered meaning to life—a profound and simple faith inspired by the belief of the simple Russian folk (not unlike the romanticism that was later to send such European seekers as Dietrich Bonhoeffer and Simone Weil to Harlem churches in search of authentic American religion), purged of the superficialities of Orthodoxy, and based on his own reading, translation, and interpretation of the Gospels. "I lived in the world for fifty-five years," he summarizes in his introduction to What I Believe (1884), "and after the first fourteen or fifteen years of childhood I was for thirty-five years a nihilist in the real meaning of that word, . . . a nihilist in the sense of an absence of any belief. Five years ago I came to believe in Christ's teaching, and my life suddenly changed" (307). In sum, Tolstoy's religious writings, his principal occupation during the years between the completion of Anna Karenina and the publication of The Death of Ivan Ilych (1886), mention his loss of faith and years of nihilism as the prerequisite, but he is concerned almost entirely with the recovery of his faith and its nature.

⌒⌒⌒

The difference is immediately clear when we turn to the celebrated spiritual autobiography by a younger contemporary of Tolstoy, Edmund Gosse's Father and Son (1907). The bulk of A Confession is devoted to Tolstoy's renewal of faith from age fifty to fifty-five; his life up to that point is reported hastily as mere background. Father and Son, in contrast, covers only the years from 1849 to 1867—from Gosse's birth up to his departure from home in Devon to London, where for the first time he lived independently and worked as a librarian in the British Museum. Gosse (1849–1928), the son of the zoologist Philip Gosse, was a distinguished translator, critic, and literary historian who, among other accomplishments, introduced Henrik Ibsen to the English public through his translations and a life of the Norwegian dramatist (1907). Gosse had already written an admiring positivistic biography of his father (1890), focusing on his scientific achievements (principally in the field of marine biology). Father and Son, in contrast, is explicitly not an autobiography, eschewing such aspects as "the cold and shrouded details of my uninteresting school life."[36]

"This book is the record of a struggle between two temperaments, two consciences and almost two epochs," it begins (1). Gosse portrays his parents, who based their every action and belief on a literal reading of the Scriptures, as "perhaps the latest consistent exemplars...of a state of soul once not uncommon in Protestant Europe" (15). "Here was perfect purity, perfect intrepidity, perfect abnegation; yet there was also narrowness, isolation, an absence of perspective, let it be boldly admitted, an absence of humanity." It was his parents' "Great Scheme" and his mother's aspiration that his life be dedicated "to the manifest and uninterrupted and uncompromised 'service of the Lord'" (289). Contrary to the common assumption that a life so wholly dedicated to religion is dreary, Gosse stresses that his early childhood prior to his mother's death was "cheerful and often gay" (29).

Gosse exposes with frankness and subtlety the first cracks in the wall of his faith, the earliest stirrings of doubt in his mind, which began at age six when he realized for the first time—as the result of an utterly trivial mistake his father made—that his father was not omniscient (36); and, for equally innocent reasons, that he could deceive his parents. "My Father, as a deity, as a natural force of immense prestige, fell in my eyes to a human level" (38). About the same time he began to question the efficacy of prayer, simply because he was told not to pray for simple things like toys. The happiest hours in this childhood dominated by "rigid and iconoclastic literalness" (71) and by incessant religious instruction came at those times "when the spectre of Religion ceased to overshadow us for a little while, when my Father forgot the Apocalypse and dropped his austere phraseology" to sing or laugh.

Gosse's life changed upon his mother's death in his seventh year and the family's ensuing move from London to Devonshire. "I do not think that at any part of our lives my Father and I were drawn so close to one another as we were in that summer of 1857" (90). But 1857 was also a year of scientific crisis, when his father, attending meetings at the British Museum and the Royal Society, became aware of the ideas of evolution which had been growing for the past thirty years.

> There is a peculiar agony in the paradox that truth has two forms, each of them indisputable, yet each antagonistic to the other. It was this discovery, that there were two theories of physical life, each of which was true, but the truth of each incompatible with the truth of the other, which shook the spirit of my Father with perturbation. (111)

In the unrealistic hope of settling the scientific controversy he wrote his ill-fated *Omphalos*, whose crudely literalist and fanatical interpretation of the Creation—he argued among other things that Adam, though he came from no womb, had a navel, the *omphalos* of the title—provoked ridicule among scientists and in the popular press.[37]

Disappointed in his hope of reconciling science and religion, the elder Gosse retreated into the community of "Saints," the Wesleyan Brethren, in their Devonshire village and into his collections and study of marine biology. Gradually his troubled mind formed the idea that his son was an *âme d'élite*, "a being to whom the mysteries of salvation had been divinely revealed" (167), and he insisted on having him at age ten examined, baptized, and accepted into the religious community as an adult—scenes that Gosse describes with comic irony. "I saw myself imprisoned forever in the religious system which had caught me and would whirl my helpless spirit as in the concentric wheels of my nightly vision" (217). Yet through it all and despite his seeming meekness the boy "clung to a hard nut of individuality, deep down in my childish nature" (219).

His life changed yet again when his father married for a second time and his stepmother, devout but no fanatic, encouraged the boy to lead a more normal, healthy life. While he did not resort to open rebellion and, "young coward that I was, let sleeping dogmas lie" (246), he began to rebel in trivial ways against the tyranny of the religious life. Fascinated by his first glimpse of illustrations of the Greek gods, he was appalled by his father's "Puritan fury." "My Father's prestige was by this time considerably lessened in my mind" (277).

When the boy was sent off to an academy run by the Plymouth Brethren, he was exposed for the first time to secular poetry, and specifically to the poems of Christopher Marlowe. This extension of his intellectual horizons did not stir doubts in his young mind. "On the contrary, at first there came a considerable quickening of fervour" (319). But his father, on discovering among Edmund's books a volume containing Marlowe's *Hero and Leander*, burned it, arguing that his son's landlady, when he went off to London, would immediately mark him as a profligate should she find such a sinful book in his possession. "I began to perceive, without animosity, the strange narrowness of my Father's system" (319). Though still not inclined to skepticism and doubt, he began to wonder about the doctrines of other churches, believing that it was unlikely that "a secret of such stupendous importance should have been entrusted to a little group of Plymouth Brethren, and have been hidden from millions of disinterested and pious theologians" (320). He returned to his last year at school "full of strange discords" (324) and conflating Keats and the Book of Revelation, John Wesley's hymns and Shakespeare. "In my hot and silly brain, Jesus and Pan held sway together, as in a wayside chapel discordantly and impishly consecrated to Pagan and to Christian rites" (324). One summer afternoon, "the highest moment of my religious life, the apex of my striving after holiness" (326), he prayed fervently for an epiphany. Nothing happened. Evening came. The bell rang for tea.

"The Lord has not come, the Lord will never come," I muttered, and in my heart the artificial edifice of extravagant faith began to totter and crumble. From that moment forth my Father and I, though the fact was long successfully concealed from him and even from myself, walked in opposite hemispheres of the soul, with "the thick o' the world between us." (326–27)

Gosse's account of his youthful doubts ends at this point. He leaves for London, his faith undermined and his belief in his father's authority dashed. An elegiac tone pervades the pages of the epilogue—a refrain, he stresses, that he was to repeat over and over as the years passed: "what a charming companion, what a delightful parent, what a courteous and engaging friend, my Father would have been, and would pre-eminently have been to me, if it had not been for this stringent piety which ruined it all" (348). Gosse loved and respected his father, but given his father's inflexible views no compromise was possible. It was a case of "Everything or Nothing," the book ends;

and thus desperately challenged, the young man's conscience threw off once for all the yoke of his "dedication," and, as respectfully as he could, without parade or remonstrance, he took a human being's privilege to fashion his inner life for himself.

The stupendous success of the book signals a new climate of opinion marking the beginning of the twentieth century. The first edition and five further impressions sold out within the first year. Having almost immediately established itself as a classic of English literature, it was rapidly translated into other languages. His book was "a call to people," as he wrote to an admiring reader, "to face the fact that the old faith is now impossible to sincere and intelligent minds, and that we must courageously face the difficulty of following entirely different ideals in moving towards the higher life."[38]

꩜

Such "deconversion" experiences as Gosse's were not uncommon in the second half of the nineteenth century. Robert Graves, for instance, recalls in his autobiography: "I had great religious fervor, which persisted until shortly after my confirmation at the age of sixteen, and remember the incredulity with which I first heard that there actually were people, people baptized like myself into the Church of England, who did not believe in Jesus's divinity. I had never met an unbeliever."[39] However, the accounts were usually brief statements, often in obituary notices of secularists in freethinking journals, rather than detailed literary narratives.[40] But similar experiences gradually began to make themselves felt in the literary works of the period, as writers, having lost their faith through their reading of Nietzsche as well as the other scholars of doubt, began to look back at their earliest years in a new way. Childhood and youth were now analyzed as the period during which doubt leading to a final loss of faith began. This was a new development, conspicuously different from the attitudes of those earlier contemporaries Gustave Flaubert (1821–80), George Eliot (1819–80), and Theodor Fontane (1819–98). Flaubert, the son of a surgeon and himself initially a student of law, had grown up in a wholly secular atmosphere. Eliot (Mary Ann Evans), liberated at an early age from the religious views of her Warwickshire peers, was translating David Friedrich Strauss's freethinking *Life of Jesus* in her early twenties. Fontane, the son of an apothecary, was educated in rationalistic Berlin and worked there as a pharmacist and minor civil servant before becoming a journalist and independent writer. Although Fontane outlived the others by two decades and produced his finest novels in the 1890s, the views of all three were determined by the skepticism of their intellectual generation—a skepticism that was born of rationalism rather than Darwinism, that they took for granted as their intellectual heritage, and that saturated the texture of their social fabrics.

The extremes of absolute deconversion and of deconversion followed by reconversion, as represented in the contrasting autobiographical accounts of Gosse and Tolstoy, exemplify the principal patterns evident in several of the major novels of lost faith that begin to be written and published at the beginning of the twentieth century.

CHAPTER THREE

Theologians of the Profane

His insights are those of a theologian marooned in the realm of the profane.
—*Gershom Scholem, Walter Benjamin*

S kepticism did not come naturally to writers born into intensely religious
families and often intended, like Gosse, for religious careers—writers
of generations late enough, moreover, to have their attitudes and impressions shaped by the controversies precipitated by *The Origin of Species.*
If we consider three representative English, French, and German novels—
Samuel Butler's *The Way of All Flesh*, Roger Martin du Gard's *Jean Barois*,
and Hermann Hesse's *Demian*—surprising parallels become evident despite
significant differences of nationality, generation, and composition. Butler's
novel, written in the decade from 1873 to 1884, appeared posthumously in
1903; Martin du Gard began writing his book in 1910, and it was published
in 1913; and Hesse's work, written in 1917, appeared in 1919. These works
were not the impassioned first novels of inexperienced young authors. None
of the three men undertook their highly autobiographical novels until their
maturity (in their thirties and forties), at a point in their lives when they
were able to look back with critical detachment at their childhood and youth
in deeply pious families during an era shaped by the spiritual tensions of the
years following Strauss's *Life of Jesus*, Darwin's *The Origin of Species*, and
the other works that shook the foundations of conventional religious belief.

From Faith to Alienation: Samuel Butler's *The Way of All Flesh*

Samuel Butler (1835–1902) was a well-traveled and well-published author
by the time he wrote *The Way of All Flesh*. The scion of a distinguished

ecclesiastical family—his grandfather was Dr. Samuel Butler, the headmaster of the Shrewsbury School and bishop of Lichfield; his father the Reverend Thomas Butler—he was brought up in an atmosphere of middle-class evangelicalism. Educated at Shrewsbury, he studied for holy orders at St. John's College, Cambridge, but on graduation in 1858 refused ordination because of religious doubts. A year later he emigrated to New Zealand where he spent several years as a successful sheep breeder and wrote his first book on his experiences. Returning to England in 1864, he studied painting and exhibited at the Royal Academy. (A devoted connoisseur of music, Butler also composed and published pieces for the piano as well as cantatas and oratorios after the manner of Handel.) In 1872 he enjoyed his greatest success as a writer with *Erewhon,* his satirical attack on modern society; in *The Fair Haven* (1873) he lampooned established religion and the belief in miracles. During the following decade, while writing and rewriting *The Way of All Flesh,* he visited Canada and participated in the Darwinian controversy with a series of tracts, including *Life and Habit* (1877) and *Evolution Old and New* (1879), in which he developed his own theory of evolution.

Challenged by his close friend Eliza Mary Ann Savage, whom he had met in his art classes, to write a novel better than *Middlemarch,* he undertook *The Way of All Flesh,* which in the eyes of one critic "is the most directly autobiographical Bildungsroman in English before *Sons and Lovers* and Joyce's *Portrait.*"[1] But the novel differs from the traditional bildungsroman in an important respect: it looks back to the three generations preceding the hero's birth in order to illustrate Butler's views on evolution. He rejected Darwinian natural selection in favor of his theory of the "Continued" or "Evolutionary Personality," which recalls past existences, and an "unconscious memory" handed down from generation to generation. These views are expounded from time to time by the narrator.

> It would almost seem as if a transmitted education of some generations is necessary for the due enjoyment of great wealth. . . . a certain kind of good fortune generally attends self-made men to the last. It is their children of the first, or first and second, generation who are in greater danger, for the race can no more repeat its most successful performances suddenly and without its ebbings and flowings of success than the individual can do so, and the more brilliant the success in any one generation, the greater as a general rule the subsequent exhaustion until time has been allowed for recovery.[2]

The novel is introduced by sixteen chapters of what amounts to a brief family saga covering three generations of the family preceding the hero's birth

in 1835 (the year of Butler's own birth)—a saga suggested by the generalizing title, which replaced the original manuscript title "Ernest Pontifex."
Butler is intent upon demonstrating the deviation of the family from the
pristine grace, natural piety, and artistic talents of John Pontifex until its
regeneration in the person of his great-grandson Ernest, the protagonist of
the novel.[3]

John Pontifex is by profession a carpenter and a man of natural spirituality, whose innate artistic abilities show up in his gifted drawings and
his skill as an organ builder and church organist. His son George—in whose
depiction Butler allowed himself a wicked caricature of his grandfather, the
headmaster—becomes a successful and prosperous publisher of religious
books, a tyrannical father, and pretentious art connoisseur, in whom his
father's artistic abilities have degenerated to nothing more than the admiration and purchase of second-rate copies of Italian paintings. For business reasons—he is precisely of a generation with, and shares the pious
hypocrisy of, the banker Bulstrode in *Middlemarch*—he determines that his
son Theobald is to be a clergyman. "It was seemly that Mr Pontifex, the
well-known publisher of religious books, should devote at least one of his
sons to the Church; this might tend to bring business, or at any rate to keep
it in the firm" (chap. 7; 30). Theobald, while resolute in his faith, feels no
call to become a clergyman and tries to rebel. But when his father threatens
to cut him off without a penny, he gives in. Following his ordination, he
serves a period as curate, marries Christina, a young woman who shares his
simple and devout faith, and eventually obtains a rectorship at Battersby-
on-the-Hill where in due course his son Ernest is born.[4] Only at this point
does the autobiographical bildungsroman begin.

In keeping with Butler's evolutionary project to show how Ernest manages to cast off the oppressive family burden of evangelical piety and to
recover his great-grandfather's virtues, the early chapters—the novel is allegedly the first-person account by Edward Overton, a family friend who
knows the principals and has access to their documents—portray the dull
weight of religiosity in the Pontifex household. Ernest is taught to kneel
almost before he can crawl and to mouth the Lord's prayer and the general confession as soon as he can speak, and it is taken for granted that he
will become a clergyman. When Overton visits on a Sunday, he witnesses
the unbending rigor with which the Sabbath is observed by the family, the
absolute and stern faith of father and mother, and their keen "scent for possible mischief" (chap. 26; 110). How was it possible, Overton reflects, "that
a child only a little past five years old, trained in such an atmosphere of
prayers and hymns and sums and happy Sunday evenings—to say nothing

of daily repeated beatings over the said prayers and hymns... should grow up in any healthy or vigorous development?" (chap. 26; 108–9).

Ernest's miserable years at Dr. Skinner's Roughborough Grammar School (modeled after Butler's own unhappy time at Shrewsbury) are relieved only by the attentions of his aunt Alethea, who moves to Roughborough in order to provide moral support for the nephew in whom she recognizes signs of promise. (Alethea, whose name means "truth," is the only unspoiled sibling among George Pontifex's children.) With her encouragement Ernest takes up the great-grandfatherly practice of carpentry and organ building. When Alethea dies, she wills her considerable estate to Ernest, to be held secretly in escrow by Overton until Ernest is twenty-eight years old. Finishing Roughborough without distinction, he enters Emmanuel College, Cambridge, to prepare for his ordination.

"More explicitly than any other Bildungsroman," Jerome Buckley has suggested," the novel is grounded in the intellectual history of the Victorian period, and the fortunes of nineteenth-century Anglicanism are directly related to the action and the characters."[5] This claim is borne out by Ernest's experiences in 1858, as he is reading for his ordination. "Up to this time, though not religiously inclined, he had never doubted the truth of anything that had been told him about Christianity. He had never seen anyone who doubted, nor read anything that raised a suspicion in his mind as to the historical character of the miracles recorded in the Old and New Testaments" (chap. 47; 208). In this period of quiet just before the controversies of 1859–60, we are told, the sole signs of spiritual activity at Cambridge were evident in the Simeonite movement, in which vestiges of the earlier evangelical awakening still survived. Ernest is contemptuous of that unkempt band of religious enthusiasts until he wanders out of curiosity into a sermon by the fiery preacher from London Gideon Hawke. Profoundly moved by the occasion, the labile Ernest feels that he has reached a turning point in his life. When he visits his parents in Battersby, much to their chagrin he uses his newfound ultra-evangelical views to criticize their ecclesiastical doctrines (chap. 50).

Upon his ordination as a deacon, he accepts a curacy in central London. But there, in another of his "snipe-like changes of flight," he encounters the Oxford-trained senior curate Pryer and other friends from the Church of England, who soon convince him that the High Church, "and even Rome itself" (chap. 51; 235), has more to offer than he has previously acknowledged. Under Pryer's tutelage, in which the naive Ernest fails to recognize the homoerotic element, he learns the tenets of the High Church: the role of the priest as spiritual guide, the need for confession, the requirement of

celibacy, and the Bible as a stumbling block that can only confuse the laity
(chap. 52). In his eagerness to put his new ideas into practice, he moves
into a poor neighborhood near Drury Lane and entrusts Pryer with his small
inheritance to support plans for a College of Spiritual Pathology. Gradually
becoming disenchanted with Pryer's views and finding himself too poorly informed to convert his neighbors from Methodism to the Church of England,
he is stunned by a conversation in which a freethinking tinker, Mr. Shaw,
exposes Ernest's basic ignorance of the Gospels and mindless acceptance of
various doctrines, including the resurrection.

Ernest is as naive in personal relationships as in his theology. In his utter
inexperience, believing that a young woman in his house, Miss Maitland,
is a prostitute like her neighbor Miss Snow, Ernest propositions her and is
arrested for sexual assault. Sentenced to six months' hard labor, he promptly
succumbs to brain fever, from which he awakens with wholly new feelings.
Disclaimed by his family, he learns that Pryer has absconded with all his
money. Loathing his previous life, he forsakes the clergy and, in another of
his rapid changes, gives up his faith. "Only a year ago he had bounded forth
to welcome Mr Hawke's sermon; since then he had bounded after a College
of Spiritual Pathology; now he was in full cry after rationalism pure and
simple" (chap. 64; 285).

At this point, two-thirds of the way through the novel and with his religious faith devastated, Ernest's spiritual education is complete and he has
attained a new, albeit still inchoate, ethical belief. "He had lost his faith in
Christianity, but his faith in something—he knew not what, but that there
was a something as yet but darkly known, which made right right and wrong
wrong—his faith in this grew stronger and stronger daily" (chap. 68; 304).[6]
The remainder of the book deals with his experience of life: success and failure in business, an ill-conceived marriage with children and divorce. When
he is twenty-eight years old, he is rescued by a deus ex machina—or, in this
case, by a goddess named Fortuna. Overton hands over his now considerably
increased trust fund from Aunt Alethea, and Ernest is able to enjoy growing success as the author of religious-critical essays and a life of absolute
emancipation—from family attachments, from conventional views, from
economic dependence. "I am an Ishmael by instinct as much as by accident
of circumstances," he tells Overton, "but if I keep out of society I shall be
less vulnerable than Ishmaels generally are" (chap. 84; 396). Ernest had early
given up his two children for adoption but provided well for their futures. His
daughter Alice, a robust young mother, and his son Georgie, a sailor, carry
on the family evolution into the fifth generation, healthy but unmarked
by Ernest's problematic nature. "He is in a very solitary position," Ernest's

publisher confirms. "He has formed no alliances, and has made enemies not only of the religious world but of the literary and scientific brotherhood as well" (chap. 86; 419).

Its pronounced allegorical elements place Butler's novel firmly in the tradition of such works as John Bunyan's *Pilgrim's Progress*. Many of the names—Pontifex, Theobald, Christina, Alethea, Roughborough, Emmanuel College, and others—are clearly allegorical, as are the frequent polar juxta-positions of persons: the good and bad fathers (John Pontifex vs. George and Theobald), the whore and the virgin (Miss Snow and Miss Maitland), Low and High Church (Mr. Hawke and Deacon Pryer)—and, ultimately, the com-plementary pairing of Ernest and Overton as youthful and mature versions of the same Butlerian personality. Yet in its profound and detailed psycho-logical analysis of the process of religious disenchantment, leading from abject integration into the religious community to the critical alienation of the outsider, it is utterly modern. Unlike the poems, which simply gave expression to the feelings of doubt, or like the earlier novels, which took doubt for granted without any analysis of its sources, Butler's novel depicts the evolution of experiences common to a generation of thoughtful young people—the way of *all* flesh—in the second half of the nineteenth century.

From Faith to Doubt: Roger Martin du Gard's *Jean Barois*

Roger Martin du Gard's *Jean Barois* differs in several revealing respects from *The Way of All Flesh*. First, Butler basically thought of his novel as the story of an individual, "Ernest Pontifex," yet gave it a generalizing title, which was justified by the family saga prefixed to the hero's life and the theory of evo-lution incorporated in the text. Martin du Gard, in contrast, intended to give his novel the universalizing title "S'Affranchir?" ("Emancipation?" or "Self-Liberation?") but succumbed to the publishers' insistence—"shamefully," he later felt, because it betrayed his real intentions—on using the hero's name more conventionally as the title.[7] Second, Butler's novel takes place in a Protestant milieu, extending from Low Church evangelicalism to High Anglican ritual, while Martin du Gard is concerned with fin de siècle French Catholicism. Third, Ernest Pontifex's liberation enables him to retreat into an Ishmael-like privacy and individualism that the Romans treasured as *otium* but that strikes many modern readers as selfish and self-indulgent. Jean Barois, in contrast, is "emancipated" to play an active role as a jour-nalist and propagandist in the Dreyfus Affair and the other intellectual crises preceding World War I. Fourth, Butler saw history as evolution—not by Darwinian selection, as we observed, but by an unconscious family memory which enables Ernest to recover and preserve the qualities of his great-grandfather, though they have been weakened and disfigured for two generations in his grandfather and father. Martin du Gard, in contrast, held a more pessimistic view of history as an atavistic process, a cyclical recurrence, according to which the individual, despite all efforts to liberate himself, is destined to relapse into regressive beliefs.[8] Both Jean Barois and his father, therefore, experience deathbed reconversions to a religious faith from which their science and rationalism earlier seemed to free them. Finally, *The Way of All Flesh*, for all its irony and social criticism, is presented as a straightforward narrative in the tradition of the bildungsroman. *Jean Barois*, in contrast, is an experimental novel consisting of dialogues introduced by brief scenarios and interrupted at intervals by reportage and collage-like documentations, all written in a style that the author called "rapid, changing, urgent, cinematographic."[9]

Yet despite these differences the lives of the two protagonists, Ernest Pontifex and Jean Barois, display remarkable similarities in the major sections dealing with their childhood and youth. *Jean Barois* is organized in three parts. Part 1 follows its hero's life from his childhood faith in a pious household by way of his student years with their religious doubts and their resolution to the death of his father and Jean's marriage, his work as a science teacher and tensions in the marriage stemming from religious conflicts, and the dissolution of his marriage following the birth of his daughter Marie.[10]

Part 2 deals with the founding of the liberal journal *The Sower* (*Le Semeur*) and the public response to the Dreyfus Affair. Barois, emerging from the 1890s as a prominent freethinker, is now widely sought after as a lecturer on such topics as "The Universal Crisis of Religions." His public appearances culminate with a lecture on "The Future of Disbelief" ("L'Avenir de l'incroyance"), which is reproduced in full. A few months later, when he is still in his early forties, a carriage accident nearly costs Barois his life and causes him spontaneously to utter a prayer to the Virgin Mary. Shocked by his momentary relapse into religious faith, he sets down his last will and testament, affirming his lack of belief in an immortal soul and asserting that good and evil are nothing but arbitrary distinctions.[11] This document is meant to offset and to outweigh any subsequent conversion precipitated by the infirmities of old age. (The author, since he was too young to have experienced the Dreyfus Affair directly, spent six months of intense labor on this section working ten hours a day; during the ten preceding years he had collected and analyzed the relevant documentary evidence, some of which was incorporated by montage into the novel.)[12] The section has been widely and justly praised for its vivid portrayal of the public response to that great polarizing crisis of French civilization. Henri Peyre has reasonably claimed that it offers, "better than any other novel written on that tragic civil war, which tore irretrievably the conscience of France and moved that of the world, an accurate, yet a significant and stylized, account of the events then lived and of the problems involved."[13]

Part 3 depicts the later years of Barois's life, when he finds himself and his views shared with the older liberal Dreyfusards forced into opposition by a new generation of young Catholic nationalist intellectuals, who regard them with an amused contempt. As his journal loses its readers, Barois becomes discouraged and depressed. (The author regarded this section—not just "the aging of the intelligence, the senile evolution in the domain of ideas," but above all "the tragic aging of man, in his body and in his heart, his physical decline, this mortal anguish in the face of disease, the hopelessness of age and death"—as "incontestably" the best part of his novel.)[14] The novel ends, as Barois earlier feared, with his reconversion and death, following which his daughter, now a novice, with the acquiescence of the officiating priest burns his last will and testament, thus symbolically eradicating the entire meaning of her father's life.

The parallels to *The Way of All Flesh* are confined essentially to part 1, for after the disintegration of their ill-fated marriages the careers of the two young men diverge dramatically. Ernest Pontifex withdraws into a life of Ishmael-like isolation, at odds with the religious, scientific, and literary worlds, while Jean Barois enters public life as a prominent spokesman of the liberal left. When we lose sight of Ernest, we have every reason to believe that he will continue, like Butler himself, on his path of idiosyncratic independence. We leave Jean, in contrast, on his deathbed following his pathetic reconversion stemming from fear, loneliness, and the infirmities of old age. But part 1 of *Jean Barois* constitutes an account of the gradual loss of religious faith that is as painfully explicit as the similar account in *The Way of All Flesh*—indeed the most vivid account altogether, according to many critics, of the great struggle between Catholicism and science in France between 1880 and 1910.[15] These reports of spiritual development leading from faith to unbelief distinguish these two novels from those earlier nineteenth-century works in which Victorian doubt prevailed or the loss of faith was posited as a fact rather than as a process.

The loss of faith is an obsessive theme in Martin du Gard's fictional oeuvre.[16] In his early novel *Becoming!* (*Devenir!* 1908)—note the infinitive form of the title, which anticipates the discarded title "S'Affranchir?"—the hero quarrels with his mother when he forsakes the religious beliefs of his childhood, but the break is simply presented in a few lines as a fact, as in most nineteenth-century novels, and not developed psychologically at length. The novella *L'Une de nous* (1910; One of us), part of an unfinished novel, exposes a young woman's religious disillusionment resulting from an unhappy marriage and a lifetime of disappointed hopes and unmitigated suffering. And in his multivolume epic novel *Les Thibault* (1922–40), for which he was awarded the Nobel Prize in 1937, "the grand theme of the individual wedged between history and God," as Camus put it with elegant precision, "is orchestrated in a symphonic manner."[17] The conflict between faith and science, he continues, "which so greatly agitated the beginning of the century, causes less stir today. Yet we are living its consequences, announced in *Jean Barois*" (xviii). Indeed, the novel amounts to "a dossier of a religious crisis" (xvii).

Jean is the son of a pietistically devout mother and a freethinking physician father. Raised by a pious grandmother following his mother's early death, Jean is severely afflicted at age twelve by the hereditary tuberculosis that killed his mother, an illness attributed by his grandmother to spiritual weakness rather than heredity. Although his illness is exacerbated when she insists on taking the boy to Lourdes in search of a divine miracle, he is eventually cured by his father's rational treatment: healthful food, fresh air, restorative rest. Already here, though he does not yet understand it, Jean is whiplashed between faith and reason. Three years later, when Jean, now healthy and enjoying the free exercise of his mind, begins to think about the moral issues of evil and injustice in the world, his first religious doubts arise. When he questions his priest, the abbé responds with the rote answers of the church: that evil is a necessary condition of good, that trial and temptation are needed for the betterment of man, and so forth. Discouraging further introspection and meditation, the abbé urges Jean to strive for spiritual health through action.

Jean's spiritual doubts intensify when he goes to Paris to study medicine and the natural sciences, where the laws of the universe are analyzed with no reference to God. Readings in theology and biblical history lead him to perceive contradictions in Catholic doctrine as well as inadequacies in the Gospel accounts. Yet, as he confides to his new friend, the Swiss abbé Schertz, he still wants to keep his faith and needs religion just as he needs food and rest. Schertz points out that only the dogma of Catholicism is being undermined by science and reason; personal faith remains intact. He offers Jean a "symbolist compromise," by which the less than credible incidents of the Bible are simply interpreted figuratively. But he encourages Jean to retain his faith because, he argues, human nature requires the sense of organized community that is offered by Catholicism (and not by Protestantism). Jean is dismayed when his freethinking father makes a deathbed reconversion. Despite his misgivings about the difference in their beliefs, and with the encouragement of the abbé Schertz, he marries his devout childhood friend Cécile.

Several years later, now a teacher of natural science at a Catholic school in Paris, Jean recapitulates his religious development in a letter to Schertz (a development whose three stages correspond with striking precision to those of Ernest Pontifex's growth). The first stage of unthinking faith ended when he realized at age seventeen that there were anomalies in "revealed" religion. Following his acquaintance with Schertz, he then clung eagerly for a time to the liberal understanding of Catholicism and the symbolist interpretation of the Bible. This, together with his wife's faith, provided him for a time with peace of mind and respect for religion. But the old doubts resurfaced. He saw that Catholicism becomes meaningless if it is stripped of those very sacraments and ceremonies that are unacceptable to the modern mind. He soon discovered that the faith of his childhood had receded from him and that, in fact, he had now reached the point of absolute denial and atheism. His new views produce violent disagreements with his profoundly devout wife, and his teaching of evolution eventually brings him into conflict with the clerical authorities of his school. He resigns from his position and, weary of acceding constantly to his wife's demands that he at least observe the motions of a practicing Catholic, arranges a formal separation. As part 1 ends, Jean has been liberated for his new career as a publicist for freethinkers.

Martin du Gard insisted that he had nothing in common with Jean Barois: "Eh bien, non! Je ne suis pas du tout Jean Barois."[18] We can readily accept that disclaimer. To be sure, a few fictional details, especially concerning Barois's youth, come from the author's life, to the extent that this most private of writers has admitted us into his autobiography.[19] The atmosphere of Barois's childhood owes much to Martin du Gard's memories of vacation visits to his great-grandmother in Clermont. The figure of the abbé Schertz is based on Martin du Gard's teacher at the École Fénelon, Marcel Hébert, to whom the author has proclaimed his indebtedness,[20] who introduced the future writer to the works of Tolstoy—Martin du Gard came to regard *War and Peace* as his "master book" ("le maître livre")[21]—and to whom the novel is dedicated with the concern that "[y]our religious sensibility can only be wounded by certain tendencies of this book." Barois's difficulties with the school authorities are anticipated by Hébert's own forced resignation as director of the École Fénelon and subsequent defrocking because of the liberal views expressed in his *Souvenirs d'Assise* (1899), a dialogue contrasting true faith with the transitory forms of the church. (Is it possible that Martin du Gard's use of the dialogue form in *Jean Barois* was suggested by this important work of his venerated teacher and friend?)

Otherwise Barois bears little similarity to his author. Barois (born 1866) is made fifteen years older than Martin du Gard (1881–1958) so that he can experience the Dreyfus Affair as a mature and independent intellectual; accordingly he comes to maturity in an age significantly more devout than the fin de siècle. Barois spends his boyhood in a small town embraced by the mystical Catholicism of his grandmother and, later, with pious family friends, rather than in Paris with a family characterized by "polished indifference" to a religion accepted simply as another social institution.[22] Barois studies science and medicine rather than, like his creator, history and archaeology. Above all, Martin du Gard's spiritual development followed a somewhat different course—a course much closer to that of Edmund Gosse (whose *Father and Son* was acclaimed in France and awarded a prize by the Académie Française in 1913). He belonged to a family of practicing Catholics, "with a very pious mother, the company of priests, of devout friends,"[23] and observed the formalities of the church, taking communion and the sacraments at Easter. He even succumbed briefly to an "unhealthy mysticism," he confesses, and experienced "crises of tears at certain sermons."[24] But as he walked away from the altar after his first communion—very much like Gosse shortly before the end of *Father and Son*— he suddenly felt a wave of sadness and disappointment because he had undergone no great spiritual transformation or interior illumination. This moment was the first fissure in his faith—a fissure widened by his introduction to philosophy at the École Fénelon, his acquaintance with Marcel Hébert, and his reading in such contemporaries as Renan, Ibsen, and Hippolyte Taine.

The final rupture took place in 1901 while he was a student at the École des Chartes—a period of awakening for which his letters of that year provide the best account. It was then that, for the first time, he seriously read the Bible (like Butler's Ernest). Horrified in the Old Testament by the "bestial physiognomy of this cruel God,"[25] he was led by his study of the New Testament to see in a wholly new light "the instructions of the church, this entire complex administration of prayers, of ceremonies, of rites, of symbolic sacraments, of obligations of every sort," which he now rejected "with indifferent contempt."[26] He had come to understand that "the church, as it is...is in perpetual opposition to the teaching of Jesus."[27] As the elderly Doctor Philip in the later novel *Summer 1914* (1936) was to describe the first of the three great crises in modern French culture, he discovered, in reading the four Gospels from start to finish, that they were "a tissue of contradictions."[28]

For this reason, as he wrote in August 1901 to his former confessor and friend
Marcel Hébert, it seemed impossible for him to remain any longer a practicing Catholic.[29] The mild hypocrisy which was the only means by which
a doubting priest (like Hébert) could reconcile reason and faith was out of
the question for a lay person who was free to follow his own moral law. Yet
he wanted to prove through irreproachable conduct that one can "deviate"
(s'écarter) from the religion of the church and its God without becoming an
atheist.[30] He never returned to the church, as does Barois with his deathbed
confession.

It was this difference, no doubt, that led Martin du Gard to believe that
his concession regarding the title of the novel was "shameful." For in an
important sense the hero of the novel is not Barois but, as Camus and other
critics have observed, Marc-Elie Luce, whose death scene is juxtaposed in
radical contrast to Barois's in the final pages of the novel.[31] Luce, whose very
name suggests enlightenment, is a respected scholar and philosopher who
holds the chair of history of religion at the Collège de France and, at the same
time, functions actively as a member of the Senate, to which he was elected
as an independent. A generation older than Barois and his collaborators of
The Sower, he agrees to lend his voice and authority to their enterprise
and soon leads the campaign in defense of Dreyfus. The son of a Protestant
minister, he began as a student of theology but soon gave it up, feeling no call
(vocation), unable to accept any specific religious creed, and retaining from
religion nothing but his fervent interest in moral questions. Unlike Barois,
who asks God's forgiveness for his earlier role as "a sower of doubts" (355; 1:
549), Luce experiences no last-minute reconversion and informs the priest
who attends his deathbed that "a man should attain happiness without
being duped by any sort of mumbo-jumbo through truth alone."[32] Luce
comes much closer to the author's own life and ideal than does Barois; and
"S'Affranchir?"—the original title of the novel—while perhaps "primary,
and ponderous, and a little vulgar,"[33] clearly expresses the theme of the
work as exemplified by Luce. Indeed, Martin du Gard later confessed that
"Luce is my man."[34]

However, since the conflict between religion and science (along with the
Dreyfus Affair) constituted one of the two principal themes of this exemplary novel of ideas, it was necessary to focus on a more typical protagonist
who experiences deconversion and a subsequent shameful reconversion to
blind submission. Luce provides the keenest analysis of Barois's dilemma.

One day his Catholic education foundered on the rock of science; almost
all intelligent young men have that experience. But, unfortunately, the

moral code which we have in the blood and of which we are so proud
has been transmitted to us through many mystical-minded generations.
How can we renounce so noble an inheritance? It's a painful process.
Not every man succeeds in strengthening his intellect enough for it to
ride out the storm, when all the winds of instinct and waves of memory
bear down on it. Those sentimental yearnings of the human heart—how
strong they are, for all their futility! (355–56; 1: 549)

In this novel religion appears primarily as the realm of women and of men
weakened by illness. All four generations of Barois women—Jean's grandmother, his mother and mother-in-law, his wife Cécile, and his daughter
Marie, who becomes a nun—adhere mindlessly to the church and its doctrines. The two representative men of science—Jean's father and Jean himself—retreat, when weakened by infirmity and threatened by death, from
their freethinking atheism, which was produced by rationalism, and make
deathbed conversions that appear to invalidate their lifelong convictions.
Reason enough for Martin du Gard to find it "shameful" that he seemed to
make a hero of Barois by giving the novel his name, rather than stressing
the representative nature of his ignominious and cowardly conversion.

From Faith to Community: Hermann Hesse's *Demian*

In his contribution to the memorial issue of the *Nouvelle Revue Française,*
the theater historian Philippe van Tieghem (1898–1969) recalled that, in the
years immediately following World War I, many young French intellectuals
returning from the war regarded Martin du Gard's novel as their "Baruch"—
the French idiom designating the most urgent new literary discovery.[35] "As-
tu lu *Jean Barois?*" became the shibboleth of a generation, the criterion that
determined whether or not one belonged to the group. They confessed to
one another that even Barois's terrified prayer to the Virgin Mary made sense
to freethinking soldiers who had faced death in the trenches.

Across the Rhine the same status was achieved by *Demian,* a novel
that appeared anonymously in 1919 and by 1922 had gone through fifty-six
printings. It was revealed only a year after publication, and after the novel
had won a prize for first novels, that this angry young man's novel, which
had captured the minds and mood of a generation, was actually the work
of Hermann Hesse. The forty-two-year-old Hesse was already known to an
earlier generation of prewar readers as the author of entertaining realistic
tales and novels and of poems featuring a neoromantic mood of bittersweet
melancholy. Now—anonymously, so that it would not be burdened by his

earlier reputation—he had produced this powerful work that incisively explained the collective psyche of a generation, the expressionist generation that had launched itself with an almost mystical fervor into World War I. What had brought about this astonishing transformation?

Hesse (1877–1962) was the scion of a Swabian family distinguished by two generations of missionary work. His grandfather Hermann Gundert, who had spent over twenty years on the Malabar coast of India, was a noted scholar of international reputation. Fluent in some thirty ancient and modern languages, he produced a standard Malayalam-English dictionary and entertained a flow of visitors from East and West who came to the small southwest German town of Calw, where he directed the Calw Missionary Press. Hesse's father, Johannes Hesse, was a Baltic German from Estonia, who had also spent four years as a missionary on the Malabar coast. Compelled for reasons of health to return to Europe, he was reassigned by the Basel Missionary Society to assist Dr. Gundert in Calw. There he met and married Gundert's widowed daughter, Marie Isenberg, and continued after Gundert's death to direct the Missionary Press. Accordingly Hermann Hesse and his five siblings grew up in a profoundly religious atmosphere of pietist Protestantism, tempered by the living presence of comparative religion represented by his grandfather, his parents, their visitors, their books, and the household décor.[36] There, as Hesse later described it in his essay "My Belief" (1931),

> I encountered Christianity in a unique and rigid form, decisive in my life, a meager and transitory form now outdated and almost extinct. I encountered it as a pietistically tinged Protestantism, and the experience was deep and strong: the lives of my grandparents and parents were entirely controlled by the Kingdom of God and stood in its service.[37]

But, as in the childhood of Martin du Gard, doubts soon arose. "However grand and noble was this Christianity as lived by my elders—as service and sacrifice, as community and commitment—the confessional and in part sectarian forms in which we children came to know it were very early questionable in my eyes and in part completely intolerable." He found the world of Indian religion and poetry far more inviting than "this narrow and pinched form of Christianity, with these somewhat mawkish hymns, these generally so boring ministers and sermons." Later, Hesse continues, he regarded himself as a person with a profound religious feeling. But his personal religion often changed in form, "never suddenly in the sense of a conversion but always slowly as growth and development" (177–80).

Hesse was expected to follow the path that would lead by way of one of the distinguished Swabian preparatory schools to the University of Tübingen and then to the clergy or an academic career. But given his rebellious resistance to organized religion, tensions inevitably arose. In 1890 he was sent off to the Latin School at Göppingen near Stuttgart (an experience depicted in several chapters of *Demian*), where he prepared for the state board examinations that opened the way to the "seminaries" of Württemberg. Admitted in 1891 to Maulbronn, a former Cistercian monastery, within half a year the troubled youth ran away and slumped into a mood of such abject depression that his parents removed him. Following two more years of misbegotten attempts at other schools and several months working as an apprentice in a tower-clock workshop, Hesse acquired a position in a Tübingen bookstore and for the next eight years—first in Tübingen, then in Basel—advanced in the profession of antique book dealer while he read voraciously, giving himself the education he had resisted at school. At the same time he was writing poems and rather precious *poèmes en prose*. While his early works attracted a certain amount of critical attention from readers including Rainer Maria Rilke, it was not until 1904 that he achieved his first broad acclaim as well as a measure of financial independence with *Peter Camenzind*, a novel in the tradition of the nineteenth-century bildungsroman. He gave up his job as a book dealer, married, raised a family of three children, and turned out a series of successful and popular novels on timely subjects (the German school system, the stresses of modern marriage, the lives of artists).

Then in 1916 his life underwent a drastic change for the worse. Hesse had moved his family to Switzerland in 1912, and it was from there that he observed with growing despair the war hysteria that was prevalent in both France and Germany. When he attacked the war mentality in a series of articles, many of his former friends and readers in Germany turned against him with vile denunciations. This rude awakening was exacerbated by personal difficulties. In 1916 his father died, his youngest son became seriously ill, and his wife was afflicted with an emotional disturbance so severe that it required her commitment to a mental institution. These pressures persuaded Hesse, toward the end of 1916, to entrust himself to the psychoanalytical care of Dr. Josef B. Lang, a disciple of C. G. Jung.

The sessions with Lang, which extended into 1917, produced a pronounced sense of spiritual liberation. Hitherto oppressed by feelings that conflicted with Judeo-Christian notions of good and evil, of right and wrong, Hesse learned to acknowledge their existence in his own soul and in the world. Instead of forcing his thoughts and emotions into patterns prescribed by society, he decided to accept the "chaos" of his own consciousness, where the boundary between good and evil did not seem nearly so sharp and clear as in conventional ethics. The immediate product of this psychic release was the novel *Demian* (1919), which Hesse wrote in a few weeks in 1917. The radical ethical ideas of the novel were formulated more systematically in two essays on Dostoevsky published in the volume *In Sight of Chaos* (1920), which T. S. Eliot cited in his notes to *The Waste Land.*

Unlike *Jean Barois*, a realistic third-person account with a clear historical context, *Demian* is a first-person narrative with no historical background. Instead of realistic detail it features a world of dreams, visions, and symbols. Whereas Martin du Gard dated his hero's birth fifteen years earlier than his own in order to accommodate the Dreyfus Affair, Hesse shifted his symbolic autobiography forward by as many years so that his protagonists could move directly from childhood and youth to the battlefields of World War I. But in both works the hero evolves from a childhood of pietist devotion toward a Nietzschean posture "beyond good and evil." As in *Jean Barois*, whose true hero is Marc-Elie Luce, *Demian*'s spiritual center is not Emil Sinclair, whose life story provides the narrative framework, but the shadowy figure of his boyhood friend Max Demian, who exemplifies the ideal toward which Sinclair aspires.[38]

In his narrative, Emil Sinclair recounts certain crucial episodes from his life between the ages of ten and twenty (from about 1905 to 1915). Sinclair's boyhood revolves around his ambivalent friendship with Max Demian (chaps. 1–3). When he goes off to boarding school he slumps at first into profligacy. But the ethereal love he conceives for a girl glimpsed in the park and the mystical pronouncements of a new friend, the renegade theologian Pistorius, gradually steady his uncertainties (chaps. 4–6). At the university he encounters Demian again, is introduced into his community of kindred spirits, and enters into an ambiguous relationship with his friend's mother, Frau Eva.[39] This year of happiness is ended by the war, which claims Demian as a victim but leads Sinclair to the final stage of spiritual independence in which he no longer has need of the external mentors who have supported him up to this point in his life (chaps. 7–8).

When we meet the ten-year-old Emil Sinclair, he has just become aware of the "Two Worlds" between which he is torn: not the realms of faith and reason, as in *Jean Barois*, but the "light" world of home—a world of reason, of Christian piety and duty, of order and security—and the "dark" world outside, with its irrationality, its drunkenness, its violence. At home Sinclair regularly celebrates the evening devotions with his parents: prayers, songs, and blessings shared reverently by the entire household. His father, whose career is never specified, is a man of considerable learning and knowledge of religious history, his mother a woman of gentle piety. Even the house in which the family lives was once part of a Christian monastery and features on the keystone above the entrance an image of a sparrowhawk.

Sinclair's entanglement in the "dark" world of sin comes about when, to impress an older boy, he foolishly lies that he has committed a petty crime—he boasts that he stole apples from a farmer's orchard—and suddenly finds himself blackmailed by the other boy, who threatens him with the police. "It was my sin that I had given the devil my hand."[40] At the same time, the incident creates "the first rift in the righteousness [*Heiligkeit*] of my father" (115) because Sinclair feels a sense of superiority over his father, who fails in all his wisdom to comprehend what has happened to his son. (We are reminded of Gosse's childhood epiphany of doubt regarding his father's infallibility.)

After several weeks of torment he is finally, and by unspecified means, liberated by Demian, a mysterious youth who has moved with his recently widowed mother to Sinclair's town. One day, Demian suggests to Sinclair that the biblical story of Cain, which has been discussed in Bible class, could be interpreted quite differently from the official version: the mark of Cain was in actuality based on the respect, even fear, that many people feel for certain strong and gifted individuals, who seemed to be distinguished as though by a mysterious sign from others. To rationalize their fear before such superiority, people invented the story that these men had in fact murdered someone, perhaps a brother, and been marked by God for their crime. (Demian's reading is clearly Nietzschean, adapting Strauss's method of mythic interpretation.) Sinclair is intrigued and troubled by this possibility, which confirms his early doubts about the infallibility of official Christianity, but he is still too young to tear himself loose from the security of his family. He spends another year or more in a state of childhood innocence and happiness, not even speaking to his liberator.

Several years later, Sinclair is again brought in contact with Demian, whom he has been stealthily observing from afar and who is surrounded by rumors and gossip. It is reported that he and his mother do not attend any church, indeed that they may be Jews or even Muslims! For practical reasons—in Germany at that time, confirmation was still a necessary prerequisite for many careers—Demian is sent to confirmation classes at school. But since he has delayed for two years, he is put into the same class as the younger Sinclair. There, for the first time, Sinclair becomes more closely acquainted with the youth who earlier rescued him from his blackmailer.

By this time, Sinclair reports, his faith in matters of religion had acquired several gaps (154). While troubled, like the fifteen-year-old Jean Barois, by

questions of evil and injustice, he did not join the unthinking scoffers because he still felt a profound reverence for the religious dimension of life.
"But Demian"—not unlike the freethinking tinker in *The Way of All Flesh*—
"had accustomed me to regard and interpret the tales and articles of faith
more freely, more personally, more playfully, more imaginatively." Demian
tells him, one day, that there is an alternative to the usual view of the two
thieves on the crosses with Jesus at Golgotha. Surely, he argues, the one
you would trust would not be the weeping repentant but the other one, who
has character enough to stand by his principles and actions. In a sudden
epiphany Sinclair's inchoate feelings, triggered by his childhood awareness
of two worlds, come together in the realization that we must accept and
revere the world in all its aspects and not simply its arbitrarily partitioned
official half—that we need "in addition to the service of God also a service of
the Devil" (156). The confirmation class has prepared Sinclair, he realizes,
to be accepted not into the church but into "an order of thought and personality, that must exist somewhere on earth and for whose representative or
messenger I took my friend" (159–50).

In Hesse's depiction, Sinclair's spiritual development takes anything
but a smooth course. He suffers many pendulations between the extremes.
When Demian goes off to the university and Sinclair to boarding school in
another town, they lose touch for several years. Sinclair initially falls into a
state of profligacy, drinking heavily and neglecting his studies. He is rescued
from those depths by his iconicizing image of a girl with which he falls in
love and repeatedly tries to capture in paint. Seeking a renewed contact with
Demian, he draws from memory the image of the hawk recalled from the
keystone of his house, showing it breaking its way out of the world-egg, and
mails it off. Some time later he finds on his school desk a note referring
to his drawing and saying that the deity toward whom the bird is flying is
named Abraxas. At the same time, he learns from a new teaching adjunct
(who presumably knew Demian at the university and delivered the note)
that Abraxas is the ancient name of a Gnostic deity "which had the symbolic task of uniting the divine and the devilish" (186). Shortly before he
leaves school, and still obsessed with the image of Abraxas, Sinclair meets
Pistorius (the name under which Hesse introduced his psychoanalyst, J. B.
Lang, into several of his works), a church organist and lapsed student of
theology, with whom he has a number of discussions on the history of religion, myth, and mysteries. (Pistorius with his mythological interpretation
of Christ and the Bible represents in Sinclair's development a close parallel
to the abbé Schertz with his "symbolist compromise" in Jean Barois's life.)
By this time Sinclair has reached a point in his spiritual development at

which he recognizes the beauty and power of the religious dimension in human life as exemplified by the group surrounding Demian and Frau Eva, but firmly rejects all the rituals and false piety of the conventional church as well as all rigid systems of morality. "I have always only suffered from morality" (194).

At this point Sinclair's spiritual development is virtually complete. When he goes off to the university, he again encounters Demian and now meets his friend's mother, Frau Eva, with whom he promptly becomes infatuated. In the community surrounding Demian and Frau Eva he meets believers of various faiths, including Buddhists who wish to convert Europe and disciples of Tolstoy. It is Sinclair's period of happiness, "the first fulfillment of my life and my admittance into the league" (249). Then war breaks out. Demian is called to arms and Sinclair soon follows. On the battlefield in Flanders in the spring of 1915, Sinclair has a vision (based on images from the biblical Revelation) of a mighty goddess in the heavens who bears the features of Frau Eva and from whose forehead thousands of stars burst forth. The vision is in fact triggered by the exploding mortar shell that wounds Sinclair and sends him off to the field hospital, where he finds Demian on the pallet next to his. Passing on a kiss from Frau Eva, Demian dies, but he promises Sinclair that he will always come to him if summoned—if only Sinclair will listen deep within his own soul.

The theme of the novel, which like *Jean Barois* is essentially the story of faith lost and the quest for a new faith, is reflected in a form and language largely determined by religious images. The episodes of Sinclair's life are patterned explicitly on Christian motifs and metaphors. Sinclair is first thrust out of the paradise of his childhood because he claims to have stolen forbidden apples; he looks back longingly at the security of his parents' world as at "a lost paradise"; and his expeditions into the "dark" world are related to the parable of the Prodigal Son. Demian, Sinclair, and the others who rebel against the world of their fathers bear "the mark of Cain" and feel more sympathy for the unrepentant thief of the Gospels than for the remorseful man on the third cross. Sinclair's acquaintance with Abraxas, the deity of good and evil, is related in a chapter entitled "Jacob's Struggle with the Angel." And the entire novel—the narrative of a disciple revolving around a Christ-like figure—is based on the gospel form.

The two central symbols in the second half of the book are likewise religious but no longer conventional Christian ones. The bird breaking its way out of an egg, an image of spiritual rebirth that recurs constantly from the first page to the last, is borrowed by way of Johann Jakob Bachofen from late Roman cultism; but here the symbol has been redefined in such a way

as to exemplify the theme of the novel. The egg represents the dualistic
world that insists on arbitrary distinctions between good and evil, a world
that must be shattered if a new reality is to be born. Abraxas, the god of
good and evil to whom Sinclair is introduced by Demian and Pistorius, is a
central Gnostic deity. Frau Eva, finally, is a Christian archetype colored by
the Jungian conception of *anima*.

Theologies of the Profane

Three novels written under such diverse historical circumstances obviously
display considerable differences. For Butler, born in 1835 and writing *The
Way of All Flesh* in the 1870s, the most powerful influence affecting his
re-vision of the Christian faith was the theory of evolution, while for the
two younger writers the Higher Criticism of the Bible, the new studies of
mythology, and Nietzsche's ethics moved into the foreground. As a result,
Ernest Pontifex loses his faith in traditional Christian ideas and rituals,
but he professes until the end his growing faith in "something" that distinguishes right from wrong. In contrast, Jean Barois, in his last will and
testament, and Emil Sinclair, with his faith in Abraxas, commit themselves
explicitly to an ethics "beyond good and evil." Ernest emerges from his loss
of faith as a new Ishmael, determined to stand apart from a society whose
views he no longer shares and from a religion to which he can dedicate
nothing but critical essays. Jean, in contrast, enters public life and engages
himself actively with a group of like-minded freethinkers until, outflanked
and declared irrelevant by a still younger generation, he weakens and reverts
to the faith of his childhood. Sinclair, finally, allies himself with an invisible
community of the elect, who have been cast into the role of leaders of the
new world yet to be born from the ruins of a past trampled by the war. Pontifex is chastened by the realization that his theological education has taught
him nothing about the Bible, but this insight provokes him to nothing more
than a critique of the institutions of the church. A similar exposure to the
Bible leads Barois to his symbolist compromise and Sinclair to his mythic
interpretations of the biblical stories. And the three works display distinct
generational differences with regard to their literary form. *The Way of All
Flesh* falls squarely into the tradition of the realistic bildungsroman with
powerful ironic overtones. *Jean Barois* is an experimental novel exploiting
all the devices of the early twentieth century: montage, reportage, dialogue,
and cinematographic speed. *Demian*, finally, reflects the techniques of magical realism, of Symbolism, and of myth that characterized the Expressionist
generation whose feelings and thoughts it sought to portray.

Yet for all the differences among them, the three novels are related by pronounced similarities—similarities produced in large part by generational factors. There is absolutely no evidence of any intellectual or literary influence: Martin du Gard does not mention Samuel Butler, whose novel was not translated into French until 1921; Hesse read (and reviewed) *The Way of All Flesh* and *Jean Barois* only in the late 1920s and 1930s when those works first appeared in German. The similarities stem rather from the fact that all three writers shared similar childhood experiences—even mystical emotions—in homes with traditions of pietist devotion, with notably pious mothers, and, in the case of Butler and Hesse, with fathers and grandfathers who were active theologians. Indeed, Butler and Hesse were intended, until their rebellion, for clerical careers. All three soon experienced tensions with the faith of their childhood, tensions that provide the themes of their respective novels: a tension between church and reality (Butler/Ernest), between faith and reason (Martin du Gard/Barois), and between the worlds of good and evil (Hesse/Sinclair). For all three protagonists (and presumably their authors) the gradual, wavering, and painful loss of childhood faith, followed by the movement toward new modes of faith, constitutes the principal theme of their early lives. (What happens later, as we have seen, diverges from case to case.) For these reasons it is not unreasonable to regard them, to use Gershom Scholem's happy term, as theologians of the profane.[41] Despite their loss of conventional faith, they were so profoundly shaped by the religious experiences of the late nineteenth century that they were incapable of describing even their secularization in other than religious terms.

⌒∞⌒

The enormous success of *Demian* and *Jean Barois* tells us that the young postwar generations of France and Germany saw their own spiritual crises captured in novels representing the rebellion of youth against its fathers. That success may also be due in part to the fact that the books are entirely open-ended. Jean Barois and Marc-Elie Luce both die at the end of Martin du Gard's novel, and the reader is left to wonder which road European youth will now take—whether it will relapse like Barois into an outmoded faith or gaze courageously into an unknown future like Luce. Matters look no simpler four years later. At the end of his magnum opus, the eight-volume *roman-fleuve Les Thibault* (1922–40), Martin du Gard stresses the state of confusion facing European youth in a world shattered by World War I. In the diary notices that the dying Antoine Thibault leaves for his infant nephew Paul, he writes about the enormous changes that his nephew will see as he grows to maturity. "Morally there will be a violent break with the past," he prophesies in tones reminiscent of *Demian*, "and all the old standards will be scrapped. The world will pass through a phase of growing pains, with bouts of fever, convulsions, sudden improvement and relapses; and reach a new equilibrium in the end, but only after many, many years. It will be a hard birth, the birth of your New World." But he warns his nephew not to shirk the responsibility of thinking for himself. It is always tempting, he writes, "to let oneself be caught up in a great wave of collective enthusiasm, to embrace some comforting doctrine because it makes things easy.... For it is precisely when his mind is most beset with doubts that a man is liable, in his desire to find an escape at all costs from perplexity, to clutch at any ready-made creed that offers reassurance." [42]

When we lose sight of Sinclair at the end of his account, we have no idea in which direction his spiritual impetus will lead him if and when he emerges unscathed from the war. For Sinclair, for those with the mark of Cain, the community of awakened or awakening ones, humanity is "a distant future, toward which we were all underway, whose image no one knew, whose laws were written nowhere" (237). At this point in the development of Hesse's chiliastic vision, [43] he still believed optimistically in the possibility of a spiritual rebirth of humanity as a whole. Humanity at present might still be toiling in the mires of despair, but within sight on the horizon lay hope. He expressed this conviction succinctly in a letter of 1917 to Romain Rolland: "I believe not in Europe, but only in humanity: in a kingdom of the soul on earth in which all peoples participate and for whose most noble expression we are indebted to Asia." [44] As yet the ideal is not clearly defined: it is "a subterranean, timeless world of values and of the spirit" [45] and "an international world of thought, of inner freedom, of intellectual conscience." [46] Demian and his group regard the outbreak of the war as a harbinger of this rebirth: "The New is beginning, and for those who cling to the Old, the New will be terrible" (251). The war itself is only a distraction that conceals the vast transformations taking place beneath the surface: "Far below something was growing. Something like a new humanity" (254). Demian and his friends look forward to a rebirth of humanity that is felt to be imminent but that they have thus far experienced only in their dreams and visions. As Hesse put it in his essay "The Brothers Karamazov, or The Decline of Europe" (1919), which captured T. S. Eliot's attention: the decline is "a turning away from every fixed morality and ethic in favor of a universal understanding, a universal validation, a new, dangerous, terrifying sanctity." [47]

Once the previously sustaining religious belief has failed, men and women seek surrogates. As Emerson observed (in his essay "The Sovereignty of Ethics," 1878), "Man does not live by bread alone, but by faith, by ed-ucation, by sympathy."[48] In the more severe words of a twentieth-century philosopher, humankind appears to be "condemned to meaning."[49] Karl Jaspers puts it more cynically: "The absurd faiths of the modern era, ranging from astrology to theosophy, and from National Socialism to Bolshevism, suggest that superstition has no less power over the human mind today than it had formerly."[50] It will be my project in the following chapters to describe a few of these theologies of the profane, the various "modes of faith" that attracted many thoughtful Europeans in the decades before and after World War I.

PART TWO

New Modes of Faith

All we have gained then by our unbelief
Is a life of doubt diversified by faith,
For one of faith diversified by doubt.
—*Robert Browning, "Bishop Blougram's Apology"*

CHAPTER FOUR

The Religion of Art

Nietzsche and Dostoevsky were not the first thinkers to proclaim that God was dead. In *The Phenomenology of Spirit* (1807) Hegel built the death of God into his system as a necessary precondition for the final stage of human consciousness which he called "absolute knowing " (*das absolute Wissen*). Of relevance here is the fact that the statement occurs in the penultimate chapter, "Revealed Religion." The chapter, which immediately follows a section entitled "Religion of Art" (*Kunst-Religion*), opens with the sentence: "Through the religion of art, Spirit has emerged from the form of *substance* into that of the *subject*"[1]—at the point, in other words, when a belief accepted by the whole society was being displaced by a radical individualism. According to Hegel's historical sequence, the religion of art appeared at the moment in time when the ethical spirit of Greek antiquity was giving way to the Roman legal sense of an abstract right—at the moment, in short, when religion had lost any sense of faith and adhered to empty ritual.

It is unnecessary for our purposes to consider the differences between Hegel's view and the more general Romantic conception of art as the most appropriate vehicle for the expression of religion, which legitimated the widespread image of the museum as a "temple" of art.[2] Hegel's view belongs to a different tradition, which extends in German intellectual history at least from Schiller to Nietzsche and regards art not as an expression of but as a substitute for religion. From a wholly different standpoint Walter Benjamin observed: "With the advent of the first truly revolutionary means of reproduction, photography, simultaneously with the rise of socialism, art sensed the approaching crisis which has become evident a century later...[and] reacted with the doctrine of *l'art pour l'art*, that is, with a theology of art."[3] Benjamin goes on to argue that this produced a "negative

theology in the form of the idea of 'pure' art, which not only denied any
social function of art but also any categorizing by subject matter."

The turn from religion to art characterized many writers associated with
l'art pour l'art toward the end of the nineteenth century, for whom cultic or
liturgical ritual offered an aesthetic model: Baudelaire, Mallarmé, Verlaine.[4]
In a programmatic statement titled "Modernity" (1890) the Austrian journalist, dramatist, and theoretician Hermann Bahr observed shrewdly that
"[a] wild torment permeates the age and the pain is no longer bearable."

> The cry for a savior is widespread and the crucified are everywhere....
> That salvation will come from the suffering and grace from despair, that it
> will dawn after this terrible darkness and that art will come among men—
> such a resurrection, glorious and blessed, is the belief of modernity.[5]

In many cases, to be sure, the aestheticization of art was not accompanied
by a pronounced crisis of faith; one does not readily associate Oscar Wilde,
for instance, with a religious crisis. In several cases, however, it is possible
to observe in precise detail the movement from religion to art, from priest
to *poeta vates*.

Stefan George: Art as Ritual

Stefan George is almost wholly unknown outside Germany today, even
among specialists in modern poetry. In Germany, however, he is widely
regarded among cognoscenti as the initiator of a "new poetry" that broke
radically with the Romantic traditions of the past. "In each one of you," he
told his followers, "I must first kill off the entire nineteenth century"[6]—by
which he meant principally the epigonal circle of Munich poets promoted
by King Maximilian II of Bavaria.

Because of the hagiographic accounts by disciples who have haloed his
figure, because of the distortions stemming from his temporary cooptation
by the National Socialists, and because of the lack of biographical information, it is difficult to obtain an objective picture of George's early years;[7]
indeed, the most accurate record of his development is his poetry. Stefan
George (1868–1933), known locally as Etienne, was born in Büdesheim and
grew up in the town of Bingen, just across one of the most scenic bends of the
Rhine, in a devoutly Catholic and bilingual family. (His great-grandfather
had come to Germany from Lorraine, and George himself was undecided
at first whether he should become a French or a German poet.) As he re-
lates in the short prose piece "Der kindliche Kalender,"[8] the rhythm of his

early life in the Catholic Rhineland was determined by the ecclesiastical calendar: from Christmas, Candlemas, and the Fasching carnival through the Eastertime festivities, Corpus Christi, Pentecost, and St. John's Day back around to Advent, each holiday tied to agricultural practices meaningful to the son of a prosperous vintner and wine merchant in a famous wine region. Another poem ("Verjährte Fahrten I") recalls a pilgrimage to Walldürrn in Baden, where the children hoped to "rescue ourselves from our anguish at the place of grace" ("Wollten uns aus unsren nöten / Retten an dem gnadenort," 1: 38).[9] He later told Ernst Robert Curtius that "[g]enuine Catholicism is something venerable, pure, and right. I lived in it myself up to my eighteenth year. Then the transformation took place within me."[10] George had nothing but contempt for the "religious wave" at the turn of the century. "People want to have everything too cheaply," he told the scholar-critic. "The distress will have to get much worse" (125). He worried about the "vague religious backwash" of Christian and Hindu ingredients that attracted many in the years immediately before World War I (126). And he was equally suspicious of "all this Catholicizing" that swept across Europe after the war (127). We will return to what he called his "transformation." For the moment, however, it is important to establish the strong Catholic basis in George's life and thought, for it determines the conspicuous ritual and liturgical element in his poetry.[11]

The actor and dramatist Georg Fuchs, a classmate of George's at the eminent Ludwig-Georg Gymnasium in Darmstadt where George's religious instruction continued to be strictly supervised, recalled that already in his teens the poet understood the "magically consecrational power of ritual," that he cultivated his elegant German in a "high priestly" manner, and that he initiated a few select friends into a "consecrational alliance" (Weihebündnis) with a ritual involving bowing, kneeling, and sprinkling with sand—a ceremony, Fuchs confesses, that transformed the bowling alley where this took place into an "initiatory temple" (Einweihungstempel).[12] George also invented and wrote poems in a secret language that he called IMRI (a hidden allusion to the biblical INRI?) and that had the same sacerdotal function as the Latin of the Mass. Fuchs took it for granted that George, after his gymnasium years, would enter the priesthood. Indeed, even after he lost his faith George stylized his appearance and bearing into a hieratic habitus. The photographic images that George carefully controlled do nothing to contradict that impression.[13]

But George did not enter the priesthood. Following his graduation and with his father's support he embarked on a study trip lasting almost two years. He hoped to improve his knowledge of languages, but a more

immediate desire was to escape what in the poem "Franken" (Franks, from
Der Siebente Ring) he later called "the avoided regions where my disgust
swelled up in the face of all that they praised and practiced; I ridiculed their
gods and they mine."

> Hier die gemiednen gaue wo der ekel
> Mir schwoll vor allem was man pries und übte·
> Ich ihrer und sie meiner götter lachten.
> (1: 235)

His travels took him to London, Switzerland, Italy, Paris, Spain, Copen-
hagen, and back to Paris where he was invited to attend Mallarmé's *mardi
soirs* and met many of the new French poets. (George was to become one of
the earliest German advocates and translators of French Symbolist poetry.)
By the time he arrived back in Germany and took up his studies in Berlin,
he had become completely alienated from the Catholic faith of his youth
and attuned to a new sense of the dignity and calling of the poet.

This alienation implied no hostility. The early poems that he grouped
under the title "Von einer Reise 1888–89" (From a journey 1888–89)[14] sound
a note of sincere regret at his loss of faith. In "Die Glocken" (The bells)
the ringing of the church bells—a frequent symbol in George's poems for
religious faith—awakens memories of childhood devotion and beginning
doubt:

> Als ich schwach war da liess euer klingen
> Vor reue des herzens saiten zerspringen
> Und alle stärke es von mir trug
> In der frage: klingt wahrheit ihr oder trug?

> [When I was weak your ringing caused / the strings of my heart to break
> from remorse / and it bore away all my strength / in the question: do you
> sound truth or deception?] (2: 493)

Another poem from the same period, "Seefahrt" (Lake trip), depicts a boat
ride with friends across a lake as bells from nearby villages sound the Ave.
They enter a church where they hear the litanies and observe the women
telling their rosaries. His friends scoff and they hasten away as it grows dark.

> Doch mich verlezt ihr spottend wort
> Bin ich auch nicht viel besser selber—

[But their mocking words offend me / yet I am not much better myself.] (2: 497)

"Herzensnacht," which might best be translated as Saint John of the Cross's "dark night of the soul," expresses the sorrow of a life deprived of faith:

Das trübe leben das mich umschliesst
Füllt meine seele nicht aus
Sie ist ein einsames haus
Um das ein nebelmeer rings sich ergiesst.

[The gloomy life that surrounds me / does not fill my soul; / it is an empty house / enclosed roundabout by a sea of fog.] (2: 475)

It has been widely recognized that George's Catholic background, even after he lost its informing faith, provided the material for the powerful sense of ritual that pervades his poetry and shaped his life—what has aptly been termed his "aesthetic Catholicism."[15] Indeed, George was almost Roman in his emphasis on ritual at the expense of faith. The titles of his volumes— from the early *Hymns* (*Hymnen*, 1890) and *Pilgrimages* (*Pilgerfahrten*, 1891) to the final *The New Kingdom* (*Das Neue Reich*, 1928)—betray this indebtedness, as did his costume and demeanor and the strict observance of his "circle" (*Kreis*) with its reverential disciples who addressed him as "master" (*Meister*). This self-stylization has been almost worshipfully imitated by his followers and ridiculed by George's enemies.[16]

What matters in the present context, however, is not the ritualization of the poetry and the stylization of the life but the poet's turn from religious faith: first, in the 1890s, to the cult of art; then to the secularization of his religiosity into a mystical cult of revelation; and finally to the proclamation of a new "secret Germany" of the spirit. Hence his conviction that poetry should not be interpreted but accepted on its own terms as a revelation.[17]

George's aesthetic turn is strikingly evident in the appearance of his books, of which the first several small volumes were printed in private editions of only one hundred copies for distribution to select friends. While still a teenager he had created for his poems a stylized roman script that was distinctly different from the fraktur used in most books of the period or the handwriting taught in the schools. To achieve the appearance of a classical ductus he gave up the capitalization of substantives which is normal in German; reduced the letters *k* and *t* and all other letters with tails (*d f g h l p q*) in such manner that they did not extend above or below the line; wrote the letter *e* like the Greek epsilon (ϵ); and simplified punctuation by omitting all commas and replacing everything but full stops (. : !) with a center dot (·). The resulting script, which resembles Carolingian minuscule, was reproduced in the typeface of his volumes. The effect was enhanced when, beginning with the volume *The Year of the Soul* (*Das Jahr der Seele*, 1897), the graphic artist Melchior Lechter began to design George's now distinctive books. Amidst the often undistinguished or cheap gilt volumes being published around the turn of the century, George's works stood out as works of art in themselves.

The preciosity of the script and design reflect the subject matter of the poems.[18] George had concluded the last poem in his early works ("The Schoolboy") with the wish to encounter nature: bodies, flowers, clouds, and waves. That is what he set out to accomplish in his first two collections, *Hymns* (1890) and *Pilgrimages* (1891). But by the end of the second volume he had come to the reluctant conclusion that a poetry of severe simplicity was not possible in the German language as he had inherited it, ravaged as it was by what he regarded as the miserable poetry of the nineteenth century. The concluding poem, "The Clasp" ("Die Spange"), states that conviction symbolically.

> Ich wollte sie aus kühlem eisen
> Und wie ein glatter fester streif·
> Doch war im schacht auf allen gleisen
> So kein metall zum gusse reif.

> Nun aber soll sie also sein:
> Wie eine grosse fremde dolde
> Geformt aus feuerrotem golde
> Und reichem blitzendem gestein.

> [I wanted it (to be made) of cool iron / and like a smooth firm band; / but in the shaft on all the tracks / there was no such metal ready for casting. / So now it shall be like this: / like a large exotic (flower) cluster / formed from fire-red gold / and rich glittering stones.]

The shift from the bright vowels of the first strophe to the dark ones of the second suggests in sound the difference between the severe ideal and the lush substitute.[19]

George's next volume, *Algabal* (1892), exemplified this shift from simple nature to exotic constructs. Algabal was the Roman emperor Varius Avitus (204–222), of whom George had been made aware by Huysmans's novel *À rebours* (1884). As a child in Syria Varius was a priest of the sun god Elagabal. When he became emperor in 218, he adopted the name of the god, changing it to Heliogabalus, and proclaiming his deity supreme among the gods of Rome until he was assassinated by his soldiers. George's Algabal has an underground kingdom where "my garden requires neither air nor warmth" ("Mein garten bedarf nicht luft und nicht wärme," 1: 47). Its lifeless flocks of birds have never seen a springtime; its trees consist of charcoal; and its ever-gray light knows neither morning nor evening. Yet the artificiality of this hermetically enclosed realm does not ultimately suffice. The cycle ends with one of the programmatic poems that often open and close George's volumes: in "Augury" ("Vogelschau") the poet recalls the flight of exotic birds suggesting the atmosphere of *Algabal*—multicolored jays, parrots, hummingbirds, ravens, and jackdaws—and concludes in the present tense with more homely swallows that now fill the air, a hint of his future turn to less wondrous subjects:

> Schwalben seh ich wieder fliegen·
> Schnee- und silberweisse schar·
> Wie sie sich im winde wiegen
> In dem winde kalt und klar.

> [I see swallows flying again, / snow- and silverwhite flocks; / how they float in the wind, / in the wind cold and clear.] (1: 59)

The later works of the 1890s seek in a different manner to transmute the stuff of history and nature into art. The next volume (1895) contains, as its tripartite title suggests, books of serene bucolics (*Hirten- und Preisgedichte*), of medieval sagas and songs (*Sagen und Sänge*), and of oriental matters (*Hängende Gärten*). That excursion into the past is succeeded in *The Year of the Soul* (*Das Jahr der Seele*, 1897)—by far his most popular and most purely lyrical volume—by a return to nature: a domesticated nature shaped to his aesthetic ends, as in the famous opening poem: "Komm in den totgesagten park und schau" ("Come in the park they say is dead and look"), which is regarded by some as "one of the loveliest poems in the German language."[20] George's detached attitude toward nature, in which according to several witnesses he felt distinctly uncomfortable and alien, is suggested by the noun "park" and verb "look": he is at ease only in the controlled landscape of a park or garden, and even there he proposes to do no more than to contemplate it aesthetically. He suggests to his companion—the only volume in which the poems are addressed to a woman or, more generally perhaps, to womankind—that she take the deep yellow of the season, the soft gray of birch and box tree, the still unwilted late roses, and weave them into a wreath:

> Dort nimm das tiefe gelb· das weiche grau
> Von birken und von buchs· der wind ist lau·
> Die späten rosen welkten noch nicht ganz·
> Erlese küsse sie und flicht den kranz.
> (1: 121)

This opening poem, which portrays the weaving of the fall foliage into a simulated "autumn face" ("verwinde leicht im herbstlichen Gesicht"), serves as an apt introduction to the artificial world of the park.[21] The cycle works its way through the sequence of seasons—from fall through winter and, skipping springtime, to summer. The volume ends on the same note of melancholy resignation with which it began. "Do you still want to look for the full colors of earlier days on the bare grounds" of autumn ("Willst du noch länger auf den kahlen böden / Nach frühern vollen farben spähn")? Our days vanish quickly, "but all things that we called flowers / assemble at the dead spring" ("Doch alle dinge die wir blumen nannten / Versammeln sich am toten quell," 1: 167).

The title poem of the next volume, *The Tapestry of Life* (*Der Teppich des Lebens*, 1899), also privileges the beauty of the figured tapestry over that of the living world. In the fabric he discerns human, animal, and vegetable life revolving in a dance framed by stars. No one understands the mystery of the intertwined figures and designs, which come to life one evening and reveal their meaning.

> Sie ist nach willen nicht: ist nicht für jede
> Gewohne stunde: ist kein schatz der gilde.
> Sie wird den vielen nie und nie durch rede
> Sie wird den seltnen selten im gebilde.

> [It doesn't (respond) on demand: is not for every / common hour: is no treasure for the guild. / It is never (revealed) to the many and never through speech; / it is (revealed) to the few and rarely through its image.] (1: 190)

George's poems of the 1890s amounted to an attempt, through the turn to an absolute art, to counteract what the poet regarded as the cultural vulgarity of the new German Empire and to create an aesthetic world preferable to mere reality. George returned from Paris in 1889, having rejected the Catholicism of his youth, with a new appreciation for the poet's calling and with the mission of renewing poetry and art in Germany. In 1892, with his friend Carl August Klein, whom he met at the University of Berlin, he founded the journal *Blätter für die Kunst.* (Already during his school years in Darmstadt, in response to Bismarck's *Kulturkampf,* George and a few other classmates had produced a short-lived literary journal with the title *Rosen und Disteln* [Roses and thistles], in which all allusions to religion and politics were rigorously excluded for the sake of "more serious forms of poetry."][22] The editors state in their program that their journal "desires a SPIRITUAL ART [*GEISTIGE KUNST*] based on the new manner of perception and creation—an art for art's sake—and is thus opposed to that exhausted and inferior school derived from a false conception of reality."[23] The same initiative is evident in his translation of Baudelaire's *Fleurs du mal* (1891; 2nd ed., 1901), which he undertook, as he states in the preface, "not from any desire to introduce a foreign writer but for the fundamental sheer joy in creating form" (2: 233). George adapts Baudelaire's poems in a manner intended to play down their notorious theme of *spleen* in favor of *idéal* (which he translated as *Vergeistigung*), thus transforming Baudelaire into a poet of "fervent spirituality" (*glühende geistigkeit*). To accomplish this, he included only 118 of the original 151 poems, omitting the famous prefatory "Au lecteur" and softening in others "the repulsive and negative images" that attracted the younger generation. "In poetry," he wrote elsewhere, "as in all art activity, anyone who is still affected by the addiction to 'say' something, to want to 'accomplish' something, is not worthy of entering even the forecourt of art.... The value of poetry is determined not by its meaning (otherwise it would be something like wisdom, erudition) but its form."[24] However, in the course of the decade it became evident to George that his ideal of the spiritual life could not be satisfied by poetry alone, no matter how absolute and pure it might be. Contemplating a former leper house on the outskirts of Munich, George remarked bitterly: "We who bear the divine secrets of the nation in our hearts and who are called upon to bear witness to them: we belong out here. We ought to settle outside the gates of this profane and godless people that desecrated everything, and we ought to die here as the protectors of the eternal light!"[25] Accordingly, his mission after the turn of the century took on a new prophetic character.[26]

The final poem of *The Year of the Soul* (1897) ended, as we saw, on a note of melancholy resignation as the flowers gathered at the dead spring. But in the opening poem of the next volume, *The Tapestry of Life* (1900), we suddenly hear a new tone.

> Ich forschte bleichen eifers nach dem horte
> Nach strofen drinnen tiefste kümmernis
> Und dinge rollten dampf und ungewiss -
> Da trat ein nackter engel durch die pforte:
>
> [I was searching with pale eagerness for the treasure, / for strophes of deepest grief, / and earthly things rolled with dull uncertainly—/ then a naked angel stepped through the portal.] (1: 172)

The angel wore no crown, his voice resembled the poet's, and when the poet knelt the angel (clearly an image of the poet's higher self) also knelt. But his message was a new one: "Das schöne leben sendet mich an dich / Als boten" (The life of beauty sends me to you / as its messenger). The religious angels of George's Catholic childhood have been secularized into an angel representing the aesthetic ideal.[27] In his preface to a new edition of *Hymnen, Pilgerfahrten, Algabal* (1899), which had appeared only a few months earlier, George noted a change in the German public, "a new desire for beauty" ("ein neues schönheitsverlangen," 1: 6) exemplified by the recent upsurge of painting and the decorative arts. (George is referring to the artistic revival of *Jugendstil*.) In his life, he continued, there had been bad days and many a harsh and shrill tone. But now a good spirit is holding the scales level and he is prepared to do everything the angel wishes.

> In meinem leben rannen schlimme tage
> Und manche töne hallten rauh und schrill.
> Nun hält ein guter geist die rechte waage
> Nun tu ich alles was der engel will.
> (1: 173)

For too long he has been thirsting for happiness, but he no longer wishes to be oppressed by the yoke of a Lord whose service is too gloomy and lonely. Then the angel appears in the path of the aggrieved poet.

> Zu lange dürst ich schon nach eurem glücke.
> Dass mich des herren joch nicht mehr bedrücke!

Zu düster und zu einsam war sein dienst
Als du mir schmerzlichem am weg erschienst.
(1: 174)

The angel, as "friend and leader and ferryman" ("Ich bin freund und führer dir und ferge," 1: 176), conducts the poet to a mountaintop from which he can survey humanity below: the hordes seeking profit and pleasure, other swarms following the cross, and a smaller band attracted by the glory of classical Greece ("Hellas ewig unsre liebe")—the proper company for the poet. Neither material life nor Christianity is the realm of the angel, who never speaks of sin or ethics ("Du sprichst mir nie von sünde oder sitte," 1: 176) but proclaims an aesthetic kingdom of beauty.

⟨∾⟩

Every spiritual kingdom needs a deity, an object of worship for the cult of aesthetic religion. Because George had rejected the God of his Catholic youth, he required a new one. His longing produced precisely such a deity. This next chapter in George's life and thought, its central episode, is strange and difficult for us to understand. But it constituted a turning point in the poet's life. Late in 1901 in the center of Munich, George saw and admired a startlingly beautiful youth of thirteen—an encounter that he described several years later in Dantesque tones.

> We had just passed the midday zenith of our life and we were concerned when we contemplated our immediate future. We were moving toward a distorted humanity grown cold. . . . When we saw Maximin for the first time in our city he was still in his childhood years. He came striding toward us from the Victory Arch with the undeterrable firmness of a young fencer and with the mien of supreme commanding power mitigated by that liveliness and melancholy that had entered the countenances of people only after centuries of Christian cultivation. We recognized in him the representative of an all-mighty youth as we had seen it in our dreams.[28]

A few months later he encountered the same youth and asked if he could have him photographed. In January 1903 George met the boy again, became acquainted with his parents, and thereafter saw him frequently at home, in his own apartments, and at literary gatherings. Maximilian Kronberger (1888–1904), the son of a brewer, was himself an aspiring poet and admirer of George. The relationship lasted little over a year because in April 1904

Maximilian suddenly died of meningitis, one day before his sixteenth birthday. But the youth, whom George and his friends called Maximin, was
transfigured into the deity of the new cult of aesthetics proclaimed by the
angel of the earlier poems.

We must understand this in a very literal sense. For George, the appari-
tion of Maximin was an epiphany, the second embodiment of God on earth
after Jesus. This is made amply clear in the central section of *The Seventh
Ring* entitled simply "Maximin," around which the other sections revolve.
The twenty-one poems, which move from Maximin's Advent to his death
and spiritual assimilation ("Einverleibung," which in some copies George
entitled "Kommunion"),[29] begin with the straightforward statement:

> Dem bist du kind· dem freund.
> Ich seh in dir den Gott
> Den schauernd ich erkannt
> Dem meine andacht gilt.

> [For one you're a child, for another a friend. / I see in you the God /
> whom I acknowledge, trembling, / and for whom my reverence is
> reserved.] (1: 279)

The poet has longed for Him just as once the people called for a savior (1:
279). When His eye glows, dead trees come to life and the rigid earth is
revived (1: 280). Now that He has appeared, the poet can emerge from the
valley of darkness and look into the new land. As the angel's song resounds,
His mouth sears the poet's lips and the poet kneels down and prays ("Knie
hin und bete!" 1: 281). The poet quotes the words that Maximin allegedly
uttered upon his death:

> 'Lass mich in die himmel entschweben!
> Du heb dich vom grund als gesunder!
> Bezeuge und preise mein wunder
> Und harre noch unten im leben!'

> ["Let me float away into the heavens. / Do thou rise up from the ground
> as healed. / Bear witness and praise my wonder / and tarry below for a
> while in life."] (1: 282)

The poet consoles himself and his friends that "you too have heard the call
of a god /and a god's mouth has kissed you" ("Auch ihr habt eines gottes ruf

vernommen / Und eines gottes mund hat euch geküsst," 1: 284). Later the
poet prays to Maximin:

Du wachst über uns
in deiner unnahbaren glorie:
Schon wurdest du eins
mit dem Wort das von oben uns sprach.

[You watch over us / in your unapproachable glory: / already you have
become one / with the Word that spoke to us from above.] (1: 285)

In *The Tapestry of Life* the appearance of the angel in the poet's hour
of despair proclaimed an aesthetic kingdom of art and the epiphany of its
god. In *The Seventh Ring* the god manifests himself in the earthly form
of Maximin. George's next (and last) two slim volumes, *The Star of the
Covenant* (1914) and *The New Kingdom* (1928), are concerned essentially
with the establishment of the cult of the new deity and his aesthetic state.
The Star of the Covenant, looking back toward the preceding volume, begins
with a prayer to Maximin:

DU STETS NOCH ANFANG UNS UND END UND MITTE
Auf deine bahn hienieden˙ Herr der Wende˙
Dringt unser preis hinan zu deinem sterne.

[Thou, ever our beginning and our end and middle / on your course here
below, Lord of the turn, / our praise rises up to your star.] (1: 350)

But at the end the poet apostrophizes his disciples of the cult devoted to the
new deity: "You are the foundation as I now praise you" ("IHR SEID DIE
GRÜNDUNG WIE ICH JEZT EUCH PREISE," 1: 390). In the "Final Chorus"
("Schlusschor") the disciples rejoice that God's path has been opened to
them, His land laid out for them, His strength in their breasts, His salvation
poured over them, and His joy blossomed within them ("Gottes pfad ist uns
geweitet . . . Gottes glück ist uns erblüht," 1: 394).

There is no need to sketch yet again the history of the George circle in the
years until his death in 1933.[30] By 1907 and *The Seventh Ring* the course
of development relevant in the present context was complete: from the

young poet's crisis of faith and his rejection of Catholicism to his turn to the religion of art, the angel's annunciation of the aesthetic kingdom, and the epiphany of its new deity. George's personal development from poet to seer to apostle is paralleled by the transformation of his group from circle to covenant to state, which in a late poem he called the "secret Germany" ("Geheimes Deutschland," 1: 425).

George's tendency toward proud isolation and coterie building was evident as early as his years at Darmstadt, where he inducted Georg Fuchs and a few select friends into his quasi-religious cult. Indeed, the power of George's personality, his aura, was so strong that it struck some as oppressive: the young Hugo von Hofmannsthal, while admiring the older poet, consciously withdrew from his influence, writing that he could "kill without touching."[31] The impulse to group formation grew increasingly strong as George became less satisfied with a life solipsistically dedicated to his own poetry. *Blätter für die Kunst* announced on its title page that it was meant for "a close circle of readers invited by the members." *The Star of the Covenant* (where the "star" is clearly Maximin)[32] was initially intended as a "secret book" ("geheimbuch") for "friends of the closer circle" ("freunde des engern bezirks").[33] The "Headings and Dedications" of *The Year of the Soul* contain thumbnail sketches of sixteen of the friends associated with the *Blätter für die Kunst* or who had gathered around him in Berlin and Munich. George's educational mission took place at the expense of his poetry, which after 1900 became increasingly exhortatory and prophetic and less prolific. Yet the number and quality of followers attracted by his personality and his message of intellectual and cultural elitism are astonishing, even if they did not exhaustively exemplify what Friedrich Wolters, in the subtitle of his hagiographic biography, rather presumptuously called "German Intellectual History since 1890." In addition to some of the most prominent literary scholars of the early twentieth century—Friedrich Gundolf and Max Kommerell—such artists as Melchior Lechter and Reinhold and Sabine Lepsius were attracted to George's "circle" along with the Dutch poet Albert Verwey, the cultural historians Ernst Kantorowicz and Friedrich Wolters, and the philosopher Georg Simmel. Perhaps the name most familiar outside Germany is that of Claus von Stauffenberg, the noble young officer who attempted in the plot of July 1944 to assassinate Hitler.

George lived a life of fierce and peripatetic independence, residing occasionally at home in Bingen but more often in hotels or with friends in Berlin, Munich, Heidelberg, and elsewhere. After 1900 he spent less and less time abroad, seeing his mission in Germany. He published his volumes in small editions and read his poems exclusively in closed gatherings. With Karl

Wolfskehl he edited a three-volume anthology, *Deutsche Dichtung* (1900–1902), which looked back across what he considered the trivial poetry of the nineteenth century to the great era of Goethe. He declined all public honors apart from the Goethe Prize, which was awarded to him in 1927. In 1933, refusing to become president of the German Poetry Academy established by the Nazis, he left Germany and went to Switzerland, where he died a few months later, dedicated fervently yet quixotically to his ideal of a homeland guided by the spiritual ideals of a "secret Germany."

Paul Valéry: Art as Order

Paul Valéry was arguably the leading intellectual among major poets of the twentieth century, acknowledged even by philosophers as "one of the few modern poets of whom it can be said without exaggeration that they were also significant thinkers."[34] Other prominent poets, such as T. S. Eliot and Gottfried Benn, devoted considerable energy to criticism and essays on a variety of topics. But none was so obsessively dedicated to matters of pure mind as was the French *académicien*, who once remarked to Teilhard de Chardin that, if he had to choose between spiritualism and materialism, he would choose the latter "because the spiritual is the doctrine that requires the least intellect."[35] In the oeuvre of none other was the volume of actual poetry so slight, especially in proportion to the vast analytical prose ranging across literature, music, painting, philosophy, politics, history, education, mathematics, psychology—in sum, every field of intellectual endeavor. Poems constitute only two hundred of the almost three thousand pages in the two-volume Pléiade edition of his works, not to mention the thousands of pages of notebooks that he filled daily and compulsively for more than fifty years. Moreover, in the life of none other was the work of poetry concentrated in such brief spurts of creative energy. Apart from the Symbolist phase of his youth (1888–92), from which he selected and revised twenty-one poems for his *Album de vers anciens* (1920), his poetic production was essentially limited to the years around the two world wars. His relatively few major poems were composed during and immediately after World War I: the five-hundred-line poetic monologue *La Jeune Parque* (1917) and the twenty-one poems of *Charmes* (1922). World War II, in turn, produced in response the impressive translation of Virgil's *Bucoliques* (1942–44; first published 1953).

This is not to say that his poetic activity ceased absolutely between those periods: the myth of Valéry's "Grand Silence" was no more than that—a myth. The interwar years saw the appearance of a few "pièces diverses" as

well as two operatic libretti and several poetic dialogues. But the relatively
few poems that established his fame and stature as the widely acknowledged "Poète d'État" of France—notably *La Jeune Parque* and *Le Cimetière
marin*—were essentially the product of World War I. As he waited to find
out if he would be called to arms, he told his friend Albert Coste in 1915, he
initially suffered from inactivity. "The time was too stressful to continue
any long-winded exercises. So do you know what I am doing? I am refitting,
repainting, and varnishing some old verses. It's a ridiculous activity, rather
Chinese, but traditional: during every terrible epoch of humanity, one always sees some gentleman seated in a corner attending to his handwriting
and stringing pearls."[36] In a similar vein, apropos of *La Jeune Parque*, he
wrote a year later to André Breton that he was composing some verses, "a
duty and a stratagem, a long forgotten game. Why? There are reasons. Among
others, the state of war is too exciting to permit, alongside itself, rigorously
conducted analyses." He imagined that the "superannuated poetry" that he
undertook was like "a work carried out in the age of Latin verse. There were
rhetoricians, in those days, at the time of Attila and Gaiseric, who chewed
over their hexameters in a corner."[37]

Paul Valéry (1871–1945) was born at Sète, west of Marseilles on the
Mediterranean coast, a town with a hillside cemetery overlooking the sea,
as celebrated in *Le Cimetière marin*.[38] Following school in Sète and lycée in
nearby Montpellier, he received his baccalauréat in 1888 and enrolled in the
law faculty of the University of Montpellier. Here he wrote and published
his first poems and met two of his lifelong friends, Pierre Louÿs and André
Gide. Through them he became acquainted with the poetry of Mallarmé,
which influenced him profoundly, and soon met the master himself. Then
in 1892, just when he seemed to be on the point of a remarkable career—he
had received his *licence en droit* and already published, in Louÿs's journal
La Conque, a number of poems that had brought him a rapid and gratifying
recognition—Valéry experienced a spiritual crisis known in biographical
accounts as the Night of Genoa. During a visit to his mother's family in
Genoa, on a night when his room was repeatedly illuminated by a dramatic
lightning storm, "my entire destiny played itself out in my head. I am
between Myself and Me."[39]

It is likely that the Genoan night represented the culmination of several
factors.[40] For reasons that remain unclear in the life of this intensely private
man, he had lost his previously ardent religious faith. In his late teens
Valéry was a devout Catholic, "almost an idolater," as he confessed to Pierre
Louÿs.[41] "He adores this religion," he wrote of himself in the third person,
"which makes beauty one of its dogmas, and Art the most magnificent of its

apostles. He adores above all his own private Catholicism—a bit Spanish, quite Wagnerian and Gothic."[42] He loved high masses in the cathedral of Montpellier, and he believed—"this is my entire metaphysics and ethics— that God exists and the devil too, but within us."[43] Suddenly the frequent allusions to his religion cease, along with the rhapsodic effusions about Catholic masses. (But for the rest of his life, as we shall see, Valéry continued to use theological terminology to refer to other matters, and specifically poetry.)

In addition, in the summer of 1892 Valéry was recovering from an un-happy love affair, and—law degree in hand—family circumstances now made it necessary for him to begin to support himself. His brief personal acquain-tance with the venerated Mallarmé provoked doubts in his mind about his poetic ability. And his study of Poe's *Eureka* persuaded him that his com-pelling interest in the human intellect could best be pursued by means other than poetry. All these factors appear to have come together in the fall of 1892—whether or not on that specific night in Genoa—to change his life plan. In any case, as he recalled in 1921, "I had ceased writing verse and al-most given up reading. Novels and poems, in my opinion, were only impure and half-unconscious applications of a few properties inherent in the great secrets I hoped some day to discover, basing this hope on the unremitting assurance that they must necessarily exist."[44]

The self-boycott was not absolute; Valéry did in fact write and publish a few poems over the next several years. For the most part, however, he shifted his attention from poetry to mind, the pure intellect—a shift exemplified by two important prose works. In 1894 he wrote on commission his "Intro-duction à la méthode de Léonard de Vinci." At age twenty-three, he later confessed, he admired Leonardo more than he understood him. "I regarded him as the principal character of that Intellectual Comedy which has still to find its poet and would, in my judgment, be far more valuable than *La Comédie Humaine*; more so, even, than *The Divine Comedy*."[45] By putting Leonardo ahead of Balzac and Dante, Valéry elevated intellectual analysis to heights beyond poetry. His Leonardo, to be sure, has little to do with the historical figure: "I propose to imagine a man whose activities are so diverse that if I postulate a ruling idea behind them all, there could be none more universal. And I want this man to possess an infinitely keen perception of the difference of things, the adventures of which perception might well be called analysis."[46] The next year, in "La Soirée avec Monsieur Teste" (1895), Valéry sought to sketch "the portrait of a mind as much occupied with it-self as a virtuoso may be with the debates between his instrument and his talent."[47] He wrote his book at a time when "for me literature was suspect, even the fairly precise works of poetry" (3). The protagonist's name—Teste suggests both *tête* (head, consciousness) and Latin *testis* (witness)—points to his cerebrality and his function as the analytical observer of the world (67, 90). The early celebration of Leonardo anticipates Valéry's later enthusiasm for Goethe's universal genius and his turn to the figure of the legendary Renaissance magus for his last major work, the dramatic sketches of *Mon Faust* (1945).

During the next two decades, now married and supporting his family first as a civil servant at the Ministry of War and then as secretary to the director of the Havas Press Agency, Valéry devoted himself principally to studies in a variety of scientific fields, which he recorded assiduously in his voluminous notebooks, and entered eagerly into the cultural life of Paris (where in February 1896 he met Stefan George at Mallarmé's apartment). It was not until 1912, when Gide, Louÿs, and the publisher Gallimard encouraged him to collect his early poems for publication, that Valéry returned gradually to poetry. He began by extensively revising his early poems, which were eventually published in the *Album de vers anciens* (1920), and he undertook his magnificent poetic depiction of the growth of human (female) consciousness, *La Jeune Parque,* which underwent some hundred drafts before it was finally published in 1917. His work on *La Jeune Parque,* in turn, stimulated the production of some entirely new poems, twenty-one of which he gathered for the volume *Charmes* (1922). At this point, when he was being unanimously hailed as France's greatest living poet, Valéry in effect gave up poetry to play the role of the national *homme de lettres.* He wrote essays, introductions to various volumes, and poetic dialogues on such topics as architecture (*Eupalinos ou l'Architecte*) and dance (*L'Âme et la danse*). He lectured all over Europe and was elected to the Académie Française and appointed to the chair of poetics at the Collège de France. Upon his death in 1945 his funeral was celebrated as a state ceremony with national honors.

c○○っ

Valéry's poetry stands distinctly apart from the Surrealism promulgated in numerous manifestos by his friend André Breton. The automatic writing through which the Surrealists sought to capture images of the unconscious traced its heritage back by way of Dada and Apollinaire to Rimbaud and Baudelaire. But no seaway bears the *Bateau ivre* to the *Cimetière marin,* and *La Jeune Parque* plucks no *Fleurs du mal* for her bouquet. The tightly controlled strophes of Valéry's highly cerebral poems look back, rather, at the evocative symbols and metaphors of Mallarmé's hermetic products. In contrast to the spontaneity of Surrealist poetry, Valéry cultivated order, attention, consciousness, discipline. Hence his fondness for the sonnet, which constitutes over half of the twenty-one poems of *Album de vers anciens* and six of the twenty-one *Charmes*. "Eternal glory to the inventor of the sonnet," he exclaimed, whose structure "tends to give to each verse of a finite and brief system a distinct function and a role in a progression."[48]

Poetic order is achieved only by constant revision and lengthy elaboration, motivated by an "ethics of form" of the sort, as he recalled, that was not uncommon among poets before the turn of the century. "Neither the Idol of Beauty nor the superstition of literary Eternity had yet been ruined, and the belief in Posterity had not been fully abolished."[49] Valéry goes on to confess that he too, at the critical age when the human intellect is formed, had contracted this ill, "this perverse taste for unlimited revision, and this acceptance of the reversible state of works." The Symbolists, in their intellectual rigor, had rejected scientific dogma, which was no longer fashionable, and no longer accepted religious dogma. But they found a surrogate for their faith in aesthetics, where they sensed "in the profound and meticulous cult of the ensemble of the arts an unequivocal discipline, and perhaps even a truth. Little was lacking for the establishment of a kind of religion."[50]

For Valéry, poetry replaced religion as the new theology. Even in the 1920s, he ascertained in his notes for a lecture called "Poésie Pure" (1927), one could detect in the public at large an often passionate interest "in these virtually theological discussions" about aesthetic theory. "For me, Poetry ought to be the Paradise of Language," he wrote in a review of a new translation of the *Spiritual Canticles* of Saint John of the Cross.[51] "Poets venture into the Enchanted Forest of Language expressly to lose themselves, to intoxicate themselves on their bewilderment, seeking crossroads of signification, unanticipated echoes, strange encounters."[52] Poetry constitutes a world unto itself, an absolute place, or—to use the term that Valéry frequently repeats—its own "universe." In an Oxford lecture entitled "Poésie et pensée abstraite" (1939) he contrasted the musical universe with the poetic one. "The poetic universe is not so powerfully and easily created. It exists, but the poet is deprived of the immense advantages that the musician possesses."[53] The musician has at his disposal a group of tools made expressly for his art, but the poet must borrow his language from the public voice. Poetry "demands or suggests a wholly different 'Universe': a universe of reciprocal relations, analogous to the world of sounds, in which the musical thought is born and moves. In this poetic universe, resonance outweighs causality, and 'form,' far from disappearing into its effect, is required by it.

The Idea reclaims its voice."[54] By "sensation of a universe" Valéry means that the poem or poetic state enables us to perceive "a *world*, or complete system of relationships," among its beings, things, events, and actions.[55]

What stimulates the poet to create such a poetic universe, an absolute system of language? "Disorder is essential to 'creation,'" Valéry maintained in the first sentence of his theses on "l'Invention esthétique" (1938), "inasmuch as the latter defines itself through a certain 'order.'"[56] We have seen that Valéry was inspired to his major works of poetry by the disorder of war. "I had lost my freedom of spirit," he wrote in 1917—around the time that he completed *La Jeune Parque* and began *Le Cimetière marin*—and bidden farewell to philosophical speculations. "I found that the means of struggling against the imagining of events and the all-consuming activity of impotence was to commit oneself to a difficult game: to make for oneself an endless task, burdened with conditions and clauses, wholly constrained by strict observance. I took poetry for my private charter. I accepted the most classical restrictions. I imposed, moreover, the continuity of harmony, the exactitude of syntax, the precise determination of words, which were sorted, weighed, and selected one by one."[57]

Equally devastating, as he makes clear in his essay "The Intellectual Crisis" ("La Crise de l'esprit," 1919), was the disorder of modern civilization produced by the war. "We [modern] civilizations now know that we are mortal," the first letter begins—not unlike the vanished civilizations of the Bible. "We see that the abyss of history is large enough for the whole world" and swallows both mind and body: "spiritual Persepolis is no less ravaged than material Susa."[58] Why these reflections at this point in history? "An extraordinary tremor has passed through the marrow of Europe," and this "mental disorder" (989) has caused Europe to resuscitate innumerable intellectual and spiritual systems of the past: dogmas, philosophies, ideals, including all the nuances of Christianity and positivism—the familiar products of an anxiety pendulating between nightmare and the real. The military crisis of the war is now past. The economic crisis has emerged at full strength. But the subtler intellectual crisis is more difficult to grasp. "There is the lost illusion of a European culture and the demonstration of the incapacity of knowledge to save anything" (990). Desire and renunciation are equally ridiculed, and creeds are confounded: "Cross against Cross, Crescent against Crescent" (991).

The intellectual crisis is especially grave because of the sorry condition in which it found its patient. Valéry does no more than sketch generally the state of Europe on the eve of the war; but a disequilibrium of that degree indicates a "disorder of the perfect state" (991)—a disorder consisting of "the free coexistence in all cultivated minds of the most dissimilar ideas, the most contradictory principles of life and knowledge" (992). A modern "intellectual Hamlet," contemplating the millions of ghosts on the battle-fields of Europe and meditating on the life and death of the eternal verities, would vacillate between the two dangers still menacing the world: order and disorder. If he picks up a skull, it might be Leonardo's, whose vision of a flying man was coopted in the war for purposes he never envisaged; or Leibniz's, whose dream of universal peace was sadly shattered; or "Kant, who begat Hegel, who begat Marx, who begat..." (993). In the face of such confusions, Hamlet is at a loss. "And I, he asks, I, the European mind, what am I going to become?" (993). Wearied by his production, exhausted by his attempts, frustrated by his responsibilities and his transcendent ideals, he asks himself if like Polonius and Laertes and Rosenkranz he should commit himself to a movement. "Adieu, phantoms! The world has no further need of you. Nor of me. The world, which baptizes with the name of progress its tendency toward a fatal precision, is seeking to unite with the blessings of life the advantages of death" (994).

No poem more vividly exemplifies both Valéry's general theory of poetry as a self-enclosed universe and the specific themes and images of his essay "The Intellectual Crisis" than Le Cimetière marin, which he was com-posing at precisely the same time—his most popular and most frequently anthologized and interpreted poem, and, next to La Jeune Parque, arguably his greatest and most mysterious one. It would be fruitless, after almost a century of interpretations, to analyze yet again this sublime achievement of modern poetry. For our purposes two aspects are significant.[59]

The famous first strophe contains the three essential elements of the poem: nature (the sea and sun), death (the cemetery), and the poet's con-sciousness.

Ce toit tranquille, où marchent des colombes,
Entre les pins palpite, entre les tombes;
Midi le juste y compose de feux
La mer, la mer, toujours recommencée!
Ô récompense après une pensée
Qu'un long regard sur le calme des dieux![60]

[This quiet roof, where the doves are walking, / trembles between the pines, between the tombs; / Equitable midday composes there with fires / the sea, the sea, ever renewed! / O what a reward, after a thought, / a long gaze at the calm of the gods!]

The seemingly paradoxical opening line, as well as other subsequent images, becomes luminously clear when one looks at Valéry's ink drawing of the cemetery as viewed from a vantage point higher on the hillside. To anyone gazing down across the vaults and trees, the sea, dotted with small white sails, appears to hover above the cemetery, and, indeed, it fills the upper two-thirds of the drawing.[61] The doves on the roof, accordingly, are the sails on the sea, sparkling in the noonday sun—"equitable" because at the midday solstice it is perfectly still and in balance—as glimpsed between the pines and the tombs. The poet, troubled by his thoughts, now turns for consolation to timeless nature.

The twenty-four strophes of the poem fall easily into three groups of eight.[62] The first group elaborates, in a series of brilliant images, the theme of a scintillating nature that in the calm of midday is timeless, peaceful, still—a Temple of Time ("Temple du Temps") that the poet, disdaining the concerns of human life, seeks to enter.

> Beau ciel, vrai ciel, regarde-moi qui change!
> Après tant d'orgueil, après tant d'étrange
> Oisiveté, mais pleine de pouvoir,
> Je m'abandonne à ce brillant espace.

> [Lovely heaven, true heaven, look at me as I change! / After so much pride, after so much indolence / strange but filled with power, / I give myself up to this radiant space.]

In the second group of strophes the poet's attention shifts from the sea to the cemetery, wondering what attracts him to this bony ground ("Quel front l'attire à cette terre osseuse"). Thinking of the departed ones who lie enclosed there, he concludes that the place, where "the faithful sea sleeps on my tombs" ("La mer fidèle y dort sur mes tombeaux"), pleases him. As he watches over the white tombs, which remind him of a flock of sheep, he asks the sea—apostrophized as the "splendid bitch" of a watchdog—to ward off all such Christian images as "the cautious doves" (of the Holy Ghost), vain dreams (of immortality), and curious angels. In this timeless, isolated, absolute realm "life is immense, being drunk with absence" ("La vie est vaste, étant ivre d'absence"). The dead are well concealed in their earth; the world is motionless at the solstice.

In this "perfect diadem" of nature, the single disturbing element is the human consciousness of the poet: "I am within you the secret change" ("Je suis en toi le secret changement"). (Valéry is reiterating here a theme prevalent in European thought at least since Dostoevsky's *Notes from Underground* and recently reechoed by Unamuno in his *Tragic Sense of Life*—namely that consciousness is a disease.) His regrets, doubts, and constraints are "the flaw in your magnificent diamond" ("le défaut de ton grand diamant"). He realizes that the dead, who previously seemed to him to be so peaceful in their tombs, have actually dissolved into a dense absence ("fondu dans une absence épaisse"), drained by the red clay of the earth. With an allusion to the traditional *ubi sunt* motif, he now asks where their souls have gone. In the sublime impersonality of death, what happens to everything singular and personal?

In the last group of strophes the poet turns from the departed dead to his own consciousness. Will his own "great soul" still sing when it too has been transformed into vapor? Gazing at the empty skulls and "uninhabited heads" of his forefathers, he realizes that immortality is nothing but "a lovely lie and a pious ruse" ("Le beau mensonge et la pieuse ruse"). The worms do not care for those who sleep beneath the earth; they feast on life! The true worm is human consciousness, whether manifested as love or hatred of oneself. In a famous strophe (21) the poet recalls Zeno's paradox and decides that no logic can contest the fact that the arrow (of consciousness) has pierced his flesh. The last three strophes hail life and the future. The poet exhorts his body to shatter its pensive mold ("Brisez, mon corps, cette forme pensive!") and to drink in the wind, which has begun to stir, bringing back to life the motionless sea, where now the boats are breaking with their prows the roof of the sea. "The wind is rising," the final strophe begins; "one must try to live."

> Le vent se lève!... Il faut tenter de vivre!
> L'air immense ouvre et referme mon livre,
> La vague en poudre ose jaillir des rocs!
> Envolez-vous, pages tout éblouies!
> Rompez, vague! Rompez d'eaux réjouies
> Ce toit tranquille où picoraient des focs!

> (The wind is rising... one must try to live. / The immense air opens and closes my book, / boldly the wave bursts powderlike upon the rocks. / Fly away, pages resplendent! / Break, waves! Break with joyous waters / that tranquil roof where the jibs are foraging!)

It seems evident, first, that *Le Cimetière marin* amounts to a poetic response to the problems raised by Valéry's essay on the intellectual crisis of

Europe. The poem in its rigorous form constitutes a symbol of order as a defense against the disorder of war and the postwar turmoil: the "récompense après une pensée" of the opening strophe. Further, it is difficult to avoid associating the skulls that the poet contemplates (strophes 18–19) with the skulls of the discarded intellectual tradition (represented by Leonardo, Leibniz, and Kant) that Hamlet picks up: the specific cemetery of Sète symbolizes the vast cemetery of postwar Europe. In this historical situation, the poet is tempted to turn away from the tumultuous present into the timeless realm of poetry.

The absolute and totally self-contained nature of the pure poetic realm to which the poet retreats is signified, first, by the circular form of the work, which begins and ends with "ce toit tranquil." The last line of the poem returns us to the first line.[63] Within this poetic realm, as we saw, religion is banished because its consolations have turned out to be false. Pure poetry is the surrogate for lost faith. This "universe," in turn, is governed by its own system of relationships, which are sustained by a series of "resonant" (to use Valéry's term) images and metaphors. The tranquillity of nature at the noonday solstice is suggested by a series of words which "resonate" with one another: "calme," "pur," "paix," "se repose," "purs," "stable," "calme," "sommeil," "pur," "sereine," among others. The tranquillity of nature is initially carried over into the realm of death, the cemetery, but it is gradually qualified by images of enclosure ("fermé," "caché"), absence (strophes 9, 12), and dissolution ("défait," "essence," "fondu"). The dream as knowledge ("le Songe est savoir") has become "vain dreams" ("les songes vains") and dreams with the colors of lies ("un songe/Qui n'aura plus ces couleurs de mensonge"). The consolation of death and the dream of immortality have been exposed as illusory.

The tranquillity of the first two groups of strophes, whose flow is interrupted only by occasional exclamations or questions, changes abruptly toward the end, where the grammar becomes conspicuously disjunctive and where continuity of image is replaced by violent oppositions. The first line of strophe 21—"Zénon! Cruel Zénon! Zénon d'Élée!"—is echoed in the first line of the following strophe by "Non, non!" and the exclamation "Debout!" (Get up!) retracts the "Achille immobile" (made immobile by Zeno's paradox) of the preceding line. The "non, non," in turn, is answered by the life-affirming "Oui!" that opens the penultimate strophe. And when the poet, in the final strophe, celebrates the wind that stirs the waves of the previously tranquil sea, that "opens and shuts my book" and carries off its pages, dazzled by the light, we sense the doubts of the thinker Valéry, the affirmer of pure intellect, about the value of poetry.

The poem, which began as a retreat into an aesthetic order in the face of historical disorder, leads the poet at the end back into action. Stillness has given way to movement, timelessness to temporality, and death to life. The poem has affirmed its epigraph from Pindar's third Pythian ode: "Dear soul, do not seek everlasting life, but exhaust what is practicable."

"Literature changes the author," Valéry wrote in the collection of aphorisms *Autres Rhumbs* (1927). "With each of the movements that draw it out of him, he undergoes an alteration. Once achieved, it reacts once again upon him. He makes himself, for instance, into the person who was capable of producing it."[64] Valéry's great poem seems to anticipate his turn away from poetry barely two years later, following the publication of *Charmes*. But in the hundreds of pages of lectures, essays, notes, and reviews that he produced during the next two decades, he meditated almost obsessively on the nature and function of pure poetry, and on the glorious contribution that his own slender poetic oeuvre made to that ideal.

⋘∘⋙

The differences between Valéry and his near contemporary George are vast: in France, the contented family man with steady employment and in Germany the peripatetic bachelor of homoerotic tendencies; the lover of the radiant Mediterranean landscape of his youth versus the denizen of dark northern European cities; the grand poet-of-state who later addressed thousands and the withdrawn cult leader who chanted his poems to a small group of devoted followers; the one discouraged from his poetic enterprise by the overwhelming example of Mallarmé and the other fortified by that same example in his sense of poetic mission. Yet for all the differences, equally pronounced similarities link the two great poets. Both were devout Catholics in their youth who lost their faith for nonarticulated reasons. Both were contemptuous critics of their respective societies and cultures. While George emphasized the rituals of religion in an effort to shape his poetry and life, Valéry sought order in nature and pure intellect to offset the disorder of the world. Ultimately, however, both turned to their belief in an absolute poetry to replace the lost faith of their youth. We can observe yet a third variation of the same aesthetic type when we turn to a writer of the next generation in Ireland.

James Joyce: Art as Escape

It is tempting to compare Joyce (1882–1941) with his contemporary, Roger Martin du Gard, because of the conspicuous parallels in their lives as well as their early novels. Martin du Gard's recollection that he grew up in a Catholic society "with a very pious mother, the company of priests, of devout friends" (see chap. 3) might be applied equally well to Joyce.[65] Although his father was anticlerical, his early governess—Mrs. "Dante" Hearn Conway—was a person of conspicuous piety from whom he learned to make the sign of the cross and to pray. For his own edification and his siblings' he turned the story of Adam and Eve into a play in which he himself assumed the role of the serpent. Like his French contemporary, as a young boy Joyce enjoyed the usual Catholic religious instruction. He served as an altar boy, was confirmed, studied the rituals of the Mass as he contemplated a priestly career, and even—in analogy to what Martin du Gard called his own "unhealthy mysticism"—wrote hymns to the Virgin Mary and served as prefect in his school's Sodality of the Blessed Virgin. His entire education—with the exception of a few months at the Christian Brothers' school in Dublin—took place in Jesuit institutions: from Clongowes Wood College to University College, Dublin. He later remarked "for the sake of precision" that he should be designated not so much a Catholic as a Jesuit.[66]

Like Martin du Gard, who experienced "crises of tears at certain sermons," Joyce at age fourteen attended a spiritual retreat at Belvedere College where the hell-and-damnation sermons elicited from him a response of terrified contrition. Similarly, his faith began to erode not so much because of his reading as from doubts arising from his first encounter with a prostitute and his passion for life. Like the hero of Martin du Gard's early novel *Devenir!* and in an equally autobiographical passage, Joyce's fictional alter ego Stephen Dedalus quarrels with his mother for his refusal to do his Easter duty. Like Martin du Gard, finally, Joyce left the church while retaining the forms and images of Catholicism in his works. All in all, Joyce's *A Portrait of the Artist as a Young Man* (1916), as well as its ur-form *Stephen Hero*, has much in common with *Jean Barois* as well as the novels of Samuel Butler and Hermann Hesse, being heavily autobiographical and "based on a literal transcript of the first twenty years of Joyce's life."[67]

But in other important respects Joyce was much closer to the poets of *l'art pour l'art*. While Martin du Gard entertained a "symbolist compromise" (that is, a mythic interpretation of the Bible), Joyce like Stefan George before him, secularized and incorporated the liturgy and its images into his literary vocabulary.[68] As Richard Ellmann precisely observes, "Christianity had subtly evolved in his mind from a religion into a system of metaphors."[69] *A Portrait* closely resembles the works of George and Valéry to the extent that it shows how the hero's crisis of faith leads to a new religion of art rather than to political engagement or social criticism or the vague dream of a community of the spirit, as was the case in the novels.[70]

The underlying tension of the novel, the opposition between church and art, between Christian and pagan, is suggested by the hero's name, Stephen Dedalus. Saint Stephen, for whom Stephen's Green in Dublin was named— "my green," as Dedalus reminds us[71]—is the archetypal Christian: the first martyr, stoned to death after he enraged the Sanhedrin by accusing them of being "stiff-necked" and of murdering Jesus (Acts 6–7), an apt image for Stephen's growing religious skepticism and criticism of the ruling church authorities. Daedalus (still the spelling in *Stephen Hero*), in contrast, is the archetypal artist, as signaled in the epigraph to the novel, a line from Ovid's *Metamorphoses* (8.188): *et ignotas animum dimittit in artes* (and he applies his mind to unknown arts). The line introduces a long passage in which Daedalus, having constructed the labyrinth to contain the Minotaur, "alters the laws of nature" (*naturamque novat*) by inventing wings with which he and his ill-fated son Icarus flee from Crete. It is Daedalus the creative artist, longing to escape his imprisonment on the island of Crete, that Joyce has in mind as the model for the hero of his novel, who at the end is prepared to leave his spiritual imprisonment (of family, church, country) on his own island: Ireland. Many images, such as the long aimless walks that Stephen undertakes—his "devious course up and down the streets" (96)—evoke the labyrinth that Daedalus constructed and in which King Minos imprisoned him to prevent his escape. The novel, which begins with an epigraph from the *Metamorphoses,* ends with an allusion to Ovid's figure, for the last line amounts to an apostrophe by the aspiring young artist to the Daedalus of antiquity: "Old father, old artificer, stand me now and ever in good stead." His name, in short, anticipates and summarizes the trajectory of the novel, which leads Stephen Dedalus from his devout Catholic childhood to his rejection of the church and self-discovery as an artist.[72] Indeed, his classmates with unwitting premonition refer to him as "The Dedalus." The polarity between Christian and pagan resounds throughout the novel, culminating in the great disquisition on aesthetics in chapter 5, which juxtaposes Aristotle and Saint Thomas Aquinas.

Before Stephen can commit himself to the pagan pole of his nature and set out on his Daedalean flight from the labyrinth of Ireland, he must reject the call of Saint Stephen. He spends his early years surrounded and embraced, virtually smothered, by the Catholic culture of family and school. The opening chapter is dominated by claustrophobic scenes in the restrictive Jesuit Clongowes Wood College to which his anticlerical father sends him for the pragmatic reason that the Jesuits will "be of service to him in after years. They are the fellows that can get you a position" (72). (Those scenes are interrupted only by the acrimonious religious quarrel that breaks out over Christmas dinner when Stephen goes home for the holidays.) We learn that "all through his boyhood he had mused upon that which he had so often thought to be his destiny" (147) and that in his "proud musings" he had often "seen himself as a priest wielding calmly and humbly the awful power of which angels and saints stood in reverence" (141). Even as a boy the obsession is so self-evident that, when he sits down to write a love poem, "from force of habit he had written at the top of the first page the initial letters of the jesuit motto: A.M.D.G." (71; *ad majorem Dei gloriam*, "to the greater glory of God"). Yet already then his rebellious spirit asserts itself, as when he insists—even at the risk of a beating by school bullies—that the heretical and immoral Byron is a better poet than the devout "rhymester" Tennyson. The second chapter ends when Stephen, in the embrace of a prostitute, finally surrenders to the desires of the flesh.

Following that "first violent sin" (97) Stephen sinks for a time into "a cold lucid indifference" and stoops to "the evil of hypocrisy" (98) to conceal his sin. But in the course of the spiritual retreat that occupies most of chapter 3, the terrifying sermon on death and judgment with its evocations of the material and spiritual torments of hell convince him that "against his sin, foul and secret, the whole wrath of God was aimed. The preacher's knife had probed deeply into his diseased conscience and he felt now that his soul was festering in sin" (107). He realizes that, like Lucifer, he has been guilty of the sin of pride: *non serviam* (109).[73] Tormented by conscience and terrified by the visions of punishments awaiting him, Stephen goes to a nearby church and makes his confession for the first time in eight months. When he attends mass the next morning and takes communion, the host upon his tongue (131) symbolically parallels and annuls the prostitute's kiss at the end of the preceding chapter.

Returning to the bosom of the church, Stephen now enters a period of piety, prayer, and self-mortification, becoming convinced that "frequent and violent temptations were a proof that the citadel of the soul had not fallen and that the devil raged to make it fall" (137). His conspicuous devotion brings him to the attention of his Jesuit teachers, and the director summons him to his study to ask if he has ever felt that he has a vocation to the priesthood (140). The conversation arouses in Stephen all his boyhood dreams of becoming a priest. "He listened in reverent silence now to the priest's appeal and through the words he heard even more distinctly a voice bidding him approach, offering him secret knowledge and secret power" (142). Yet even as he descends the steps from the director's study he is troubled by thoughts of the "grave and ordered and passionless life that awaited him," and all his instincts rebel, "stronger than education or piety" (143). At that moment he realizes with sharp clarity:

> He would never swing the thurible before the tabernacle as priest. His destiny was to be elusive of social or religious orders. The wisdom of the priest's appeal did not touch him to the quick. He was destined to learn his own wisdom apart from others or to learn the wisdom of others himself wandering among the snares of the world. (144)

The "snares of the world" belong to the cluster of images employed in the novel to symbolize the labyrinth, and so we are again in the Daedalean world. As a group of his schoolmates calls out to him, "The Dedalus," his name suddenly seems to be prophetic of his own destiny. "Now, at the name of the fabulous artificer, he seemed to hear the noise of dim waves and to see a winged form flying above the waves and slowly climbing the air" (149). A few minutes later, as he walks along the seashore listening to "the call of life to his soul not the dull gross voice of the world of duties and despair" (150), he sees a girl standing in the water like "a strange and beautiful seabird" (151) and succumbs wholly to the magic of life and the world.

The last chapter finds Stephen at the university, a move to which his mother is opposed, knowing that it will fortify him in his turn away from the church. The break with his family comes soon enough. As he reports to his friend Cranly, he quarrels with his mother because of his refusal hypocritically to attend communion on Easter. He makes it clear that he has become an agnostic rather than an atheist: "I neither believe in it [the Eucharist] nor disbelieve in it" (206). "I will not serve," he insists, echoing the words of Lucifer. "I will not serve that in which I no longer believe whether it call itself my home, my fatherland or my church" (213). Yet he also has no intention of becoming a Protestant. "I said that I had lost the faith, Stephen answered, but not that I had lost selfrespect. What kind of liberation would that be to forsake an absurdity which is logical and coherent and to embrace one which is illogical and incoherent?" (210). As Cranly shrewdly observes, Stephen's mind is still "supersaturated" with religion despite his disbelief. Like Joyce himself, following his spiritual liberation Stephen secularizes the familiar Catholic images for his own purposes. In his great disquisition on aesthetics (184–87) Aquinas furnishes the vocabulary with which Stephen defines his wholly secular theory—"applied Aquinas," as he quips, or an aestheticized theology in which Aquinas's three requirements for beauty, *integritas*, *consonantia, claritas*, become the "wholeness, harmony, and radiance" familiar from Joyce's epiphanies. He is furious with his girl for flirting with a young priest. "To him she would unveil her soul's shy nakedness, to one who was but schooled in the discharging of a formal rite rather than to him, a priest of the eternal imagination, transmuting the daily bread of experience into the radiant body of everliving life" (192).

Following the breaks with family and church it remains only for Stephen to make the break with Ireland, for—again with the image of a labyrinth— "when the soul of a man is born in this country there are nets flung at it to hold it back from flight" (177). When we leave him on the last page of his account he is preparing to go abroad "to encounter for the millionth time the reality of experience" (218). Appropriately enough, to support him in his project he calls on the "old father, old artificer," Daedalus. The shift from Saint Stephen to Daedalus exemplifies perfectly the shift from a lost faith to a commitment to art that constitutes the principal theme of the novel. (When Dedalus reappears two year later in *Ulysses* [1922], he is wholly the artist without the religious qualms whose development Joyce portrayed in the earlier novel.) The continuing use of secularized religious images is justified by the fact that Stephen's commitment to religion was so total during his early years. More than any other novel of the twentieth century, Joyce's *Portrait* represents the turn to art as a clear surrogate for the loss of religious faith.[74] Yet in his secularization of ecclesiastical ritual and in his self-stylization as a priest—indeed, even in his use of Daedalus/Icarus to signify his break and flight from home—Joyce surprisingly resembles that altogether different German poet, Stefan George, who in the early stages of his development also turned to the religion of art and evolved a theology of aesthetics.[75] But whereas George eventually moved beyond art to cultivate a "secret Germany" of the élite not unlike the community idealized by Hesse in *Demian*, Joyce resembled Valéry in his continuing pursuit of an absolute art to replace the reality of Europe *entre deux guerres*.

⟨ornament⟩

CHAPTER FIVE

Pilgrimages to India

The Discovery of India

While Joyce, like his Stephen Dedalus, fled eastward from Ireland to continental Europe in the decade preceding World War I, other European thinkers, writers, and artists were crisscrossing India on cultural pilgrimages in search of the paradise they regarded as lost in Western civilization—in the days when a trip to India meant weeks at sea and not just hours in a jet. At the turn of the century Pierre Loti embarked on his quest for Vedic wisdom on the subcontinent. Three years later the young German adventurer Waldemar Bonsels spent five months on the Malabar coast. In 1905 Max Dauthendey embarked on a Cook's tour around the world, which took him to India for one month. In 1908 Stefan Zweig arrived for a four-month tour of India, Ceylon, and Burma. In 1910 the artist Melchior Lechter and the poet Karl Wolfskehl, both members of Stefan George's inner circle, set sail on a six-month journey to the East. In 1911 Hermann Hesse and the painter Hans Sturzenegger departed on a similar expedition, and that same year Hermann von Keyserling set out on his famous voyage around the world, which began with several months in India. It was not only the French and Germans who made the trip to India. In October 1912 E. M. Forster arrived for the first of his three sojourns in India. But the British writers, as members of the ruling colonial power, looked on the land with different eyes from those of the French and German cultural tourists.[1]

These journeyers to the East, who recorded their impressions in essays, journals, novels, and poems, sailed not simply through the Suez Canal and across the Indian Ocean, the Arabian Sea and the Bay of Bengal, but also on a sea of literary myth and philosophical speculation extending back for centuries. Following the purely mythical legends and rumors that reached Europe during the Middle Ages, generations of traders and missionaries

sent back reports regarding the geography, languages, and religions of the
mysterious East. The first European to propose India as a foundational element of world culture was Johann Gottfried Herder, whose *Ideas toward
a Philosophy of the History of Humankind* (*Ideen zu einer Philosophie der
Geschichte der Menschheit*, 1783) included a chapter called "Indostan" (bk.
11, chap. 4), in which he maintains that Indians are concerned from childhood on and at every moment of their lives with their culture, thanks to
the many customs and festivals, the various gods and fairy tales and sacred places that surround them. He admires the "patient calm and gentle
obedience" that in his opinion characterize the Indian character. But their
very character also exposed Indians to the depredations of Europeans, who
have eagerly seized the riches that the subcontinent has to offer. (Herder's
image determined down to the present the German view of Indians as a
gentle, peaceful, and spiritually advanced people.)[2] A few years later Kalidasa's drama *Sakuntala* (translated by Georg Forster in 1791 from William
Jones's English adaptation) made such an impression on Goethe that he immediately appropriated one of its theatrical devices for the "Prelude in the
Theater" in *Faust*.

Thanks largely to the poetic vision of Novalis (Friedrich von Hardenberg)
and the critical energies of Friedrich Schlegel, India became a central image
in German Romanticism.[3] At the beginning of *The Disciples at Sais* (*Die
Lehrlinge zu Sais*, 1798) Novalis speaks of "sacred Sanskrit," which—unlike
other languages, which do not understand themselves—"speaks in order to
speak because speaking is its joy and its essence."[4] In a talk to his friends
in Jena called *Christendom or Europe* (*Die Christenheit oder Europa*, 1799)
Novalis, contrasting poetry with academic learning and philosophy, extols
"a bejeweled India over against the cold, dead mountain peaks of study
room rationality."[5] During his years in Paris (1802–4), Novalis's close friend
Friedrich Schlegel dedicated himself to the study of Sanskrit and read the
works of Indian religion and philosophy in the original, an enterprise that
produced his book *Über die Sprache und Weisheit der Indier* (1808; On the
language and wisdom of the Indians). According to Schlegel no language,
including Greek, is philosophically so lucid and precise as Sanskrit. He
hopes that the single-minded obsession with the Greeks, which in past
centuries distracted the European mind from seriousness and higher truth,
may be offset by an acquaintance with Oriental antiquity, which can lead
us back to knowledge of the divine.

While Novalis died early (1801) and Schlegel turned away from the Orient after his conversion to Catholicism, their enthusiasm and insights were
furthered in a more disciplined manner by the scholarly researches of such

Orientalists as Friedrich Majer, who was indebted to Herder, and Franz Bopp, who published in 1816 a book on conjugational systems in Sanskrit and other languages, demonstrating for the first time the common origin of the Indo-European languages and laying the basis for the modern study of comparative philology. August Wilhelm Schlegel, whom his brother termed "the first German Brahman," became professor of Sanskrit at the University of Bonn where he hoped to establish a "Benares on the Rhine."[6] Although the literary interest in India dwindled for a time, scholars like Majer, Bopp, and A. W. Schlegel founded the scholarly field of Indology, which thrived in Germany throughout the nineteenth century.

Arthur Schopenhauer (1788–1860) provided an important link between the Romantic image of India and the twentieth century.[7] Schopenhauer was introduced to Indian antiquity by Friedrich Majer, whom he met in 1813–14 at his mother's home in Weimar and who alerted the young philosopher to a Latin translation of the Upanishads published in 1801 by the celebrated French Orientalist Abraham-Hyacinthe Anquetil-Duperron (1731–1805) under the title *Oupnek'hat*.[8] "How the Oupnekhat is filled throughout with the breath of the Vedic spirit," Schopenhauer exclaimed.[9] Two years later he confided in his notes that "my theory would never have been able to arise before the Upanishads, Plato, and Kant simultaneously cast their rays into a single human mind."[10] He reiterated that assertion in the "Critique of the Kantian Philosophy" appended to the second edition (1844) of his magnum opus *The World as Will and Idea (Die Welt als Wille und Vorstellung*, 1819), confirming that he was indebted "for the best of my own development—besides the impression of the visible world—to the work of Kant, the sacred writings of the Hindus, and Plato."[11] Schopenhauer stated definitively and repeatedly that it was the ancient Hindu doctrine of the Upanishads and not Buddhism that attracted him.[12] What caught his attention? Essentially the analogy he perceived between his conception of "will" and "idea" (the Kantian distinction between *Ding an sich* and phenomenon) and the Hindu notion of *brahman* as essential reality and *maya* as illusory appearance. Almost at the beginning of *The World as Will and Idea* (bk. 1, section 3) we read that

> Kant opposed what has been recognized as mere phenomenon [*Erscheinung*] to the thing-in-itself; the ancient wisdom of the Indians states: "it is *maya*, the veil of illusion, that shrouds the eyes of mortals and lets them see a world of which one can say neither that it is nor that it is not: for it resembles a dream, resembles the glitter of the sun on the sand which the wanderer takes from afar to be a body of water, or also the

discarded piece of rope that he takes to be a serpent." (These metaphors can be found repeatedly in numerous places in the Vedas and Puranas.)[13]

Schopenhauer was not the only German philosopher to look toward India. But Kant referred to India almost wholly in the context of his lectures on physical geography and anthropology—not in his philosophical works. Schelling turned to India only in his late writings on mythology (*Philosophie der Mythologie*, 1842) and revelation (*Philosophie der Offenbarung*, 1854)— that is, much later than Schopenhauer. And Hegel, basing his opinions on biased reports by officers of the East India Company, held a notoriously negative view of India, which he regarded as a realm outside of world history and thus historically irrelevant; and of Hinduism, which he criticized as an undisciplined effusion of the human fantasy and hence as philosophically irrelevant.[14] Schopenhauer's works, eclipsed during his lifetime by Hegel and Hegelianism, enjoyed a resurgence after his death when they were enthusiastically received by the young Nietzsche in his *Untimely Observations* and by Paul Deussen, Nietzsche's classmate at Schulpforta and a leading historian of Indian philosophy, in his magisterial studies of the Vedanta.[15] Schopenhauer was soon read and incorporated by the many writers, artists, and thinkers who made pilgrimages to India at the beginning of the twentieth century.

Another important factor shaping the image of India in European thought of the late nineteenth century was the influence of the theosophical movement, which sought to revitalize the study of comparative religion and philosophy and professed to offer, through the mystical means of spiritualism and occultism, access to the hidden mysteries of nature and to an understanding of the universe as an integrated and interdependent whole.[16] In 1875 the Theosophical Society was founded in New York by Henry Steel Olcott as president and Helena Petrovna Blavatsky as secretary-general. Madame Blavatsky (1831–91), known to her followers as "the Sphinx of the nineteenth century," popularized her ideas sensationally through her controversial book *Isis Unveiled* (1877), which purported to draw on ancient wisdom handed down over the centuries by "Eastern adepts" in order to provide nothing less than "A Master-Key to the Mysteries of Ancient and Modern Science and Theology." The "mahatmas," whom she claimed to have encountered in Tibet in the 1850s, showed her that

by combining science with religion, the existence of God and immortality of man's spirit may be demonstrated like a problem of Euclid. For the first time we received the assurance that the Oriental philosophy has room for no other faith than an absolute and immovable faith in the omnipotence of man's own immortal self.[17]

In response to the struggle between materialism and the spiritual aspirations of mankind, it was her endeavor in the two volumes of her work (devoted respectively to "Science" and "Theology") to liberate mankind from the tyranny of false theology and the assumed infallibility of science (xlv). It is necessary to "interrogate nature instead of prescribing laws for her guidance" (628).

In 1879, she and Colonel Olcott moved the headquarters of the Theosophical Society to India, to the suburb of Adyar outside Madras, where they were enthusiastically welcomed by the Hindus. In 1885 Madame Blavatsky returned to Europe, where the British freethinker and socialist Annie Besant (1847–1933) became her ardent disciple. Following Madame Blavatsky's death in 1891, Annie Besant went to India and founded the Central Hindu College at Benares. When Colonel Olcott died in 1907, she moved to Madras and became president of the Theosophical Society. The movement, now with a more pronounced Hindu emphasis, flourished under her leadership, and the headquarters of the society at Adyar soon became a stop *de rigueur* on the itinerary of European cultural pilgrims in India.

Other factors contributed to the new awareness of India. Annie Besant was active in the Home Rule movement, which had been growing in strength ever since the first Indian national congress met in Bombay in 1885. The opening decade of the new century was marked by anarchy, terrorism, and assassinations as Indian radicals sought to regain power from the British. Apart from politics, the cultural world was alerted to developments in India in 1913 when the Nobel Prize in literature was awarded to the Indian poet, dramatist, novelist, and philosopher Rabindranath Tagore (1861–1941), who in 1901 founded a school intended to become a meeting ground between East and West and who became a familiar figure in Europe and the United States as a cultural ambassador. There was also, finally, a flood of mainly second-rate novels by English writers about life in the Raj—a flood for which Kipling's *Kim* and other stories provided the most familiar examples.[18]

For these various reasons, India emerged as a favored goal for cultural pilgrimages among European seekers after a surrogate for their lost faith.[19] The strength of the wave can be judged by the reaction of Stefan George, a vigorous opponent of all mysticism, to Melchior Lechter's travel journals. "The imminent danger for the world is Hinduism," he complained to Ernst Robert Curtius in 1912.[20]

Two Early Pilgrims

Pierre Loti (the pen name of Julien Viaud, 1850–1923) achieved his early fame
as the author of frankly autobiographical romances based on his travels and
experiences in the French navy, which he entered at age seventeen and from
which he retired with the rank of captain.[21] It was on the basis of those
early works, notably *Pêcheur d'Islande* (1886), a novel about life among the
Breton fishermen known to Loti from his youth, that in 1891 he was elected
to membership in the Académie Française. Gradually, however, Loti abandoned all pretense of fiction and wrote a series of first-person travel narratives with such titles as *Au Maroc* (1890) and *Jérusalem* (1895), in which, as
in the early *Propos d'exil* (1887), a principal topos was the glaring contrast between the cultures of Europe and Asia. In 1899 Loti was temporarily assigned
to the Ministry of Foreign Affairs, in whose service he made a trip to India
charged with various minor commissions from the French government.

His account of that trip, *India (without the English)* (*L'Inde [sans les
anglais]*, 1903), was an immediate international success, necessitating more
than fifty editions by 1911.[22] (Loti's work is exceptional among the scores
of works dealing with France-in-Asia because almost all the others concern
Indochina and not India proper.[23] Loti himself had earlier, in 1883, been
on assignment in French Indochina and written a series of critical articles
on the Annam War.) His very title represents an implicit protest against
English colonial policies.[24] The account, based on Loti's diary notes from a
six-month stay in India beginning in December 1899, is the lyrical, sensuous,
and readable narrative of a journey beginning in Ceylon and zigzagging across
the subcontinent: from the southwestern province of Travancore ("L'Inde
charmante" never visited by tourists, 139), by way of the lagoons of Cochin
to Madurai, Pondichéry, and on to Hyderabad; then north to Udaipur and the
"beautiful rose-colored city" of Jaipur in the "famine-starved" northwest;
south again to Madras; then back north to Agra, Delhi, and Benares, where
the book ends.

The popularity of the work is easy to understand. Loti visits most of the
main tourist attractions:[25] the ruins of Golconda and the vanished cities of
Gwalior and Amber; the grottos of Shiva at Ellora (Eluru) and the mountain shrine of Trichinopoly (Tiruchirapalli); the decaying French colony at
Pondichéry, the huge temple of the Juggernaut (Krishna) on the Bay of Bengal, the "charme de féerie et horreur dantesque" of Jaipur (320), the Taj
Mahal at Agra ("l'une des merveilles classiques de la terre," 378), and the
holy Ganges at Benares. At many places he gains special access to otherwise

forbidden temples and palaces by permission of kings, princes, and ma-
harajahs, to whom he sometimes has commissions (for instance, to deliver
a French decoration to the maharajah of Travancore). At other times he
is turned away by Brahman and Muslim clerics who do not wish their
precincts to be defiled by the touch of infidels. Lyrical descriptions of the
lush jungle scenery alternate with detailed depictions of the cities. He visits
the ancient Jewish quarter of Mattancheri; attends performances of classical Sanskrit dramas by the renowned actress Baladoni; is entertained by
the dances of skilled *bajadères* and the delicate music of the finest Indian
musicians; witnesses festivals featuring the transport of a great statue of
Vishnu or a huge boat of Shiva and Parvati; and visits pottery factories and
carpet weaveries. He appreciates the seductive beauty of the women in their
saris and the handsome grace of the men; at the same time he is aware of
corpses at the edge of the cities and the widespread starvation. He observes
the differences between north and south, between Muslim and Hindu. "For
anyone coming like me from Brahman India, what first strikes the attention
is the absolute change in the conception of religious monuments. Mosques
replace pagodas, a sober, precise, and graceful art succeeding enormity and
profusion" (369). Loti registers the dissonant elements noted by most travelers to India: the tawdry Westernization, the inequities of the caste system,
the screaming contrasts between the luxury of the princes and the poverty
of the people, the filth of the streets and rivers, the danger of huge bats and
cobras. Yet he remains cool, objective, nonjudgmental throughout.

For all its surface appeal as a travel book, Loti's voyage also constitutes an
inner search. The descendant of devout Huguenots and during his childhood
a pious believer and daily reader of the Bible, Loti lost his faith in the
manner now familiar among intellectuals of the late nineteenth century.[26]
"In my infancy I had a glowing faith, a passionate enthusiasm for Christ—
then I passed through several phases."[27] Doubts stirred in his mind by his
exposure to science, the boredom he felt during long Sunday sermons, and
above all—shades of Roger Martin du Gard—the sharp disappointment of his
confirmation from which he had expected grand sensations and revelations:
all these factors produced an early religious crisis which was intensified
by his experiences and love affair as a young ensign in Turkey. A brief
flirtation with Catholicism in a Trappist monastery failed to satisfy his
religious yearning, and his confusions were intensified by his voyage in 1894
to the Holy Land. The spiritual vacuum created by his loss of religious faith
produced in turn an obsession with and fears about death.[28] So in his journey
to India we recognize yet another attempt to discover spiritual satisfaction.

Virtually on the first page Loti tells us that he is going to India, "the cradle of human thought and prayer," to supplicate the "keepers of Aryan wisdom" to give him "in place of the ineffable Christian faith that has vanished at least their more austere faith in an indefinite prolongation of the human soul" (4). His entire touristic and anthropological account is punctuated by the record of that inner pilgrimage, which ultimately gives shape to a work that otherwise would have no more goal or purpose than a Baedeker. Almost immediately after his arrival in India, when he visits his first Brahman temple and is not allowed to enter, he gets the impression of idolatry and hostility. How childishly naive, he believes, was his hope of finding "a little light in the religion of our great ancestors" (39). A few days later, near the southwestern city of Trivandrum where he is the guest of the maharajah, he is quartered in gardens that house the ministries, hospitals, banks, schools, and Christian churches. "It was not to see all this that I came to Travancore, and I am beginning to understand how difficult it is to get in touch with Brahman India, that deeper India, even here where I feel it so close to me, always living and immutable, agitating me with its mystery" (64). A week later, leaving Travancore, he is dismayed to realize that he has not yet penetrated the inner core (*intimité*) of India and has divined nothing of the Brahmanism of which this province is one of the centers (99). It is closed to Europeans, despite the unfailingly gracious reception by the people. He recalls his childish dream of gaining insight into the "intangible truth" (*l'insaisissable vérité*) of the faith that the Brahmans guard so fiercely. "But no; here, as everywhere else, I would have been the eternal stranger, the perpetual wanderer who only knows how to delight his eyes at aspects of people and things" (133–34). He is grateful when he reaches Pondichéry, "ce petit coin de vieille France" on the Gulf of Bengal where he can feel at home again (227).

Loti's pessimism deepens as he travels north from the lush southern "India of the Great Palms" into "Famished India" of the northwest because the "ancestor of our Europe" is now a country of ruins (271). When he finally manages to get on friendly terms with two young Brahman priests at the great temple in "the white city of Udaipur," he sees that his hope of gaining any insights from them was chimerical because their Brahmanism "has been obscured, from generation to generation, by the abuse of rituals and observances; they no longer know the hidden meaning of the symbols" (279).

Loti initially intended at this point in his trip to take up residence in the house of the Theosophical Society at Madras, of which he had heard great reports. But he was dismayed by his first conversation with two of them—a Hindu educated in European universities and Colonel Olcott himself, then president of the society[29]—who offered no consolation for his obsessive thoughts about death. " 'Prayer,' they said. 'But who is listening to it? Man is alone with his responsibility. . . . You must pray to yourself through your deeds.' " During the following silence, "one of the saddest silences that my life ever passed through," Loti felt that his last vague beliefs were falling from him one by one, "with the imperceptible rustlings of things falling into the void." Was it for this that he had come to India, he wonders, "to the ancient primal hearth of human religions," if one found nothing but a Brahmanism wrapped in idolatry along with spiritualist writings available all over the world (352)? Deciding not to stay at Madras, Loti goes back north past Agra to Benares where in the "Maison des Sages" he meets Annie Besant, "a European woman who escaped from the turmoil of the West."[30] She tells him that true theosophists have no doctrines and dogmas. "Our friends at Madras"—that is, Olcott and his followers—tend toward Buddhism, whose coldness, she intuits, offended Loti's mystical soul. It is necessary only to seek an antimaterialist, spiritual truth with all possible means. But if he chooses to stay, she warns, he must not hate them if they deprive him of any unconscious hopes which, unbeknownst to him, still sustain him (412).

Loti does not describe the process that follows, but he remains in Benares, going down to the river each morning to observe the faithful at their ablutions, witnessing funeral ceremonies, conversing with aged pundits, visiting the Golden Temple, and resting on the ancient stone bench where Buddha sat. And gradually his views change.

> Formerly, attached desperately as I was to the Christian conception of life, I had disdained the study of this doctrine which offended all my human tenderness; not long ago, at Madras, I rejected it—in its coldest and cruelest Buddhist form, to be sure. But recently it has grown on me, almost from hour to hour, in its primal integrity as it was enunciated at the beginning of time by our great mysterious ancestors. And after experiencing terrifying things that I neither can nor wish to depict, I sense that I have resigned myself to whatever consolation it is still able to offer. (436)

Loti suspects that his present mood will pass and that the world will reclaim him once he has left the immediate influence of Benares. "But the new seed that has been planted in my soul is destined to thrive there and will surely lead me back to Benares" (436).

The book ends with Loti's address "To my unknown brethren." "I have sworn the oath that was asked of me, and the Sages of the silent little house have taken me as one of their disciples" (454). He will make no attempt in his book to express what they have taught him—only to report on the trivial incidents of his journey. But he wants his readers to know that "more consolation is to be found in the Vedic doctrines than one initially supposes; and the consolation obtained there cannot be destroyed by reason, like that of the revealed religions" (455). The Sages at Benares alone are capable of giving access to those profound mysteries of life and death and, specifically, the continuation of life beyond terrestrial destruction. On this solemn note Loti concludes his account, which begins as little more than a colorful and sensitive travelogue and gradually reveals itself as a key document in the search of European intellectuals for an Indian surrogate to replace their lost Christian faith and, in the process, establishes a pattern evident in many subsequent accounts. This pattern includes, as we have seen, a gradual shift from depression to exaltation, awe at a landscape of primal paradise mixed with irritation at the commercialization of the temples, criticism of the British and the Europeanization of the cities, contrasts of Eastern religions and Christianity, and ritual visits to the theaters and the Theosophical Society.

Waldemar Bonsels (1881–1952) might well be called the German Loti. Like his French counterpart he left home at seventeen to begin a lifetime of wandering—though hardly the regimented travels of the naval officer. His works, unknown today, were sensationally popular during his lifetime. His fairy tale for children, *The Adventures of Maja the Bee* (1912), was an international bestseller, and in the 1930s he was one of the most widely read writers, whose works—including novels, children's stories, and travel books—were translated into two dozen languages.[31] Bonsels's *An Indian Journey* (*Indienfahrt*, 1916) was as spectacular a success as Loti's *India*, having been translated by 1922 into French, Finnish, Swedish, Dutch, Russian, and English; selling over the decades more than half a million copies; and in the late twentieth century being included in the Manesse series of quality reprints. In the United States it even appeared, with notes and vocabulary, in an edition for use in school and college German courses.[32]

An Indian Journey, actually composed in 1912, was based on Bonsels's months in India from October 1903 to April 1904. Prior to its writing he had already made use of his impressions of the Indian landscape and atmosphere in a potboiler churned out in two weeks jointly (each writing alternate chapters) with his friend Hans Hahn: *Aimee: Die Abenteuer einer Tänzerin* (1908; Aimee: the adventures of a dancer). The last four chapters of the novel, which begins in Munich and moves with adventures and murders along the way from Budapest to Chicago and Calcutta, take place in the town of Cannanore on the Malabar coast, where Aimee has been brought by the local maharajah and followed by two German admirers. The story ends bloodily when Aimee is stabbed to death by a jealous rival, the Indian girl Atala, who then leaps into the sea, leaving her German beloved to be found guilty of the murder.

An Indian Journey differs from Loti's India inasmuch as it is restricted geographically to a tiny section of the country on the southwestern Malabar coast. Bonsels's trip begins in Cannanore and ends just one hundred miles to the north in Mangalore, to which Bonsels proceeds by an indirect route that leads him inland through the jungles and hills of the Western Ghats. Bonsels, a young man in his early twenties with adequate funds at his disposal, takes up his account when he arrives in Cannanore after some ten months in India, during which he has apparently also visited Bombay and the ancient town of Bijapur. Accompanied by his servant Panja, his cook Pascha, and his dog Elias, he rents a bungalow on the edge of town and settles in for a stay of several months during which he encounters few other Europeans but observes the fishermen at work, engages in nocturnal dialogues with his monkey Huc, and witnesses epic battles between cats, rats, and snakes. After a time he sets out with his household on the journey to Mangalore, meeting along the way the primitive Dravidian peoples of the jungle, falling ill for weeks with fever, being taken out of the swamps to recover on the hills where he has a dialogue with the hill monkey Gong, and finally enjoying the hospitality of a petty Hindu king before making his way back to the coast. At Mangalore, through the mediation of a local English official, he meets the cultured Brahman Mangesche Rao, who has been dismissed from his position at the English College for suspected sedition. The account ends when Rao is poisoned by radical Brahmans who resent his ties to the British and his attempts to create a unified and independent India, whereupon the disenchanted Bonsels prepares to return to Germany.

The adventure story is also, like Loti's, a journey of self-discovery. Europe recedes in Bonsels's memory "like a noisy, ugly dream full of needless excitedness," and he wants to escape the "harried and arbitrary nature of European busyness."[33] He has come to the East, he tells us, driven by a "painful restlessness" which compels him to "measure the essence of God" (19) with the unconscious goal of gaining eternity. His pilgrimage, he continues, is a search for order, "the sister of knowledge," and "the connections between the spirits of the dead and the living." A wise Brahman understands his restless compulsion to wander. Some people are driven by their plenitude and others by their vacuity, he says. The latter bring nothing home but emptiness; "but the others, the rich ones, give while seeking, and the compulsion of their wandering often helps those they meet" (227). Contemptuous of the German missionaries on the Malabar coast, he wonders "whether a temple is a suitable place for a textile factory" of the sort established by the mission in Cannanore (50). In Mangalore he resents being grouped as a German along with "these prophets of holy simplicity" (223), whose intellectual background was inadequate to "take up the spiritual battle with the cultivated representatives of Hinduism" (215) and who, in turn, had only contempt for what they regarded as the "pagan blindness" of the Brahmans and Buddhists.

Everywhere he turns Bonsels finds "the poetic brilliance of the Vedas and the spirit of Kalidasa" (48) as well as the mystery which most foreign reporters on India claim to have been lost. He encounters the true spirit of India in his drunken dialogue with his monkey Huc, who explains to him the nature of freedom and the freedom of nature. "Do you believe that for a single hour of peaceful communion with the happy beings of the jungle we would not give up all the frivolities that engage you throughout your entire hasty day?" (60–61). Deep in the jungle, Bonsels recalls lines from the Upanishads:

He who takes Brahman as understanding
and does not turn away from Brahman,
sheds all evils from himself while still alive
and all wishes will be fulfilled.
(68)

"To the heavenly worlds of the Upanishad and their light no spiritual ray is alien," he reflects. "There is only obedient and quiet meditation or a restless revolution." Such thoughts as these inspire his restlessness and drive him to search for "the heart of the ancient realm" (69). Watching a young Dravidian girl die from a cobra bite, he is dismayed at human impotence and wonders where we can obtain the power of which we have vague premonitions in our desire for fulfillment (90). Wracked by fever, he recognizes with utter lucidity that "the thirst that raged through his body was the thirst of his soul for knowledge" (105). In his feverish dreams he imagines a conversation with his own projected ego. Later, gazing from a mountain pass toward the distant ruins of Bijapur, he is moved (again like Loti) to musings on death, rejecting the European Romantic conception in favor of the Indian understanding. "Dying is a duty, just as is living.... The people of India die more easily, more self-evidently and, as it were, less ceremoniously than we. They leave all concern for their future welfare to the deity" (146).

Recalling a lovely panther he shot, the commanding presence of a tiger glimpsed in the jungle, and the wisdom of the monkey Huc, he becomes aware of human arrogance. "It seemed to me once again as though the spirit of this land and its ancient peoples appeared and addressed me" (162). The culmination of his spiritual journey is attained when the Brahman Rao teaches Bonsels that "Brahman is the light of the spirit and bliss without suffering. Brahman is joy, primal knowledge, a homogeneous mass of understanding, consisting of blissfulness, accessible through the consciousness, equipped with the loftiest insight" (231). In sum, we seem to be dealing again with a spiritual pilgrimage embedded in a trip to India characterized by vivid depictions of landscape, animals, and people, and enlivened at the end by a plot exemplifying religious and political tensions in India.[34]

But the book, unlike Loti's, is almost a total fabrication. Bonsels did indeed spend five months in India—in the service of the very Basel Mission on which he heaps such scorn.[35] Having completed his business apprenticeship in a textile factory in Bielefeld and then worked as a salesman for a publishing company in Karlsruhe, Bonsels applied in 1902 for a position with the Basel Mission, which for many years had been active on the Malabar coast. After the freedom of his previous life he felt a certain dread at the regimentation of mission routine. Yet afflicted as he was by the Indophoria prevalent in early twentieth-century Germany, the impecunious young man was eager to grasp any means to finance a trip to India.

He arrived in Bombay on 18 October 1903, and, after spending the mission's funds with profligate abandon on posh hotels, proceeded by train and oxcart by way of Bangalore and Madras to Cannanore, where in early November he took up his duties in the mission textile factory. He lived alone in a large old house with a slave, Daniel, and his early letters were euphoric with delight at being in India. But within two weeks he was bored with the "deadening conformity" of his work and having difficulties with other members of the mission. By the end of the month he had negotiated a transfer to Mangalore where he arrived in January 1904. Here too he felt himself to be an outsider, resigned in February, and left India a month later by way of Bombay. In an open letter entitled *My Resignation from the Basel Mission Industry and Its Reasons* (1904) Bonsels sought to put the best light on his behavior.[36] His interpretation was challenged by an officer of the mission, who denied that Bonsels, apart from short excursions out from Cannanore and Mangalore, had seen much of the jungle during his months in India or had any close contacts with English agents, Brahmans, or rajahs.[37] Indeed, apart from towns through which he passed on the trip to and from Bombay, he saw little of India apart from the two coastal towns.

Whatever the truth of the disputed details, it is clear that the story could not have happened as related in *An Indian Journey*. Bonsels was not an adventurer of independent means but the dissatisfied and impecunious employee of the Basel Mission. He knew neither Hindustani nor any other local languages, and his English was barely serviceable—certainly not adequate for philosophical conversations with the Brahman Rao. He was hardly in a position to threaten natives with his gun or, in a mood of irritation, to strike the half-caste secretary of an English official, as does his literary persona. He did not spend over a year traveling throughout the subcontinent but barely five months limited mainly to the Malabar coast. While there is no reason to question the validity of his accounts of the landscape, it is clear that other episodes in the book are literary clichés: the child killed by a cobra; the fight between a cobra and a mongoose; the jungle king riding on his elephant (whom the author promoted, if indeed he even had such an encounter, from a minor tribal chieftain); and the attempted liberation of the king's slave-mistress, who prefers to remain in bondage. The conversations with the monkeys Huc and Gong amount to commonplaces of fable literature. The tale of the missionary who frightens off a threatening tiger by playing hymns on his harmonium was an anecdote widely recounted in the missionary community.[38] His account of the political activities of the Brahman Rao was fabricated from contemporary news reports to make the book, written years later, seem up to date. The long dream involving his vision, seen from his own grave, of a girl and a huge blue flower is surely based on one of the most famous episodes in German Romantic literature: the blue flower in Novalis's novel *Heinrich von Ofterdingen*. The monk from Kashmir seeking the unattainable is reminiscent of the Tibetan lama in Kipling's *Kim*. Much of the philosophical content is based on reading that Bonsels undertook in the years following his trip. Above all, the analogy to Loti's *India* seems unmistakable.[39]

Bonsels wrote his book in part, no doubt, to capitalize on the wave of interest in India stirred up by Loti, Tagore, and other publications of the early 1900s; by the excitement generated by the radical political developments in the English colony; and by commonplaces about India prevalent since Herder. It constitutes an adroit mixture of adventure, politics, and travel flavored with the necessary ingredient of the search for spiritual meaning— a spiritual dimension of which the twenty-four-year-old Bonsels gave absolutely no indication during his actual stay in India. The immense popularity of the work attests, then, both to the considerable interest in accounts of spiritual pilgrimages to India and to the tested success of the quest pattern underlying Pierre Loti's French model, which Bonsels skillfully adapted for a gullible German public some eight years after his actual sojourn on the subcontinent.

The German Diarists

Max Dauthendey (1867–1918) arrived in India on 19 January 1906 in the course of a six-month Cook's tour around the world paid for by money his Swedish wife Annie borrowed from her family.[40] Dauthendey was not from a poor family. His father owned a fashionable photography shop in Würzburg and had made a considerable fortune from chemical innovations for his profession. Dauthendey was expected to take over the family business, but the budding artist (before his poetic ambitions awoke) rebelled and left home. He parted on friendly terms with his father, who until his death in 1896 supported his son on his wanderings around Europe.[41] His inheritance enabled Dauthendey and his new wife to make the first of his overseas trips—a misbegotten expedition to Mexico in 1897. But he managed to spend money faster than he acquired it and was thus obliged for years to finance his grand plans by often hasty writing and borrowing from family, friends, and publishers.

Dauthendey's early poems—in such volumes as *Ultraviolett* (1893), the poetic drama *Sehnsucht* (1895; Longing), and the epic *Phallus* (1896)—impressed Stefan George, who attracted the young poet as an occasional contributor to *Blätter für die Kunst*. The poems, characterized by a drastic synesthesia through which he sought to capture in language the fragrances, colors, and sounds of nature, anticipated by a generation the experiments of the expressionists. During these years, as he poured out vast quantities of poems, stories, dramas, and other writings, Dauthendey traveled widely—first throughout Europe and later on the eagerly awaited trip around the world that took him to the East. He had longed for that goal ever since his boyhood when he heard one of his father's customers talk about Java and wished for a book about Java as his Christmas gift.[42] His interest in the East, while not pursued in any systematic manner, was further fired by desultory readings in Schopenhauer, Pierre Loti, and others.

Dauthendey's journey to India was motivated quite differently than were those of Loti, Bonsels, and subsequent German writers. In the first place, he felt none of the Europe-weariness of the kind prevalent around the turn of the century. Indeed, on his trip around the world, whenever he felt homesick for Europe, he renewed his energies by going down to the engine room of the ship and contemplating there "the European zeitgeist embodied in steel and iron."[43] Nor did he feel any of the conventional Franco-German hostility to

Americans or the British, of whom he said that they understood Asian art and culture better than other Europeans.[44]

In the second place, there was no powerful religious motivation.[45] "My mother's family was rigorously religious and belonged to the pious sect of the Moravians," he stated in his autobiography.[46] But his mother died when he was only six years old, and his father had a more relaxed attitude toward religion. He saw to it that his children attended church, and Dauthendey's earliest poems display a certain conventional religious sentiment. But he gradually accepted his father's belief that the universe is not ruled by a personal God but informed by a divine spark (*Gottesfunken*) that he named with the Hegelian term "der Weltgeist."[47] (It was only in the last months of his life, in 1917–18 while interned on Java, that he experienced a revelation and conversion to Christianity.)

Unlike Loti and many later German travelers, Dauthendey had no interest in the theosophists, some of whom he had encountered in Munich vegetarian restaurants in 1892: "these people with pale faces and large, spiritual eyes had an off-putting effect on me," he noted in his biography, like the deep-sea flora and fauna that one can see behind glass in an aquarium. "These theosophists, it seemed to me, longed out of the barrenness of an existence without fantasy for the fantasy-flower of life."[48]

In general, he later summarized, "I undertook all my trips from the need to see lands and peoples," but he never felt the least desire to settle permanently anywhere outside Germany.[49] Elsewhere he explains his Kantian ideal of "sacred purposelessness" (*heilige Zwecklosigkeit*): "The only goal that the writer should uphold is to empathize with the life of the universe and to let not just his own life but all the phenomena of life flow into his heart."[50]

The month in India (19 January to 18 February 1906) took him from Bombay by way of Jaipur, Delhi, Agra, and Lucknow to Benares; then northward to the Himalayas and Darjeeling; and finally from Calcutta across the Bay of Bengal to Burma and back again to Madras and Ceylon, whence he continued on his trip to China, Japan, Honolulu, and the United States. Dauthendey kept no journal during his trip; and his attempt at writing what was supposed to be a lighthearted account by a "Cook Passenger around the World" gets no farther than Bombay before it breaks off.[51] The most immediate register of his impressions can be seen in the many postcards and letters he sent to his wife back in Germany, in at least one of which he inscribes (with total ignorance of the geography of central and southern India) the ritual praise of India as a paradise. "India is with the exception of the Himalayas almost entirely level, like a splendid garden with ancient trees that arch like green temples, and beneath them the naked brown Indians and white herons and thick purple blossoms: it produces the impression of paradise."[52]

The earliest literary harvest from his trip was a collection of "twelve Asiatic novellas" published under the title *Lingam* (1909), almost all of which deal, as the title suggests, with sexual love. But with one exception all the tales concern Indians and the native inhabitants of other Asian lands (Burma, Malaya, China, and Japan). Despite the carefully observed atmosphere and scenery the stories reflect nothing about the reactions of a European traveler to the East.

With his next book, *Die geflügelte Erde* (1910; The winged earth), we encounter a different situation altogether. A theme pervading the entire volume, as the subtitle indicates, is the love the poet feels for his wife at home in Germany as he travels the seven seas in his voyage around the world ("Ein Lied der Liebe und der Wunder um sieben Meere"). While Dauthendey kept no journal and worked only with a few photographs, postcards, and memories, the volume amounts to an amazingly vivid and detailed account of his trip.[53] It was only after his return, while telling his wife about the trip, that he realized how much he had seen. "Only then did many sights awaken, which I did not realize I had registered; images and landscapes and incidents came out of my unconscious into consciousness as, in my mind, I composed the world trip once again for her eyes at home."[54]

The work constitutes a 470-page poetic diary in free verse (with internal and end rhymes), for which he hoped to win the Nobel Prize. Some 130 of the roughly page-long poems deal with his experiences in India and another two dozen with the visit to Madras and Ceylon.[55] The arrival in Bombay is depicted with the kind of colorful detail that charactcrizcs the entire work.

Der Dampfer schnaubte laut mit seiner Pfeife, dann ging's wie Todessteife
    um das Schiff,
Es hat die Anker eingehaut und es entschlief.
Bombay lag dort am Kai, breit, langgestreckt, mit großen, steinernen
    Hotelpalästen,
Und festen Hafenbauten, von Schornsteinrauch und Sonnennebel
    zugedeckt;
Und alle Fenster schauten glatt, als krochen ihre Häuser platt vorm
    Mammon auch in Indien auf dem Bauch.

[The steamer snorted loudly with its pipe; then a deathlike stiffness
went through the ship. / It struck its anchor and fell asleep. / Bombay lay
there at the quai, broad, stretched out, with large stone palatial

hotels, / And sturdy harbor buildings, covered with chimney smoke and
morning mist; / And all the windows looked flat, as though their houses
were creeping on their bellies before Mammon even in India.| (42)

The poet is struck by the "human masks" (*Menschenmasken*), the "long
colorful stripes of caste marks that cross the foreheads, cheeks, ears of all
the brown people, poor and rich alike, vertically and horizontally" (43).
We get detailed descriptions of the Hotel Tajmahal in Bombay, the telegraph
office, the street life, the elegant dinners in the hotel, and the various tourist
attractions in a land that "seemed paved with prayers" ("Der mit Gebeten
wie gepflastert schien," 45). In the searing heat the Europeans sit in their
hotels, in evening dress with collars extending to their ears, while he would
prefer to wear "nature's most elegant garb, / the brown skin color of naked
Indians" ("der Natur vornehmste Kleidung, / Die braune Leibesfarbe nackter
Indier," 46). When the *bajadère* dance theater is closed, he is taken to a local
"coolie theater" (*Kulitheater*, 64–70), where he witnesses scenes, including
the dance of a *Kulibajadere*, that impressed him so greatly that he also
described them in one of the stories of *Lingam*. Traveling on to Jaipur, he
tells the history of "the rose-red city" (77) that Loti depicted so vividly, with
its "Palace of the Winds" and "Living Statues."

   After a few days in Delhi he moves on to Agra and visits the Taj Mahal,
"the tenderest monument of love" ("das zärtlichste Denkmal der Liebe,"
106), whose cupola by moonlight looks like "a white mountain supported
neither by wall nor stone" ("Wie ein weißer Berg, dem nicht Mauer, nicht
Stein einen Halt gab," 107). From Jaipur he travels to Benares where from
the bridge across the Ganges "it seemed to me as though I heard names
from the Vedic books and echoes from the cathedral of wisdom. / Longing,
which is always underway, paused here for a moment, piously caught, / and
breathed the glorious spirit of the holy river."

   Mir war, als hörte ich aus Vedabüchern Namen und Echos aus der Weisheit
      Dom.
   Sehnsucht, die immer reist, blieb einen Augenblick hier fromm gefangen
   Und atmete den hehren Geist vom heiligen Strom.
   (127)

Dauthendey is moved by Benares, a city already called "the almighty" six
hundred years before Christ and before anyone thought of Rome as "eternal"
(128). He visits the Golden Temple, observes cremations on the Ganges, and
goes to Buddha's former residence at Sarnath. His reflections on the life

and thought of Buddha lead the loving Westerner finally to the observation, bold-printed for emphasis, that "Only in the arms of a loving woman, which grasp you to her heart, / can you find true nirvana."

Nur beim geliebten Weib, nur in den Armen, die ans Herz dich binden,
Kannst du das wirkliche Nirwana finden.
(149)

The trip to Darjeeling takes him within sight of Mount Everest, "the earth's outermost finiteness" ("an der Erde äußerster Endlichkeit," 156), but he experiences his true epiphany—like others to come—at daybreak on Tigerhill, where "at a distance through the snow a blood-red star digs its way, / as though you see a scarlet bird sweeping down from golden heights" ("Gräbt sich von fern durch den Schnee ein blutroter Stern, / Als siehst du aus goldener Höh' einen scharlachnen Vogel fegen," 159).

Dauthendey remains only briefly in Calcutta, "the merchants' city with its broad Indian-European streets" (166), before sailing for Burma. Back in India a short time later, he finds Madras "in European vestments" ("in europäischer Gewandung," 207) and is shocked by the elephantiasis that afflicts so many of the people. Given his antipathy toward theosophists, he does not make the ritual visit to the Theosophical Society and soon goes on to Ceylon, the "glittering island," where he visits the Temple of the Holy Tooth. Sailing from Colombo on an English ship, "once again on European territory, with European women in their spring hats and clothes of the latest fashions,"

Ich seufzte, weil jetzt die einfachen indischen Lappen verschwanden und die nackten, braunen Gestalten, die sich vorher zwei Monate vor meine Blicke hinmalten.

[I sighed because now the simple Indian rags disappeared along with the naked brown shapes which for two months painted themselves before my eyes.] (235)

⟨∞⟩

It is a pity that Stefan Zweig (1882–1942) kept no journal and wrote no thorough account of his trip to India in 1908–9.[56] The brilliant young critic-translator-biographer was encouraged to visit India by that multifaceted genius Walter Rathenau, who told him that it was impossible for anyone to understand Europe who had not been outside that continent. "You are a free man. Use your freedom!... Why don't you travel to India and America?"[57] Taking this advice, Zweig set off almost immediately on a four-month tour of India, Ceylon, Burma, and Indonesia. However, he saw India not as something "romantic" in rosy colors—an uncritical generalization that he unfairly attributes to Pierre Loti—but as an admonition to the human race. "It was not the splendid temples, the weathered palaces, not the Himalayan landscapes that gave me the greatest sense of inner development on this trip, but the people I got to know—people of another kind and world than a writer tends to encounter in the European inland" (214).

It is only from his two newspaper reports—on Gwalior and Benares (1909)—that we get a sense of Zweig's gift of observation. In "Benares: City of a Thousand Temples" he portrays the religion that fills the city without himself being drawn to it. There, he begins, "the river itself is the sanctuary [*Heiligtum*], the eternally self-renewing wonder of atonement."[58] The river is the great equalizer, for it accepts the sins of the living and the ashes of the dead; it welcomes the most renowned princes as well as the poorest of the poor. "Sins are equal in all the castes" (254). Hence Benares, like Jerusalem and Mecca and Rome, is a "magical magnet of faith" (255). Yet the ultimate secret of any religion, he continues, lies silent and mysterious beyond the possibilities of language. "Here in Benares one has premonitions of the power of this alien religion which can live only in this people, just as this people seems to live only for it" (259). Ultimately, therefore, Zweig resigns himself to observation from without. "Strangeness, unsurmountable strangeness is the final sensation vis-à-vis all the feelings of this people.... One can peer into their houses, read their books, visit their temples. Yet their inner life remains incomprehensibly alien" (260). And on this note of resignation Zweig's all too succinct impressions of India end.

Melchior Lechter, the graphic artist who designed Stefan George's books from *The Year of the Soul* (1897) down to but not including *The Star of the Covenant* (1914), developed strong mystical leanings that eventually led to a break with the Master. His travel account was nothing but "a vague religious backwash made up of Christian and Hindu ingredients," according to George.[59] Lechter's *Diary of the Trip to India* (1912)—a handsome leather-bound folio volume privately printed in an edition of only 333 copies, with an elaborate border on each of its 208 unnumbered pages[60]—constitutes an almost day-by-day account of the trip that the artist made with Karl

Wolfskehl from 30 September 1910, when he left Berlin, until 2 April 1911, when he set sail from India for the trip back to Germany. (Wolfskehl became ill with dysentery and returned in late December.) The account, written with the eye of a visual artist who constantly photographed scenes and sketched his impressions, shows a distinct progress from his initial disappointment— at the rain, the heat, the rats, the filth, the illness—to an ecstatic state of rapture by the end of his five-month stay.

Arriving on 22 October in Colombo (Ceylon), Lechter finds that "the first view disappointed." Two days later he is dismayed by the "disgusting" thievery around the temples of Buddha. He complains about the trivialized Buddhism that he encounters in the temples. Yet when he contemplates the luxuriant landscape "the image of paradise forces itself violently upon me" (28 Oct.). He attends theatrical and dance performances and converses with priests about Buddhism and theosophy and the differences between mysticism and occultism. By the time he leaves Ceylon for the subcontinent toward the end of November, he has found the atmosphere he sought: "There is reverence here, there is time for reflection" ("Hier ist andacht, hier ist einkehr," 16 Nov.).

Arriving in Madras, he finds the temples so "glorious" that he feels giddy at "this phenomenal work of Indian spirit" (22 Nov.). While the city is altogether too Europeanized, the air has such *limpidezza* that it would have pleased Nietzsche. He makes the ritual visit to Annie Besant at Adyar to discuss theosophy and visits the Seven Pagodas, which he finds spectacular. From Madras he sails across to Burma, "an Eden for a colorist" (26 Dec.), and is impressed by the "confusing abundance" of Rangoon. Returning to India in a "floating prison" with no company but card-playing Britons and Americans, he arrives on 22 January in Calcutta, a city altogether too Europeanized and modern, where even the women dance badly. A high point of the trip comes when he travels north to Darjeeling and views the sunrise from Tigerhill, where he experiences an epiphany like that of Dauthendey. "It seems to me as though I were hovering above the earth in eternal regions. . . . Behind these icy, inexorable peaks lies a sacral land" (29 Jan.).

Traveling down to Benares, he is struck by the impression that Hindu architecture is more spiritual, more imaginative, than the Buddhist buildings he saw in the south. In "holy, mystical Benares" he visits the Golden Temple and the offices of the Theosophical Society (from which Annie Besant has now moved to the headquarters in Madras). Then, moving west toward Delhi, he is amazed by the temple at Khajreha, which impresses him as being the source for the shape of Christian cruciform churches: "Make a pilgrimage there and look! . . . Who in Europe knows about it? When I think about these works, where is the much praised Renaissance left? Their style is chewed over and over, it is, ach, so boring, incapable of development, and impoverished" (16 Feb.). The Taj Mahal, in contrast, strikes him as "tedious to the point of yawning. Cold, hard, lacking imagination. No character, no ideas" (20 Feb.). The much praised marble intarsias amount to an "insane waste of effort without effect." In Lahore he buys a manuscript of the Bhagavad Gita illustrated with forty rather primitive miniatures and then goes south again to Delhi, where he admires the gait and gowns of the Indian girls and women. "Here one sees that European women simply don't know how to walk" (8 Mar.). A few days later he is in Bombay, dismayed at the "repulsive pettiness and stinking, creeping lousiness" of the Europeanized culture in India. "Oh how I am disgusted by the mendacious, modern, Christian European man" (12 Mar.).

From Madura he sails back to Ceylon, where he is disappointed by Anuradhapura after the experience of India. Pierre Loti, he concludes, beautified the town in his account, which opens *L'Inde (sans les Anglais)*. Summing up his experiences, he now senses that India is ultimately an incomprehensible land. "You are far, yet alive in the vaults of my inner being: from now on you belong in a different manner to the reveries that summon me, to the powers to which I am subject."

                                      ᴄᴏ

It is one of the ironies of Hermann Hesse's *Out of India (Aus Indien, 1913)* that the author never set foot on the subcontinent. His trip in the fall of 1911 took him from the Malayan peninsula to Sumatra and finally to Ceylon before dysentery and disenchantment drove him back home again after only two months in the East. Twelve years later, in a frank self-assessment, he hesitated to recommend the book to his friend and fellow India enthusiast Romain Rolland. "The book is poor and the trip itself was on the whole a disappointment.... At the time, when weary of Europe I had fled to the Indies, I found there nothing but the seduction of the exotic. This physical exoticism kept me away from the spirit of India, which I knew and was seeking even then, more than it brought me close to it."[61]

India was a goal toward which Hesse had long been aspiring.[62] "From the time I was a child I breathed in and absorbed the spiritual side of India just as deeply as Christianity," he recalled.[63] Yet his trip, as he realized in retrospect, was not so much a search for India as a flight from home. The thirty-four-year-old father of three, tied down for years in an increasingly unhappy marriage and frustrated by the demands of supporting his family through his writing, had become restless. His trip was also more generally a flight from Europe, he later realized. "I was fleeing it and almost hated it in its garish tastelessness, its noisy fairground busyness, its hectic restlessness, its crude boorish addiction to enjoyment."[64]

Setting out with such confused and self-centered feelings as these, Hesse was poorly prepared for any direct encounter with the East. He wanted not so much to become acquainted with an exotic land as, rather, through his response to the foreign to make discoveries about himself.[65] In fact, he was almost pettily impatient with the discomforts of travel: the weather, the filth in the cities, the primitive accommodations in the countryside, the poverty and beggars.

Crossing from the Malayan peninsula to Sumatra on a Dutch coastal steamer, Hesse reflects, as he reports in *Out of India,* that Europeans coming to the Malayan islands with any other reasons than business always entertain the secret hope of finding a land of primitive paradise innocence. "Pure romantics will occasionally find these paradises and will believe for a while, bribed by the good-natured childishness of most Malayans, that they are partial shareholders in a delightful primal condition."[66] Hesse thought that he had found such a paradise when he and three European companions traveled into the jungle and spent several days at a riverside camp:

Und bin für Augenblicke tigerwach
Und froh, wie ich's in Knabenzeiten
Und seit den Knabenzeiten nie mehr war.[67]

[For a few moments I am tiger-alert / and as happy as I was in childhood / but never again since then.]

The last stage of his trip takes Hesse to Ceylon, where he is initially depressed in Kandy by "all the depravity and shortcomings of a foreigners-town systematically ruined by all-too-wealthy Englishmen" (3: 836). But out in the countryside, the sight of the primitive nature-people inspires him with "an atavistic contentment and sense of home" (3: 836). Visiting a Buddhist temple, he admires the fresco representations of the life of Buddha and is reminded of Giotto's painting of Saint Francis at Assisi. In Kandy, though already sick with dysentery, he visits the Temple of the Holy Tooth where he is annoyed by the beggars and by the priests with their gold and ivory, sandalwood and silver, and ancient holy books whose Sanskrit texts they can no longer read. The famous tooth reminds him of relics in European churches. He respects the simple faith of the people, who have travestied the pure teachings of Buddha and put in its place "a gigantic structure of helpless piety, of foolishly hearty prayers and sacrifices, of touchingly mistaken human foolishness and childishness" (3: 841). Yet in comparison with their simple piety, "what can we do, we clever and intellectual people from the West, who are much closer to the source of Buddha's knowledge and all knowledge?" (3: 841). "The Buddhism of Ceylon is nice to photograph and to write newspaper articles about; beyond that it is nothing but one of the many touching and grotesque forms in which helpless human suffering expresses its distress and its need for spirit and strength" (3: 842).

To celebrate his departure from India in a worthy manner, he climbs the tallest mountain of Ceylon, the 2,500-meter Pedrotallagalla. Here finally, gazing out over the valley of Nurelia, he experiences an epiphany like those of Dauthendey and Lechter on Tigerhill in the north and admires the island on which ancient Indian legends located paradise. Yet this view of paradise— a constant leitmotif in European accounts of India—reaffirms his sense that he has come all this distance only to confront himself.

> We come to the South and East full of longing, driven by a dark and grateful premonition of home, and we find here a paradise, the abundance and rich luxuriance of all natural gifts. We find the pure, simple, childlike people of paradise. But we ourselves are different; we are alien here and without any rights of citizenship; we lost our paradise long ago, and the new one that we wish to build is not to be found along the equator and on the warm seas of the East. It lies within us and in our own northern future. (3: 845)

What Northern Europeans in their intellectualized and individualized culture only rarely experience, Hesse continues later (3: 850)—say, while listening to Bach—that sense of belonging to a community and of drawing strength from a magical source is available every day to the Buddhist in the cool portico of his temple.

Hesse came to the East, then, in flight from European civilization and with the romantic hope of finding a lost paradise. His experiences were dominated to a considerable extent by disappointed expectations and by his annoyance at the Westernization that he observed in the cities. In January 1912 he summed it up: "I had gone to see the primeval forest, to caress the crocodiles and catch butterflies, and found quite incidentally and without looking something much lovelier: the Chinese cities of Indochina and the Chinese people, the first real cultural people that I have seen."[68] It was ten years later before he realized the difference.

Previously my reading, searching, and sympathies were restricted exclusively to the philosophical aspect of India—the purely intellectual,
Vedantic and Buddhistic aspect. The Upanishads, the sayings of Buddha,
and the Bhagavad Gita were the focal point of this world. Only recently
have I approached the actual religious India of the gods, of Vishnu and
Indra, Brahma and Krishna. And now Buddhism appears to me more
and more as a kind of very pure, highly bred reformation—a purification
and spiritualization that has no flaw but its great zealousness, with which
it destroys image-worlds for which it can offer no replacement.[69]

It was this new vision of India that he sought to depict in his novel *Siddhartha* (1922).

Hesse reviewed Count Hermann von Keyserling's *Travel Diary of a Philosopher* (*Das Reisetagebuch eines Philosophen*, 1918) in the journal *Vivos Voco*
(Nov. 1920), giving it the highest praise. "On the whole this is the most significant book that has appeared in Germany for years. To begin with the
central point: Keyserling, while perhaps not the first European, is the first
European scholar and philosopher who has truly understood India."[70] He
immediately alerted his friend Romain Rolland to its significance, attribut-
ing to it the astonishing postwar revival of interest in Asia among German
youth.[71] It contains, Hesse reported, some very superficial pages but others of great beauty. In 1920 Keyserling founded a "School of Wisdom" at
Darmstadt to teach the Hindu methods of meditation and sponsored annual
meetings attended by such figures as Leo Baeck, C. G. Jung, Ernst Troeltsch,
and Rabindranath Tagore. While Hesse believed that "interior liberation"
of the Asian sort was perhaps the only viable alternative to bolshevism,
he nonetheless repudiated any kind of political action and the possible ex-
ploitation of Eastern thought.

Keyserling (1880–1946) made his trip around the world in 1911–12 and
wrote his book the following year. The outbreak of war prevented its scheduled publication in 1914, and no doubt its delayed publication in the period
of spiritual confusion following the war accounted in no small measure
for its immense impact.[72] The book is based extensively on Keyserling's
detailed travel diaries, but the author invites us to read the work like a
novel: "an inwardly coherent poetic work created from the inside outward"
(xxx). Keyserling admits frankly that he undertook his journey to escape his
"natural man" (848). At age thirty-two he had still been too "dependent on

independence," seeking desperately to preserve his freedom by constant transformations. After earning his doctorate in geology in 1902 at the University of Vienna, he spent three years in Paris composing his first philosophical work (*Das Gefüge der Welt*, 1906) and then attempted unsuccessfully to be licensed to teach philosophy at the University of Berlin. Shortly thereafter he withdrew to his family estate in Estonia for what was to be a life of study and contemplation. He soon came to feel, however, that he was too young to settle down as a finished personality, but Europe no longer offered enough to further his development. What he desired was not new material but fresh responses. So in October 1911 he set out on the yearlong trip around the world that produced his *Travel Diary of a Philosopher*. As a result of his trip he can now accept his own being, feeling himself to be at one with his time and jointly responsible for its fate. What matters, he has learned, is to live for others, not for oneself. "The bodhisattva, not the sage, exemplifies the goal of human progress" (858).

It would be difficult to imagine a work that differs more radically from the travel accounts of Pierre Loti, Max Dauthendey, and Melchior Lechter, whose visual imaginations so vividly depicted the external world of India. In his title the emphasis definitely lies on the word *philosopher*. Keyserling, his *Wanderjahre* behind him, was on a quest not for external impressions but, rather, for inner self-realization. Accordingly, his journal tells us remarkably little about people and places. We find few names, no dates, and nothing about travel companions, who are occasionally characterized by their nationalities. The account amounts, rather, to a record of his response to the stimuli that he received in India—a response that is lively, varied, provocative, and often captivating. Every experience becomes a springboard to flights of speculation—anthropological, ethical, metaphysical.

Upon his arrival in Ceylon he is immediately struck by the lush vegetation that dominates the hothouse atmosphere of the country and becomes a leitmotif of his thought. Hinduism in its incredible richness and with its fertile proliferation of deities can be comprehended only as a "vegetative process" (34). The famous Buddhist tolerance, but also its caste system, are explained by the model of vegetation according to which all parts of the plant, from root to blossom, are of equal value (49–50). Nirvana is simply the escape from nature and its fecundity (45–46). He is inspired by his experiences to comparative speculations: on Buddhist joy and the European-Nietzschean tragic sense of life (36); on the similarities between the phenomenologies of Buddha and Ernst Mach (42–43). Buddhism, he reflects, is more tolerant than Christianity because Buddha was an aristocrat (like Keyserling) and therefore harbored none of the resentments that Nietzsche attributed to the proletarian followers of the proletarian Christ (52–53). Christianity is ultimately superior because attachment to one's fellow man is better than Buddhist detachment (62). Yet the average Buddhist is better than the average Christian because the Buddhist goal of golden mediocrity is easier to achieve than the lofty Christian ideal (63–64).

Keyserling's lively, combinatory, and restlessly ruminating mind is guilty at times of romanticizing India. He is enchanted by the worship practices of these "gentle brown people with the long bluish-glistening hair and wonderfully lovely hands" (54). He makes the inevitable allusions to paradise. "Here was rooted the truth content of the image of paradise" (89). As he makes his way across the subcontinent, we hear nothing about the modes of transportation that fascinated the naval officer Loti, the colorful scenes that attracted Lechter, or the discomforts of travel that irritated Hesse. The temples of Madurai inspire him, rather, to thoughts on the spirit and advantages of polytheism—because it reflects the varied disunity of the psyche (which he sees also reflected in the work of such geniuses as Goethe and Shakespeare and in the institution of Catholicism with its saints, 108)—in contrast to monotheism, which deprives and narrows the world. When Keyserling observes the dances, he does not respond sensually, as did Loti and Dauthendey, but sees in them an expression of India's creativeness and its wealth of natural shapes (122). Similarly the Seven Pagodas, which brought out the artist in Melchior Lechter, produce no descriptions but only reflections on eternity and transitoriness. "My spurred imagination races ahead of time" (127).

At the invitation of Annie Besant, who by this time had moved from Benares to Madras, Keyserling spent a longer period (and some seventy pages of his text) as a guest at the headquarters of the Theosophical Society in Adyar. Here he contemplates the occidental character of theosophy and the truth content of occultism; he meditates on the essence of yoga and on concentration as the technical basis of all progress. While acknowledging the achievements of theosophy, he is aware of its weaknesses—notably its externalization of the religious impulse in humankind. Eventually moving on, he admires (like Loti) the eloquence of the stones in the sacred caves of Ellora and comes, like Loti and Lechter before him, to prefer the richness and variety of Hindu art to the art of the "protestant" sects of Buddhism and Jainism (199). He regards Indian Buddhism as a degenerate form of the religion as it exists in Ceylon. At Udaipur he inspects the erotic art of the palace, ponders amidst the ruins of Chitor the heroic age of India, and admires the knightly culture of Jaipur, which is reminiscent of the European Middle Ages. Venturing as far west as Lahore and Peshawar (modern Pakistan), he gets a taste of Central Asia before heading back to Delhi, whose imperial atmosphere reminds him of Rome. He feels instinctively at home in northern Islamic culture because Jews, Christians, and Muslims alike share a common faith going back to Moses. Indeed, in their orientation toward the external world the Muslims, like Christians, are basically occidentals (248–49). Like Loti, but unlike Lechter, he finds that the Taj Mahal is "perhaps the greatest of all works of art" which the creative human spirit has produced (250), conceding at the same time that he judges art "only as a direct expression of what is metaphysically real" (256).

At Holy Benares he again spends a longer period, maintaining that every Christian theologian should sacrifice a year of study and spend it on the Ganges, where true reverence still prevails—unlike Europe where only its pale reflection survives (264). Only the Hindu understands the meaning of faith and knows that faith is the precondition for cognition (281–83). In the West, especially since the Reformation, reason and intellect have destroyed faith and, in its place, instilled the notion of sin, which the older and wiser Hindus eschew. To be sure, there is also much superstition in Benares; but in a fully cultivated person Hindu belief creates the loftiest humanity that is imaginable.

Why has this knowledge remained unknown in Europe? Because few people have visited India—at least an India *sans les Anglais*—and because faith has no system that can be learned from books alone. The greatest Indian *rishis* are wiser than the most renowned Western thinkers. Plato, Goethe, Hegel, Nietzsche had fleeting moments of luminous insight but did not live their lives in profundity. The most important factor is concentration: India's absolute advantage over the West is the fundamental recognition that culture in any true sense is achieved not by breadth but by depth, and depth depends upon concentration. Western man must learn to read the surface as a mirror of depth. Keyserling adds many pages of thoughts on meditation and concentration, concluding that the heart of yoga is the ability to get beyond one's humanity as determined by nature alone. "Increasingly I am experiencing in the Indian manner, seeing the world and life in the light of the spiritual sun of Hindustan" (337).

Leaving Benares for Gaya, the holiest site of Buddhism, Keyserling understands that Buddhism is a good alternative for those weary of the incredible richness and variety of Hinduism. He regards the famous bo tree as the holiest place in the entire world because Buddha, a man who had to work his way up to godliness, is greater than Jesus, who was born a god. In the Himalayas, finally, he feels that man is close to the godhead. Like Dauthendey and Lechter, he experiences there a sunrise epiphany. "It was as though I had already reached my goal, as though I had already crawled out of the larva of my humanness" (393). He is curious to see how long this new person will last, which—come what may—he will never quite lose when he comes back down to earth.

The sojourn in India now moves quickly to its end. In Calcutta, Keyserling meets the Tagores: the painter Abenindranath and the poet Rabindranath, who impresses him as being "a visitor from a higher, more spiritual world" (402). In the Tagores' palace he experiences Indian music, contrasting it with European program music, which mistakenly attempts to portray through sound qualities that are not music. He sails across the Bay of Bengal to Burma, reflecting that what he has seen and experienced in India "summons again and again the myth of the Golden Age into our consciousness" (418).

The *Travel Diary*, which was soon translated into French (1919), English (1925), and other languages, made Keyserling famous throughout Europe. Its impact twenty years later can be measured by the impression that it made on an idiosyncratic American travel writer and admirer of Madame Blavatsky. In a tribute written to Keyserling on his sixtieth birthday (1940) Henry Miller praised him as one of the few philosophers who actually philosophize. He recalled that he read *The Travel Diary* during a sea voyage and was interested especially in the section on China and India.

> I saw the philosopher in his undershirt, a frail weather-beaten man, puzzled, ravished, perplexed, roving amidst a fauna and flora which were constantly changing and shifting; I saw that he was most extraordinarily fallible, permeable, malleable. I rejoiced for him, and even enjoyed his occasional discomfiture.[73]

In these travel accounts by a naval officer, an unhappy mission worker, a poet, an artist, two writers, and a philosopher we get seven wholly different responses to the experience of India. But in almost every case they share a set of basic characteristics. (Dauthendey and Zweig represent the occasional exception.) The author states at the outset that his trip is a search for a new belief to replace a lost Christian faith and the degenerate values of early twentieth-century Europe. They find a primal paradise in India; but it is a paradise that has been lost amidst the temple ruins covering the subcontinent and that is sensed only fleetingly in mountaintop epiphanies. Yet all of them hope that at least a fragment of the elevating experience will survive and accompany them on their returns to their European destinies. In sum, the pilgrimage to India inevitably leads back to Europe, and the mythic East is replaced by other surrogates both real and surreal: by politics, by myth, and by utopia.

The Anglo-Indian Angle

Loti and his German followers visited, and were enchanted or disappointed by, an India of the imagination based on myth, legend, and literature—an India, moreover, *sans les Anglais.* English travelers, in contrast, sailed out to the East with a wholly different mindset: to bring Western law and order to a colony with which England had maintained trade relations since the early seventeenth century and where it currently enjoyed political hegemony. "Carrying England to India," or "Anglicanism," was ridiculed by G. Lowes Dickinson in the articles he wrote for the *Manchester Guardian* (1912–13).[74] "When the civilian and military officials on the outward bound ships go to church," he joked, "they are not thinking of religion. They are thinking of the social system" (4).

The extended official presence of England had produced ever since the late eighteenth century a voluminous Anglo-Indian literature comprising plays, poems, and hundreds of stories and novels.[75] The difference between the Franco-German pilgrimages and the English official assignments is evident if we briefly consider, in conclusion, the finest late product of that genre, E. M. Forster's *Passage to India* (1924).

Forster made the first of his three visits to India in 1912–13—not on any official assignment or romantic quest but to visit a friend. "My connection with India is peculiar and personal," he related in a talk entitled "Three Countries" (1959).

> It started because I made friends with an Indian, and but for him I might never have gone to his country, or written about it.... It is on this basis of personal relationship that my connection with that strange country rests. I didn't go there to govern it or to make money or to improve people. I went there to see a friend.[76]

In the course of that first six-month stay Forster traveled across the subcontinent, from Bombay eastward to Bengal and from the Punjab down to Hyderabad, recording his impressions in his journals and in letters to his mother, some of which were later included in his nonfiction book about India, *The Hill of Devi* (1953).[77] While he dutifully writes about the Taj Mahal

(147) and attends a mystery play about Krishna (153–54), he is depressed by the swarms of Americans in Udaipur (166) and finds Jaipur—the "rose-red city" that enchanted Loti and Dauthendey—"fraudulent... a laid-out town, painted blotting-paper pink" (208).

Forster almost always moves quickly beyond the ritual descriptions to the personal relations within the Anglo-Indian community or between English and Indians that interest him.

> There! yet another description of the Taj has been written. After that,
> I won't go on to describe the Fort, which we visited this morning....
> Plans are all in the melting pot again—it scarcely seems worthwhile
> mentioning. Bob is in one of his fidgety moods.... (148)

Forster is irked by both his compatriots and the Indians. As he notes on 2 December, "Nowgong a small Cantonment and a bore; polo; officers' wives with hideous voices and faces of that even pink. Though not more attracted to Indians than I was, I'm irritated by my countrymen even more" (156). The next day he encounters "another fool, but well-bred and amiable. Theosophist of the silliest sort...." India, he concedes, "is full of such wonders, but she can't give them to me" (193). While his Cambridge friend Dickinson, Forster's travel companion on the ship outward bound for India, recorded his view of the trip in a series of newspaper articles, Forster saved his impressions for his novel. He began *A Passage to India* (1924) immediately following his return but left it in fragmentary form. He took up the project again in 1922–23 after a second visit to India—this time in an official capacity as temporary replacement for the private secretary to the rajah of what was then known as Dewas State Senior (Central India). By this time he had read widely on India and published eight essays and some thirty-two reviews on various Indian subjects.[78]

In a certain sense Forster's classic work amounts to a sublimation of the archetypal Anglo-Indian novel, which has a readily recognizable pattern.

> A typical novel generally begin with a voyage, bringing the hero, more
> often the heroine, to the shores of India. On her arrival in a Presidency
> town or a mofussil "station" she is welcomed by a father, aunt, or some
> distant relation, and invariably causes a flutter in the small Anglo-Indian
> colony there. She becomes the belle of the season, is much sought after,
> and goes through the usual round of Anglo-Indian gaieties. There follow
> accounts of *burra-khanas,* shooting-parties (generally tiger-hunts), pic-
> nics, visits to places of historical interest, balls and dances with their

kala-juggas, and race-meetings. There are scandals and gossips at the
club regarding her "doings," interlaced with love-rivalries and misunderstandings, and finally everything ends in a happy marriage. A baboo,
a begum, a nawab or a rajah, or a political agitator is thrown in for local
colour, or to supply the villain indispensable to a work of fiction. There
are, of course, many variations of the theme, but this may be taken as a
skeleton of a typical Anglo-Indian novel.[79]

It takes little imagination to detect here the pattern underlying *A Passage
to India.* Adela Quested is the heroine who, accompanied by Mrs. Moore,
comes out to India—very much an India *avec les Anglais*—to visit her fiancé, Ronny Heaslop (Mrs. Moore's son from an earlier marriage). Adela's
romantic views create a stir in the tight, arrogant Anglo-Indian community
of the local station, which Mrs. Moore also shocks by her friendship with
the young Indian physician Aziz and a local renegade, the school principal
Mr. Fielding. The novel features visits to a mosque and a Hindu festival
celebrating the birth of Krishna; polo games and a "Bridge Party" at the
club in a (failed) attempt to bridge the gap between the English and those
whom they dismissively term their "Aryan Brothers";[80] the ritual expedition to the local sight, the Marabar Caves; the excitement and dissension
between Anglos and Indians caused by Aziz's arrest and trial for rape on the
basis of what turns out to be Adela's mistaken (probably on the basis of a
"hallucination") and subsequently retracted accusation.

But Forster inverts and ironizes the familiar scheme. Mrs. Moore is sent
away by her son before her unorthodox views and her insistence on Aziz's innocence can become a public scandal, and she dies on shipboard. The bigoted
and career-oriented Ronny breaks his engagement to Adela, who returns
to England. The freethinking principal Fielding, who is (falsely) rumored to
have had an illicit relationship with Adela, also goes home for a vacation
and marries Mrs. Moore's daughter. Aziz loses his position but finds another
in a native state. Rather than the happy resolution of difficulties, the novel
ends with exacerbated racial tensions that reflect the increasing volatility
of the political situation leading eventually to Indian independence.

There is no need here to offer yet another interpretation of the much-
analyzed and problematic work or another appreciation of the subtlety with
which Forster portrays his various English, Hindu, and Muslim types. In
fact, the novel betrays a more subtle understanding of, and sympathy for,
the Indian religions than do most of the works previously discussed. What
matters in the present context is that the novel—in contradistinction to the
French and German works but typically for Anglo-Indian fiction—can in no

way be construed as a quest for a surrogate faith. As far as his personal views are concerned, in the article "What I Believe" (1939) the admirer of Erasmus and Montaigne made clear his own skepticism. "I do not believe in Belief," it begins. "Faith, to my mind, is a stiffening process, a sort of mental starch, which ought to be applied as sparingly as possible."[81] Indeed, his views as set forth in an address entitled "Art for Art's Sake" (1949) are closer to those of the poets in chapter 4, above. "Works of Art, in my opinion, are the only objects in the material universe to possess internal order, and that is why though I don't believe that only Art matters, I do believe in Art for Art's sake."[82]

Fielding more than any other character represents Forster's attitude vis-à-vis the Anglo-Indians. Dickinson portrayed himself and Forster to a Frenchman on the ship bound for India: "We don't 'belong,' and they know it. We are outside the system. At bottom we are dangerous, like foreigners. And they don't quite approve of our being let loose in India."[83] The fictional Fielding tells a Muslim friend: "The truth is that the West doesn't bother much over belief and disbelief in these days."[84] He himself came to India because he needed a job. "I cannot tell you why England is here or whether she ought to be here. It's beyond me." Yet Fielding is the only English character with a certain insight into India, with the awareness that the Indian gracefulness and restfulness of gesture are "the social equivalent of Yoga" (245).

Forster treats Adela, the figure with the symbolic surname ("Quested"), with an irony suggested by her very first words, which express the romantic desire "to see the *real* India" (17). (Forster acknowledged that "I don't myself like the phrase 'the real India.' I suspect it. It always makes me prick up my ears.")[85] But "we aren't even seeing the other side of the world," she complains to Mrs. Moore after they have wasted an evening at a performance of *Cousin Kate* at the Anglo-Indian Chandrapore Club. When she tells the English ladies at the club that she wants to meet Indians, they are astonished. "Wanting to see Indians! How new that sounds!" (20). They instruct her that, as an Englishwoman, she is superior to them. "Don't forget that. You're superior to everyone in India except one or two of the Ranis, and they're on an equality" (35). The Indians, in turn—the Hindus, Muslims, Sikhs, Parsis, Jains, and others—are united only by their common abuse and contempt of the English (100).

Mrs. Moore—whom in her affection for the Indian people some critics have identified with Annie Besant and who becomes in the mind of the crowd outside the courthouse a Hindu goddess, "Esmiss Esmoor"[86]— presents a different case. It is only after her arrival in India that she begins to think about religion. "Mrs. Moore felt that she had made a mistake in mentioning God, but she found him increasingly difficult to avoid as she grew older, and he had been constantly in her thoughts since she entered India, though oddly he satisfied her less" (46). After her terrifying experience in the darkness and echoes of the cave and its mystery, she is wholly disenchanted with "poor little talkative Christianity" (144), which now seems altogether inadequate.

Adela and Mrs. Moore fail to realize that India, "seemingly so mysterious," in fact permits no mystery or privacy because its conventions have such compelling force (43). A cynical Indian remarks bitterly that "the so-called spirituality of India" amounts to nothing more than the inability to coordinate, to keep engagements, to catch trains (106). Even the normally epiphanic moments lose their charm under Forster's ironic gaze. When Adela and Mrs. Moore are taken to the Marabar Caves, they eagerly await the sunrise (like Dauthendey and Lechter before them).

> Colour throbbed and mounted behind a pattern of trees, grew in intensity, was yet bright, incredibly brighter, strained from without against the globe of the air. They awaited the miracle. But at the supreme moment, when night should have died and day lived, nothing occurred. It was as if virtue had failed in the celestial fount. The hues in the east decayed, the hills seemed dimmer though in fact better lit, and a profound disappointment entered with the morning breeze. Why, when the chamber was prepared, did the bridegroom not enter with trumpets and shawms, as humanity expects? The sun rose without splendour. (131)

When Adela, beginning to have doubts about her accusation of Aziz, realizes that she must testify in the trial against him, she thinks: "Truly Anglo-India had caught her with a vengeance and perhaps it served her right for having tried to take up a line of her own" (191). Before Ronny breaks their engagement, she broods that henceforth she will have to meet the other insolent Anglo-Indian clubwomen, "year after year, until one of their husbands was superannuated" (191). After "years of intellectualism" Adela resumes her "morning kneel to Christianity" (205). Her "last Indian adventure" is the crowning disenchantment: her Indian servant follows her onto the ship at Bombay and attempts to blackmail her with the allegation that she has been Fielding's mistress.

In part 3 Fielding and Aziz are briefly reunited two years later in the Native Province where Aziz is now employed. Though they still trust each other, their respective views have hardened, they lack true understanding of each other, and during their last hours together "they wrangled about politics" (314). Without the English, Fielding now insists, "Indians go to seed at once." Aziz responds angrily that the English should clear out. "We wanted to know you ten years back—now it's too late" (315). Although they promise while on a farewell ride to remain friends, the images tell a different story: "the horses didn't want it—they swerved apart; the earth didn't want it, sending up rocks through which riders must pass single file" (316). All the voices of India—temples, jails, palaces, birds spoke with a hundred voices "'No, not yet,' and the sky said 'No, not there.'" The most magnificent specimen of Anglo-Indian fiction, which began in irony, ends in resignation.

⸾⸾⸾

It is a fact of literary history that Forster borrowed the title of his novel from Walt Whitman's poem "Passage to India" (from the fifth edition of *Leaves of Grass*, 1871). If Forster took the poem at all seriously, then he clearly had something more in mind than criticism of what Kipling had notoriously called "The White Man's Burden." Whitman's poem begins as a hymn in praise of three great technological achievements—the laying of the Atlantic cable in 1866, the opening of the Suez Canal in 1869, and the completion of the Union Pacific Railroad that same year—which for the first time globalized the entire world.

> Passage to India!
> Lo, soul, seest thou not God's purpose from the first?
> The earth to be spann'd, connected by network,
> The races, neighbors, to marry and be given in marriage,
> The oceans to be cross'd, the distant brought near,
> The lands to be welded together.[87]

But technology alone does not suffice, Whitman realizes. After the seas have all been crossed "Tying the East to the Western sea, / The road between Europe and Asia" (344), the poem continues, "Finally shall come the poet worthy that name." Then at last in a grand poetic vision

> All these separations and gaps shall be taken up and hook'd and link'd together,
> The whole earth, this cold, impassive, voiceless earth, shall be completely justified,
> Trinitas divine shall be gloriously accomplish'd and compacted by the true son of God, the poet.
> (345)

This, it would appear, Forster saw as his mission: to expose the ultimate unity underlying the complexities and apparent differences of the societies he depicts:

> Old occult Brahma interminably far back, the tender and junior Buddha,
> Central and southern empires and all their belongings, possessors,
> The wars of Tamerlane, the reign of Aurungzebe,
> The traders, rulers, explorers, Moslems, Venetians, Byzantium, the Arabs,
>   Portuguese....
> (346)

Forster's figures fail in the end to connect. Whitman, however, points the way beyond the poet's quest for meaning, the vision achieved only in an art for art's sake. The ultimate circumnavigation of the world involves nothing less than "the voyage of his mind's return, / To reason's early paradise" (347)—in short, to a social and philosophical resolution. Following the inevitable disappointment in their pilgrimages to India, it was therefore to politics and myth that the writers turned after the failure of the retreat into art for art's sake and the flight from Europe.

CHAPTER SIX

The God That Failed

A free-floating "faith" longing for an object was, according to Thomas Mann in the chapter "On Faith" in his *Reflections of a Nonpolitical Man* (1918), the hallmark of the age at the end of World War I. "One must *believe*. And in what? In faith itself! would be the correct answer. For it is actually a kind of l'art pour l'art, a kind of faith as gesture and aestheticism.... It is faith in politics, in progress, in mankind and its perfectibility."[1] Mann was describing the mythophilic German, whom he labels Gothic Man: "the man of the new intolerance, the new antihumanism of the mind, the new unity and decisiveness, of faith in faith" (496). But his analysis applies equally well to the internationally minded socialists and communists who were emerging in Germany and other countries in opposition to the nationalists of Fascist and Nazi tendency. In both cases the impulse and structure of belief were essentially theological, and the political faith a surrogate for religious belief. As Roger Martin du Gard put it in the *Epilogue* (1940) to *Les Thibault*, "it is precisely when his mind is most beset with doubts that a man is liable, in his desire to find an escape at all costs from perplexity, to clutch at any ready-made creed that offers reassurance" (980). Many former socialists and communists recalled this longing for a quasi-religious faith when they sought to explain the attraction of the Party in the 1920s. "Whether or not Marxist Communism may be regarded as a kind of 'religion,'" wrote one historian of philosophy, "it remains a fact that it represents a movement of faith that for many people is a substitute for religion."[2]

Richard Crossman came up with the inspired title *The God That Failed* (1949) for his anthology of autobiographical essays by six writers who were initially attracted to and then turned away from communism. He recognized that "despair and loneliness were the main motives for conversion to

Communism" among those who were left with a "Christian conscience" even though they had abandoned orthodox Christianity. The emotional need and structure of thought remained even when the substance shifted from religion to politics. "The emotional appeal of Communism lay precisely in the sacrifices—both material and spiritual—which it demanded of the convert."[3] The Christian analogy of the title recurs in the various contributions. André Gide, addressing a meeting in Paris in 1935 of the Union pour la Vérité, explained that "on account of its compromises Christianity is bankrupt." "If Christianity had really prevailed," he continued, "and if it had really fulfilled the teaching of Christ, there would today be no question of communism—there would indeed be no social problem at all."[4]

Arthur Koestler's account of his "conversion" exploits all the registers of religious doctrine. "A faith is not acquired by reasoning," it begins. "One does not fall in love with a woman, or enter the womb of a church, as a result of logical persuasion."[5] From a psychological point of view, he continues,

> there is little difference between a revolutionary and a traditionalist faith. All true faith is uncompromising, radical, purist; hence the true traditionalist is always a revolutionary zealot in conflict with pharisaian society, with the lukewarm corrupters of the creed. And vice versa: the revolutionary's Utopia, which in appearance represents a complete break with the past, is always modeled on some image of the lost Paradise, of a legendary Golden Age. (16)

Koestler became converted, he recalls, "because I was ripe for it and lived in a disintegrating society thirsting for faith" (17). The "pauperized bourgeois" of the period turned, in their despair, to either the right or the left. Koestler found his own revelation in the Communist Manifesto. "The new star of Bethlehem had risen in the East" (21). When Prince Hubertus zu Löwenstein, the lionized young German anti-Nazi, reached Hollywood in 1936 and spoke to prominent actors and actresses, he found them eager "to buy freedom for their souls with a small contribution, just like the poor souls in Tetzel's [early sixteenth-century] dispensation campaign. Communism, popularly presented, was a substitute religion [*Ersatzreligion*]."[6] It was precisely this "New Faith" of communist ideology that Czeslaw Milosz scornfully identified in his passionate attack on "the captive mind."[7] The religious analogy, which we have already observed in the turn to myth, is a basic feature among thinking Marxists (as, indeed, it was already for Karl Marx, who called his scathing critique of Bruno Bauer and other Right Hegelians *The Holy Family* [1845]).

One of the most perceptive analyses of the appeal of the socialist ideal appeared only three years after Crossman's famous collection: Whittaker Chambers's *Witness*. Chambers (1901–61) was attracted to the communist movement during his years as a student of history at Columbia University in the early 1920s. As he explains in the prefatory "Letter to My Children," "educated men become Communists chiefly for moral reasons."[8] In a world that has lost its religion, "Communists are that part of mankind which has recovered the power to live or die—to bear witness—for its faith" (9). Because the communists have recognized that the human mind is the decisive force in the world, "the Communist vision is the vision of Man without God" (9). Accordingly, "every sincere break with Communism is a religious experience" (16). The dying world of 1925—a world rent by the threat of war and the crisis of economics—as Chambers experienced it, "was without faith, hope, character, understanding of its malady or will to overcome it" (195). In contrast to other parties and movements and faiths that had failed, communism was "acutely aware of the crisis of history" (195), but "in place of desperation, it set the word: hope" (196). Communism offered the young Chambers "what nothing else in the dying world had power to offer at the same intensity—faith and a vision, something for which to live and something for which to die" (196). In Chambers's account we encounter the same elements evident in the appeal of that other great political surrogate of the 1920s, the myth of National Socialism. Both arose in response to the perceived crisis of history and, in Chambers's terms, replaced despair with a vision. The appeal of the socialist vision and its subsequent disenchantment constitute the theme of several of the finest literary works of the period *entre deux guerres*.

Martin du Gard and Socialism in Prewar Europe

"The religious impulses of the new humanity will find an outlet, a social outlet," says Meynestrel, the venerated "Pilot" of the Geneva branch of International Socialism on the eve of World War I in Roger Martin du Gard's *Summer 1914* (1936). "For the mystical aspirations of institutional religion, social aspirations will be substituted."[9] On another occasion Meynestrel clarifies his views, saying that it will not be "that pig-headed anti-clericalism, so dear to the free-thinking bourgeois of the nineteenth century, which will free the masses from the yoke of religion."

> Here again the problem is a social one. The foundations of religions are of a social character. From the earliest ages religions have derived

their chief force from the suffering of oppressed mankind. Religions have always profited from misery. Once that prop is gone, faith will steadily decline. When a happier era dawns, the existing religions will lose their hold on men. (77; 2: 85)

As it turns out, Meynestrel subsequently sabotages the efforts of his pacifist colleagues to prevent the war by a general strike because he is convinced, like Hesse's Demian, that the old world must be shattered before the new one can emerge. Common to all the young revolutionaries in Martin du Gard's novel, perhaps the finest fictional depiction of socialist aspirations in the prewar era,[10] is the sense that socialism has replaced religion as the object of the human need for faith. "A revolutionary," exclaims the militantly passionate Austrian militant Mithoerg, "is a man who *believes* [*un croyant*]" (74; 2: 82). He accuses Jacques Thibault of being a political dilettante, a playboy rationalist, a man of opinions who likes to vacillate from one side to the other. "The true revolutionary, he has that courage, because he has faith, because he believes with all his heart, without question" (75–76; 2: 83). Thibault, he is convinced at this early point in the novel, will never have that compelling revolutionary faith. "Faith is a gift of heaven, so to speak. It's not for you, *Kamerad*. You don't have it, and you'll never have it" (74; 2: 82).

In fact, he misjudges Thibault, who already at this point—28 June, the fateful day of the assassination of the crown prince in Sarajevo—is "sick of our eternal palavers! Sick and tired of all that—ideology!" (62; 2: 62) and longs for action. Six weeks later Thibault's longing for action compels him into the quixotic act that costs him his life when, in the first days of the war, he makes the futile attempt to distribute pacifist leaflets from an airplane to the massing German and French troops. "His sole motive was a mystical certitude that this plan of his, for which he was ready to give up his life, was now the one and only way of rousing the masses from their torpor, of abruptly changing the course of events and countering the forces that had combined against the toilers of the earth, against fraternity and justice" (655; 2: 659).

Summer 1914, the seventh and longest of Martin du Gard's eight-volume *roman-fleuve*, *Les Thibault*, covers the weeks from 28 June to 10 August 1914—from the events at Sarajevo to the first days of the war. While the vast novel is narrated almost entirely from the point of view of Jacques Thibault, the action moves from city to city, showing the activity of young socialists in Geneva, Paris, and Berlin, Jacques's trip as a secret courier, an international gathering of socialists in Brussels, antiwar demonstrations in Berlin and Paris, and Jacques's late, hectic adventure in Basel. In addition to a large cast of new characters, several subplots are carried over from earlier volumes, revolving around Jacques's brother Antoine and the family Fontanin. We witness Antoine's single-minded dedication to his medical career and the final days of his current love affair; we attend the death of Jérôme Fontanin, surrounded by his amorous and financial scandals; we follow the frantic attempts of Jérôme's pious wife to redeem her husband's reputation, Jacques's friendship with their son Daniel, and his love affair with their daughter Jenny.

Above all, the novel focuses on the frenetic political activities of the socialists in various countries as they seek passionately but ineffectively to forestall the war gathering its seemingly inevitable momentum.[11] (The author has well learned the lesson of his favorite novel, Tolstoy's *War and Peace*, concerning the confusion and irrelevance of individuals in the face of history.) As a result, we do not follow here the development of Jacques Thibault's faith in socialism: it is already a fait accompli when the work begins. Indeed, the period between his sudden departure from Paris three years earlier and his reappearance in Switzerland, where he has established himself with moderate success as a writer and journalist, remains mysterious. We know only from the opening pages of volume 3 (*La Belle Saison*), as he confesses to his older brother, that he felt he was stifling in Paris. "Everything they make me do is loathsome, sickening! My teachers! My classmates! Their infatuations, their favorite books! The contemporary authors! Oh, if only someone in the world could guess what I am, me—what I want to do" (264; 1: 819).[12] Between his disappearance and his reemergence as the central consciousness in *Summer 1914* we hear only rumors about his life and catch a glimpse of him in volume 6 (*The Father's Death*).

Paradoxically, it is in the last chapter of that volume, almost as a transition to *Summer 1914*, that we find a profound exchange on religion—but between *Antoine* and the priest who has just buried his father. Antoine assures the priest that he lacks any sense of religion (853; 1: 1377). It is not so much that he has lost the faith of his childhood, he continues; he never had it—only the unthinking repetitions of a child (859; 1: 1382–83). He concedes that there may be in human beings a generalized urge to believe. "It is even possible that the efforts of modern minds—and I am thinking of those who are furthest from any literal faith—tend obscurely to reassemble the elements of a religion, to bring together certain notions which, taken as a whole, would constitute an entity that differs little from many Christians' idea of God" (854; 1: 1378). At this point, shortly before the end of volume 6, Antoine is stating a position that is not at all far from the one that his brother later expounds for the benefit of Jenny Fontanin.

In *Summer 1914* Jacques has become reunited in a sudden and mutual
passion with the beloved woman of his youth, whom he left without ex-
planation or farewells three years earlier. He wants her to understand the
values for which he is now struggling. It becomes clear that socialism is the
object to which his religious impulses have attached themselves. "Don't
imagine it was an impulse of blind philanthropy that swept me into the
revolutionary movement. No, I went through a long phase of doubt, of spiritual loneliness—a terrible time!" (360; 2: 368). In his youth he held firm
but vague notions about the brotherhood of man and the victory of truth
and justice. "A fool's paradise, as I very soon found out, and then everything
seemed to go dark inside me. That was the most appalling period of my life;
I let myself sin, I touched the lowest depth of despair. Well, it was the revolutionary ideal that saved me then." Jean's experiences, after he deserted
his prosperous bourgeois family to work as a dockhand in Germany and as
a machine-tender in Italy, familiarized him with the injustices of the existing social system. He came to the conviction that a new social system
was needed, a new order ruled by the proletariat, which would restore to
the individual not only his rightful share of the profits but also his human
dignity. Jacques understands human nature well enough to anticipate that
the first results of the revolution will be disappointing—that workers, once
liberated, will initially seek the basest forms of satisfaction. "Men's lower
instincts will need to be appeased before any real spiritual progress [*la culture spirituelle*] is feasible.... Before their souls become enlightened" (364;
2: 372). But his almost divine faith in socialism is indomitable.

Among these prewar socialists the spectrum of views regarding means
extends from the absolute pacifism of Jacques Thibault by way of the cal-
culating militarism of Meynestrel to the violent brutality of Mithoerg, but
their goal is identical: an idealized vision of a perfect society, in which all
men will share equally in the benefits and joy of a socialized humankind.
Jacques seeks to explain his views to his politically indifferent brother, who
is committed only to his scientific work.

> "When we say that the revolution will abolish the proletarian condition,
> that's what's meant. In the view of true revolutionaries, the revolution
> shouldn't merely give the worker a more comfortable life; above all, it
> should change the relations between men and their work, so that the
> work itself becomes more 'human,' instead of being a dreary, never-
> ending round of toil. The worker should have leisure, and cease being a
> mere tool; should have time to think about himself and make the most of
> his abilities, his human qualities. Yes, he should become, so far as in him

lies—and his capacities for that are far less limited than people think—a man with a mind, a personality, of his own." (150–51; 2: 158–59)

But Antoine, who is troubled neither by his comfortable social status in the *haute bourgeoisie* nor by his inherited wealth, is not convinced by his brother's revolutionary rhetoric. "Atavism, upbringing, the natural bent of your mind—all pull you in the opposite direction," he thinks, like the Martin du Gard of *Jean Barois*. "Just wait; very likely when you're forty you'll be more of a 'damned bourgeois' than I am!" (186; 2: 195).

In the end, to be sure, the ideal of an international socialism rapidly gives way before the nationalistic fervor that infects even the socialists in France, Germany, Belgium, and elsewhere when the war actually breaks out. Jacques's quixotic final act—indeed, his only real act in the entire novel—takes on a poignantly ironic aspect: his plane crashes and burns before he can distribute a single leaflet, and the severely wounded Jacques is shot as a German spy by retreating French troops.

The utter uselessness of the war, which destroys the values of the past and corrupts the ideals of the present, is reiterated in the *Epilogue* (1940), which constitutes the last volume of *Les Thibault*[13] and reflects the viewpoint that Martin du Gard had reached by 1937 when he received the Nobel Prize: that

> in this century, when everyone "believes" and "asserts," it is perhaps useful that there should be some who "hesitate," "put in doubt," and "question"—independent minds that escape the fascination of partisan ideologies and whose constant care is to develop their individual consciences in order to maintain a spirit of "inquiry" as objective, liberal, and fair-minded as is humanly possible.[14]

Jacques's idealistic socialist views are represented here only in their passionate appropriation by his beloved Jenny, who has borne the child they conceived during their brief affair. Antoine, on the point of death from poisoning by mustard gas, has been brought by his wartime experiences to a position much closer to the views of his dead brother, whom he now appreciates more than he was capable of doing before. In a long conversation with his former mentor (chap. 13), the elderly Doctor Philip gloomily foretells the death of nineteenth-century liberalism, but Antoine argues that the collapse of capitalism will enable a new world order to arise from the ruins of civilization. Socialism, he maintains in the diary of his last weeks, will not be its inspiration. Dejected by his perusal of some copies of the socialist

newspaper *Humanité*, Antoine is struck by "the sorry figure cut by our Socialists. . . . Their tone is that of narrow party men. Nothing really fine can
come of such ideas, or of people professing them; these Socialist demagogues
are débris from the pre-war age, and must be swept away like so much other
refuse" (998; 2: 999–1000). He sees nothing good coming from the republican brand of imperialism represented by Clemenceau and speculates that
"perhaps it is in conquered Germany that the true, the coming, socialism
will strike root first. Precisely because it's a defeated country" (998; 2: 1000).

Alfred Döblin and Socialism in Germany

Just as Martin du Gard was writing the closing pages of *Epilogue* in the late
1930s, the German physician-novelist Alfred Döblin, exiled in France, was
exposing the futility of Antoine Thibault's hope in the two thousand pages
of his monumental "narrative work" (*Erzählwerk*) *November 1918* (1939–
50). Döblin's trilogy—now acknowledged along with Hermann Broch's *The
Death of Vergil* (1945), Hermann Hesse's *The Glass Bead Game* (1946), and
Thomas Mann's *Doktor Faustus* (1947) to be one of the landmark works
of German literature in exile—begins as though in conscious counterpoint
to, and as an extension of, Martin du Gard's *roman-fleuve*. Indeed, the very
title consisting of month and year suggests the parallel. The first volume
begins in Alsace, in the same landscape where Jacques Thibault dies at the
end of *Summer 1914*. The opening scenes take place in a military hospital,
like the one where Antoine Thibault is treated toward the end of *Epilogue*
before being transferred to the civilian hospital where he dies. And it begins
on 10 November 1918, only a week before the last entry in Antoine's diary.
But at that point the similarities end, and even the opening pages of the
first volume amount to a ringing refutation of Antoine Thibault's dream
of a socialist Germany. (There is no evidence that Döblin was personally
acquainted with Martin du Gard or knew his *roman-fleuve*, although it is
unlikely that he could have remained unaware of the Nobel Prize awarded
to his French contemporary in 1937.)

Though both were socialist in name, the movements in France and Germany took entirely different paths. French syndicalists, in keeping with the
principles of Georges Sorel's *Réflexions sur la violence* (1910), believed in the
economic pressure of general strikes to precipitate a social revolution that
would bring government and industry under the control of the labor unions.
The German Social Democrats, in contrast, eschewed economic socialism
and its violence in favor of the gradualism of parliamentary participation.
Emerging in 1875 through a fusion of Ferdinand Lassalle's Universal German

Working Men's Association and its more militant rival, the Social Democratic Party of Wilhelm Liebknecht and August Bebel, the Social Democrats rejected the theory of a dictatorship of the proletariat to be achieved through the destruction of the bourgeois state, as proclaimed by Karl Marx with the founding of the International Working Men's Association (First International). Instead they hoped to take over the existing state through action as a parliamentary party, thereby establishing the model for the social democracy as proclaimed by most national parties of the Second International (established in 1900). The resolution was not achieved immediately. The 1890s witnessed ideological battles between the "revisionism" as set forth by Eduard Bernstein in *Evolutionary Socialism* (*Die Voraussetzungen des Sozialismus und die Aufgaben der Sozialdemokratie*, 1896) and the "revolutionary spontaneity" expounded by Rosa Luxemburg in *Reform or Revolution* (*Sozialreform oder Revolution?* 1899). A compromise position between the two extremes was occupied by Karl Kautsky, the leading spokesman of the Social Democratic movement before World War I. In such works as *The Class Struggle* (*Das Erfurter Programm*, 1892) and *The Social Revolution* (*Die soziale Revolution*, 1902) Kautsky offered a defense of Marxist theory while in practice applying the pragmatic politics of the revisionists.[15]

The struggle continued into the war years until in 1915 the Independent Social Democrats under Kautsky and the more radical Marxist Spartakus League under Karl Liebknecht broke away from the majority party led by Friedrich Ebert, essentially a bureaucrat with support among the people. Luxemburg had been imprisoned as early as 1914 for her antiwar activities, and Liebknecht was arrested in 1916 when he exhorted the troops in Berlin to refuse to fight. Liebknecht was released on 22 October 1918, and Luxemburg on 9 November that same year. In the meantime Ebert, the leader of the majority Social Democrats, profoundly fearing any Russian victory, repudiated the pacifism of the radical left and, through his support for the war effort, won the confidence of the government. As a result he was well positioned at war's end to become chancellor and then president of the new German Republic.

⁂

Alfred Döblin (1878–1957), an almost exact contemporary of Roger Martin du Gard, was born in the Baltic port of Stettin at the mouth of the Oder River. When Döblin was ten years old his father, an unsuccessful small businessman, deserted the family and emigrated to the United States with his mistress. Döblin's mother, from a prosperous Jewish family, moved with her five children to Berlin, where she was supported by one of her brothers. In view of their limited circumstances, the family lived in the working-class section of the city, east of Alexanderplatz, where Döblin spent almost his entire life until his emigration in 1933. Owing to the unusual circumstances, Döblin grew up identifying socially, politically, and culturally with the bourgeois ideals of his family yet sympathizing deeply with the misery of the urban proletariat among whom he lived and worked as a physician.

It is typical that his first extant writing, from the pen of the eighteen-year-old gymnasium student, was an essay advocating better treatment of women: "Modern. Ein Bild aus der Gegenwart" (1896; Modern: an image from the present).[16] Based extensively on August Bebel's *Woman and Socialism* (*Die Frau und der Sozialismus*, 1883), it surveys the position of women of the aristocracy (who are bought by their husbands, but essentially free), of the bourgeoisie (who sell themselves into marriage, but enjoy security), and in particular of the lower classes, who all too often must prostitute themselves in order to survive. In a mixture of fact and fiction that was to become the hallmark of Döblin's later great novels, the discussion is brought to life through a melodramatic narrative concerning an unemployed young seamstress named Bertha, who is consoled by her religious faith but not rescued by it from her predicament. "Prostitution is a terrible evil," the young author opines, "but *not* a necessary one. It is a consequence of capitalism" (19).

Following his graduation in 1900, the budding socialist studied medicine in Berlin and Freiburg im Breisgau, where he completed his degree in psychiatry and neurology in 1905 with a dissertation on memory disturbances. In 1911, after internships at an insane asylum near Regensburg, in the psychiatric hospital at Buch outside Berlin, and in a municipal hospital in the capital city, Döblin opened his own practice in proletarian East Berlin and was married the following year. Meanwhile he had continued his literary activities. In 1910 he was co-founder, along with Herwarth Walden, of the Expressionist journal *Der Sturm*. Three years later he published his first volume of stories and completed his first novel, *The Three Leaps of Wang-lun* (*Die drei Sprünge des Wang-lun*, 1915). Döblin, who like the socialists portrayed in *Summer 1914* became an ardent nationalist with the onset of World War I, served as a military doctor—first in Saargemünd (Lorraine) and later in the Alsatian town of Hagenau, where he witnessed the outbreak of the revolution.

Döblin's initial reaction to the revolutionary activities was skeptical, as he observed in "Revolutionary Days in Alsace" (written in December 1918), the first in a series of sardonic articles for the *Neue Rundschau*, which he soon continued under the pseudonym "Linke Poot" (North German dialect for "Left Paw"). "First thing in the morning my orderly was gone and with him twenty marks; that's how they are celebrating revolution."[17] He pokes fun at the soldiers who now carry their rifles ostentatiously in the Russian manner, with the stocks on their shoulders and barrels pointing down. Back in Berlin, he describes a parade of Social Democrats. "In the endlessly long procession, garlands with red bows, red flags, proletarian shouts, otherwise nothing that could remind me of revolution: a well-ordered petit-bourgeois event on a huge scale" (71).

Within weeks, however, his attitude began to change. In a major statement entitled "The Exorcism of the Ghosts" (written in February 1919) he confessed that he first saw in the revolution nothing but anarchy and soldiers without discipline.[18] He recalled that for years he had unsuccessfully sought contact with the various political parties in Berlin. Even though he shared the political ideals of the Social Democrats, he had none of the economic concerns of the workers and, as a physician, was regarded by them as an outsider. Now suddenly his views changed, and he briefly became an enthusiastic supporter of the 1917 revolution and of developments in the Soviet Union. Strolling through postwar Berlin, he realized that the real enemy was the traditional military in its haughty isolation from the people. Yet it was not the military that ultimately held the real power but "the industries, the technocrats, the scientists" (75). The churches and religion were equally culpable because the clerics and the feudal military had allied themselves in the service of the state. "Religiosity lives within us, but those religious figures have no life—only its history, its machinery" (77). Both religion and the state were subservient to Capital. Yet as early as March 1919, when his sister was killed by a grenade fragment during a disturbance in Lichtenberg, the "Red" section of Berlin, Döblin realized that revolution was not the proper way to the socialist goal and had to be suppressed. Faced with the anarchy that called itself "revolution," he decided that the counterrevolutionary Whites, no matter how alien their views, were better than the violent Reds.[19] Later Döblin never tired of repeating that the Germans had attempted two great revolutions that failed: the Peasants' Revolt of 1524–25 and, shortly thereafter, the wars of Reformation. In contrast to the French and English, he concluded, the Germans are apathetic, incompetent, and "revolutionarily listless" (*revolutionsunlustig*) vis-à-vis the state.[20]

Reasoning that only socialism could root out the evil at its source, Döblin joined the Independent Social Democratic Party, which he left in 1921 for the majority Social Democratic Party. During the 1920s he continued to comment on the current political situation—which in another piece he called "The German Masquerade" ("Der deutsche Maskenball,"

1920)—carefully distinguishing his democratic ideals from the violence and
economic turmoil that marked the political reality of the day.[21] And he was
active in such organizations as the Association for the Protection of German Writers (Schutzverband deutscher Schriftsteller), the leftist-communist
Group 1925, the Society of Friends of the New Russia, and the Writers' Section of the Prussian Academy.

In 1929, following the publication of three earlier novels, an epic
poem, and several volumes of political and philosophical essays, Döblin
achieved national and eventually worldwide fame with his masterpiece
Berlin Alexanderplatz.[22] Because his hero, the ex-convict Franz Biberkopf,
rejects any association with the Party, the novel was attacked in the radical
communist journal *Linkskurve* (December 1929) as being openly hostile to
the organized class battle of the proletariat. This attack prompted a response
in which Döblin broke sharply with his former leftist comrades.[23] He developed his views more fully in the "open letters to a young man" which
appeared in 1931 under the title *Knowing and Changing!* Döblin realized
that the traditional Social Democratic Party, which he had left in 1928, was
not a viable political response to the steadily strengthening Nazi movement.
Social conditions, he argues, are products of human history; "the economic
process does not take place without humankind."[24] Because the middle class
has failed, the workers are now the bearers of the formerly bourgeois ideals
of democracy and freedom (58). (Döblin never ceased to lampoon the apathy
of the intellectuals, whom he saw as all talk and no action.) Marxism attracted the workers, Döblin shrewdly recognizes, with a feeling closely akin
to the one that motivated believers of the transcendent religions (92). But
Marxism's purely economic policy of exposure and destruction cannot be
imbued after the fact with truly human qualities (98). A threefold culture is
required for a genuine revolution, for the spiritual and political renewal of
Germany through an ethical socialism: a culture embracing a religious element after the model of Protestantism; a humanistic-democratic ideal; and
a socialist vision (161). Germany's organizations and its social sense were
shaped by its military-feudal history. "The land experienced itself only as a
centrally directed mass.... A country like Germany needs nothing so much
as to turn away from its exaggerated collectivism and to turn toward the
individual and a natural society" (169). With these convictions Döblin left
Germany in 1933 for his years of exile in Switzerland and France and, from
1940 to 1945, in the United States, where he completed the vast project of
November 1918.

The last months of World War I witnessed violent military, political, and social turmoil in Germany. In March 1918, even as battles continued on the western front, Germany ended the war in the east through a peace treaty with the Russians at Brest-Litovsk. The home front and the war effort were plagued by strikes among workers protesting against the hardships brought on by four years of war. Following decisive French and British victories in July and August, the collapse of Bulgaria, and the crumbling of the Austro-Hungarian forces, the German high command realized by early October that defeat was inevitable and decided to seek a quick armistice. To this end, the military declared by fiat a constitutional monarchy, installing Prince Max of Bavaria as chancellor. Kaiser Wilhelm II, informed that he would no longer be supported by the military, abdicated on 9 November and fled to Holland. Encouraged by the sailors' mutiny, which had erupted a week earlier in the fleet at Kiel and spread rapidly to Berlin and other parts of Germany, Karl Liebknecht, leader of the radical Spartacist movement, sought to establish a soviet republic in Germany after the model of the Russian Revolution. To forestall this move, Philipp Scheidemann, one of the Social Democrats in Prince Max's cabinet, quickly proclaimed a democratic republic, where-upon Prince Max handed his office over to Friedrich Ebert, the other Social Democrat in his cabinet. The workers' and soldiers' councils, which had been established in Berlin after the model of Russian soviets, fell in behind Ebert, regarding the majority Socialists as allies. The German high command under Field Marshal Hindenburg lent its support to the new regime, through Quartermaster General Wilhelm Groener, in return for Ebert's promise to resist the revolution.

Following violent conflicts between government troops and communist demonstrators on "Bloody Friday" (6 December), Ebert persuaded the various councils to set elections for 19 January 1919 (the day following a date symbolic in Prussian history ever since the Kingdom of Prussia was established on 18 January 1701). However, on 23 December the radical sailors, disenchanted by Ebert's counterrevolutionary alliance with the military, invaded the chancellery and seized Ebert. The chancellor was freed the next day by government troops, but a few days later the left-wing Independent Socialists resigned from the government, in protest against its counterrevolutionary measures, and joined with the Spartacists to establish the official Communist Party of Germany (KPD) on 1 January 1919.

Despite the opposition of Rosa Luxemburg, who felt that the masses in Germany were not yet ripe for revolution, Liebknecht and his supporters determined to resist the government with armed force. The opportunity presented itself on 4 January 1919, when Robert Eichhorn, the police chief of

Berlin and an Independent Socialist, was dismissed and replaced by a moderate Socialist. The Communists took over the main police headquarters at Alexanderplatz, which was besieged by army troops in a bloody battle. Meanwhile, Gustav Noske had established with Ebert's acquiescence the notorious *Freikorps*, companies of demobbed right-wing soldiers, who entered Berlin and engaged in several days of bloody fighting with the Communists. On 15 January, the revolutionary forces were finally defeated, and the leaders of the Spartacists, Karl Liebknecht and Rosa Luxemburg, were caught and arrested. Later that evening they were murdered outside army headquarters in western Berlin near Bahnhof Zoo and their bodies tossed into a nearby canal. The elections held, as planned, on 19 January effectively marked the end of the social revolution although sporadic revolts from the right as well as the left continued in various parts of Germany for the next two years. Through the collaboration of Ebert and Hindenburg the existing economic and military order of imperial Germany was essentially preserved under the guise of the new democratic republic. The events of the two months from the collapse of the empire (10 November 1918) to the murder of Karl Liebknecht and Rosa Luxemburg constitute the framework and background in Döblin's epic work.

Döblin's *November 1918*

It is generally acknowledged that the events during the unsuccessful but bloody revolutionary weeks between the armistice and the murders are faithfully depicted in the two thousand pages of *November 1918*.[25] Döblin makes use of an impressive mass of documents, many of which are incorporated through quotation and montage into the text: contemporary newspaper reports, official documents, meeting protocols, journals, memoirs, biographical and historical accounts.[26] Döblin personally witnessed many of the incidents in Alsace and Berlin that he depicts. At the same time, it is also the case that his account is shaped retrospectively by the attitudes he had acquired by the time of composition twenty years after the fact: notably his rejection of his early and more radical socialist views and his conversion from atheism to Catholicism. Whereas the first three volumes are primarily political in orientation, covering in their polyphony the entire spectrum of reactions to the revolution, volume 4 depicts an essentially religious response in the persons of two central figures. As Döblin summarized his intentions in his autobiographical "Epilogue" (1948), "Two things ran side by side and together: the tragic fizzling out of the German revolution of 1918 and the dark urge of this individual human being."[27]

The trilogy in four volumes had a complicated genesis and publication history.[28] The first volume, *Citizens and Soldiers 1918* (*Bürger und Soldaten 1918*), written in Paris between late 1937 and early 1939, was published in Amsterdam in 1939, two months after the outbreak of World War II. Döblin immediately began the second volume, *A People Betrayed* (*Verratenes Volk*); but the work, completed in early 1942 in Los Angeles, had grown so large that it had to be divided into two parts, the second of which was entitled *Return of the Troops* (*Heimkehr der Fronttruppen*). Since immediate publication was out of the question, Döblin set to work on the lengthy final volume, *Karl und Rosa,* which he finished in August 1943. But his problems were still not over. The two volumes of part 2 finally appeared in 1949, and *Karl und Rosa* in 1950. But for political reasons—Döblin's portrayal of the situation in postwar Alsace-Lorraine—the French occupation authorities refused permission to reprint the first volume. So the four-volume "trilogy" as an entity appeared for the first time in 1978, for the centennial of Döblin's birth.[29] The critical reception was mixed, ranging from Hans Mayer's laudatory appreciation in *Der Spiegel*[30] to the severe condemnation by W. G. Sebald, who regarded the novel aesthetically as kitsch and politically as a "monumental alibi construction."[31] The many books and articles devoted to the novel since 1978 have increasingly supported Hans Mayer's view.[32]

The trilogy covers almost day by day the two tumultuous months from 10 November 1918 to 15 January 1919. Indeed, the section headings of part 2 simply bear dates, running from "The 22nd and 23rd of November" to "Around December 14." The novel intermingles fact and fiction in a weird configuration. Historical narrative gives way to phantasmagoric visions of such figures as the late medieval mystic Johannes Tauler and Satan. Tragic destinies take their course in drastic counterpoint to comic burlesques. Döblin follows an impressive account of the huge Communist demonstration in the Berlin Tiergarten on 6 January with a grotesque Dance of the Dead that same evening, in which the statues of thirty-two past rulers of Brandenburg and Prussia climb down from their pedestals to discuss the events of the day. Rosa Luxemburg is visited in her prison cell by the ghost of her dead lover as well as a seductive Satan. As historian, in sum, Döblin is closer to Herodotus than to Thucydides, with his acceptance of wonders, his willingness to digress, and his interest in the role of sex in human affairs.

The general framework afforded by the fictionalized historical events from the armistice to the murders of the two Communist leaders is filled out by accounts revolving around five groups of figures. We witness the frantic maneuvering of Ebert and his political and military associates (Scheidemann, Groener, Noske, and others). We are privy to the hopes and anguish of Woodrow Wilson as he sets out on the futile crusade to obtain consensus on his Fourteen Points and the League of Nations (in volume 3). We observe the personal and political tensions within the radical groups surrounding Karl Liebknecht and Rosa Luxemburg (especially in volume 4). On the purely fictional level Döblin tells the humorous story of the dramatist Erwin Stauffer, who—twenty years after the fact—meets the daughter he never knew he had and is reunited with the beloved woman from whom he has been separated through the machinations of his former wife. Following a comedy of errors and misunderstandings and utterly oblivious to the political turmoil surrounding them, they all live happily ever after.

The central story, with which volume 1 opens and volume 4 concludes, is that of Dr. Friedrich Becker, a former teacher of Greek in a Berlin gymnasium and a war hero, whose life is changed by the severe emotional and physical battle wounds from which he is slowly recovering, first in Alsace and then in Berlin. Becker's story is paralleled by those of his roommate in the military hospital in Alsace, Lieutenant Hans Maus, and their nurse, Hilde, with whom they both have affairs and with whom Maus eventually settles down in a thoroughly bourgeois marriage. When Becker returns to his teaching position in Berlin, he becomes involved in a scandal surrounding the homoerotic affair between the school's director and a student—an affair that causes Becker to be charged with political and moral turpitude. When the director is beaten to death by the boy's enraged father, his son runs away and joins the revolutionary forces occupying police headquarters in January 1919. The previously apolitical Becker goes there to find him but is moved by the suffering of the fighters—not by their politics but out of human solidarity—to join their resistance, for which he is subsequently arrested and imprisoned for three years. Troubled ever since his wounding by visionary conversations with the Alsatian monk Johannes Tauler and with Satan, who assumes various forms (a South American dandy, a lion, a mouse), Becker emerges from prison to become an itinerant evangelist, wandering around the Germany of the 1920s preaching the overthrow of contemporary Christianity, which he regards as an attack on true religion and God.[33] At the moment of his death he is rescued from his despair by a mystical vision of redemption, but his unclaimed body is dumped into the harbor by the criminals with whom he was associated in his final degradation.

The first volume, *Citizens and Soldiers*, introduces or at least mentions most of the major figures of the trilogy. But in the two weeks covered by the action—from 10 November to 25 November—no single figure emerges as central. The volume presents us, rather, with a kaleidoscopic and polyperspectival image of the incipient German revolution—first in Alsace and then in Berlin—which parallels Döblin's earlier essay "Revolutionary Days in Alsace."[34] (The microcosmic setting of a small town in Alsace permits the author to focus initially on individual responses to the revolution before he moves to the larger stage of Berlin.)[35] Döblin sought to expose the meaning of the revolution at every level of political consciousness, and not simply among those who were politically sophisticated and active. Few participants are spared from his satire. For the soldiers the revolution amounts to an opportunity to sit around eating and drinking with red bands on their arms and without any responsibility to their officers. The civilian population is opportunistic, looting the military barracks and hospital as soon as the soldiers withdraw. The French nationalist Maurice Barrès suspects that the revolution is nothing but a deceptive maneuver by the military. "If it wasn't made by the generals, it certainly came at a convenient moment for them" (1: 335). In Strasbourg, which is utterly bourgeois and thoroughly French, the revolution fails miserably. As red flags flutter on the cathedral, the citizens wait eagerly for the arrival of the French troops while the native German populace huddles nervously behind shuttered windows, anxious to see what fate the future has in store for them (1: 339). Jacques Peirotes, the socialist mayor of Strasbourg, informs the revolutionary sailors from Kiel: "Just because you come from Wilhelmshaven, you mustn't believe that you know more about socialism than I do. Socialism's way must be prepared. Here there is nothing to be accomplished. Not now. Socialism doesn't come from you and from me but from the masses. Show me the masses" (1: 155). Döblin makes fun of the intellectuals in Berlin who pay lip service to the revolution. "They demanded all this [progressive programs], and since they were only intellectual workers, they didn't have to concern themselves with the ordinary details or, heaven forbid, with execution. That was left to politics and the parties, which in turn they basically rejected and attacked from every side" (1: 286). They set sail on "the open sea of world betterment, where the sirens lured, where Scylla and Charybdis waited to smash them, and where a goddess lurked, a demoness, to transform them from clever men into fools." In general the people regarded dubiously "this new monster—the revolution which looked so similar to war" (1: 250).

Against the background of the revolution portrayed with caustic skepticism, Döblin depicts the arrival of a contingent of mutinying sailors in Strasbourg and the small town of the military hospital; their ineffective soldier's councils; and, a few days later, the withdrawal of German troops back across the Rhine. We see the reaction of representative groups and individuals to these developments: the hospital staff, the officers, the military chaplain, the local citizens and workers in Strasbourg and Hagenau, bands of marauding soldiers, deserters, war profiteers and black marketers in Berlin. The narrative is punctuated from time to time by vignettes of such historical figures as Marshal Foch, Maurice Barrès, General Ludendorff, and others. And we are introduced tentatively to a few figures who will gradually become central in the later volumes: notably Friedrich Becker, Hans Maus, Hilde, and Stauffer. (A few other stories are begun, only to be dropped later with no development.) In this multilinear volume Döblin is concerned above all—much like Martin du Gard in *Summer 1914*—with communicating a sense of the impact of the revolution on people from every social stratum.

Following the depiction of the revolution on the individual level, the scene shifts to Berlin and to larger historical figures. Volumes 2 and 3 continue the satiric critique of socialism. *A People Betrayed* shows how the people are duped by their leaders. Ebert sells out the socialist revolution by turning against his former allies on the left and joining forces with the old guard, "How was he supposed to appear against the ultraradicals, the Spartacists, who distrusted him, hated him. And rightfully so, he thought with satisfaction; he himself had contempt for the idiots" (2: 296). The Spartacists, in turn, waste their time in idle theoretical debates rather than acting. "Bloody Rosa" rages against the independents, demanding "destruction of capitalism, annulling of all war debts, confiscation of all foodstuffs" (2: 296), while Liebknecht stirs up the masses against Ebert and the "Kaiser socialists" (2: 446). "The workers at least have their socialism," a fellow teacher tells the returning Becker, "and for purposes of complaining they get it presented to them in several varieties—as majority, independents, Spartakus. Finally everybody will have his own party. That's the primal condition, and we are no longer very far from that point" (2: 95–96). In one of his grotesque visionary passages Döblin personifies Revolution, who "in other countries acted like a Fury, hurled firebrands, and frightened people out of their houses; but in Germany, grown ever smaller, she wanders around like a flower girl in torn skirts, trembling from the cold, with blue fingers, and seeks shelter" (2: 281).

In a section headed "Private Revolution" Döblin depicts the chaos reigning in Berlin as the people loot shops in the name of a socialist "expropriation" (2: 139). A black market in ration cards flourishes. "They were both revolutionaries, as befits dismissed munitions workers, and nothing meant more to them than to put something over on capitalism," is the justification of one couple (2: 142). Meanwhile speculators thrive in the name of socialism. "Originally the world was not allocated, and today it has also not yet been allocated," opines a one-time revolutionary socialist in czarist Russia whose war profiteering has brought him enormous wealth. "In my humble opinion it still is open to everyone" (2: 318). "Socialism is the crown, the blossom of human development," he concludes, to which his flunky reverently choruses: "Finally I can honestly say: I too am a socialist" (2: 318).

It is Döblin's implicit argument that the mindless turn to socialism in its various manifestations was a futile attempt to escape the chaos created by the loss of religious faith. The dramatist Stauffer's former mistress, who has emigrated to America, observes shrewdly that "over there we live with more reality: more coldly, but also less quixotically. It seems to me that your Europe no longer has any proper religion; religion doesn't agree with it. So they make religion out of everything, like a deserted lover who casts himself around the neck of a whore" (3: 379).

In volume 4 the political situation deteriorates into a comic grotesqueness as the futility of socialism is exposed. When Becker goes into police headquarters, now occupied by the revolutionary forces, to rescue one of his students, he sees the hopeless situation of the rebels. "To the misery of their proletarian existence they now have the misfortune of following confused ideas and being betrayed" (4: 555). The mutinying sailors are reduced to stealing bed linens from the Berlin palace (4: 110). On an island off the German coast a madman imitates the revolution on the mainland, proclaiming himself a revolutionary ruler (4: 243). The sailors who attempt to take over the Ministry of War in Berlin are turned away by an undersecretary because they lack the proper signature on their order (4: 305). Without officers, the revolutionary soldiers are chaotic. "There's an image of the German revolution," observes one figure. "People who can't drive get into an automobile but kick out the chauffeur" (4: 321). Meanwhile, the conservative military officers in the Hotel Eden make fun of the "democratic swine" (4: 575). The revolutionaries take over the state printing press in order to obtain money to fund their activities. "But they didn't get the lovely millions. Why not? The bills were stored in the vaults, and the revolutionaries didn't have the keys. And, after all, a German revolutionary will not steal and break in" (4: 448). As this "revolution" goes on, most citizens of Berlin go about their daily affairs with little acknowledgment of the violence taking place in the heart of the city. "Everybody did exactly what was on his mind at the moment— climbed into a streetcar, crossed a square, stood in front of a shop window and contemplated the displays.... They held their newspapers in front of their noses, and in the newspapers were reports about the terrible things that were happening only a quarter-hour away" (4: 565).

In hiding shortly before his capture, Karl Liebknecht deplores the opportunities lost by his party.

> We had the most magnificent platform in the world and found ourselves
> in a situation that won't return: after a lost imperialistic war in which
> our natural enemies, the enemies of socialism, had been compromised
> and ruined and suffered bankruptcy. We only needed to exploit this sit
> uation and to do what was necessary at that moment. To do it radically
> and completely and wholly, without any theories and program, but only
> what the moment and the situation require, and in the view of every per
> ceptive person in the land.... Our impact would have been immense....
> Instead we trivialized ourselves through theories and dogmas. We nar
> rowed ourselves to a sect. (4: 535)

In their futility Karl and Rosa talk about religion, not politics, and Karl
sings the praises of Satan in Milton's *Paradise Lost* so passionately that
Rosa exclaims that they should henceforth call themselves Satanists, not
Spartacists (4: 582). Their brutal murder represents with gory symbolism
the death of the socialist movement in Germany.

In the midst of this chaos only Becker and Rosa Luxemburg achieve
tranquillity through a religious conversion. (Döblin's assumption of Rosa
Luxemburg's last-minute conversion, triggered by visions of her dead lover
and Satan, which is developed as a parallel to Becker's, has been a subject of
controversy among critics and biographers.)[36] In the course of the tetralogy
Becker, who is tormented by a growing sense of his own ethical responsibility for the war, undergoes a remarkable three-stage development, which
is signaled by distinct prefigurations: from his initial position of a Faustian
spiritual alienation, by way of an Antigone-like rebellion against the state,
to a Christlike redemptive self-sacrifice.[37] "Something extraordinary had
happened. He, the atheist, pantheist, admirer of the Greeks, heathen, had
returned to the faith of his mother, at the end of this crisis which looked
more like a sickness than an experience" (4: 180). He achieves no sudden
redemption. "I am having a hard time learning to be a Christian," he tells
his friend Maus close to the end of the novel. "Again and again I fall into
the mistake of believing that I have Christianity and can go walking with
it as though it were a book under my arm. But that's not how it is. My
Christianity is like a tropical rainfall. The ground dries out again after a
short time" (4: 555). Becker has come to the realization, as he explains to
Maus and Hilde, that nothing has changed. The war is over, but the peace
agreements are meaningless. "Whether we like it or not, we've got to go

back to the causes of the war and draw the consequences. Because anyone can see at a glance that the old causes are still in force" (4: 627).

So Becker, who becomes known as the "Red Pastor," sets out to prepare the way for the new Noah who will restore the degenerate world (4: 640). "He outtrumped the socialist slogan, that religion is opium, by charging that the degenerate Christianity here in Germany is no religion at all but only an attack on religion, intended to open the way for a new heathenism. It ought to be cleared away" (4: 648). When Becker dies, he is visited by visions in which Satan vies with the angel Antoniel for his soul. (Similarly, Rosa is saved from Satan at the last minute by the cherub of her vision.) The novel that began as a political struggle between past and future, between the old order and the socialist future, has become a moral battle of good and evil.

Another disenchanted follower of the God that failed, Döblin leaves us with the sobering implication that the world cannot be redeemed by socialism, which amounts to no more than a pathetic surrogate for faith lost. The novel, to be sure, contains a substantial criticism of the reactionary old order in Germany; but Döblin is most bitterly disappointed by the failure of the socialism in whose goals he for a time believed. For the newly converted exile in California, Germany could have been saved after World War I only by a new *imitatio Christi:* not by politics but by religion, and not society as a whole but only individual by individual. The failure to learn the lesson of the past and to undo the evils that led to that war, Döblin believes, opened the way for Hitler and the tragedy of mid-century Europe.

Ignazio Silone and Communism in Italy

Unlike Martin du Gard and Döblin, who observed the political situation in France and Germany without being participants, Ignazio Silone (pseudonym for Romolo Tranquilli, 1900–1978) was an active member of the Italian Communist Party for ten years. In his contribution to *The God That Failed* he depicts the outrageous social and political injustices in his native Abruzzi that drove him, at age seventeen, to the Socialist Youth Federation in Rome, where he worked as a journalist for the socialist newspaper *Avan-Guardia*. Representing the federation, he attended the meeting of the Italian Socialist Party in 1921 where the left wing, led by Antonio Gramsci, Palmiro Togliatti, and others, broke away to form the Italian Communist Party. As a member of the new Party, Silone gradually became aware of the "notable differences of opinion between Russian Bolshevism, formed in an atmosphere in which political liberty and a differentiated social structure were both alien concepts, and the Left-Wing Socialist groups of the Western countries."[38]

He was increasingly dismayed by the degeneration of the Communist International into tyranny and bureaucracy, into fanaticism, centralization, and abstraction. In 1927, at a meeting of the International in Moscow, Silone was outspokenly offended by the hypocrisy of the Stalinists, who demanded that the foreign representatives condemn a document by Trotsky without ever having read it. Yet he remained within the Party, even going underground and finally into exile in Switzerland, until in 1931 he was formally ousted for criticizing Moscow's expulsion of three other comrades.

Like Koestler, Silone underscored the quasi-religious appeal of communism. "For me to join the Party of Proletarian Revolution was not just a simple matter of signing up with a political organization; it meant a conversion, a complete dedication." He compares the psychological mechanism through which the individual becomes progressively identified with the collective organization to the one "used in certain religious orders and military colleges" (98–99). Because of this religious indoctrination the departure from the Party is always a wrenching experience: "something of it remains and leaves a mark on the character which lasts all one's life" (113). In that respect, Silone suggests, ex-communists are like ex-priests. And for that reason, he concedes, the literary work to which he turned following his political career stemmed from "an absolute necessity to testify, an urgent need to free myself from an obsession, to state the meaning and define the limits of a painful but decisive break, and of a vaster allegiance that still continues" (81). Despite his disenchantment with communism, Silone's faith in socialism "remained more alive than ever in me," staying essentially "what it was when I first revolted against the old social order" (113). While rejecting the socialist-communist abstractions and scientific theories, Silone regarded socialist values as permanent; and "on a group of values one can found a culture, a civilization, a new way of living together among men" (114).[39]

While Silone wrote no single vast work like *Summer 1914* or *November 1918*, most of his novels revolve around the same central theme of allegiance and disaffection. The action of *Bread and Wine* (*Pane e vino*, 1937) takes place in autumn 1935 as Mussolini is preparing his invasion of Ethiopia. The revolutionist Pietro Spina has just returned illegally to Fascist Italy after fifteen years as a loyal Party member, including several years of political exile in various countries.[40] Sick of the abstractions of political theory, which always bored him, he has returned to Italy, he explains, "for air"

(47). While he was living abroad, Italy "slowly became an abstraction for me and an incubus. I really needed to feel my feet on the ground once more" (40). His return is a desperate attempt to recapture the lost reality of his past and to escape the "professionalism" that marked the Party (96). This pragmatic quality, which incapacitates Pietro Spina as a theoretician, makes him all the more sensitive to issues of right and wrong. He comes to realize increasingly that "morality can live and flourish only in practical life.... The evil to be fought is not that sad abstraction which is called the devil; the evil is everything which prevents millions of men from acting like human beings" (264).

To conceal himself from the authorities he dons clerical garb, a natural disguise for the seminary-trained young man. Assuming the identity of a priest named Don Paolo Spada, he goes into hiding in a remote mountain village. Later he leaves his mountain retreat and goes to Rome, where he meets clandestinely with a Communist cell in the sewers of the city. Many of Pietro Spina's personal qualities and much of the plot—in radical contradistinction to the protagonists of Martin du Gard and Döblin—are determined by his role as what I have elsewhere termed a fictional trans-figuration of Jesus:[41] he is introduced by a John the Baptist figure, Don Benedetto, who helps to shape his ideas; becomes renowned in the mountain village for "miracles" of healing; is regarded by the simple peasants as the reincarnation of Jesus; meets clandestinely with groups interested in his teaching; criticizes the official "church" (Party dogma); explains his faith in a new kingdom on earth in the form of parables that can be appreciated by the peasants and workers; partakes of a Last Supper of bread and wine; and is betrayed by the Judas-like priest Don Poccirilli. (At the end Spina is not crucified but escapes into the mountains; he does not die until the sequel *The Seed beneath the Snow* [1945], which takes place in the four months following his disappearance.)

According to the now-familiar pattern the Party functions as a clear surrogate for the church, an analogy that Silone repeatedly exploits in the course of the novel, as in the recollections of Pietro Spina's friend Luigi Murica, who recalls the romantic allure of his early political activities.

> "In the group we read poorly printed newspapers and pamphlets preaching hate of tyranny and announcing as a certainty, as inevitable and not far off, the advent of the revolution which was to establish fraternity and justice among men. It was sort of a weekly dream, secret and forbidden, in which we communicated and which made us forget our daily misery. It was like the rites of a hidden religion." (239)

The analogy between church and Party is anything but gratuitous because it helps to explain both Pietro Spina's decision to leave the church and his subsequent disenchantment with the Party.

> He had left the Church not because he no longer believed in the dogmas or the efficiency of the sacraments but because it had seemed to him that the Church was identified with the corrupt, wicked and cruel society which it should have been fighting. When he became a socialist, that was all that drove him. He was not yet a Marxist. (95)

In effect, he exchanged one form of order for another. Yet the community whose rule he now accepts has also become what he calls a "synagogue"—an institution existing more for the sake of its dogma than for the people it was intended to help. Contemptuous of all moral values as petit bourgeois prejudices, the organization has become its own supreme value. "Have I then not fled the opportunism of a decadent church to fall into the Machiavellianism of a sect?" (96). The analogy between church and Party is symbolized by the leitmotif of weaving introduced in the first paragraph of the novel. As Don Benedetto's sister Marta sits at her loom, "the shuttle jumped back and forth in the warp of black and red wool, from left to right and from right to left" (11). This emblematic act suggests that left and right, red and black, Party and church are interwoven just as inextricably in Pietro Spina's mind as in Marta's fabric.

If abstraction is the great evil that Pietro Spina detects first in the church and then in the Party, its opposite is human solidarity, whose supreme image is neither the Christian Mass nor the meeting of the Party cell, but the sharing of bread and wine in the simple act of companionship. "The bread is made from many ears of grain," Pietro tells his friend Luigi Murica. "Therefore it signifies unity. The wine is made from many grapes, and therefore it, too, signifies unity. A unity of similar things, equal and united. Therefore it means truth and brotherhood, too; these are things which go well together" (270). This sense of community, as opposed to the arid formalism of the Party, is the true meaning of communism for the people. Speaking of the peasants in *Bread and Wine*, the author remarks: "To them, Socialism just meant being together" (149).

Spina's rejection of the communism to which he was once fiercely committed, his rejection of the Party's abstractions, and his turn to purely human relationships is equivalent to Jesus' condemnation of the Pharisees and his teaching of brotherly love. A man who "hungers and thirsts after righteousness" in Fascist Italy of 1935 is exposed to all the dangers that threatened

Jesus in the Jerusalem of the early first century. When Spina is ashamed and annoyed at the necessity of assuming a disguise and changing his name, Don Benedetto reminds him that "the Scriptures are full of clandestine life," citing the flight into Egypt and the occasions when Jesus hid himself from the Judaeans. This "religious apologia for the clandestine life made Pietro more serene and illuminated his face with childlike joy" (230).

Silone's novel represents a stage well beyond that of the first two works we considered. Whereas *Summer 1914* portrayed the growth and optimism of socialism in France before World War I, and *November 1918* the appeal and failure of the socialist revolution in Germany just after that war, *Bread and Wine* depicts the conversion and defection of a dedicated Communist in Fascist Italy of the early 1930s. Yet a common denominator links all three works: the authors clearly saw the appeal of socialism initially as a response to the loss of religious faith—and eventually as yet another God that failed.

His novel *A Handful of Blackberries* (*Una manciata di more*, 1952) returns to the same basic theme but carries it to extremes of grotesque comedy without the *imitatio Christi* and fictional transfiguration of Jesus that shaped *Bread and Wine*. (The very title refers not symbolically to a secularization of communion as in the earlier novel but to the sharing of simple fruits of the field that one figure offers to another.) The parallel of church and Party in Italy immediately following World War II is exposed weirdly in the association of the Catholic-Communist "Red Churchwomen" who take as their emblem, despite the clergy's taboo and the Party's embarrassment, the image of a Jesus dressed in a red robe and exposing a heart on which the hammer and sickle are engraved in gold.[42] Don Alfredo, a prominent member of the rural Party, falls into disgrace and is charged with nostalgia for the past and retarding progress when his clock, which stopped at the instant of the Liberation, starts going again—backward, in the direction of the past (295–96). As in *November 1918*, ordinary people are untouched by lofty politics—here the shift from fascism to communism—and simply look out for themselves. "Our part of the country is all ears," a local official explains. "The Party changes its name, but the ears remain and serve the new Party" (294). He complains at the cost of having the town's draperies dyed red and at the tinsmith's price for making the new hammer and sickle. "All these new-fangled emblems—what use will I be able to make of them, a few years from now? Mind you, I'm not criticizing them. For me one Party is as good as another" (294). To be on the safe side he keeps the crown of the former monarchy in reserve. "When an emblem falls into momentary disuse, I always put it away safely. You never know" (297).

All this goes to explain why Rocco de Donatis, the central figure of the often episodic and anecdotal novel, forsakes the Party in order to commit himself to the simple people for whose sake he initially appealed successively to Catholicism and communism. The son of an impoverished aristocratic family, Rocco was once tempted by the priesthood and still remains on close terms with his boyhood friend Don Nicola, the village priest. "Rocco was born with an evident vocation for religious life," Don Nicola recalls. "He was the object of the clearest call from God that I have ever witnessed" (84). But in a sudden epiphany Rocco realized that the people attending mass were insipid and that the common people did not come near the church. Yet in the denial of his vocation he "demanded from secular life the absolute quality that he could have found only in a monastery" (84). In order to fight the social injustices and political farces he has witnessed in his mountain community, he turns to the Communists, joins the Party, works with a student group in Turin, and is eventually imprisoned by the Fascists. Shortly before the Liberation he comes back from the north to head the local partisans and soon thereafter emerges as a rigorous leader of the revolutionary Party, where he also converts and wins the love of Stella, a young Jewish refugee from Vienna.

During his wartime imprisonment Rocco became aware of dissension within the Party ranks. "The struggle against the Fascist dictatorship had by then dwindled to secondary importance, the prevailing need being to discover, and persecute, heretics of all kinds, following the tumultuous internal vicissitudes of the Russian (Bolshevist) Communist Party" (116). While Rocco initially admires the fanaticism of Oscar, the Party disciplinarian among the political prisoners, he gradually becomes disenchanted. In the turmoil of Liberation he sees that priests and Italian army officers are indiscriminately killed by the partisans. On a trip to Poland and Russia as a Party representative after the war, Rocco is told of the forced labor camps operated by the Communists. Later he is criticized by Oscar for reading forbidden books—Bukharin and Trotsky, among others—and for remaining on good terms with ostracized friends of his youth. "You already knew that Martino had been expelled from the Party in exile for ideological deviation?" Oscar challenges him. "In spite of that, you have become his friend?" (118).

These insights gradually lead him to break with the Party. "The Party was a great thing when it had to live underground," he tells Stella. "Then we were persecuted; now in our turn we are becoming persecutors" (138). The decision is not an easy one, and he postpones his break, staying in the Party while withdrawing from all public activity, no longer speaking at meetings or writing articles for the Party newspapers. Stella tries to persuade him to stay despite his disillusionment. "The Party still corresponds to the strong, virile, active part of you," she tells him (145), warning that he might otherwise give way to an inherited tendency to despair, melancholy, pessimism. Rocco discovers that he cannot simply leave the Party. As Martino observes, "When the Party isn't able to deport or shoot its deserters, it tries at least to kill them morally. It tries to dishonor them, discredit them, cover them with odium and ridicule. It accuses them of infamous motives, vices and crimes" (279). Oscar tricks Stella into unwittingly betraying Rocco, an act that drives her into despair and into an almost mortal illness.

When the novel ends, Martino has been forced again to flee for a crime of which he is innocent. The former Catholic marries the Jewess Stella, having come to the realization that love is a stronger bond than religion or politics: "*Amo ergo sum*," says Rocco, the former seminarian (246). The recent "Liberation" was, after all, no true liberation of people and minds— merely the substitution of a new authority and dogma for an old one. But Rocco has not lost his faith in humankind. At a celebration that Rocco calls both civic and religious—"We don't recognize the distinction" (309)—he proposes a toast "To the future Liberation."

⁓∞⁓

All three writers, then, share with the contributors to Richard Crossman's anthology and with other former Communists the understanding that socialism/communism constituted for many of its believers in the first half of the twentieth century a surrogate for lost religious faith. Liberals on the left sought their consolation in the seeming solidarity of the Party, its dogma, its rituals, and its promise of a brighter future. Hence the commitment of Jacques Thibault, the naive opportunism of many lower-class Germans at the end of World War I as observed by Friedrich Becker, and the Party activity of Pietro Spina and Rocco de Donatis. Their quasi-religious belief in the Party made its failures especially poignant for the heroes of Martin du Gard's *roman-fleuve*, for Döblin's Liebknecht and Luxemburg, and for Silone's protagonists. At the same time, their religious commitment explains the mystical visions and reconversions that accompany the deaths of Friedrich Becker and Rosa Luxemburg as well as the turn to simple human solidarity at the end of Silone's novels. The God that failed gives way to the humanity that endures and to a vision sometimes satisfied by myth. In his brilliant essay "The Future of Secular Religions," Raymond Aron recognized that fascism/nazism, just as much as socialism/communism, constituted another of those "doctrines which in the souls of our contemporaries take the place of vanished faith and situate the salvation of humanity here on earth, in the distant future, under the form of a still-to-be-created social order."[43] Or as T. S. Eliot put it in his lectures on "the idea of a Christian society" (1939), "If you will not have God (and He is a jealous God), you should pay your respects to Hitler and Stalin."[44]

⚜

CHAPTER SEVEN
─────────────

The Hunger for Myth

"History Is Bunk!"

When Henry Ford took the witness stand in July 1919 (in his libel suit against the *Chicago Tribune*) and declared that "History is Bunk!" his statement marked the symbolic end of a century in which history had ruled the Western mind.[1] The nineteenth century has rightfully been called historiography's "Golden Age."[2] It was not only the era of the great historians in Germany, France, and England[3] and of such imposing serial collections of source materials as the *Recueil des historiens des Gaules et de la France* (1738–1904), the *Monumenta Germaniae Historica* (1819–1969), and the "Roll Series" of *Chronicles and Memorials of Great Britain and Ireland during the Middle Ages* (1858–1911). History invaded every field of academic thought—philosophy, theology, law, and the natural sciences.[4] Historians played prominent roles in the public life of their countries. Leopold von Ranke advised the kings of Prussia and Bavaria while Adolphe Thiers and François Guizot served as minister and prime minister in the government of King Louis Philippe. The works of Thomas Macaulay and Theodor Mommsen enjoyed an unprecedented public success.

But by the beginning of the twentieth century this euphoria was beginning to wane. In 1872 Nietzsche struck a blow against academic history in his "Untimely Thoughts" on "the use and disadvantage of history for life," where he lists five reasons why the "oversaturation" of his age in history is "hostile and dangerous for life."[5] The personality is weakened by history's differentiation between internal and external life; history creates the illusion that the present age possesses a higher degree of justice than other ages; it disturbs natural instincts and prevents the individual from maturing; it implants a belief in stages of human history and the sense that the present age is epigonal; and, as a result, an age becomes ironic and even cynical about itself. "Historical education is actually a kind of congenital gray-hairedness," he continues (1: 258), railing against the "dissolutions of the sense of history from which the present suffers" (1: 275) and the "vehemence" of its historicism (1: 265), which has undermined the vibrant power of life. Nietzsche is not hostile to all history—merely to academic history as taught and practiced in the schools and universities. Indeed, he maintains, history is essential for the health of any people: as *monumental* history, which provides us with the sense that the grandeur of earlier ages is still attainable by humankind; as *antiquarian* history, which preserves memories of our origins to be regarded with piety; and as *critical* history, which enables us to break with the past in order to live our lives in the present.

The Great War, into which the nations blundered and which they stubbornly maintained for four long, bloody years despite all the historical erudition of their leaders, effectively destroyed any belief that history holds lessons for the present. Hermann Hesse, in a 1918 essay "World History," concluded that "the world history that [his teachers] set before us was a kind of swindle of adults to diminish and belittle us."[6] In one of the savagely satirical pieces he wrote in 1920 Alfred Döblin observed that readers were slowly catching on to the tricks of the historians. "After ten pages of their books one can tell to which party they belong. Also whether they pray to Maria, Jahwe, or anyone else."[7] In 1928, Paul Valéry reiterated and intensified Nietzsche's views, arguing in the opening words of his brief note "On History" that "history is the most dangerous product that the chemistry of the intellect has devised," because it causes us to dream, enervates the peoples, engenders false memories, exaggerates their reflections, keeps open old wounds, torments them in their repose, produces a delirium of grandeur or of persecution, and makes nations bitter, haughty, insufferable, and vain. "History justifies whatever one wishes." [8]

If history holds no lessons to replace religious faith, where are we to turn? Nietzsche hinted at one direction in his comments on "monumental" history.

> As long as the soul of historiography lies in the great impulses that a strong individual can derive from it, as long as the past must be described as worthy of emulation, as imitable and possible for a second time, it is in danger of being shifted, reinterpreted into the realm of the beautiful and thereby brought closer to free invention. Indeed, there are ages that are totally unable to distinguish between a monumental past and a mythic fiction, because precisely the same impulses can be taken from the one realm as from the other.[9]

Half a century later this identification of history and myth inspired several prominent scholars associated with the circle surrounding the poet Stefan George to produce biographies of "monumental" figures that focus not so much on biographical "fact" as on the meaning those figures provide for the present: Ernst Bertram's *Nietzsche* (1918), which proclaims itself in the subtitle as an "essay in mythology" ("Versuch einer Mythologie"); Ernst Kantorowicz's paean to the medieval Emperor Friedrich of Hohenstaufen *Kaiser Friedrich der Zweite* (1928); or Friedrich Gundolf's biographies *Goethe* (1916) and *Cäsar: Geschichte seines Ruhms* (1924; Caesar: the story of his fame).[10]

A related initiative was announced by the philosopher Theodor Lessing in a controversial work defining history as the attempt to give meaning to what is basically meaningless (*Geschichte als Sinngebung des Sinnlosen,* 1916), which bears a subtitle reminiscent of Nietzsche: "The Birth of History from Myth" (*Die Geburt der Geschichte aus dem Mythos*). "History is a never-ending human mythic poem," Lessing asserts, born from the consolatory self-healings of human despair and blended with wishes and ideals.[11] Lessing takes it for granted that this Nietzschean history-as-myth functions as a surrogate for religion. "Modern man cannot dispense with such fabrications. For they are the last remnants of his waning religious impulses. Powers of faith necessary for life stand behind them. It is false when they appear disguised as the investigation of reality" (28–29). Carl Schmitt published a "political theology" (*Politische Theologie,* 1922) based on the premise that "all significant concepts of the modern theory of the state are secularized theological concepts not only because of their historical development...but also because of their systematic structure."[12]

Oswald Spengler's "morphology of world history," *The Decline of the West* (*Der Untergang des Abendlandes,* 1918–22), shares the same tendency. In the preface to volume 2 he mentions the predecessors to whom he feels himself most deeply indebted: Goethe for his method, and Nietzsche for the formulation of his questions. "It is a scholarly prejudice," he clarifies, "that myths and representations of deities are a creation of primitive peoples and that 'with progressing culture' the human soul loses its myth-shaping power. The opposite is the case."[13] Spengler maintains that "every myth of grand format stands at the beginning of an awakening spiritual age." The external sources of motifs and elements on which myth scholarship has expended its energy are historically superficial and have no deeper significance. What matters is the *numen,* the primal shape of the world-perception manifest in the myth (515). This search for the mythic basis of every culture governs Spengler's morphology and endows his work with its structure, which can be called mythic rather than logical, inasmuch as it sees each culture in terms of a seasonal cycle leading from spring (youth) through summer (maturing consciousness) and fall (mature intelligence) to winter (decline).

Findings of positivistic biblical history persuaded many theologians at the turn of the century to concede some of the power of religion to myth.[14] At the end of the nineteenth century, Martin Kähler in his study of the so-called historical Jesus and the historic biblical Christ (*Der sogenannte historische Jesus und der geschichtliche biblische Christus*, 1892) concluded that the sources of information are neither adequate nor reliable enough to permit the reconstruction of any valid biography of Jesus. Yet all questions of validity aside, he continued, it is not the historical Jesus who has been of inspirational value to millions of believers, but the Christ of faith as depicted in the New Testament.

In response to the growing suspicion that Jesus never lived and to ac-count for the details of his portrayal in the Gospels, scholars of the history of religions school suggested that many passages in the New Testament were composed simply in order to fulfill prophecies or "myths" set forth in the Old Testament. As the scientific study of mythology and folklore inspired by Sir James Frazer's *The Golden Bough* (1890) exposed scholars to the vast body of world myths, it became possible for scholars to identify a mythic source for virtually every motif in the New Testament. In a se-ries of books beginning with *Christianity and Mythology* (1900), John M. Robertson argued that Christianity marked essentially the reemergence of an older Semitic cult of Joshua. Arthur Drews, widely celebrated in prewar Germany for his public lectures, published a hotly debated study entitled *The Christ-myth* (*Die Christusmythe*, 1909), in which he argued that "it is the fundamental error of liberal theology to think that the development of the Christian church took its rise from a historical individual, from the man Jesus" (epilogue). The mythic theory of Christianity survived World War I and into the 1920s, when it received a fresh impetus from the various studies of the Christ archetype and Christian symbols carried out by C. G. Jung and such followers as P. L. Couchoud, whose sensationally successful *Le mystère de Jésus* (1924) suggested that the story of Jesus was no more than the product of a collective mystical experience.

Taking his cue from Frazer, T. S. Eliot claimed in "*Ulysses*, Order, and Myth" (1923) that Joyce's "parallel use of the Odyssey" had the importance of a scientific discovery. "In using the myth, in manipulating a continuous parallel between contemporaneity and antiquity, Mr. Joyce is pursuing a method which others must pursue after him. . . . It is simply a way of con-trolling, of ordering, of giving a shape and a significance to the immense panorama of futility and anarchy which is contemporary history."[15] Since Joyce—and, indeed, well before *Ulysses* (1922)—countless writers have used the same device to shape modern fictions based on such historical, mythic, or legendary figures as Odysseus, Jesus, Virgil, Ovid, Parzival, and Faust, among others.[16] But in nineteenth-century Germany an entirely different meaning emerged, known by the Greco-Latin vocables as *Mythus* or *Mythos,* which came to full flower during the 1920s and 1930s. This meaning appears to have a unique connection with conservative political thought—in particular, Italian Fascism and German National Socialism—and explicitly played on religious associations, offering itself as a substitute for lost faith.[17]

The Myth of *Mythos*

In 1930 the philosopher Erich Unger began a study entitled "Reality, Mythos, Knowledge" with the observation that the word "Mythos," which only a few decades earlier had no representative significance, seemed to have become "virtually an expression of the cultural mood of the times."[18] Unger was referring to the ambivalence of an age that felt a great affinity to myth and, at the same time, regarded it with a certain alienation. "It is as though one noticed a profound and unbridgeable opposition separating the cultural atmosphere of our epoch from something remote and different, which is designated by the quality 'mythos,' and as though one felt compelled to enter into some sort of cognitive or experiential relationship to this quality because it perhaps contains something that we are lacking" (3–4). Unger was hardly the only observer struck by the incantational power of myth. When Alfred Rosenberg began to assemble his "evaluation of the spiritual-intellectual form struggles" of the 1920s, that muddled evangelist of National Socialism contemplated various titles. The first version of 1922 was still called simply a "Philosophy of Germanic Art." Three years later the title had a more resolute sound: "Race and Honor." It was not until 1928 that the work got the notorious title under which it was published in 1930 and which for fifteen years decorated successive editions: *The Myth of the Twentieth Century* (*Der Mythus des 20. Jahrhunderts*).[19]

The phenomenon that Harry Levin called German "mythophilia," and which he contrasted to the mythoclastic skepticism of the French, astounded foreign observers as early as the 1920s.[20] The myth scholar Karl Kerényi recalled that he had little understanding for "'mythos' in the sense in which, in Germany between the two world wars, it became an incomprehensible, at once ridiculous and fateful power, acknowledged even by

Thomas Mann." Kerényi concedes that his rejection possibly indicates the absence in his character of certain elements that are present in Germans. "Nowhere had I encountered 'mythos' as a special power—only 'mythology.'"[21] How does it happen that a term, which only a few decades earlier had lacked any representative value, suddenly in Germany became a "special power," acknowledged by such radically different temperaments as Alfred Rosenberg and Thomas Mann? We are not concerned here with the individual components or partial myths of which the confused Nazi myth was composed and whose provenience has been analyzed by various critics.[22] It is a question of semantics. How did the word *Mythos* get the associations that it assumed in Germany—its powerful rhetorical effect in popular cultural philosophy, in daily speech, and ultimately in politics?

Etymologically the Greek vocable *mythos* means "speech," "language," "narrative," and therefore exists only in and by means of language. We do not need to agree with Max Müller that myth is a "disease of language" in order to define it with Paul Valéry as "that which exists and subsists only by having words for its cause."[23] The modern "veneration of myth" identified by a series of talks entitled "The Reality of Myth" sponsored in 1965 by Bavarian Radio can exist only when the concept "myth" exists.[24] But the concept is a relatively recent one in European languages and thought.

The eighteenth century was acquainted with mythology, but not with myth. Such representative reference works as Adelung's *Grammatisch-kritisches Wörterbuch* (2nd ed., 1798) and Sulzer's *Allgemeine Theorie der schönen Künste* (2nd ed., 1792) contain only the rubric "Mythologie." Mythology does not signify "veneration for myth" but, at most, knowledge about myths. The Age of Enlightenment was not very much interested even in mythology. When Benjamin Hederich published his *Gründliches mythologisches Lexikon* in 1724, he assumed strong reservations on the part of his public and defended his undertaking against the "theological zeal" of those who take too literally the biblical admonition that one should not heed fables.[25] Anticipating a general indifference among the educated, he introduced a number of practical reasons why, say, the philosophicus, the philologicus, the artist, or the traveling cavalier ought to have some acquaintance with "this learned gallantry." For Hederich, the classical myths are nothing but pleasant fables behind which are hidden "in part true stories, in part natural events, but in part only good moral teachings" (xi). Johann Joachim Schwabe, who in 1770 reedited the original *Lexikon*—"Hederich" remained one of the richest sources of material for generations of German writers from Goethe on and well into the nineteenth century—had little patience with

Hederich's imaginative readings of the old fables. Nevertheless he made no effort to eliminate the moralizing and naturalizing interpretations. "To be sure, I don't like them," he confesses, "but they may well appeal to others" (v).

That turned out to be the case. It is one achievement of German Romanticism that it overcame the eighteenth-century hostility to myth.[26] In general, the Romantics as well as their successors interested themselves in what would today be called mythology: knowledge about ancient myths as an expression of religious or philosophical thinking of primitive peoples. The form *mythos* or *mythus* occurs occasionally in the first half of the nineteenth century, but the meaning varies as greatly as the lexical form.[27] For the literary theorist Friedrich Schlegel, in agreement with Aristotle's *Poetics*, *mythos* means no more than epic or dramatic action.[28] The theologian David Friedrich Strauss identified *mythus* as "any nonhistorical narrative in which a religious community recognizes a component of its sacred foundation."[29] In general, the feminine form *Mythe* prevails in dictionaries of the nineteenth century, bearing the primary meaning of "fable about the gods" or "unverified narrative."

All in all, then, the nineteenth century knew of no "myth" for which one should feel reverence. The public was acquainted with *Mythe* in the sense of a specific mythological tale. The specialized dictionaries of philosophical and theological concepts use *Mythus* also as the designation for something like the fanciful-anthropomorphic "protophilosophy" of primitive peoples.[30] And occasionally the word occurs in the modern meaning of a conventional lie, as we know it from such titles as *The Myth and Reality of Our Urban Problems, The Myth of Mental Illness, The Suburban Myth, The Myth of the Titanic, Body Myths*, and so on. French speakers call a liar simply a *mythomane*. The semantic difference between German *Mythos* and English *myth*, French *mythe*, or Italian *mito* can be most clearly recognized if one tries to translate the title of Alfred Rosenberg's influential volume. "The Myth of the Twentieth Century" means in English almost exactly the opposite of what Germans in the 1920s and 1930s understood under *Der Mythus des 20. Jahrhunderts:* not the creation of a valid and life-sustaining truth, but the unmasking of an obvious lie.

If we consult the evidence of the dictionaries, it appears that the significant shift in the popular German usage occurred in the first third of the twentieth century. In the first edition of the standard *Sprach-Brockhaus* (1935) the more resonant form *Mythos* has wholly driven out the softer *Mythe*. And next to the primary meaning of myth as a story about the gods, a second and wholly new meaning has intruded, which is otherwise lacking in the European languages: myth is now regarded as a "vivid, life-renewing idea" ("bildhafte, lebenerneuernde Idee") and not restricted to primitive peoples. This simple change in the second syllable (still retained in the edition of 1970) contains in all lexical concision an important chapter of German cultural history.

The Rebirth of Myth

In his essay "Richard Wagner and the *Ring of the Nibelung*" (1937), Thomas Mann speaks of an opposition between "the Wagnerian and the Goethean manner of dealing with myth." It is not so much a question of the obvious difference in mythological spheres: dragons, giants, and dwarves in the *Ring* cycle and sphinxes, griffons, and nymphs in *Faust; urgermanisch* here and *ureuropäisch* there. The difference exposes, rather, a fundamental antagonism of artistic attitudes and opinions. Goethe "does not celebrate myth; he plays with it." Nothing, Mann concludes, could be less Wagnerian than Goethe's "ironic manner of conjuring myth."[31] With this distinction between Wagner's "celebration" of myth and Goethe's ironizations, Mann seems to have in mind the same difference between myth and mythology to which Kerényi was alluding. Irony presupposes a certain degree of detachment. The artist who plays with mythic or mythological elements with a sophisticated awareness feels no "reverence" for myth; rather, he has knowledge about myth—that is to say, he is practicing mythology.

Modern literary works displaying mythic components should more accurately be designated, because of the consciously ironic handling of those elements, as mythological and not as mythic. The frequent allusions in Eliot's *Waste Land* to such figures as Philomela or Tiresias serve to express the differences between the skeptical Europe of the 1920s and an ancient Greece that still believed in myth, rather than any similarity. The many writers from Goethe by way of Thomas Mann, Joyce, and André Gide to Günter Grass, Jean-Paul Sartre, and John Updike, all of whom use mythological themes and motifs ironically, do not therefore contribute to the development of the myth concept.[32] If we wish to trace the development of *myth*, we must turn away from the line of mythological scholars and writers and begin at the other pole—with Richard Wagner.[33]

In his *Message to My Friends* (1851), Wagner describes the homesickness that filled him during his Swiss exile.[34] In compensation he immersed himself in the primal (*urheimisch*) element that was still alive in the poetic works of the past. Here we are dealing with something quite remote from the ironized mythology in Thomas Mann's sense. Wagner thought he could make out the "fundament of ancient ur-German myth" behind the mythological surface of medieval poems. "What I discovered here was no longer the historically conventional figure in which the clothing interests us more than its true shape: the true, naked human being in whom I could recognize every seething of blood, every twitch of the powerful muscles, in its unrestricted, freest movements—the *true man*." Where history offers us only external circumstances, myth reveals man as "the involuntary creator of his circumstances." This myth is far from the mythology of the eighteenth or the *Mythe* of the nineteenth century. Mythology, as well as *Mythe*, is historically conventional, whereas *Mythos* is eternally true. Mythology claims no validity for the present; in myth we recognize the ideal of humankind in its naked reality. It is evident that we are confronted here not only with a new word but with a new concept corresponding to the awakening national consciousness of the Germans. Wagner's *Mythus* is not historically conditioned, as was previously *Mythe*, but eternally valid as a model; no longer dead in the past, but throbbing, quivering in the present; no longer mere matter, but living organism.[35] Only this vital conception of myth, in contrast to the earlier definition of *Mythe*, justifies the botanical metaphors that frequently characterize it. For Wagner myth is a "root" (*Wurzel*) with "seed," "stem," and "branches," whose "fruit" nourishes the people.[36]

It is well known that Nietzsche hailed Wagner as the creator of a new myth. In his *Philosophie der Mythologie* (1842) Friedrich Schelling had developed a theory of mythic thinking; but for Schelling this thinking was always restricted to humanity in the earliest stages of its development.[37] Nietzsche, in contrast, ascribes the power of mythic thinking to a contemporary. "The poetic quality in Wagner manifests itself in the circumstance that he thinks in visual and perceptible processes, not in concepts; that is to say, he thinks mythically, just as the populace [*das Volk*] has always thought."[38] As for Wagner, here too myth is the mark of a living culture. "Without myth every culture loses its healthy creative natural power: only a horizon surrounded by myths rounds off an entire cultural movement into unity."[39] Consistent with that understanding, organic metaphors show up in Nietzsche's language as well: in his eyes, myth "blooms" "with colors" and "with fragrance" before "its leaves wither" and the "discolored and ravaged flowers" are borne away by the winds.[40]

This utterly original conception of myth as a blossoming organism on which the health of the people depends justifies, in turn, the gastronomical motif that occurs in Wagner's language, when he speaks of myth as "nourishment" and as a "fruit" that nurtures the people. In his treatise *Opera and*

Drama (1851) Wagner sketches the destiny of the German people, whose native myth has been undermined by Christian religious views.

> The people formerly comprehended only the indigenous in myth. Now that the understanding of the indigenous was lost, it sought surrogates in ever new alien things. Ravenously it devoured everything foreign and uncommon: its nourishment-crazed fantasy exhausted all possibilities of the human imagination, only to squander them in incredibly varied adventures.[41]

In *The Birth of Tragedy* Nietzsche appropriates the gastronomic motif, projecting a disconsolate image of contemporary man. "Now mythless man, constantly starving, stands amidst all pasts, digging and burrowing for roots, even when he has to dig for them in the most remote antiquities." He asks rhetorically if the feverish and eerie stirring of present-day culture is "something other than the greedy grasping and groping for food of a famished man."[42]

In and of itself the gastronomic motif is of no particular significance. But it exemplifies the process of making absolute that is necessary before myth can become truly dangerous. The organic conception of myth with its characteristic botanical metaphors shows that for Wagner and Nietzsche the concept is on the point of liberating itself from conventional mythology. Specific mythological figures like Siegfried or Dionysos can neither "bloom" nor bear "fruit." Such vegetative activity is reserved for a myth that has been transformed into a "root." And only through the metaphorical shift from *Mythe* as shape to *Mythos* as root can one avoid, when using the gastronomical motif, the image of intellectual cannibalism which otherwise would involuntarily suggest itself. Only in language does myth as "root" claim the same degree of reality as, say, a turnip for which one can actually hunger and which truly nourishes. And only in German, thanks to the associations that have accumulated around the concept since Wagner and Nietzsche, is it possible to "hunger" for myth. The nourishment-crazed, myth-eating German, restlessly grubbing for edible roots, strikes the speaker of English as no less outlandish than the American who—in a common figure of speech—"explodes" a myth strikes a German. The different metaphors stem from wholly different understandings of the concept. One "hungers" for what is organic, living; but one "explodes" what is technically constructible. If we were dealing simply with a phenomenon of cultural philosophy, this semantic curiosity would produce nothing but a linguistic *pointe*. But because language determines our thoughts and because politics is above all an affair of language, dire potentialities are exposed. A people that has once accepted this gastronomical rhetoric sees no major culinary miracle if, in the witch's kitchen of the 1920s, the mythic roots are prepared à la Rosenberg—that is, spiced with the equally mythic sauces of blood.

With Wagner and Nietzsche we are dealing with a myth which, according to Thomas Mann, can actually be "celebrated." But to the extent that the myth is celebrated as a living organism, Wagner and Nietzsche turn against the rationalist myth scholarship of the nineteenth century, which totally extirpated primal mythos.[43] Wagner rages against "anatomical science" but also against Christianity, which laid its hands on the "root" of myth in order to deprive it of its "lushly productive artistic power."[44] And Nietzsche concludes resignedly: "It is the fate of every myth to creep gradually into the confinement of an allegedly historical reality and to be treated by some later age as a one-time fact with a claim to historicity." Scientific myth research, Nietzsche jeers, "begins anxiously to defend the credibility of myths but to resist any natural life and proliferation of it."[45] Here, clearly and for the first time, the concept of myth departs from traditional European mythology and myth research. We see how the longing for myth resulted first from a dissatisfaction with the rationalistic civilization of the present and how it corresponds to the ideal of a new national consciousness.[46]

The Proliferation of Myth

After the turn of the century, many signs suggested that myth had become absolute, thanks to Wagner and Nietzsche, and had become a free-floating power that arrived just in time to encounter the growing irrationalism of the epoch. Hermann Hesse's *Peter Camenzind* (1904) opens with a Nietzschean statement that has been called inconceivable outside the German cultural world around the turn of the century:[47] "In the beginning was the myth. Just as the great god composed and struggled for expression in the souls of the Indians, the Greeks and Germanic peoples, so too it continues to compose daily in the soul of every child."[48] In the circle surrounding the poet Stefan George myth had become a conjuration formula, whispered for its talismanic power.[49] In Ernst Bertram's *Nietzsche* myth no longer designates a component of a comprehensive theory of gods but "everything that we can state about the nature of man, whose memory has come down to the living." Bertram appropriates from Nietzsche the dialectical opposition of myth and rationality. "Our over-alert and monitoring reason, today just as formerly, has its immovable limits wherever a myth wants to establish itself." But mythic vision succeeds in discovering the living myth ever anew. "Despite all accumulated knowledge, all methods, all justified deliberation, we know only what we see, and we see only what we are and because we are."[50]

The first volume of Spengler's "morphological" philosophy of history displays a similar inversion of concepts. For Spengler, as for Wagner and Nietzsche, myth is organic, the initial formative act of an awakening spirituality.[51] Spengler's own "Faustian mythology"—like Bertram's "mythology" of Nietzsche—is the systematization of a myth of modern man that has been declared absolute, a "mythic organism" in contrast to the "fragmentary saga shapings" of primitive peoples. The veneration of myth in the service of an awakening national consciousness goes hand in hand with a devaluation of conventional mythology.

Under these circumstances many people must have felt like the heroine of Albrecht Schaeffer's novel *Elli or the Seven Steps*, who attends an evening discussion of young Berlin intellectuals: "Elli heard the words, she knew them, but each one—such as shape, form, mythos, the heroic, bodily, blood, originary, formation—was instantly alienated within its context along with the context itself; they were sheer riddles, hieroglyphs of the ear, a secret language."[52]

In the 1920s myth penetrated the public consciousness as a magical shibboleth. Virtually every branch of scholarship—and not only in Germany—turned to mythology with a euphoric joy of discovery: C. G. Jung's depth psychology, the mass psychology of Wilhelm Wundt, the demythologizing biblical research of Rudolf Bultmann, Bronislaw Malinowski's anthropology, or Ernst Cassirer's philosophy. This scholarly interest furthered, in turn, the rediscovery of the mythological writings of such Romantic thinkers as Bachofen and Schelling, which were reprinted in the 1920s. Efforts of this sort assured the myth concept of a new scholarly validity. But along with these researches, which used the word *myth* in a technical and responsible manner, various works of popular philosophy made a less conscientious use of the term: Rudolf Kayser's *Zeit ohne Mythos* (1923; An age without myth) or Arthur Liebert's *Mythus und Kultur* (1925). In 1928 Hugo von Hofmannsthal observed that "if this present age is anything, it is mythic—I know no other term for an existence that fulfills itself before such vast horizons."[53] Two years earlier, Hofmannsthal had explored this phenomenon thoroughly: "Now as before the disquiet is general, doubt and confusion growing rather than declining.... We attempt to struggle through to clarity, to recognize what has fallen and what is still upright; but the ordering sense within us, which alone would be capable of such judgments, has been profoundly damaged." Amidst this general decline of values only myth is capable of restoring order: "The myth of our European existence, the creation of our spiritual world (without which there can be no religious world), the positing of cosmos against chaos."[54]

The spiritual despair of the 1920s, as well as the "hunger for wholeness" to which Peter Gay devotes a chapter of his study of Weimar culture, was also evident abroad.[55] Prominent writers in England and the United States—Yeats, Eliot, Pound, Lawrence—often looked favorably upon fascism as a response to the political confusions of the age. But their cultural snobbism saved the foreigners from so "folkish" a concept as *Mythos.*

In Germany, in contrast, the hunger for myth itself became the greatest myth of the 1920s, a common denominator which held together the most varied movements of the age. Everywhere there were calls for a "new myth" as a defense against the rationalist deconstruction of life. And ever since Wagner and Nietzsche this call had been associated almost routinely with organic metaphors. In Ludwig Klages's eclectic polemic on "the spirit as adversary of the soul" (*Der Geist als Widersacher der Seele*, 1929–32), for instance, we hear of the "jungle of myth" which the Greeks "cleared away with the ax-blows of the mind." The Greeks were "the first to set foot on the path to disaster, which with the clearing of jungles—in both a literal and a metaphorical sense—is nearing its end."[56] For Arthur Liebert in *Mythus und Kultur* myth is "a natural and organic externalization of religious consciousness," and the author rages against the scientific mentality which regards myth as nothing but an "object of investigation." "Whereas the mythic consciousness is transfigured by myth," we read, "the scientific mind tries to explain it."[57] Rudolf Kayser's elegiac writing about the "age without myth" uses the same dialectics and metaphors. Myth, which Kayser takes to be "cognition of spiritual essence," results from processes not within the conscious spirit but beneath it: "in the vegetative, in the soul, which is the organ that bears the pain of the spirit."[58] In his magisterial study of Graecophilia in the Age of Goethe, Walther Rehm appropriated the same image, explicitly presenting it as a surrogate for faith: "As a mythus, as a substitute for religion [*Religions-Ersatz*] this belief has the destiny of growth, blooming, and withering."[59] In her almost contemporaneous work on the same subject the British scholar E. M. Butler took a more skeptical view, speaking of "the insidious disease of mythomania" that in her opinion corrupted the German love of Greece.[60] Even Gerbrand Dekker's otherwise scholarly investigation of the later Schelling's thought culminates in a chapter called "The New Myth," which displays the usual range of metaphors. "We human beings of the present have become rootless plants which, driven here and there by the wind, hover free above the earth, which for us has become a dead, rigidified world of things."[61] Myth, whose death is attributed here to Descartes's rationalism, is root, plant, basis, *dynamis,* even *energeia.*[62]

In Wagner and Nietzsche the concept of myth had begun to become absolute, but it was still rooted in the individual legends of Germanic and Greek mythology. The myth concept of the 1920s is ominous because it has become a structure without contents, a wish image, a vague surrogate for religious longings, a negative reaction against rationalism and "chaos." Rudolf Kayser writes that Europe's new god, whose myth will not be peaceful and pastoral, is still nameless, and Kayser explicitly refuses "to name this god, to describe this myth."[63] "But it will break its way in, Eurasian in structure," he prophesies (95). According to Kayser's dialectics, the end of mythlessness is determined by the age's recognition of the absence of myth: "Like every myth, it emerges from need" (97).

There was no lack of warning voices which recognized the danger of such an empty concept. It is—to retain the gastronomic metaphor—as though one wanted to torment a starving man with classic menus and recipes. Although Gerbrand Dekker regards it as a "gratifying sign" that understanding for the enduring significance of myth is beginning to increase, he cautions against a "relapse into paganism." He sees that "many a modern man no longer has confidence in his own mind, which he blames for the rigidification of his worldview." Philosophy therefore has the responsibility of coming to terms with "the daemonic as the dynamic basis of life," so that it will not be left to the *Dunkelmänner* (shady characters) to seduce modern man in his "demonics gone astray."[64] To counteract the encroachment of myth into all forms of intellectual life, Ernst Cassirer devoted the second volume of his *Philosophy of Symbolic Forms* to "mythic thinking" (*Das mythische Denken,* 1925). He observed that the distinction between mythos and logos was being effaced, that myth had already laid claim to a place in the realm of pure methodology, and that the view was being advanced by its purveyors that no logical boundary can be drawn between myth and history. "If this thesis is correct, then not only history itself but the entire system of human sciences [*Geisteswissenschaften*] based upon it as one of its foundations would be removed from the realm of science and handed over to the realm of myth." Such encroachments of myth upon science can be warded off, Cassirer continues, only if one has come to understand myth within its own sphere. "Its true conquest must be based on its recognition and acknowledgment. Only through the analysis of its intellectual structure can its characteristic meaning, on the one hand, and its limits, on the other, be determined."[65] Even Kayser realizes that the "adventurousness" of a mythless age creates space for "all sorts of weird cultural entrepreneurs." Among these dubious "knights of the great transformation" he lists theosophists, faith healers, prophets of salvation, anabaptists, enthusiasts, and dadaists.[66] But for every appetite there is a cook whose secret recipe stills the hunger. Alfred Rosenberg's book, as we shall see, is distinguished from its title on from the other cultural-philosophical writings of the 1920s, for it not only offers an analysis of the spiritual hunger but promises the redeeming "myth of the twentieth century."

Up to this point, then, the following stages of development are evident. First, Romanticism overcame the myth-hostile view of the eighteenth century, which saw in mythology nothing but pleasant tales of the Greeks and Romans, by pointing to mythology as an expression of the cultural thinking of primitive peoples. Second, Wagner and Nietzsche applied the concept of mythic thinking to the present and introduced the word *Mythus* as the designation for this vitalistic cultural will of the people (*das Volk*) in contrast to the rigidified mythology of the past. Third, German cultural philosophy of the early twentieth century appropriated and even intensified this organic concept along with its botanical and gastronomic metaphors by liberating myth completely from all its ties to any historical mythology, thus transforming it into a free-floating energy of great rhetorical magic. Not until myth had become absolute and wholly emptied of any content was the fourth stage possible: the appropriation of the concept by any movement that promised to fill the evacuated structure with a new content. Every age and every land brings forth prophets of an irrational salvation. But only in Germany of the 1920s, and as a result of the process outlined here, was the concept "myth" distilled as the quintessence of such wishful dreams. Myth—at least so it seems from our historical standpoint—inevitably presented itself as the new shibboleth.

The Myth of National Socialism

Rosenberg's befuddled book begins like all glorifications of myth with a lament about the loss of center. "All present-day external struggles for power are effects of an inner breakdown. All systems of government of 1914 have collapsed, even if they formally continue to exist at least in part. But the social, religious, philosophical beliefs and values have also fallen apart. No supreme principle, no highest idea uncontestedly rules the life of the peoples."[67] But "the power that sacrificed itself from 1914 to 1918 now wants to shape itself" (701). Rosenberg proposes a solution in his discussion of "the coming kingdom" (book 3: "Das kommende Reich"). "The greatest task of our century," he proclaims in a chapter entitled "German People's

Church [*Volkskirche*] and School," "is the longing to give the Nordic racial soul [*Rassenseele*] its form as a German church under the sign of the folk myth [*Volksmythus*]" (614-15). This German church of the future will dispense with the trappings of the Roman Church with its sermons about the lamb of God, its teachings about the "fulfillment" of the Old Testament, and its wonders and rituals. It will liberate the Nordic race from Roman soothsayers and Jewish rabbis, replacing the crucifixion with "the fiery spirit of education" (*den lehrenden Feuergeist*, 616).

Rosenberg already detects signs of hope. "The blood that died is beginning to come alive. In its mystic sign a new cell growth of the German people's soul [*Volksseele*] is taking place." It is the old organic rhetoric, translated from botanical into zoological terms. But in the course of this hematogenic process, it should be noted, *blood* becomes virtually a code word for "race." Rosenberg regards it as the duty of the twentieth century "to create a new human type from a new life myth." This new myth is "the other—'truer'—stream of a genuinely growing (organic) search for truth, in contrast to the scholastic-logical-mechanical striving for 'absolute cognition'" (691).[68] With the fresh mythic insight into a life totality of spirit and will, "the organic philosophy of our age withdraws from the tyranny of the rational schemes" (697).[69]

Rosenberg's eclectic work amounts to hardly more than a compilation of various partial myths that were already long present—outside Germany as well—and that he disdains as falsifications. What is new about it is that now the concept "myth" is introduced to shape the disparate parts into a whole: the myth of the Third Kingdom (*Drittes Reich*), of the Total State, of German Man, and—last but not least—of Blood (*Blutmythus*). It would be possible to write a semantic and rhetorical history of blood. Ever since Goethe's Mephistopheles, blood has been regarded in German cultural history as "a very special juice" ("ein ganz besondrer Saft"),[70] and it long played a significant role in Christian symbolism. But many early writers asked themselves, like Novalis in his *Spiritual Songs* (*Geistliche Lieder*): "Who can say that he understands blood?" ("Wer kann sagen, / Daß er das Blut versteht?").[71] Any proper rhetoric of blood would begin with Wagner and lead by way of the enormously popular effusions of Julius Langbehn (*Rembrandt als Erzieher* [1890], which contains a section called "The Power of Blood"),[72] and Stefan George's address to his disciples "sprung from ancient blood" ("sprossen von geblüt"),[73] down to the last page of Oswald Spengler's *Decline of the West*, where an end is foretold to the dictatorship of money through the "cosmic floods of the eternal blood." But two points should be noted.

In the first place, Rosenberg would scarcely have enjoyed such a great success with his "myth of blood" if the public had not already been accustomed to an organic conception of myth. Even such foreign Germanophiles as Joseph-Arthur de Gobineau and Houston Stewart Chamberlain pay their respects to blood in their pan-Germanic propagandistic writings. But because the organic concept of myth was lacking outside Germany, the veneration of blood was never able to concentrate itself into a "myth of blood." In contrast, as early as 1925 the nationalist conservative poet-essayist Friedrich Georg Jünger wrote that life is "above all blood-related [*blutmäßig*]; that is, component of a community of blood of whose life core it constitutes a part."[74] The following lines from the year 1932 show how easy it is for a rhetorically trained thinker to shift from the botanical to the zoological: "More important than all vivisection of intellectualism is the growth of a national myth: a myth that is not sweated out of the nerves, but that blooms from the blood. For not rationalism but myth creates life."[75] Similarly Friedrich Georg Jünger wrote that "life … withers if it cuts off [its native] roots or seeks to nourish itself from alien roots. Above all it is blood-like—that is, a component of a community of blood in whose life kernel it shares."[76] The literature of the Nazi period is rife with examples. Hans Friedrich Blunck, herald of the "Nordic Renaissance" and early president of the Nazi Writers Union (Reichsschriftumskammer), asked in a poem "Why You Lived!" ("Warum du lebtest!" 1940), and responded with the answer: "in order to celebrate your lofty ancestors in your blood" ("Um die hohen Ahnen / In deinem Blut zu feiern").[77]

In the second place, the concept of myth offered Rosenberg a magical rhetoric and a dialectical structure of thought which appealed specifically to one of the constituencies which Nazism hoped to attract: the middle-class audiences educated in the tradition of bourgeois humanism, of Wagnerian opera and the Nietzschean myth of the *Übermensch*. The fact that Rosenberg subsumed his ideas under this collective heading shows that myth was now regarded quintessentially as "authoritative word." If myth is still alive and if it expresses the collective will of the people, then the individual in uncertain times can rely on myth as the model for living and dispense with individual freedom. This ominous possibility was present earlier. Rudolf Kayser traced the anarchy of the 1920s back to this individualism without content, and he saw in myth the only way out of the chaos generated by rationalistic freedom. "Cunningly and without our doing," he writes at the end of his book, "a word has crept into these pages, which deal with mythic and legal bonds—a word that anachronistically denies these bonds: freedom."[78]

Myth, in sum, possesses in addition to its structure and metaphors its own logic, according to which freedom is suddenly transformed into its opposite. This association of mythic faith with the renunciation of individual freedom crops up with notable frequency. Gerbrand Dekker echoes the same refrain. "We seek through the return to myth to renew the intimate connection with Mother Nature, to which we would perhaps be prepared to sacrifice even our spiritual freedom, won with such difficulty."[79] Myth, therefore, is not simply expression; it is also exhortation. The individual needs only to surrender will-lessly to myth and all responsibility is taken from him, for through that surrender he fulfills his destiny. As Alfred Döblin shrewdly observed, "It was [the Nazis'] intention in their dictatorial state to replace Christianity with the horrible nonsense of Rosenberg's myth."[80]

The demand for a will-less surrender to the myth of blood emerges from Rosenberg's book just as clearly as from Alfred Baeumler's exegesis of that work. Baeumler explicitly rejects the myth scholarship of the nineteenth century, "which allowed itself to be seduced by doubt and criticism to equate all myths with one another."[81] The earlier scholarly neutrality, which was nothing but a lack of faith, was responsible for the "dissolution" (Auflösung) of the age. Faith in true myth will lead German man back into the living center of the worldview. "Under worldview [Weltanschauung] National Socialism understands that unity of spiritual attitude, determined by racial predisposition, in which the possibility of mastering all problems of life and of thought is grounded" (101). Myth, originally viewed as the free expression of religious belief, has been degraded by National Socialism to the political declaration of faith. "All that is great and belonging to us in the past, all that is present strength, which bears the future in it, Rosenberg condenses into the concept of myth," writes Baeumler. "Myth is the reality-creating dream of a soul; not a subjective dreaming, but an objective shaping of that which will be" (69). The expression of the religious faith of primitive peoples reveals itself unexpectedly as the Five-Year-Plan of a modern totalitarian state.

There is perhaps no more flagrant example of the National Socialist violation of the German language and thought than this political appropriation of myth. Heinrich Schmidt refers in the entry on Mythus in his Philosophisches Wörterbuch (10th ed., 1943) explicitly to Rosenberg: "The racial significance of myth as the underlying political-philosophical power was ultimately recognized by National Socialism in the consideration of its political-philosophical dynamic." The pathological proliferation of organic myth can even be traced graphically by means of the standard bibliographies. For the last decade of the nineteenth century Kayser's Vollständiges

Bücherlexikon cites a single title under the rubric "Mythus." The five-year periods from 1907 to 1920 show respectively three or four titles. The growing hunger for myth in the 1920s announces itself with some twenty titles in the keyword index. After 1930 the line leaps dizzily upward with more than sixty titles, until it sinks back in the 1940s to about twenty-five—a level that has remained constant in the past few decades.

The Ambivalence of Myth

Thomas Mann's revealing correspondence with Karl Kerényi begins in 1934—that is to say, in the thick of the period of most intensive German mythophilia—with the concession that his interest in myth awakened late: "It is a product of my maturity and was not at all present in my youth."[82] The gradually growing interest corresponds, he continues, "to a taste that in time turned away from what is bourgeois-individual and toward the typical, general, and human." He welcomes Kerényi's plan to write a treatise on "the return of the modern novel to myth" and suggests Alfred Döblin's works as a further example (634). Seven years later he writes to Kerényi from Princeton: "At this time what should more appropriately be my element than myth plus psychology? For a long time I have been a passionate friend of this combination; indeed, psychology is the means of wresting myth from the hands of the fascist 'shady characters' [*Dunkelmänner* or *obscuri viri*] and 'refunctioning' it into the humane" (651). He reiterates the same thought seven months later. "We must take myth away from intellectual fascism and re-function it into the humane" (653).[83] He regarded his *Joseph* tetralogy (1933–42), written during the very period that saw the gradual shift in his attitude, as an attempt to "relate the birth of the Ego from the mythic collective." The figures of his novel, who for the most part organize their daily lives according to prefigurative patterns handed down from generations past, suggest an obvious analogy to the situation of modern men and women, who "remain caught with a significant part of their being in the mythic, in the collective."[84]

Hermann Broch was quick to recognize the mythic element in Mann's novels, calling "the retransformation of a chaotic being into a mythic organon . . . [Mann's] literary problem and human mission."[85] In 1934 and again under the influence of the prevailing mythophilia, Hermann Broch asked, in a talk called "Spirit and Spirit of the Age" ("Geist und Zeitgeist"), what other word affords "so much consolation that it can be held up to the most profound despair of the heart." The answer corresponds to our expectation: it is "quite simply the myth of human being, the myth of nature and its human-divine phenomenality." If this myth existed, it would be "a sign of belief and a new confluence of values, the confluence necessary in order to put an end to the bloody disintegration of values."[86] Fifteen years later— also from Princeton—his words sound different. In his wide-ranging study *Hofmannsthal and His Age* (*Hofmannsthal und seine Zeit*), written toward the end of his life, Broch took issue with the "criminal Nazi intellectuality of blood-intoxication" and expressly disclaimed any identification of myth with modernity.

> Human development consists in the progressive discrimination of ratio- nal attitudes—distances itself, therefore, more and more from the mythic unity of the past.... What matters is not the ripeness of the world for myth—that's Nazi aesthetics—but the turning away from the decorative task of artistic activity and the emphasizing of its ethical duty.[87]

Elsewhere Broch sought to come to grips with what he called in the title of one essay "the mythic heritage of literature"[88]—the function in a post-Nazi world of myth, in which he acknowledges "the primal form of all human cognition, primal form of science, primal form of art—whereby myth is inevitably also the primal form of philosophy."[89]

In 1933–34, during his brief infatuation with the ideas of National Social- ism and in his opposition to left-wing intellectuals, the poet Gottfried Benn admired the "anthropological profundity" of the new state in its "turn from the economic to the mythic collective."[90] He praised the "Doric world" of fifth-century Athens, where the state and the individual shared "common experiences of mythic, folkish, political content" before they were corrupted by the "sinking age" of Euripides, when "myth was worn out; life and his- tory became the theme."[91] Ten years later, thoroughly disenchanted with the Nazis, Benn realized that the matriarchal goddesses of the Doric world have been displaced by the motherless Athena, goddess of reason. "There is no way back. No invocation of Ishtar, no return to the *magna mater*, no conjuration of the matriarchy, no enthroning of [Goethe's] Gretchen over Nietzsche can alter the fact that there is no longer any state of nature for us."[92] In the poem "Lost I" ("Verlorenes Ich," 1943), Benn made the same point more tersely:

> Die Welt zerdacht. Und Raum und Zeiten
> und was die Menschheit wob und wog,
> Funktion nur von Unendlichkeiten—
> die Mythe log.[93]

[The world thought to pieces. And space and time / and what humanity
wove and weighed, / nothing but a function of infinities— / the myth lied.]

In 1925 Ernst Cassirer began his investigation of "mythic thinking" (*Das
mythische Denken*; vol. 2 of *Philosophie der symbolischen Formen*, 1923–
29) with the claim that this kind of thinking did not occur, as Schelling
had assumed, only among peoples at early stages of human development,
but was a characteristic of humankind in general. Twenty years later, when
Cassirer wrote his last book in New Haven—his work in English *The Myth
of the State*—he found to his astonishment that the entire concept had
changed in the German language. Myth had formerly meant the result of
an unconscious activity and the free product of the imagination. Now he
confirmed the existence of political myths that had not grown freely but
had been artificially assembled by clever artisans. "It has been reserved
for the twentieth century, our great technical age," Cassirer concludes, "to
develop a new technique of myth."[94] His book closes with the admonition
that we must study the origins and the structure as well as the methods and
techniques of political myths so that we can fight the enemy.

Precisely the same process appears to be at work in the case of Walter Benjamin.[95] Benjamin quipped that "my thought is related to theology
as is the blotting pad to ink. It is wholly soaked with it";[96] but his emphasis shifted over time as youthful messianism gave way to mature materialism. Shortly after World War I, the young Benjamin opened a brief
"Theological-Political Fragment" (1920–21) with the statement that "only
the messiah fulfills all historical happening, in the sense that he alone re-
deems, fulfills, creates its relation to the messianic" (2: 203–4). Accordingly
Benjamin tended to see all historical phenomena in theological terms, as
in his fragment "Capitalism as Religion," which begins with the premise
that capitalism can be viewed as a religion. "Capitalism serves to satisfy
essentially the same concerns, torments, discomforts to which formerly the
so-called religions responded" (6: 100). By the 1930s, however, and in response to developments in Nazi Germany, he sounds almost like Thomas
Mann, although his image of jungle and axe goes back to Ludwig Klages.

To reclaim territories in which hitherto only madness is rampant. To
push forward with the sharpened axe of reason and without looking left
or right, so as not to fall prey to the horror that entices us from the
depths of the jungle. All the land once had to be reclaimed by reason, to
be cleared of madness and myth. The same must be done now for the
nineteenth century." (5: 570–71)

What can be clearly recognized in these five examples—Mann, Broch, Benn, Cassirer, Benjamin—is that myth has been to a certain extent disqualified. In the 1920s and 1930s all five writers shared what Broch, in his essay, called the "longing of the age for myth." The paradox of this attitude is that one cannot share and express this longing without simultaneously contributing to the "myth maturity of the world."[97] It belongs to the tragedy of German intellectuals of the Weimar period that, through their early belief in something like "the" myth, they contributed to the general public readiness to accept the first mythic construct that satisfied the conditions of the empty structure. Accordingly, in the oeuvre of many leading writers of the period—even if we disregard such overtly Nazi authors as Hans Friedrich Blunck and Hanns Johst, who wittingly sought to create in their plays and novels new myths appropriate to the prevailing ideology—we find works with a pronounced mythic tendency.[98]

In the fifty-five poems of his *Sonnets to Orpheus* (*Sonette an Orpheus,* 1923) Rainer Maria Rilke invoked the Greek ur-poet as the icon of the modern poet striving to transform nature, to capture the essential permanence of all being in its various transformations, and to embrace both life and death in his song.

> Ist er ein Hiesiger? Nein, aus beiden
> Reichen erwuchs seine weite Natur.
>
> [Is he of this world? No, his wide nature grew out of both realms.]
> (Pt. 1, no. 6)

Gerhart Hauptmann was obsessed with classical mythic themes from his early epic *Promethidenlos* (1985; Destiny of the sons of Prometheus) down to his late dramatic tetralogy based on the *Oresteia* (*Atriden-Tetralogie,* 1943–46). But the writer who exclaimed that myth was his great home ("Mythos, große Heimat!")[99] turned during the 1920s to ancient Germanic myth for the subject of his tragedy *Veland* (1925; Wayland the smith), which was based on a theme from the Norse Eddic poems. The motto to the play, tellingly, is taken from the Romantic mythophile Schelling: "The idea of the gods is essential for art. Every idea is a universe in the shape of a particular." Hermann Broch's powerful "mountain novel" *Die Verzauberung* (The bewitchment, written from 1934 to 1936 as part of a "religious trilogy") uses the paradigm of an eternal mythic process—the power of good in a matriarchal society led by a *magna mater* is overcome by the forces of evil represented by a fear-mongering false prophet who arrives from the world outside—as the pattern for a fiction dealing with the corruption of an Alpine mining village by a Hitler-like itinerant.

Most of the early enthusiasts—in most cases as a direct result of exile and their exposure to a non-German understanding of myth—subsequently changed their views. Mann wanted to deactivate myth by psychologizing it. Broch attempted to devalue the irrational basis of myth. Benn prioritized the Athenian model over the Doric. Cassirer recommended a precise analysis of the techniques with which myth is politically manipulated. Benjamin sharpened the axe of reason to attack the myth of the twentieth century. The shift of opinion is tied in part to temporal distance: in the 1940s the possibilities for the abuse of the magical incantation were easier to recognize than had been the case in the heady atmosphere of Germany ten or twenty years earlier. In part, however, the shift can be attributed to their geographical removal from the German linguistic realm, as well as to the soberly critical spirit of the American conception of myth, as the emigrants now sought to clarify their views.

In the case of the political theorist Erich Voegelin, the critique of Nazi myth was the cause rather than the effect of his emigration. Voegelin's *Political Religions* (*Die politischen Religionen*, 1938), which appeared in Vienna precisely at the moment of the Anschluss, was immediately suppressed by the Nazis. Voegelin fled to the United States, where his small book was finally reissued, along with an English translation, almost fifty years later.[100] Voegelin traces the history of ideological movements as a variety of religious expression from the Egyptian Ikhnaton by way of medieval theocracy and Hobbes's *Leviathan* down to his own present of the 1930s. In his concluding chapter, "The Temporal Community" ("Die innerweltliche Gemeinschaft"), Voegelin points out that the sense of religiosity is so strong even in secular societies that it does not crumble under the attacks of scientific criticism.

A conscious apocalypse takes the place of a naive one. In place of the system which purports to be rationally theoretical, nationally economic or sociological, one finds the "myth": the myth is consciously engendered in order to unite the masses affectively and to transpose them into politically effective states, in which they expect redemption. Since the myth is not justified by supernatural revelation and scientific criticism cannot stand its ground, there develops in the second phase a new concept of truth—Rosenberg's concept of so-called organic truth. (62–63)

170   CHAPTER SEVEN

Voegelin observes bemusedly that persons of religious disposition may understand that they are being manipulated by "the psychological technique of myth-engendering, its propaganda and social dissemination," but that they do not allow that knowledge to disturb their faith. Far from being condemned as crimes against the dignity of the person, these temporal myths are demanded as methods of "religio-ecstatic union of the individual with his God. The engendering of the myth and its propagation through the newspaper and radio, through speeches and communal festivals, gatherings and parades, the planning for and the dying in war, are the intramundane forms of the *unio mystica*" (66). In conclusion Voegelin turns his analytical eye on the function of religious symbolism and faith in the temporal community. Small wonder, in light of this shrewd unmasking of the techniques exploited by Rosenberg and other Nazi propagandists, that Voegelin had to flee from Vienna as the Germans entered Austria.

One of the most influential statements concerning the ambivalence of myth was contained in the "philosophical fragments" that Max Horkheimer and Theodor W. Adorno composed in their American exile and circulated in 1944 in hectographed typescript. Finally published in 1947, their *Dialectics of the Enlightenment* became in the 1960s and 1970s the bible of young German intellectuals associated with the Frankfurt School of critical theory.[101] The authors undertook their project in large measure in an effort to understand the appeal of what they called the "Talmi myth of the fascists" (19; alluding to the alloy of gold and brass used by jewelry makers). "The paradox of faith degenerates ultimately into a swindle, into the Myth of the Twentieth Century" (26; referring specifically to Rosenberg's book). But behind the nationalistic-heathen myths of the Nazis they thought they could make out a profounder background. (To develop their argument, to be sure, they had to resort to vast historical oversimplifications, to idiosyncratic definitions, and to a fudged distinction between myth and mythology.) It is the main thesis of the first essay that myth, which they define as "false clarity" (4), is itself already a kind of enlightenment and that the Enlightenment, in turn, reverted to mythology (6). They exemplify the first point through an analysis of the Homeric epics, and specifically through an interpretation of the episode concerning Odysseus and the Sirens (*Odyssey* 12). They go on to argue that the Enlightenment, in its program to disenchant the world by destroying myth, ended by mythifying its own tools: the positivism of Comte, theory that turns reality into abstractions, and the systematic-historical dismemberment of totality. Kantian critique was transformed into affirmation. The Nazi myth, by this reasoning, is the inevitable outcome of nationalism tending toward racism and of the modern worship of technology.

⁓

The Nazi state was destroyed in 1945, but the organic concept of myth that it resurrected survived and continued to occupy a conspicuous place in the thinking of the later twentieth century.[102] In 1953–54 the philosopher Karl Jaspers—who not by chance was at the time writing a major rehabilitation of Schelling's philosophy (1955)—engaged in a broadly publicized debate with the theologian Rudolf Bultmann (according to the subtitle of the English edition) "on the possibility of religion without myth."[103] Against Bultmann's controversial concept of "demythologization" (*Entmythologisierung*), Jaspers argues from his existential viewpoint that "the splendor and wonder of the mythical vision is to be purified, but must not be abolished. To speak of 'demythologization' is almost blasphemous" (16). "Instead of perverting and degrading mythical thinking, we need to recover and restore the language of myth. It is the language of a reality that is not empirical, but existential, whereas our mere empirical existence tends continually to be lost in the empirical, as though the latter were all of reality" (17). Jaspers's essay is of particular interest because it reinforces the idea that myth is an essentially religious concept, which when liberated from its original associations becomes a free-floating radical, capable of being exploited by such ideologies as Nazism.

In one of the more widely discussed philosophical works of the second half of the twentieth century, Hans Blumenberg opposed his concept of "work on myth" (*Arbeit am Mythos*, 1979) to the various mythoclastic efforts of the past two centuries. Blumenberg argues, in analogy to Adorno and Horkheimer, that myth—which he understands as man's attempt to come to terms with chaos—does not die out when it has been reduced to burlesque. Rather, every new claim that a myth has been laid to rest— Blumenberg cites the early Christian exultation that the great god Pan was dead—itself belongs to the "work on myth." "There is no end to myth, although there are always aesthetic acts of violence to bring about its end."[104] To drive home his point, Blumenberg ends his concluding chapter (entitled "If not *the* myth, then at least *a* . . . ") with an account of Kafka's brief parable "Prometheus," which consists of a report on four differing legends about the Titan, each claiming to end the story, only to provide in turn the basis for a new version.

In another recent "philosophy of myth" entitled "The Conquest of Chaos," Emil Angehrn argues that reason has its origin and basis in myth, from which it then seeks to liberate itself in analogy to the great creation myths beginning with a primal chaos.[105] But to the extent that reason denies the experience of the negative forces that myth and chaos represent, it also runs the risk of becoming nothing but an oppressive order. Reason can recover a suppressed darker aspect of its nature only by engaging myth. The peculiarly German nature of the obsession with myth is amusingly evident in *The Presence of Myth* by the Polish philosopher Leszek Kolakowski. In his preface to the English edition, the author observes that in 1966, when he wrote it, his philosophical language (even in Polish) was so heavily dependent on German phenomenological and existential idiom that it could later be translated smoothly into German "whereas to render it in English turned out to be an extremely arduous task."[106] Kolakowski's text, which amounts to yet another attempt to overcome "the opposition between a meaning-generating faith and an explanatory science" (6), confirms this indebtedness. Kolakowski argues that it is a mistake for philosophy to attempt to dispense with mythopoeic activity or to prioritize the "technicologico-cognitive" over the "mythologico-symbolic" function of consciousness (132) because "culture thrives both on a desire for ultimate synthesis between these two conflicting elements and on being organically unable to ensure that synthesis" (135).

In its opposition of myth and rationality, in its view of myth as the response to chaos, and in its veneration of myth as a surrogate for a lost religious faith, the contemporary mythophilia can be seen, paradoxically, as an extension of a tradition extending from Wagner and Nietzsche by way of early twentieth-century anthropology and history of religions to the Nazi apostles of myth in the 1920s and 1930s. For even as they seek to eradicate "the myth of the twentieth century," they tacitly accept the definition of myth and the structure of mythic thinking employed by Klages, Kayser, Rosenberg, and their ilk. As Günter Grass observed in his novel *Local Anaesthetic* (*örtlich betäubt*, 1969), "a new generation is growing up that is seeking a new myth."[107]

This new mythophilia, liberated from the perversions of Nazism and seeking its sources, is no longer limited to Germany.[108] Since the work in the 1950s by such scholars as Mircea Eliade, Claude Lévi-Strauss, and Roland Barthes the interest has remained steady in France.[109] In 1980 a conference was devoted to "the return of myth,"[110] and at the University of Dijon, Jean-Jacques Wunenburger has headed since that decade a research team investigating what Wunenburger has labeled "mythophoria."[111]

Myth has emerged as a conspicuous feature of New Age thinking. Perhaps the most notable proponent in the United States was Joseph Campbell, who in numerous essays and books defended "the mythic dimension"[112] of human experience and proclaimed "the power of myth." His highly acclaimed television program of that title was one of the big successes of the 1980s.[113] But Campbell was by no means alone. In *The Myths We Live By* Mary Midgley maintains that myths are not opposed to science, as is often assumed; they are, rather, "the part that decides its significance in our lives."[114] Such contemporary movements as ecology, Gaia, and the biosphere, she continues, represent efforts of men and women to reconnect with nature and our inner "wildness."

Much the same thinking is evident in other works of recent decades, of which Stephen C. Ausband's *Myth and Meaning, Myth and Order* is representative. There we read that "man embraces myths because he must. His mind seeks order everywhere in the universe, and if it cannot find order ready-made, it will impose order and believe in the order it has imposed."[115] "All myths do the same thing: they attempt to relate man in some meaningful way to the goings-on of the universe. They reflect a world that is meaningful and orderly and, when they are outgrown because man's ideas about order have changed, they have to be discarded or altered and new myths must replace them" (118). The old gastronomic refrain that Michael Hochgesang, a contemporary gourmet of culture, was intoning in 1965 appears to be no less valid today: "The hunger for myth is huge."[116]

CHAPTER EIGHT

The Longing for Utopia

A fter the religion of art had shown itself to be as ineffectual as other religions; after the searcher had returned, disillusioned, from the pilgrimage to India; after the glowing promise of socialism had been exposed as another god that failed; and after the hunger for myth had resulted in spiritual indigestion—where was the seeker for faith to look in the years of upheaval following World War I? If the inward turn to art had failed, along with the outward turn to political solutions, whether in community or myth, the obvious solution was Nowhere, the place called Nusquama, Erewhon, or—in the phrase coined by Thomas More—Utopia. But where is "nowhere"? In space? in time? in another dimension altogether?

Three Dimensions of Utopia

Every age, as a brief historical survey reveals, has added new dimensions of possibility. For all the similarity among them as counterrealities, each utopia reflects its own time as a specific response to particular historical circumstances. The utopian impulse can be traced back at least to Ezekiel and other biblical prophets who proclaimed their ecstatic visions of a messianic holy state.[1] Just as Ezekiel reacted with his vision of social justice to the destruction of Jerusalem in 587 BCE and the humiliations of the Exile, Plato in *The Republic* posited an ideal state opposed to the political turmoil during the Peloponnesian War and expressed his dismay with the system of Athenian justice that had executed Socrates. Those two early models established patterns underlying the scores of utopias written in the course of the following twenty-five hundred years. Ezekiel's vision (Ez. 40–48) is a projection into the future, and hence a temporal utopia (or, more precisely, uchronia); Plato's is a projection into another place in the present-day world, and hence a spatial utopia. Ezekiel's vision of the restored temple and land of Israel is very much a religious utopia, a "City of God" (its name as specified in the concluding sentence is to be "The Lord is there"), and establishes a model subsequently followed by Augustine in *De Civitate Dei* (413–26) and by later Christian utopists. Plato's Republic, in contrast, is very much a secular political state. But both are presented as perfect states possible in the world as we know it, delimited in space and unchanging over time. (Both visions assume that the world outside will go on as usual, representing a constant threat to the utopian city-state: hence Ezekiel's careful provision for borders and restrictions, and Plato's establishment of Guardians to protect the state against outsiders.) Both, in sum, exemplify the standard definition of utopia as a fictional work describing the political structure of a state or community.[2]

Despite these exemplary ancient models, and setting aside such popular medieval works as the fictitious letters of Prester John describing his wondrous kingdom in the Orient,[3] the utopia is essentially a modern genre, stimulated initially by the early voyages of discovery of Columbus, Vasco da Gama, Amerigo Vespucci—the direct inspiration for Thomas More's *Utopia* was the publication of Vespucci's account of his voyages in 1507—and informed by the rediscovery of Plato's works. Appropriating the dialogue form of *The Republic*, they posited, for the restless and changing world of the Renaissance, ideal counterrealities existing in eternal stasis on islands in remote and undisclosed locations: the protocommunist paradise described by Raphael Hythloday in More's *Utopia* or, a century later, the Pacific island Bensalem of Bacon's *New Atlantis* (1626) and the ideal Christian commune portrayed in Tommaso Campanella's *City of the Sun* (*Civitas Solis*, 1623). The insularity of these utopian states is illustrated visually by the maps that are often included in the early utopias: e.g., "Utopia" in the third edition of More's work (Basel, 1515); "Macaria" (the Christian community envisaged by followers of Johann Comenius)[4] in Caspar Stiblin's *Commentariolus de Eudaemonensium Republica* (Basel, 1555); or "Christianopolis" in Johann Valentin Andreae's *Reipublicae Christianopolitanae descriptio* (Strasbourg, 1619).[5] While the visions differed from writer to writer, the form remained relatively constant.

The spatial (horizontal) projections that characterized the age of exploration were joined in the late eighteenth century by a series of secularized temporal (or vertical) projections initiated by Louis-Sébastien Mercier's *L'An 2440* (1770). Mercier's work appeared, symptomatically, at the beginning of the decade in which Captain James Cook's voyage around the world (1772–75) essentially completed the map of the world, thus leaving little unexplored space for utopias in the real world of the present. (Yet as late

as 1872 Samuel Butler could still find space in the real world for the satirical utopia, or dystopia, that he anagrammatically called *Erewhon* and set
in a country resembling the New Zealand where he had experienced his
youthful adventures as a sheep breeder; others looked to the yet unexplored
regions of central Africa and South America.) As the geographical world was
being narrowed, the newly foregrounded dimension of time put an end to
the Enlightenment rationalist view of a fixed and stable reality. The political energy of the French Revolution soon found its analogy in the sense of
history that dominated the nineteenth century, in the progressive philosophies of Hegel and Marx, and in the evolutionary theories of Darwin and his
successors.[6] If utopias could no longer reasonably be located in unexplored
parts of the spatial world, they could be projected into the future of a human
race that was now understood to be constantly changing and evolving. Hence
the many socialist utopias of the nineteenth century, principally French, are
set in a future humanity—not yet present but fully realizable in the world
as we know it. Saint-Simon's *Le Nouveau Christianisme* (1825) envisages,
as its title suggests, the future realization of an eternal community of scientists, industrial workers, and artists inspired by Christian ideals. Charles
Fourier, in *Le Nouveau Monde industriel et societaire* (1829) proposes a
wildly idiosyncratic scheme according to which society would be organized
into "phalansteries" of individuals working harmoniously together in a hi-
erarchy of shifting occupations and personal relations. And Etienne Cabet's
Voyage en Icarie (1840) describes a communist society on the imaginary island of Icaria incorporating absolute equality and human brotherhood.[7] This
is still the case in Edward Bellamy's *Looking Backward* (1888), whose hero
is projected into the future and critically contemplates the Boston of 1887
from the standpoint of a harmoniously socialized Boston in the year 2000.

The startling scientific advances at the turn of the twentieth century
opened new dimensions for exploration—from the subatomic worlds implied by Max Planck's quantum theory to the mysterious universes whose
existence was suggested by Einstein's theory of relativity. These exciting
developments stimulated in the popular imagination, on the one hand,
the emergence of the genre of science fiction, leading to the Hollywood
extravaganzas set in outer space or within the human microcosm. They
exposed, on the other hand, unanticipated potentialities for the positing of
utopian visions just when Newtonian time and Copernican space seemed
to be exhausted.

The early and still classic model of this new type of utopia is H. G. Wells's
A Modern Utopia (1905). While still conventional to the extent that it re-
lies heavily on the Platonic dialogue—between the narrator and his earthly

companion; between the narrator and his utopian double[8]—to develop its ideas in systematic fashion, the novel is at the same time utterly modern in that it envisages not an isolated city or state but a totalized utopian world, a world no longer set in extensions of earthly space or historical time but in another world altogether. "No less than a planet will serve the purpose of a modern Utopia,"[9] Wells writes in full consciousness and command of the tradition in which he is operating. Once upon a time, he continues, the isolation of a mountain valley or an island sufficed to allow a polity to maintain itself intact from outward force, as in Plato's armed Republic or the isolation of Bacon's New Atlantis and More's Utopia. Even Butler's satirical Erewhon, he remarks, "found the Tibetan method of slaughtering the inquiring visitor a simple, sufficient rule" (11). But modern thought has taught us that enclosures offer no protection against such outside forces as epidemics, barbarian hordes, or economic power. Any state powerful enough to remain isolated in the modern world would be mighty enough to rule the world. "World-state, therefore, it must be. That leaves no room for a modern Utopia in Central Africa, or in South America, or round about the pole, those last refuges of ideality.... We need a planet" (12). Accordingly Wells imagines a world that is the mirror image of ours in almost every respect except for its more highly developed views on such subjects as freedom, economics, science, government, the position of women, race, and so forth.

Wells's modern utopia differs in another important respect from the perfect states envisaged by thinkers since Plato. Indeed, he confesses that "this so-called Modern Utopia is a mere story of personal adventures among Utopian philosophies" (372). The nineteenth-century utopians projected their visions into a future where they remained static and perfect. But ever since Darwin "quickened the thought of the world," Wells remarks, thinkers have come to realize that "the Modern Utopia must be not static but kinetic, must shape not as a permanent state but as a hopeful stage, leading to a long ascent of stages" (5). This is the principle that governs his "modern utopia," which has its failures along with its progress toward ever loftier goals but which is envisaged as ultimately attainable.

These, then, are the three dimensions in which the social utopia, along with such variant forms as science fiction and the fantasy, tend to occur: in geographical space, in historical time, or in otherworlds. The secondary literature on utopias is enormous, and there is no need for our present purposes to engage in the ongoing discussion regarding definition or history of the genre. We are concerned here simply and specifically with the use of the social utopia, in its three possible dimensions, as a response to the loss of faith in the period around World War I.

Utopia as Response to Social Disorder

Utopias emerge as a response to change, upheaval, or chaos in the author's world:[10] the destruction of Jerusalem and the Jewish experience of exile, or the corruption and tyranny in city-states in the late fifth-century Greek world. Thomas More was confronted with the decay of religious authority and the perversion of justice in early sixteenth-century England, while the French utopian socialists sought to come to grips with social and political turmoil in post-Napoleonic Europe.

The same principle applies in our own time. The enthusiastic revival of utopian thought in the late twentieth century was prompted by the uprisings of the 1960s in Europe and the United States, heralded by wall placards in Paris demanding "Utopia Now!" The rebellions were legitimated and encouraged by such spokesmen as Herbert Marcuse in his 1967 talk to students at the Free University of Berlin which was paradoxically titled "The End of Utopia"—paradoxical (though hardly original)[11] because for Marcuse the end of utopia is achieved through the ultimate realization of a free society, by which he meant implicitly a Freudian-Marxian society incorporating the liberation from capitalism and personal repression that he had proclaimed in *Eros and Civilization* (1955).

> Today we have the capacity to turn the world into hell, and we are well on the way to doing so. We also have the capacity to turn it into the opposite of hell. This would mean the end of utopia, that is, the refutation of those ideas and theories that use the concept of utopia to denounce certain socio-historical possibilities.[12]

The effects of the new utopian impulse rapidly manifested themselves in the United States not just in the violence of the Weather Underground or the theocratic tyranny of Waco, Texas, but in more peaceful phenomena such as the countercultural effort to establish utopian agricultural or urban communes. The popularity of the movement is suggested by the estimation that in the 1970s a tenth of all fiction published in the United States concerned imaginary societies.[13]

That critics, scholars, and editors became keenly aware of the new utopianism is evidenced by such series as "Utopian Literature," undertaken in 1971 by the Arno Press/New York Times Collection, which reprinted a large number of less-well-known social utopias mainly from the 1890s. A major colloquium called "Utopia and Melancholy" at the University of Bielefeld in 1975 resulted in a three-volume set of "interdisciplinary studies on the modern utopia"[14] with contributions by some forty scholars from half a dozen countries. The 1970s also saw the publication of important studies, principally in German, French, and English: Helmut Swoboda's *Utopia: Geschichte der Sehnsucht nach einer besseren Welt* (1972) and Michael Winter's *Compendium utopiarum: Typologie und Bibliographie literarischer Utopien* (vol. 1, 1978); Pierre Versins's popularizing thousand-page *Encyclopédie de l'utopie, des voyages extraordinaires et de la science fiction* (1972) and Raymond Trousson's *Voyages aux pays de nulle part: Histoire littéraire de la pensée utopique* (1975); Melvin Lasky's *Utopia and Revolution* (1976), Glenn Negley's bibliography *Utopian Literature* (1977), and Frank E. and Fritzie P. Manuel's *Utopian Thought in the Western World* (1979).

Following the fall of the major European communist governments around 1990 the focus shifted significantly. Because the revolutionary and countercultural utopian élan of the 1970s and 1980s had been associated with such neo-Marxist thinkers as Marcuse and Ernst Bloch and because the violence of such "utopian" groups as the Red Brigade in Italy or the Baader-Meinhof gang in Germany had dampened public support for "utopian" ideals, there was a need for reassessment and sober analysis. This was undertaken by such endeavors as *Utopian Studies*, a journal founded in 1990 by the Society for Utopian Studies at the University of Missouri–St. Louis; and the "Collection *Utopies*" edited by Michèle Madonna Desbazeille (Montréal and Paris), which publishes secondary studies (by such scholars as Raymond Trousson, among others) as well as important primary texts. *Pace* Marcuse, Utopia is far from its end in the new millennium.

In light of this historical pattern—social disruption followed by a new utopian vision—it is hardly surprising that the cataclysmic event of World War I generated its own wave of utopian escapes or dystopian (kakotopian, metopian) satires of disillusioned expectations. The Marxist philosopher Ernst Bloch is best known for his late utopian work *The Principle of Hope* (*Das Prinzip Hoffnung*, 1954–57), which was published toward the end of his long life. But his earliest work, written in the midst of World War I when the author was just thirty years old, was explicitly already an analysis of "the spirit of Utopia" (*Geist der Utopie*, 1918; revised edition 1923). In the 1963 afterword Bloch called it a work of "revolutionary Romanticism" and "a *Sturm und Drang* book entrenched and carried out by night, against the War."[15] "That is enough," he exclaims in the prefatory "Objective" composed shortly after World War I. "Now we have to begin. Life has been put in our hands" (1). The young philosopher starts with a condemnation of the war, in which the young had to fall in order to defend "foul, wretched profiteers" while the artists cravenly justified the middlemen and instigators. "The War ended, the Revolution began, and along with the Revolution, doors opened. But of course, they soon shut" (1)—precisely the process described by Döblin in *November 1918*. Observing that Marx had "purified socialist logic of all simple, false, disengaged and abstract enthusiasm" (2), Bloch deplores the stupid pathos of the most recent romantic reactions and "the decline of Western Civilization into animalistic insensibility and irreligious obliteration" (2). The present-day world has no idea of true socialism. "Here, however, in this book, a new beginning is posited, and the unlost heritage takes possession of itself" (3). The preface ends with a Dantean flourish: *Incipit vita nova*.

Having proclaimed the loss of religious faith and of true socialism as well as the inefficacy of Romantic myth, Bloch also takes note of the seduction of the East, which he traces back as far as classical antiquity. "But we also, we most of all, late Western men and women, search further; like a dream the East rises again. Our souls also, sick and empty, move according to an *ex oriente lux*" (110). With "Orient" Bloch does not have in mind anything like the journeys to India undertaken before the war: he means the Judeo-Christian religion. The utopian ideal that he projects is a socialism as purified by Marx and enlightened by the spirit of a religion rid of the centuries-long accumulation of ecclesiastical baggage. "Within such a functional correlation of disburdening and spirit, Marxism and religion, united in the will to the Kingdom, flows the ultimate master system of all the tributaries," the book concludes. "The Soul, the Messiah, and the Apocalypse, which represents the act of awakening in totality, provide the final impulses to do and to know, form the *a priori* of all politics and culture" (278). The details of Bloch's (at this early stage still rather confused) conflation of Marxism and religion are less important here than the fact that he projects his vision in "the spirit of utopia." As a philosopher, Bloch responds to the cataclysm of the war with a utopian vision, but others soon followed with historical surveys and analyses or with cultural-historical and political-scientific approaches.[16]

In 1920 the sociologist and philosopher of culture Hans Freyer discussed "the problem of utopia" in a leading German intellectual journal.[17] Writing at a time that has "enervated man and sucked up all the strength and chivalry from his body and soul" (327), Freyer locates utopia in the context of the ancient chiliastic belief in the "Third Kingdom" (before the National Socialists corrupted the term "das Dritte Reich"). In his effort to define the conceptual form "utopia" deductively, Freyer reviews the humanistic utopia of More, the Catholic utopia of Campanella, and the social utopia of Plato to illustrate his theory of "the birth of the Third Kingdom from the spirit of the objective mind" (326). He concludes that modern man in his quest for "a stronger, healthier, happier humanity" must view his utopianism as "a right of the will" (345). In his 1921 study "Plato and the Greek Utopia" the political theorist Edgar Salin, a follower of Stefan George, maintained that in its course from antiquity to the present three principal forms of utopia emerged: the Greek, the Christian, and the modern rational utopia of progress. Instead of the unrewarding consideration of the genre according to external criteria, he proposed in his preface, utopias should be interpreted from within, from their center—but with a historical view that exposes constant shifts in the meaning and form of the genre. "Every culture thinks and writes from its own needs and its own plenitude, and only from here, uniquely and organically, can the meaning of its works and words be grasped and its form enlivened as determined by its needs [als Not-Wende]."[18]

In 1922 Lewis Mumford opened his provocative Story of Utopias with the claim that "it is our utopias that make the world tolerable to us."[19] "Our fall into a chasm of disillusion" now prompts Mumford to discuss the conception of the "good life" by which modern times have been guided. "In the midst of the tepid and half-hearted discussions that continue to arise out of prohibition laws and strikes and 'peace' conferences let us break in with the injunction to talk about fundamentals—consider Utopia!" (12). Following a review of the classic utopias from Plato to H. G. Wells, Mumford concludes that "[t]he sort of thinking that has created our utopias has placed desire above reality; and so their chief fulfillment has been in the realm of fantasy" (267). It is now urgent, he argues, to bring the utopian ideas into reality—to make eutopias out of utopias. (More's punning expression, he explains, can mean either "no place" [ou-topia] or "good place" [eu-topia].) "If this dissipation of Western Civilization is to cease, the first step in reconstruction is to make over our inner world, and to give our knowledge and our projections a new foundation" (268). We should not be surprised, Mumford suggests prophetically in his concluding pages, "if the foundations of eutopia were established in ruined countries. . . . It would not be altogether without precedent if such a eutopian renascence took place in Germany, in

Austria, in Russia" (306)—regions facing realities which, in its prosperity, modern metropolitan civilization has largely neglected.

The following year J. O. Hertzler opened her *History of Utopian Thought* (1923) with the assertion: "At this moment in the history of the civilized world when social chaos and discontent are everywhere prevalent, men are analyzing social phenomena, groping about for causes, and seeking solutions for these very puzzling complications."[20] Hertzler reviews and analyzes the history of the genre from the Old Testament prophets down to Wells's *A Modern Utopia*. But the work is at the same time a symptom of the lively postwar interest in utopian thought, an interest evident wherever we look. The cultural historian Alfred Doren, lecturing in 1924 at the Warburg Institute, reviewed the history of "wish spaces and wish times," arguing that those two types of utopia amounted to an extension of ancient attitudes: Olympian-rational and daemonic-irrational. He concluded his lecture with the statement that it was intended as a

> modest contribution to the discussion of the problem that at the moment perhaps more than any other dominates the intellectual movement of the leading minds of our time, and indeed minds of quite different focus: the *space-time problem* that was the starting point for Einstein's great intellectual feat, just as it constitutes the center point of profound and witty conversations in Thomas Mann's *The Magic Mountain*.[21]

Paul Tillich's four 1951 lectures on "the political significance of utopia in the life of peoples" were written after and in response to World War II; but the author tells us that "the problem became urgent for my generation when we returned from the first world war to a Germany in which a transcendent-utopian Lutheranism was engaged in fierce conflict with the exclusively immanent utopia of a this-worldly socialism."[22] Tillich, presupposing that utopian thinking is ontologically inherent in humankind, distinguishes between the "horizontal" utopia of socialism, which won the revolution, and the "vertical" or historical attitude of Protestant piety, which rejected the socialist utopia as inauthentic. The conflict between the two alerted his generation to the problem of politics and religion, which was no longer an abstraction but had become urgently concrete. The necessity of reconciling the two positions—bestowing metaphysical meaning upon political progress and adding pragmatism to the exclusively transcendent religious view—resulted thirty years later in his lectures. It was Tillich's rejection of those two "negativities" that generated what he called "the transcendence of utopia" (575) or, in his concluding words, "the spirit of utopia that overcomes utopia"

(578). "The vertical order takes part in the horizontal order: the kingdom of God is realized in what happens in history" (577).

We find yet another possibility of intellectual-scholarly response, finally, when we turn to the major "introduction to the sociology of knowledge" that Karl Mannheim published under the title *Ideology and Utopia* (*Ideologie und Utopie*, 1929). Mannheim contrasts utopia to "ideology," which he defines in the first part of his book as "the total structure of the mind of this epoch or of this group."[23] The utopian state of mind, in contrast, is "incongruous with the state of reality within which it occurs" (173)—in other words, out of step with the ideology of the times. As a sociologist Mannheim distinguishes among four types of utopia: the orgiastic chiliasm of the Anabaptists (190), which leads to modern anarchism; the liberal-humanitarian idea (197), which gives way to the modern skepticism of science; the conservative idea (206), which takes refuge in the past and seeks to spiritualize the present through a romantic reconstruction; and the socialist-communist utopia (215), which becomes disillusioned and renounces any direct participation in the historical process. Contemplating the modern world of the 1920s, Mannheim sees two conflicting tendencies: a utopian trend struggling, in turn, against any ideology that complacently accepts the present. As an analytical sociologist he disclaims any attempt to predict the course of historical reality. He concludes his book, nevertheless, with the concern that the disappearance of utopian vision would create a static state of affairs reducing humankind to no more than a thing.

> We would be faced then with the greatest paradox imaginable, namely, that man, who has achieved the highest degree of rational mastery of existence, left without any ideals, becomes a mere creature of impulses. Thus, after a long tortuous, but heroic development, just at the highest stage of awareness, when history is ceasing to be blind fate, and is becoming more and more man's own creation, with the relinquishment of utopias, man would lose his will to shape history and therewith his ability to understand it. (236)

The impact of World War I affected writers at least as profoundly as it affected the philosophers, historians, political theorists, sociologists, and theologians, impelling them toward fictions that may be viewed as testing grounds for utopian theories. But in almost every case the writers conclude that utopia is not realizable in human history and, even were it so, it would be unsustainable. In the following pages it is my intention to examine three representative examples—and by far the most famous and widely read—among the scores of literary utopias that arose in specific response to the war[24] and that illustrate respectively the three dimensions in which literary utopias have traditionally been set.[25]

The Utopia of Space-Time: H. G. Wells's *Men Like Gods*

When H. G. Wells published *Men Like Gods* (1923) he was one of the most renowned men of letters in the English-speaking world. In his late fifties and the author of several enormously popular scientific romances, he had also written scores of influential essays on a variety of social-political-cultural issues along with several successful novels of ideas, and he had recently brought out his *Outline of History* (1920), which was to sell over two million copies during the 1920s and become perhaps his most famous work. In 1941 George Orwell speculated in an otherwise highly critical essay that "[t]hinking people who were born about the beginning of this century are in some sense Wells's own creation.... I doubt whether anyone who was writing books between 1900 and 1920, at any rate in the English language, influenced the young so much. The minds of all of us, and therefore the physical world, would be perceptibly different if Wells had never existed."[26] Despite the disparagement of many critics since Wells's notorious dispute with Henry James, his works have been admired by writers from Jorge Luis Borges to David Lodge.[27] And since the centenary of 1966 his writings have received a fairer critical appraisal. But his beginnings were hardly auspicious.

Herbert George Wells (1866–1946), the son of a failing shopkeeper and a housekeeper-lady's maid who actually supported the family, had a highly irregular education with several false "starts," which he depicted vividly in his autobiography. His mother, "a very determined little woman," thought that "to wear a black coat and tie behind a counter was the best of all possible lots attainable by man—at any rate by man at our social level." "Almost as unquestioning as her belief in Our Father and Our Saviour," he continues, "was her belief in drapers."[28] From childhood on, accordingly, she destined her youngest son for a life of stockkeeping, tidying, and measuring cloth. He was first sent to Thomas Morley's Commercial Academy near his home in Bromley, Kent, whose principal objective was the training of good clerks, and at age thirteen began the first in a series of draper's apprenticeships. Fortunately, the bright and energetic boy had early, as the result of a lengthy convalescence from a broken leg, formed the habit of voracious reading, a habit that he pursued during hours stolen from his clerking and, after 1880, with books borrowed from the extensive library in the manor house where his mother had become housekeeper. After several more "starts" at other schools and jobs, Wells's intellectual abilities began to manifest themselves. His strong examinations gained him a scholarship at the Normal School of Science in South Kensington, where from 1884 to 1887 he had the good fortune to study biology under Thomas Huxley. His academic success enabled him to obtain teaching positions, first in North Wales and then in London, where in 1890 he earned his bachelor of science. The ambitious and energetic young man began writing articles on scientific topics, published a *Textbook of Biology* (1893), and in 1895 brought out four books, including *The Time Machine*, the success of which enabled him to embark on the career which soon made him into one of England's, and indeed Europe's, best-known writers.

Wells's religious development followed a course familiar from many other late nineteenth-century examples. His mother was Low Church and believed in "God's Fatherhood" and "a hell of eternal torment" (29). Her son, however, "a prodigy of Early Impiety," lost his faith by the time he was eleven or twelve—as usual through a trivial incident: "a dream of Hell so preposterous that it blasted that undesirable resort out of my mind for ever" (45). This early revolt against "the God of Hell in his most Protestant form" developed gradually, by the time of Wells's early adolescence, into "a real fear of Christianity" (128–29). Wells's hostility toward the church and its enormous authority implied no contempt for religion as such. Indeed, "there is no author who has a more religious faith," Rebecca West shrewdly perceived in 1912.[29] This respect for religion, including Jesus the man and the teacher, constitutes one of the central themes in Wells's *Outline of History*, which draws on the ideas of Herbert Spencer (*Evolution of the Idea of God*) and James G. Frazer (*The Golden Bough*). "Religion is something that has grown up with and through human association. God has been and is still being discovered by man.... It is a part, a necessary and central part, of the history of man to describe the dawn and development of his religious ideas and their influence upon his activities."[30]

Wells was as powerfully affected by World War I as were most of his thoughtful contemporaries. "No intelligent brain that passed through the experience of the Great War emerged without being profoundly changed," he wrote in his *Experiment in Autobiography*. But the experience was not without its ambiguities. "To me, as to most people, it was a revelation of the profound instability of the social order. It was also a revelation of the possibilities of fundamental reorganization that were now open to mankind—and of certain extraordinary weaknesses in the collective mentality" (569). This shattering war experience had two surprising effects.

First, it resulted in a turn to God that astonished his friends and the readers who knew him as the outspoken agnostic and advocate of modern science. He first elaborated the record of his mental phases—the moving account of his vacillating adjustment to the wholly unanticipated phenomenon of war—in the remarkable autobiographical novel *Mr. Britling Sees It Through* (1916), which was, Wells wrote in his autobiography, "not so much a representation of myself as of my type and class," an enterprise whose insight and success are indicated by the huge popularity of the book. Wells sought "to give not only the astonishment and the sense of tragic disillusionment in a civilized mind as the cruel facts of war rose steadily to dominate everything else in life, but also the passionate desire to find some immediate reassurance amidst that whirlwind of disaster" (573). For Mr. Britling, a successful writer and intellectual who represents the educated classes in England, that reassurance was God and a turn to religion. Wells explained his views more philosophically in *God the Invisible King* (1917).

> This book sets out as forcibly and exactly as possible the religious belief of the writer. That belief is not orthodox Christianity; it is not, indeed, Christianity at all; its core nevertheless is a profound belief in a personal and intimate God. . . . The writer will be found to be sympathetic with all sincere religious feeling.[31]

Wells later confessed in his autobiography that he could not "disentangle now, perhaps at no time could I have disentangled, what was simple and direct in this theocratic phase in my life, from what was—*politic*." "At its most artificial my religiosity was a flaming heresy and not a time-serving compromise. I never came nearer to Christianity than Manicheism." He promptly wrote two more works—*Joan and Peter* (1918) and *The Undying Fire* (1919)—to respond to the public shock at his apparent reversion and to clarify his own position of deified humanism. "After *The Undying Fire*, God as a character disappears from my work, except for a brief undignified appearance . . . in *The Secret Places of the Heart* (1922)" (575–76). Ten years later, in *What Are We to Do with Our Lives* (1932) Wells made "the most explicit renunciation and apology" for what he called his phase of "terminological disingenuousness," wishing, he confesses in his autobiography, that he had never fallen into it (578).

Wells's brief "theological excursion" during the war years constituted a reconversion experience not unlike those portrayed earlier by such writers as Tolstoy and Martin du Gard. In retrospect we understand that his early experiments in utopian fiction, notably *A Modern Utopia* (1905), amounted to efforts to find surrogates for the lost religious faith of his childhood. If that is the case, then *Men Like Gods* can be seen mutatis mutandis as a similar resort following the disenchanted resurgence of faith in the years 1916–19. But before we can understand the change that has taken place, we need to consider the second result of the war experience.

Wells's initially optimistic belief that the war would also open the way to a "fundamental reorganization" of human potentialities was soon disappointed by the realities of the postwar years, as they were simultaneously being experienced in Germany by Alfred Döblin and in France by Martin du Gard. In 1918, Wells wrote in his 1926 preface to *The Outline of History*, many reasons moved him to attempt a world history.

> It was the last, the weariest, most disillusioned year of the great war. Everywhere there were unwonted privations; everywhere there was mourning. The tale of the dead and mutilated had mounted to many millions. Men felt they had come to a crisis in the world's affairs. They were too weary and heart-sick to consider complicated possibilities. They were not sure whether they were facing a disaster to civilization or the inauguration of a new phase of human association; they saw things with the simplicity of such flat alternatives, and they clung to hope. (1)

But hope soon gave way to despair in Wells's mind. "My awakening to the realities of the pseudo-settlement of 1919 was fairly rapid," he confessed in his *Experiment in Autobiography*. "At first I found it difficult to express my indignant astonishment at the simulacrum of a Peace League that was being thrust upon Europe." He was embarrassed to find that many of his friends and associates were content with this "powerless pedantic bit of stage scenery" (611). And the world leaders gave little reason for confidence. Woodrow Wilson, upon whom Wells had once pinned his hopes, turned out to be "essentially ill-informed, narrowly limited to an old-fashioned American conception of history, self-confident and profoundly self-righteous" (604). The final chapter of *The Outline of History*, in a section headed "Moral Disorder Caused by the War," begins with the statement:

> The world of the Western European civilizations in the four or five years that followed the end of the Great War was like a man who has had some very vital surgical operation very roughly performed, and who is not yet sure whether he can now go on living or whether he has not been so profoundly shocked and injured that he will presently fall down and die. It was a world dazed and stunned. . . . There was a universal hunger for

peace, a universal desire for the lost liberty and prosperity of pre-war
times, without any power of will to achieve and secure these things.
(1050)

Wells's initial enthusiasm for the League of Nations, frustrated by the realities of the 1919 agreements, gave way to his grand project for a world state
outlined at the end of his book.

The utopian dreams that had once motivated Wells and filled him with
hope now yielded to a disillusioned sense of realism. This, I believe, is the
spirit in which we must read *Men Like Gods*—not as another utopia like
A Modern Utopia but as a farewell to utopia. As Wells wrote at the end
of his *Experiment in Autobiography*, "The change from egoism to a larger
life is consequently now entirely a change of perspective; it can no longer
be a facile rejection of primary conditions and a jump into 'another world'
altogether. It is still an escape from first-hand egoism and immediacy, but
it is no longer an escape from fact" (706). While not yet a dystopia or anti-
utopia, the novel is anything but what George Orwell has called his "most
characteristic" utopia.[32] Wells acknowledges in this work that the visions
he advanced so confidently prior to World War I are in fact not capable of
realization in this world, where we must simply make do with as much
courage and realism as we can muster.[33] In this sense the novel constitutes
"an extended allegory on the theme of loss of innocence."[34] Because this
quality was not recognized and the text was often read superficially, with
no appreciation of its mythic patterns and rich intertextuality, the novel
was long dismissed by critics as simply a late and undistinguished utopia.[35]

The utopian kingdom depicted in *Men Like Gods* is often loosely but mistakenly understood as being our own world some three thousand years hence:
a simple projection, in other words—not spatial onto another planet, as in
A Modern Utopia, but temporal. But repeatedly in the course of the novel
Wells makes it clear that he has in mind another universe altogether. "We
think in terms of a space in which the space and time system, in terms of
which you think, is only a specialized case," a wise old Utopian tells Mr.
Barnstaple in virtually Einsteinean language.[36] "Your universe and ours are
two out of a great number of gravitation-time universes, which are translated together through the inexhaustible infinitude of God. They are similar
throughout, but they are identical in nothing" (295). This planet of Utopia
in its other-universe, with its controlled population of two hundred and

fifty million, emerged from its "Last Age of Confusion"—a historical period roughly equivalent to the early twentieth century in Europe—some three thousand years earlier (66). "Utopia has no parliaments, no politics, no private wealth, no business competition, no police nor prisons, no lunatics, no defectives nor cripples.... There is no rule nor government needed by adult Utopians because all the rule and government they need they have had in childhood and youth" (80). *Our education is our government,*" a Utopian proclaims. (Wells has moved appreciably beyond his *Modern Utopia* of 1905, which still required a superior class of Samurai to run things.) In this Utopia contagious diseases have been eradicated, along with many internal and external parasites of man and animals. There has been "a great cleansing of the world from noxious insects, from weeds and vermin and hostile beasts" (92). The Utopians communicate with one another not through language but by the direct projection of thoughts, using sound only for poetry and in moments of emotion, but not for the transmission of ideas. "When I think to you, the thought, *so far as it finds corresponding ideas and suitable words in your mind,* is reflected in your mind" (59). The Utopians know no worship, but they follow the ethical teachings of a Jesus-like prophet and man of great poetic power who lived long ago and died a painful death on a wheel, which for a time in their early history was turned into a symbol and exploited by cunning and aggressive demagogues (72–75). Instead of law and religion, the Utopians are governed by Five Principles of Liberty, which all follow of their free will (272). Yet this Utopia, far from settling into a state of stasis, is marching ahead at a terrifying pace. "He had always thought of Utopia as a tranquillity with everything settled for good. Even today it seemed tranquil under that level haze, but he knew that this quiet was the steadiness of a mill-race, which seems almost motionless in its quiet onrush" (171). "New powers and possibilities intoxicated the imagination of the race"—most exciting among them the idea that the limitations of space were breaking down as it became practically possible to pass from the planet Utopia to "other points in its universe of origin" (293). It is in the course of such an experiment that twelve Earthlings arrive in Utopia on a morning in July 1921.

This intrusion sets in motion the plot of *Men Like Gods.* The story is narrated from the point of view of Mr. Alfred Barnstaple, a journalist for the London *Liberal,* intelligent, curious, apolitical, antinationalist, and anti-imperialist, who has lately become so utterly disenchanted with postwar liberalism and with the world at large that he has sunk into a state of depression from which only a prolonged holiday—from work, from his family, and from the news—can redeem him. "Everywhere there was conflict, everywhere unreason; seven-eighths of the world seemed to be sinking down towards chronic disorder and social dissolution" (5). Mr. Barnstaple's gloomy meditations sound very much like Wells's thoughts in his *Experiment in Autobiography* and *Outline of History*. "At times during the world agony of the great war it had seemed that Utopia drew near to earth. The black clouds and smoke of these dark years had been shot with the light of strange hopes, with the promise of a world reborn. But the nationalists, financiers, priests and patriots had brought all those hopes to nothing" (232).

As Mr. Barnstaple drives out of London toward Maidenhead in his little yellow roadster, in sight of Windsor Castle on the left, he is passed by two speeding vehicles. Rounding the next curve, he is astonished to see neither vehicle on the clear road ahead of him. Suddenly his own car seems to strike some invisible object and he hears a sound like the snapping of a lute string.[37] When he stops and recovers from his astonishment, he finds himself in another place altogether—in the universe that turns out to be Utopia. It is later explained that two brilliant young Utopian scientists were performing experiments, "rotating some of our matter out of and then back into our universe" (295). By sheer accident Mr. Barnstaple's car along with the other two vehicles had fallen into the other universe, killing the two Utopians in the process.

The action, which lasts only three days, involves the futile attempt of some of the Earthlings to take over Utopia. While Mr. Barnstaple regards Utopia as the fulfillment of all his dreams, the others, incited by the militant Secretary of State for War Rupert Catskill (a caricature based on Winston Churchill) and the narrow-minded priest Father Amerton, are unable to think beyond their human prejudices.[38] Father Amerton, an ugly representative of orthodox Christianity, fulminates against the "hell of unbridled indulgence" that he sees in the physical grace of the naked Utopians and their culture, which has discarded such social bonds as marriage (88). Mr. Catskill, more dialectically, acknowledges the beauty and order of Utopia but assumes that the gains were accompanied by losses. "You have been getting away from conflicts and distresses," he tells his Utopian hosts. "Have you not also been getting away from the living and quivering realities of life?" (99). He admires their security but sees in it an "autumnal glory" and "decadence" and argues that degeneration is inevitable.

When some of the Utopians fall ill, defenseless against the infections that the Earthlings have brought with them, the English-American-French intruders are removed into temporary isolation on a remote Quarantine Crag, where they plot to seize some of the Utopians and hold them hostage—an occasion that offers the author an opportunity to comment on disputes like those that undermined the League of Nations. "With a mixture of pity and derision and anger, Mr. Barnstaple listened to this little band of lost human beings . . . growing more and more fierce and keen in a dispute over the claims of their three nations to 'dominate' Utopia, claims based entirely upon greeds and misconceptions" (195). "All the use these Earthlings had had for Utopia was to turn it back as speedily as possible to the aggressions, subjugations, cruelties and disorders of the Age of Confusion to which they belonged" (23). Mr. Barnstaple tries to warn the Utopians, two of whom are killed by the Earthlings' pistols. When his fellow Earthlings decide to execute Mr. Barnstaple for "treason," he makes a daring escape down the mountainside. He watches from below as the Utopians send the top of Quarantine Crag spinning off into another dimension from which some of the Earthlings—Catskill and Father Amerton among them—are eventually allowed to return to earth with their memories of Utopia totally erased.

Mr. Barnstaple is permitted to remain for a few more weeks in Utopia, to be instructed in its history, its ways, and its plans for the future. Loving Utopia, he is "passionately anxious to become a part of it" yet realizes that he is still "a strange and discordant intruder" (115). Indeed, "toward such a world as this Utopia Mr. Barnstaple had been striving weakly all his life" (310). But he comes to understand that he can serve Utopia best by returning to Earth, by going back to "our own disordered world—with knowledge, with hope and help, missionaries of a new order" (198). When Mr. Barnstaple is returned to Earth, to the very spot where, a few weeks earlier, he had fallen through a crack in space-time into Utopia, the world has not changed— indeed, the reports in the newspapers are predictably similar—but he is a changed man whose difference is evident, to the astonishment of Mrs. Barnstaple, in the fact that he has grown taller, lost his stoop, and displays a new assurance and determination. He gives up his job at *The Liberal,* telling his wife that "I don't want a safe job now. I can do better. There's other work before me" (325)—and thereby exemplifying the meaning implicit in his name (etymologically *barn-staple* suggests burning or destroying stability). The book ends at this point with no suggestion that dramatic changes are going to take place. Mr. Barnstaple intends to begin his reforms modestly at home, seeing to it "that his sons took a livelier interest in politics and science and were not so completely engulfed in the trivialities of suburban life. . . . They were living trivially in the shadow of one great catastrophe and with no security against another; they were living in a world of weak waste and shabby insufficiency" (289–90). Indeed, Mr. Barnstaple's plan for a utopia on earth sounds very much like Wells's oft-cited admonition at the end of his *Outline of History:* "Human history becomes more and more a race between education and catastrophe" (1114).

Various hints suggest that, in the fiction of the book, Utopia is an extended dream sustained by Mr. Barnstaple during the weeks of his holiday and nourished by sights and memories. "Surely this world it was, or a world the very fellow of it, that had lain deep beneath the thoughts and dreams of thousands of sane and troubled men and women in the world of disorder from which he had come" (122), he thinks shortly after his arrival in Utopia. At the end he tells his wife that he spent his holiday wandering and dreaming, "lost in a day-dream" (324). In any case, the Utopia he encounters is a place that humanity as we know it can never attain but only move toward in almost imperceptible increments. As the Earthlings' plot demonstrates, human nature has a conservative and self-serving, even self-destructive tendency that resists attempts at progress and change. *Men Like Gods*, in sum, posits an ideal toward which humanity can strive, but the circumstances— the fact that Mr. Barnstaple must return to earth and its realities and that the other Earthlings will be sent back with no memory of Utopia whatsoever— make it clear that Wells has no expectation that Utopia will ever be realized in our world. Mr. Barnstaple's physical descent from Utopia symbolizes "his descent from flights of the imagination to the uncomfortable world of reality."[39] For that reason gaps occur in the communication between the Utopians and the Earthlings—gaps that puzzle the Earthlings, who lack the concepts to understand some of the thoughts of this advanced civilization. Disillusioned by the events of World War I, Wells projected his vision into an otherworld altogether beyond human time and space. Unlike *A Modern Utopia*, it is intended not as the plan for an attainable future but as a critique of the present.[40]

The Utopia of Time: Yevgeny Zamiatin's *We*

"All of our literature is still permeated by the poisons of war," Yevgeny Zamiatin observed in 1926. "It is built on hatred—on class hatred, its components, its surrogates."[41] In an essay on H. G. Wells, Zamiatin cites the English author's prescience: "The picture of the coming world war and the unprecedented world change connected with it evidently haunted Wells continually"[42]—changes whose effects in Russia Zamiatin detailed in numerous critical essays in the immediate aftermath of the war. For the Russian writer, to be sure, "war" meant not simply or even principally the Great War that shattered Western European society but also the revolutions of 1917 that radically transformed his motherland. Years later (1936) he recalled that "[t]he huge ship of Russia had been torn from the shore by the storm and carried off into the unknown."[43] Above all, war and revolution dehumanized the individual human being. "Wars, imperialist and civil, have turned man into material for warfare, into a number, a cipher."[44] These words, written in 1919–20, foreshadowed the reduction of men and women to ciphers or "numbers" in his futuristic novel *We,* which he conceived just at that time.

Yevgeny Ivanovich Zamiatin (1884–1937) was not sustained by any religious faith in the turmoil of war and revolution. The son of a Russian Orthodox parish priest in the provincial town of Lebedyan, situated on the River Don some two hundred miles south of Moscow, he presumably received a sound religious education.[45] But since Zamiatin was conspicuously reserved about autobiographical facts, we must extrapolate from the frequent religious allusions in his writings—not just to stories of the Bible but also to the lives of the saints. In any case, his period of youthful faith was of no great duration. "The Diogenes lamp of skepticism was lit for me at the age of twelve," Zamiatin notes in one of his three brief autobiographical sketches. (The trivial incident that shattered his faith reminds us of the childhood experiences portrayed by Gosse, Martin du Gard, and Hesse. When the twelve-year-old had his eye blackened in a fight, he prayed for a miracle—for the shiner to disappear. "The miracle did not take place. I began to wonder.")[46] Zamiatin appears to be fascinated by questions of faith in the lives of other writers. When he reminds us that "Chekhov had lost the God of the church when still a very young man" because of "the fear of God" and "the obligatory performance of prayers and ritual duties" to which he had been forced as a child, it sounds very much as though he were recapitulating his own experiences.[47] In his essay on H. G. Wells, after observing that "the religion of the modern city is precise science," Zamiatin wonders at Wells's passing relapse into faith during World War I. "The socialist, the mathematician, the chemist, the automobile driver, and the airplane pilot suddenly begins to speak of God."[48]

In 1902 Zamiatin left the provinces, which he found intolerably stultifying and satirized ruthlessly in his early stories, and enrolled at the Polytechnic Institute in St. Petersburg to study naval engineering. There he joined the Bolshevik party and, in the course of a trip to the Near East, witnessed the *Potemkin* mutiny in Odessa, which he later described in the first-person account "Three Days" (1914). "In those years, being a Bolshevik meant following the line of greatest resistance, and I was a Bolshevik at that time."[49] His biographers are no doubt correct when they conjecture that Zamiatin's decision to join the party was motivated less by political conviction than by a spirit of youthful rebellion and a craving for excitement.[50] In any case, in 1905 he was arrested, beaten, jailed for several months, and then exiled to his hometown. Zamiatin's active participation in the party was short-lived: by 1908—he had meanwhile returned illegally to St. Petersburg—when he graduated with a degree in naval architecture and was appointed as a lecturer at the Polytechnic Institute, Zamiatin appears to have renounced his party membership and revolutionary activities.[51] In 1911 he was exiled for a second time on the old charges, to the village of Lachta on the Gulf of Finland—an exile, he noted wryly, to which he owed his career as a writer, for it was during those two years of isolation that he wrote the short satirical novel *A Provincial Tale* (1913), which brought him his first wide recognition.[52]

Following the general amnesty of 1913, Zamiatin returned to St. Petersburg where he continued writing while undertaking frequent trips across Russia on various shipbuilding commissions. In 1916 he was sent to England by the government to supervise the construction of Russian icebreakers. Here, apart from a brief earlier trip to Germany, he was exposed for the first time to Western capitalist culture and got a taste of the war when the Germans dropped bombs from zeppelins and airplanes. But when the revolution broke out in Russia and the czar abdicated, Zamiatin could no longer bear to remain in England. Although he got back in time to witness the October Revolution, he regretted that he had missed the more exciting February uprising. "This is the same as never having been in love and waking up one morning already married for ten years or so."[53]

Following his return to what was now called Petrograd, Zamiatin lived through "the merry eerie winter of 1917–18, when everything broke from its moorings and floated off somewhere into the unknown."[54] He resumed his teaching at the Polytechnic Institute but gave up technical work in favor of the literary life of the capital. Associated with the intellectual group known as the Scythians, who shared his romantic view of revolution, and later with the literary circle styling themselves Serapion Brothers, Zamiatin wrote political fables and critical essays, worked on the council of the House of Writers, was active in the Union of Practitioners of Imaginative Literature, helped to organize the All-Russian Union of Writers, served on the editorial board of the World Literature Publishing House, lectured on translation, taught writing courses, and became one of the most influential figures in postrevolutionary Russian literature. Yet despite all his semi-official activity as a fellow traveler, Zamiatin was disappointed in the political developments of the young Soviet Union. Recalling his romantic attraction to the Revolution of 1905, he again resorted to erotic metaphors. "The Revolution was not yet a lawful wife who jealously guarded her legal monopoly on love. The Revolution was a young, fiery-eyed mistress, and I was in love with the Revolution."[55] Now that the revolution had subsided,

Zamiatin again followed "the line of greatest resistance" by opposing a Bolshevik party that had renounced revolution and was settling comfortably into intellectual dogmatism and political authoritarianism. In 1919, long before it had become "the God that failed," he defined communism as the new religion, analyzing its stages of development in Christian terms as *prophetic, apostolic,* and *ecclesiastical,* when the belief has conquered on the *earthly* plane—like Bolshevism after the 1917 revolution.[56] At the same time, the engineer Zamiatin tended to see society in scientific terms of "energy" and "entropy." "Revolution is everywhere in everything. It is infinite.... It is a cosmic, universal law—like the laws of the conservation of energy and of the dissipation of energy (entropy)."[57] When society has lapsed into lethargy, bureaucracy, and dogmatism, it has succumbed to entropy.

His most conspicuous images for the path of energy and resistance are the Scythian, Satan, and the heretic. His essay "Scythians?" (1918) praises the "solitary, savage horseman" galloping across the steppes, hair streaming in the wind—the "eternal nomad" who loves nothing but "freedom, solitude, his horse, the wide expanse of the steppe."[58] The true revolutionary of 1905 was a Scythian. But now "it is bitter to see the Scythian bow bound to service, the centaurs in stables, freemen marching to the sounds of a band" (21–22). The Scythian is a spiritual revolutionary who works only for the distant future. "Hence to him there is one way—Golgotha—and no other, and one conceivable victory—to be crucified—and no other" (22). For Zamiatin, who like other lapsed Christians such as H. G. Wells admired Jesus Christ and had nothing but contempt for institutional Christianity, the true victor is Christ crucified. "Christ victorious in practical terms is the grand inquisitor" (22).

> The lot of the true Scythian is the thorns of the vanquished. His faith is heresy. His destiny is the destiny of Ahasuerus. His work is not for the near but for the distant future. And this work has at all times, under the laws of all the monarchies and republics, including the Soviet republic, been rewarded only by a lodging at government expense—prison. (23)

The victorious October Revolution acclaimed in official sources has not escaped the general law of entropy: "it has turned philistine." "The world is kept alive only by heretics," he maintained.

> Our symbol of faith is heresy: tomorrow is inevitably heresy to today, which has turned into a pillar of salt, and to yesterday, which has scattered to dust. Today denies yesterday, but is a denial of denial tomorrow.

> This is the constant dialectic path which in a grandiose parabola sweeps
> the world into infinity. Yesterday, the thesis; today, the antithesis; and
> tomorrow, the synthesis.[59]

But "the cunning bringer of dissonance, the teacher of doubt, Satan, has
been forever banished from the shining mansions," Zamiatin wrote in an
essay satirically entitled "Paradise" (1921).[60] Over and over again he lam-
poons contemporary Soviet writers for allowing themselves to be reduced
to eulogists of the Bolshevik dogma. "I am afraid that we shall have no genuine literature until we cure ourselves of this new brand of Catholicism,
which is as fearful as the old of every heretical word."[61] It is against this
philistinism, this dogmatism, this false "paradise," that the disenchanted
romantic revolutionary Zamiatin turned his satirical "Satanic" wrath in his
tragic anti-utopian novel *We,* where we again encounter all the ideas and
images familiar from his polemical essays.

We (Russian *My*) can be seen as an intermediate stage between the early
utopias of H. G. Wells and the later dystopian visions of Aldous Huxley's
Brave New World (1932) and George Orwell's *1984* (1948).[62] Zamiatin had
a specialist's familiarity with Wells's works. As a member of the editorial
board of the World Literature Publishing House, he edited Russian translations of French and English books, including (from 1919 on) various volumes
by the English writer and from 1924 to 1926 a twelve-volume edition of
Wells's collected works.[63] His 1922 essay on Wells cites twenty-nine novels
in addition to four volumes of fantastic tales and others works of a general
nature, all of which he appears to have read. "I know of no English writer
more of today, more contemporary than Wells," he asserts.[64] His description of the two principal characteristics of Wells's "sociofantastic novels"
essentially defines his own *We:* "the element of social satire and the element of science" (287). (Zamiatin denies that Wells's early novels are utopias
in the classic sense—the depiction of an ideal society with almost no plot
dynamics—arguing that *Men Like Gods,* written in 1922 "when the nations
of Europe have gradually begun to heal the cruel wounds of the World War,"
is his only utopia [266, 286].) Whereas Huxley and Orwell satirized political
conditions that actually existed in their day—respectively, the consumer society of capitalism and Soviet dictatorship—Zamiatin, writing his Wellsian
sociofantasy in 1920–21 before Bolshevism had degenerated into Stalinism,

was expressing his general antipathy toward every kind of depersonalizing totalitarian state, not explicitly fascist or communist ones.

Like Plato's republic and the utopias of More, Campanella, and others, Zamiatin's One State is not a total universe but an artificial enclave, protected from the elements by a glass dome and bounded by a great Green Wall, which "isolated our perfect mechanical world from the irrational, hideous world of trees, birds, animals."[65] In this thirtieth-century polity with its geometrical streets and glass houses, which arose long after the Two Hundred Years' War destroyed the ancient world of the twentieth century along with most of humankind, the citizens are identified not by names but by a system of letters and numerals: consonants and odd numbers for the men, vowels and even numbers for the women. Their depersonalization is signaled by the "We" of the title, the collective pronoun that governs all thinking and believing.

> And so, we have the scales: on the one side, a gram, on the other a ton; on one side "I," on the other "We," the One State. Is it not clear, then, that to assume that the "I" can have some "rights" in relation to the State is exactly like assuming that a gram can balance the scale against the ton? (102)

The smooth-skinned "numbers," dressed in identical gray-blue "unifs"— the color representing rationality according to Zamiatin's color imagery[66]— live according to a Table of Hours coordinated by the clock on the Great Accumulator Tower and the timepieces built into their identification tags. The Table of Hours strictly regulates their days according to the principles of Taylor, "unquestionably the greatest genius of the ancients" (31; Zamiatin is referring to Frederick Winslow Taylor [1856–1915], whose time-and-motion theories for the rational organization of labor were recommended for the Soviet Union by Lenin).[67] "Every morning, with six-wheeled precision, at the same hour and the same moment, we—millions of us—get up as one. At the same hour, in million-headed unison, we start work; and in million-headed unison we end it" (12–13). Their food consists of artificial petroleum-based substitutes. Twice a day—from sixteen to seventeen (4:00 to 5:00 p.m.) and again from twenty-one to twenty-two—the social organism breaks up into separate cells for Personal Hours. At these hours the shades may be lowered in the rooms for various private occupations, including sex—"love" has been outlawed as an individualizing factor destructive of true community— scheduled on "sexual days" by partners with whom they are "registered."

The numbers get all their news from the *One State Gazette,* sing Hymns to the One State, and recite Daily Odes to the god-like Benefactor, who is annually and ritually reelected by unanimous vote. "Our gods are here, below, with us—in the office, the kitchen, the workshop, the toilet; the gods have become like us. Ergo, we have become as gods" (61)—a refrain that appears to echo ironically the title of H. G. Wells's novel (with which Zamiatin was somehow familiar as early as 1922). At this point in their history, in the thirtieth century, One State is about to complete the construction of a spaceship named the *Integral,* by means of which they plan to "subjugate the unknown beings on other planets, who may still be living in the primitive condition of freedom, to the beneficent yoke of reason" (3) and "to make your life as divinely rational and precise as ours" (61). In a poem composed to celebrate the *Integral* the poet R-13 recalls Adam and Eve: "Those two, in paradise, were given a choice: happiness without freedom, or freedom without happiness. There was no third alternative. Those idiots chose freedom, and what came of it?" (55). The numbers of One State are once again as innocent and simple-hearted as Adam and Eve because they have renounced freedom with its discontents for the unclouded bliss of the new paradise.

In their thought and lives, the numbers ignore the hairy beings who inhabit the lush, untamed world outside the Green Wall. They do not realize that a group of revolutionaries calling themselves Mephis (abbreviated from Mephistopheles, the representative of Satanic freedom) are planning an insurrection to break down the Wall, to let the wind blow free across the earth, and to prevent the One State from extending its totalitarianizing walls to other worlds (137).

The story, which covers a period of four months preceding the test launch of the spaceship, is told in the form of forty journal entries by D-503, a thirty-two-year-old mathematician and chief engineer of the *Integral,* who begins his account initially for inclusion in the ship's cargo as a record for his "ancestors, or for beings similar to his primitive remote ancestors" (22), among whom the spaceship may land. (He is incapable of imagining that other societies could be anything other than inferior to, or more antiquated than, his own.) When we first meet him, D-503 is a totally committed supporter of "the mathematically perfect life of the One State" (4), a man whose mind abhors nothing more than the irrationality of $\sqrt{-1}$, whose physical needs are satisfied by scheduled visits of the plump, rosy O-90, and whose only personal embarrassment is caused by his conspicuously hairy hands, which suggest a disquietingly atavistic element in his character.

The action is triggered when D-503 meets the seductive, even Satanic I-330—she wears black clothing, smokes and drinks alcohol (both forbidden by the State), and plays "ancient" music on the piano—who turns out to be a member of the insurgents and approaches him in order to sabotage the *Integral* project. As a result of his obsession with I-330, D-503 for the first time in his life sees himself in the mirror as an individual, an "I." After they have slept together—symbolically and illegally, in the historical museum called the Ancient House—he thinks of himself, in one of the biblical images that permeate the novel, as a fallen angel (66). Unable to concentrate properly on his work or to deal rationally with the wholly new experience of passion and jealousy, D-503 goes to the Medical Office, where he is diagnosed as being seriously ill. "Apparently, you have developed a soul" (79). Because the affliction is incurable and can be extirpated only by surgery and because an epidemic is feared—indeed, it has already spread to O-90, who wants a child by D-503, and to U, the controller in his building who, out of her unrequited love for him, betrays the revolution—the rulers soon come up with the plan of a Great Operation to cauterize the imagination, an operation to which all numbers are expected to submit out of loyalty to the State.

At this point matters move rapidly. Unheard-of disturbances mar the annual Unanimity Day: during the ritual vote for the great Benefactor, which normally culminates in a unanimous acclamation, thousands of hands are raised in opposition, whereupon the Guardians arrest many of the dissenters. The next day signs appear around the city bearing the inscription MEPHI. At their next rendezvous in the Ancient House, I-330 conducts D-503 through a secret underground passage beyond the Wall into the world outside where for the first time he sees trees, grass, the unfiltered sun, rustling nature, and "people" of various hues, naked and covered with fur. It is only when I-330 ascends the "bare, skull-like rock" to address the assembly—the association with Golgotha thrusts itself upon us, foreshadowing her eventual sacrificial death—that D-503 realizes she is a leader of the Mephis. In the exultation of the moment he feels himself to be an "I, a separate entity, a world. I had ceased to be a component, as I had been, and became a unit" (138).

The next day he informs I-330 that he wants to leave everything behind and to flee with her beyond the Wall into the world outside. She refuses, explaining that the primitive people outside are the irrational half of human nature which the rational half within the Wall has rejected and separated, like H_2 and O. "In order to get H_2O—oceans, waterfalls, waves, storms—the two halves must unite" (143). This union can take place only if the Wall is broken down. "There are two forces in the world," she continues, "entropy and energy. One leads to blissful quietude, to happy equilibrium; the other, to destruction of equilibrium, to tormentingly endless movement. Entropy was worshiped as God by our—or, rather, your—ancestors, the Christians"

(144). She and the Mephis belong to the anti-Christians. (By now we have encountered all the images familiar from Zamiatin's other writings.) In a subsequent conversation the appalled D-503 objects that she is planning revolution although "our revolution was the final one. And there can be no others" (152). But I-330—a Hegelian like Zamiatin himself—reminds him, the mathematician, that the number of numbers is infinite. If there can be no final number, "[t]hen how can there be a final revolution? There is no final one; revolutions are infinite" (152). (This nonorthodox view of revolution, among other things, confirmed Zamiatin's reputation as an antisocialist.)

A few days later, when the *Integral* is taken for a test flight, I-330 and other Mephis are smuggled aboard in an attempt, with D-503's collaboration, to take over the spaceship and to land it somewhere beyond the Wall. But their plan has been betrayed (by U) to the Guardians, who seize control and force the ship back to its launching pad within the Wall. D-503 is summoned into the presence of the Benefactor, whose bald head gives him an uncanny resemblance to Lenin and who tries to persuade him that he has been manipulated by I-330. At this point, still uncertain, D-503 resists and meets I-330 again for a final passionate embrace. A few days later he is seized by the Guardians and taken to an auditorium for the Great Operation, which reduces him once again to an unthinking obedient number, whereupon he goes back to the Benefactor and betrays everything he knows about "the enemies of happiness" (203). That evening he watches as I-330 is tortured in a vacuum bell; the next day she will be executed along with other insurgents in the Benefactor's special machine, which kills by dissolving human matter into a puddle of pure water. In his final entry D-503 reports that "we have succeeded in erecting a temporary barrier of high-voltage waves. And I hope that we shall conquer. More than that—I am certain we shall conquer. Because Reason must prevail" (204). Certainly D-503 has been reduced by his "fantasiectomy" to a mindless cog in the great machine of the One State. But the ending leaves no assurance that reason and entropy will prevail. O-90, who out of her love for D-503 became unlawfully pregnant with their child, has escaped into the world outside, where she will presumably bring up their child in freedom. And the Wall has been breached; fighting goes on in the western part of the State; air is blowing through the city—the air that may possibly bring with it the fresh breath of human nature and a renewal of humanity through a synthesis of reason and energy.

Zamiatin's remarkably prescient anti-utopia, which shares the elements of social criticism and science that he praised in Wells's sociofantasies, expresses his disappointment with the bureaucratic dogmatism of Bolshevism, which he witnessed in the years immediately following World War I and the revolutions of 1917. It depicts a society carried to ideological extremes by a dogmatic bureaucracy that has suppressed basic human nature. As Gary Kern has summarized,

> *We* accurately presages Stalin's cult of personality ("the Benefactor"), *Pravda*'s monopoly on truth ("the State Gazette"), the travesty of one-party voting ("the Day of Unanimity"), the control of literature ("the State Union of Poets and Writers") and the Iron Curtain (or Berlin Wall), beyond which one is not allowed to go ("the Green Wall").[68]

Unlike most earlier utopias, it does not depict an ideal society—or, at least, it does so only in the opening entries before D-503 acquires a soul and begins to question its validity.[69]

In the process the novel employs a stream of religious images and analogies—paradise, Adam and Eve, the ancient Judeo-Christian God, Satan, Abraham and Isaac, Golgotha, and Christian ritual[70]—which make it clear that Zamiatin's work is also a quest for a surrogate for lost faith: the lost faith in the Christianity of his childhood, in *l'art pour l'art* of the Symbolism of his youth, in the Bolshevism of his early maturity.[71] One perceptive critic has suggested that Zamiatin's "attitude to the sanctity of the individual personality, to the irrational in man and more especially to 'Revolution' is at times hardly distinguishable from the 'faith' of the overtly religious."[72] In the last analysis his message is not pessimistic, for it implies, or at least hopes, that human nature will inevitably reassert itself, that energy will overcome entropy, that H_2 will link up with O, that $\sqrt{-1}$ despite its irrationality can be incorporated into the rationality of mathematics.

Zamiatin's novel had a remarkable publication history.[73] Although disseminated in the early 1920s through public readings, the work was not approved by the censors for publication in the Soviet Union because of its implicit and explicit criticism of the new regime. It first appeared in 1924 in English translation. Three years later it was published in Russian in an emigré monthly in Prague—but, in order to protect the author, under the pretense that it was a translation from the Czech and in a somewhat distorted version. The pretense was not effective. Zamiatin was attacked in the Soviet Union with increasing vehemence as anti-Soviet and his works were banned until in 1931, as the result of a personal request to Stalin, he was permitted to emigrate to Paris, where he died six years later. But his novel lived a life of its own: it has been translated into most major languages, including five translations into English, the language in which it has made its widest impact on world literature; and many critics agree with its designation as "the most significant anti-utopian novel of the century."[74] The full Russian text was first published in 1952 in New York; it appeared for the first time in Russia after the fall of communism.

The Utopia of Space: Gerhart Hauptmann's *Island of the Great Mother*

In 1944, toward the end of his life and still at work on his posthumously published novel *The New Christophorus* (*Der Neue Christophorus*), Gerhart Hauptmann (1862–1946) remarked that "a direct line extends from Plato's work to *The New Christophorus*."[75] In fact, from youth until old age the Nobel Prize-winning dramatist was obsessed with utopian thought, albeit in no philosophically consistent or systematic manner.[76] Recalling his schoolboy attempts to escape a hateful reality through a "cosmic-utopian dream" projected onto the moon, he observed that "[i]n every human mind one's own utopia emerges. It emerges within oneself just as naturally as, externally, hair emerges on the human head."[77] During his brief sojourn at the university of Jena (1882–83), Hauptmann was surrounded by a group of friends who founded a "Pacific Society" (Gesellschaft Pacific). Its members called themselves "Icarians" and dreamed of establishing a protocommunist community in the United States in imitation of Cabet's Icaria.[78] (The moment of disenchantment came in 1884, when one of the friends traveled to Illinois and found the original Cabet colony in a state of utter decay.) "What binds us and bound us together," he noted in a journal entry of 1895, "is a common utopia."

> Here one could say quite a bit about the nature of utopia, which is by no means only an idle game for fantasts. Everyone, no matter who, works daily at his own utopia.... And similarly the masses, the nation, humanity work at their utopia, for which not only religions offer the proof.[79]

It was during those years that Hauptmann first read Augustine's *City of God*, More's *Utopia*, Campanella's *Civitas Solis*, and especially Cabet's *Voyage en Icarie* while attending Rudolf Eucken's lectures on Plato.[80] Accordingly, it is utterly appropriate to say that a "continuity" existed between Hauptmann and "the main stream of utopian writers."[81]

Hauptmann's turn to utopianism was a direct response to his loss of faith in the Christianity he encountered in his Silesian youth. In 1878 Hauptmann—at the time an aspiring artist—dropped out of school because of poor grades and motivation. Because his family, prosperous hotel owners

in a Silesian resort village, experienced financial disaster during the great
economic crisis of the seventies, Hauptmann went to live on the farm estate
of relatives to learn agriculture. His sense of academic failure coupled with
a feeling of guilt at being a burden to his family aggravated the emotional
turmoil of the adolescent.

When Hauptmann arrived at Lohnig, he was fit prey for the hysterical
pietism that he encountered in his aunt's home. Having lost her son a year
before, the pious woman devoted herself to a cult of the dead and to an excessive Christian charity. Hauptmann found a household teeming with religious parasites. In his autobiography he recounts the stages of his religious
crisis, which was intensified by the wild sermons of itinerant preachers,
who—like evangelical versions of Joyce's priests—threatened their listeners
with the fires of hell. A sixteen-year-old with intellectual or religious re-
serves to fall back upon might not have succumbed so readily to these back-
woods hysterics. But Hauptmann had been a poor student, and his upbringing had not been religious. Since there was no responsible adult to whom
he could turn, for several months his only solace was a copy of the New
Testament. "I carried it on my heart and do not deny that I was somewhat
calmed by its constant presence."[82]

Within a year Hauptmann escaped from Lohnig and his youthful stability
reasserted itself. But the religious crisis of 1878 is important for several reasons. His forced exposure to remorseless preachers turned him against organized religion and initiated a strong and lasting anticlericalism. His exposure
to religious hysteria prompted his subsequent interest in, and serious study
of, the psychiatric aspects of religion and provided material for memorable
scenes in his powerful novel *The Fool in Christ Emanuel Quint* (*Der Narr in
Christo Emanuel Quint*, 1910).[83] Hauptmann remained a dedicated reader
of the New Testament to the end of his life, an admirer of the man Jesus,
and a fascinated student of world religions. "I regard myself as a Christian
and as a Protestant," he wrote in 1926.[84] But his disenchantment with the
extreme manifestations of Christianity and with the clergy caused him to
search for other channels for his religious energies—notably the utopianism
that soon captivated him. In his youth, Hauptmann stressed, "its purpose
initially was only to overcome the present, to mollify the suffering of time
and place, the hunger for happiness, through a work of the imagination."[85]

The utopian impulse manifests itself frequently in Hauptmann's works,
from the fragmentary drama *Helios* (1896) to the philosophical dialogues
of his unfinished novel *The New Christophorus*. But the impulse was
strongest in the years during and immediately following World War I when
Hauptmann conceived the enchanted island of his Prospero (in the drama

Indipohdi, 1921) and wrote his novel *The Island of the Great Mother* (*Die Insel der Großen Mutter*, 1924). Just as the young Hauptmann was defenseless against the excesses of religious extremism because he lacked any systematic religious training, so too his political naiveté left him unprepared for the experience of the war. In 1887 Hauptmann was a victim briefly of the political repression of the Social Democrats instigated by Bismarck's antisocialist laws. One of the members of the "Pacific Society," with whom Hauptmann was only casually acquainted, was arrested for socialist activities, and the writer was summoned to court to explain his own connections with the "Icarians." Although Hauptmann was soon acquitted, he remained on the government's list of suspicious characters because of the social criticism implicit in his early naturalistic dramas; but neither then nor subsequently did he belong to the Social Democratic Party or take any active role in politics.

Hauptmann's political ingenuousness was evidenced again in 1913 when he agreed to write a "festival play" (*Festspiel in deutschen Reimen*) to commemorate "the spirit of the Wars of Liberation of 1813" in Breslau—the first and last time that he composed any work with an explicitly political theme. The author's utter lack of understanding for the political-patriotic context of the occasion was made clear by the humorous and even ironic manner in which he treated venerable figures of German history, and he was publicly taken to task by the press and the government. A year later, swept up emotionally by the euphoria with which most German writers, artists, and intellectuals welcomed the outbreak of World War I, he wrote a number of blatantly chauvinistic verses[86] and in October 1914 signed the notorious "Manifesto of the Ninety-three," which included the assertion that "[w]ithout German militarism German culture would long ago have been exterminated from the earth."[87]

Soon his initial enthusiasm gave way to a recognition of the true horror of war. He began by seeking to "incapsulate" himself from the war. "I believe I succeeded last night in incapsulating the whole experience of war," declares the spokesman for the author's views in the fragmentary "Berlin War Novel" (*Berliner Kriegs-Roman*) that he undertook in 1916. "I can allow only as much of it to come in as seems necessary and tolerable to me." You must understand, he explains, that "everything about us is dependent on self-preservation, self-assertion."[88] A year later Hauptmann confided to his diary that "[t]he German people are the most neglected and most abused people: and for that reason alone one would have to take their side, even if one did not have to in any case."[89] His regrets about the war were accompanied by no sympathy for the opposing Americans and Russians. "Unconsciously we are longing for a powerful man," he wrote in 1917; "but it can be neither a Ludendorff nor a Hindenburg, for these people are powerful only through the grace of their Kaiser. It must be a man who derives his strength from himself, dominating, and who is borne by the ideas of his time."[90] Dismayed by Germany's defeat and the acceptance of Wilson's Fourteen Points, he mused glumly in 1918: "What a change! Perhaps nothing is left for me but to inscribe the decline of my land."[91] Even though he emerged from the war years as one of Germany's most famous personalities—the best known, according to surveys, next to Kaiser Wilhelm—and was celebrated on his sixtieth birthday in 1922 as the "people's king" in Thomas Mann's ironic phrase, he greeted the establishment of the Weimar Republic with reserve and, in his utterly apolitical stance, declined the invitation to stand for its presidency.

⌒

It was in this mood, then, and under these radically shifting circumstances that Hauptmann in 1916 began, and in 1924 completed, a novel with the revealing title: *The Island of the Great Mother or The Miracle of Île des Dames: A Tale from the Utopian Archipelago* (*Die Insel der Großen Mutter oder das Wunder von Île des Dames. Eine Geschichte aus dem utopischen Archipelagus*, 1924). The "island" of the title places Hauptmann's novel squarely in the tradition of the many poetic islands in utopian literature beginning with More's Utopia and naturalized for German literature in J. G. Schnabel's popular four-volume adventure novel *Die Insel Felsenburg* (1731–43).[92] The reference to the Great Mother (*Magna Mater* or *Bona Dea*), in turn, acknowledges Hauptmann's indebtedness to J. J. Bachofen's theories of matriarchy, with which he had become acquainted in the 1880s, and indicates the generally religious-cultural orientation of the work. "Without Bachofen I would probably never have written *The Island of the Great Mother*," the author acknowledged twenty years later.[93] The secondary title refers to the "miracle" around which the actual plot revolves. The subtitle, finally, specifies the utopian project of the novel—a utopia written expressly, like Hauptmann's boyhood dreams of adventures on the moon, as the author's response to the disorder in the world brought about by four years of war and unrelieved by any religious faith.[94]

The action begins sometime around 1905 when several lifeboats from the shipwrecked cruise ship *Kormoran* arrive at a mountain-peaked island in the South Pacific[95]—almost as though the vessel bearing Max Dauthendey or Count Keyserling on their world trip from Hong Kong to San Francisco had been wrecked en route, if the wearily disembarking survivors were poets and philosophers and not some hundred women plus a twelve-year-old boy named Phaon Stradmann. Fortunately for the survivors, the island is fertile, filled with bananas and other foods, and is repeatedly designated as "a paradise." (Hauptmann's vivid portrayal of the island was based on descriptions in Charles Darwin's *Journey of a Naturalist*, which appeared in German translation in 1910.)[96]

Under the energetic leadership of a capable fifty-five-year-old artist from Berlin, Anni Prächtel, the women—most of them young, healthy, and well educated, as befits the participants in a prewar round-the-world luxury cruise—quickly establish a "women's republic" organized into specialized teams of ten and guided by a *triummulierat* consisting of the most mature among them. In their "Ville des Dames" they build living quarters and meeting pavilions of bamboo and set up an orderly life for themselves, following a schedule determined strictly by the calendar and celebrating Sundays and festivals to mark birthdays. They pool their collective knowledge to create a Universal Lexicon. Under the direction of a Dutch-English theosophist named Laurence Hobbema and in a temple called "Notre-Dame des Dames" they practice a Greco-Indian "universal religion" along lines proposed by the anthropologist Max Müller and unconstrained by narrow-minded moralism.[97]

The women recognize the symbolism of their survival. "We have slipped back through a mesh in the net of civilization, like caught fish into the open sea," Anni Prächtel declares. "Along with our *Kormoran* another larger ship has suffered a shipwreck in our imagination, namely, the ship of civilization" (424). (It is no accident that the sunken ship of civilization is named for an aquatic bird, the cormorant, whose name is synonymous with greed and rapaciousness.) With very few exceptions the women quickly come to view their situation not as a disaster but as an opportunity. "We have often enough criticized civilization fundamentally and wished ourselves out of those contrived, complex, and yet so unspeakably shallow circumstances and back into a pure unspoiled nature," Anni remarks to her friend, the writer Rodberte Kalb. "We have returned to the bosom of nature and, if you like, into paradise. Now we don't want to waste the opportunity but to show what we're made of without the cosmetics of culture" (423). They come to have nothing but contempt for the European culture left behind in what they call "Gloomy Man Land" (Finstermannland, 545; a play on the antihumanists lampooned in the sixteenth-century *Epistulae obscurorum virorum*) and regard their gynecocracy as ideal—indeed, as the seed ground for the redemption of humankind. The only problem concerns the future: the question of progeny to embrace the new ideals.

All goes smoothly for the first year until, unexpectedly, one of the young women becomes pregnant. Babette, an impressionable and hysterical young woman chaperoned by a companion from the circle around Annie Besant, boarded the ship in Bombay where she had come under the influence of Indian mysticism. When she is interrogated by the *triummulierat*, she tells them that she was impregnated by the Indian serpent king Mukalinda, who appeared to her one night in the form of a handsome youth—an event, she says, of which she had premonitions months earlier at Benares while bathing in the Ganges. And when she returns to the settlement with her two-week-old infant, she appears to the other women "like Iris, a divine mother, surrounded by a mystical glow" (468).

The experienced wise women—Anni Prächtel, Rodberte Kalb, and Laurence Hobbema—are under no illusions and understand immediately that the "miracle" is due, despite his twelve years, to the handsome Phaon (named for the legendary boatman to whom Aphrodite gave eternal youth and beauty). But they refuse to acknowledge the fact publicly or even among themselves, citing the principle of the Code Napoléon: "La recherche de la paternité est interdite." As the president ironically observes, every civilization is based on publicly acknowledged conventional lies (494).[98] They prefer to accept Babette's version, which enables them to realize their theory of perfect matriarchy: that women can become mothers without men.

> Indeed, with this proof man was dethroned, and women had begun their exclusive rule of the world.... This would have remained forever unchanged if the hour had not come when one could get along entirely without men. The world change [*Weltwende*] had now arrived on the sacred ground of Île des Dames. (489)

In light of the "miracle" of divine conception without the intervention of men, the women of the Îles des Dames can regard themselves as wholly independent and autonomous. So they quickly incorporate the mystical union with Mukalinda into the myth of their new religion.[99]

Rapidly, thanks to the busy offices of Mukalinda, many other young women become pregnant and bear children. (After another dozen years Mukalinda is assisted every year in his mystical unions by twelve of his "Sons of Light.") This leads to further refinements of the island religion, incorporating the worship of Mukalinda with Greek and Christian elements and integrating the sacral and profane, the female and generally human. On a high plateau topping the island's mountain, inhabited by flying fish and birds of paradise, a mythic realm is discovered by Phaon and Diodata where mystical visions occur and a unicorn is spotted from time to time, the fabled beast that symbolizes virginity and sublimated sexuality. But the new fecundity means that arrangements must be made to accommodate the newborn boys. The more fanatical feminists among the women vote to send them, when they reach the age of five, to an isolated part of the island called Wild Man Land, where they grow up under the paternal supervision of Phaon. The girls remain in the matriarchal republic of Mothers Land, where they cultivate their independence and their mythic religion.

Matters go on like this for twenty years until, one day, a delegation of women visits Wild Man Land and discovers that the boys—guided by Phaon, who retained clear memories of Western civilization from his own boyhood prior to the shipwreck—have created for themselves a wholly different existence, with musical instruments, small sailboats, and other clever technical contrivances, taking as their symbol of progress the human hand. The women, in contrast, with the tacit collaboration of Phaon, have remained in a state of paradisiacal but primitive matriarchy, revolving around the cultivation of their religion. "They are beyond us," Anni Prächtel marvels. "While we were dabbling in mythology, these good-for-nothings have made fools of us" (592). She notes the symbolism of the fact that Wild Man Land is set on the western tip of the island. "In fact the West and not the East is the human Orient" (593).

The novel ends twenty years after the shipwreck when the young men finally rebel at their enforced isolation, despite Phaon's pleas that "violence is not a man-worthy action. . . . It is an animal action. . . . Through violence the action of the Holy Hand is degraded" (624). But the youths destroy the temple, planting on its grounds a banner bearing the word "Man!" and join the maenadic young women in bacchanalian orgies that culminate in the reestablishment of an anarchic society of men and women on what was once the "Île des Dames." (Hauptmann later remarked that he was inspired to some scenes by "the many lovely and often entirely naked female bodies" that he observed for years at his home on the North Sea holiday island of Hiddensee.)[100] While Anni Prächtel and Rodberte Kalb accept the new situation with ironic resignation—Laurence dies quietly following the destruction of the temple, having failed in her attempt to achieve complete spirituality—Phaon leaves the island in a small sailboat with Diodata, the only other child who once escaped the shipwreck and hence the only girl on the island who is not Phaon's offspring. (According to a suppressed epilogue that Hauptmann published in 1925, Phaon and Diodata establish themselves on a Polynesian island where Phaon later writes the autobiographical report on "the Island of the Great Mother" that constitutes the novel.)[101]

The representation of utopia as a response to the war is made explicit in the epilogue, where the narrator tells us: "How often in the frenzy of the world war I longed for Stradmann's South Sea paradise in the tropics and envied this man who had, as it were, buried himself alive in the universe with a quiet and loyal life companion" (367). The narrator's tone toward the matriarchal ideal is respectful throughout, as indeed is Phaon's attitude toward the women of the *triummulierat*. "He knew, even though he had known it only as a happy child, that the world of European civilization was not able to develop the life feeling to any approximately equivalent height" (553). Hauptmann allows his irony to emerge explicitly only with respect to the more radical feminists in the community, some of whom even propose that they kill off the infant males at birth. In the revolution that sweeps across the island at the end "the rage of the apostate Daughters of Heaven seethed against the Mothers Land" far more fiercely than that of the young men. So it is a distortion to suggest that the novel is simply a parody of the political utopia.[102]

The novel represents if anything a mythic-religious, not a political utopia.[103] It is not the matriarchal ideal and its values that Hauptmann contemplates with irony but the notion that any utopian ideal can be sustained in the real world. The claims of Eros reassert themselves and reestablish the natural human balance of man and woman with all its inevitable inequities and imperfections. Neither Phaon nor the wise women of the island destroy the utopia, but the passionate teenagers. Rodberte, for instance, disparages earlier revolutions and reformations, which achieved nothing in comparison with the liberation of "life, love, selflessness, and creativity that prevails in the suppressed realm of women" (556). And Laurence, "who had unwillingly been swept along by the great dreary stream of civilization, now knew that she had finally been lifted out of it and set apart" (481) when she reaches the Île des Dames.

Hauptmann uses his novel, and notably the conversations among the three experienced women, as a vehicle for critically reviewing many of the leading questions of the age—not unlike Thomas Mann in *The Magic Mountain*, published that same year (1924).[104] He was utterly in sympathy with the goal of the women to establish a "culture of humanity" and a "grand community of culture" to replace the predominant patriarchal society of Western civilization (445). At the same time, he was realist enough to understand that humankind is rarely adequate to the dream of utopia. Any constructed society, he implies, is bound to fail in the face of human nature.

The three writers, although Zamiatin was junior by two decades and although their national circumstances were strikingly different, share certain
basic similarities. All of them were born into severely religious families in
rather provincial conditions and rebelled at an early age. In the case of Wells
and Zamiatin that reaction against orthodox Christianity led to and was
strengthened by systematic training in modern science; in Hauptmann's
case his early experience was focused critically by his interest in the psychiatry of religious hysteria. The near contemporaries Hauptmann and Wells
turned early to utopianism as a surrogate for lost religious faith while Zamiatin found substitutes in his youthful socialist idealism and his fascination
with Wells's writings. All three, while basically apolitical, supported the
dramatically different positions of their respective nations in World War
I, but soon became disenchanted with the war, its goals, and their early
dreams. Accordingly all three sought soon after the war to express their new
positions in "utopian" works.

In *Men Like Gods* Wells did not so much reject the dreams of his earlier
works as concede the impossibility of their realization in the human world
as we know it. To do so, he used the narrative device of the outsider looking
into and describing the utopian world of which he can never be a part.[105]
Zamiatin and Hauptmann, in contrast, each selected a particular aspect of
the contemporary social dream and, by drastic extrapolation, demonstrated
the undesirability of its fulfillment. Both of their works are related from the
viewpoint of insiders, members of the utopian community, who become
disenchanted with its reality. In all three cases the result is anti-utopian, if
not necessarily dystopian in the sense of subsequent novels such as Aldous
Huxley's *Brave New World* or George Orwell's *1984*. In the last analysis,
then, the utopia, which had consoled humankind from Plato down to the
early twentieth century, turned out after World War I to offer no better
surrogate for religious despair than had the earlier avenues of art, India,
socialism, and myth.

PART THREE

Conclusion

To the surprise of Humanists and Liberal Churchmen, the abolition of God left a perceptible void. But Nature abhors vacuums. Nation, Class and Party, Culture and Art have rushed in to fill the empty niche.
—*Aldous Huxley, Time Must Have a Stop*

꧁

CHAPTER NINE

Renewals of Spirituality

Continuities

In the widely acclaimed lecture called "Science as Vocation" ("Wissenschaft als Beruf") that Max Weber delivered at the University of Munich in 1919, he observed that "liberation from the rationalism and intellectualism of science is the fundamental presupposition of life in community with the divine."[1] Central to Weber's theory is the "disenchantment" (*Entzauberung*) that characterizes a modern world determined by systematic knowledge (*Wissenschaft*, which has a much broader meaning than English "science"). "Science," according to Weber, cannot and does not seek to answer questions about the meaning and value of life. The world is "disenchanted" because "the ultimate and most sublime values have retreated from public life either into the otherworldly realm of mystic life or into the brotherliness of direct relations of individuals to one another" (272). While he himself was unwilling to make the "sacrifice of intellect" that religious faith requires, he realized that a new longing for release from the rationalism of science is "one of the fundamental watchwords to be gathered from reactions among those of our youth whose feelings are attuned to religion or who strive for religious experiences" (255).

Weber was diagnosing a phenomenon that we have often encountered in these pages. Paul Valéry observed in his essay "The Intellectual Crisis" that "an extraordinary tremor has passed through the marrow of Europe," causing Europe to reconsider discarded spiritual systems of the past, including Christianity (see chap. 4). Thomas Mann, in his *Reflections of a Nonpolitical Man*, concluded that a free-floating "faith" was the hallmark of the postwar age (see chap. 6). The enormous popularity of *Jean Barois* and *Demian* after the war—the "Baruchs" or shibboleths of youth in France and Germany respectively—provides another symptom of the turn to spirituality prompted by the shattering experiences of the recent past (see chap. 3).

This is not to suggest that there was a universal reversion to religion after World War I. We have been surveying only the literary portrayals of representative reactions to the loss of faith. Some Europeans adhered to their faith throughout the entire period (though their stories are usually less dramatic). Others compensated for any sense of spiritual emptiness by frantic immersion in the sensual satisfactions of drugs and sex and jazz, or in the single-minded pursuit of business, scholarship, the military, government, and other professional tracks. (Hermann Broch's *The Sleepwalkers* [*Die Schlafwandler*, 1932] offers an instructive analysis of such types.) Many people continued to exploit the tested surrogates that we have been exploring. James Hilton's *Lost Horizon* (1933) is exemplary for the utopian escape mechanisms that continued to attract huge audiences. Hermann Hesse's grand utopian vision of a cultural realm called Castalia, the setting for his novel *The Glass Bead Game* (*Das Glasperlenspiel*, 1943), is notable for the fact that his hero, Joseph Knecht, ultimately turns away (like Wells's Mr. Barnstaple) from the ideal he loves in order to bear its vision and values back to the real world.[2]

The Orient also continued to exert its attraction, as attested by the huge success of Hesse's novel *Siddhartha* (1922) both at the time of its publication and again among the hippies of the 1960s. The East-and-West stories and novels of W. Somerset Maugham—e.g., *The Painted Veil* (1925) or *The Narrow Corner* (1932)—as well as Thomas Mann's Indian novella *The Transposed Heads* (*Die vertauschten Köpfe*, 1940) continued to appeal to readers in the decades *entre deux guerres* even though the authors depicted Oriental mysticism ironically, rather than accepting it. Despite its title André Malraux's philosophical dialogue *The Temptation of the West* (*La tentation de l'occident*, 1926) amounts to an elegy to a fading Oriental culture and a radical critique of a Western society that has replaced understanding by critical judgment. "A.D." tells his Chinese correspondent Ling that "Europeans are weary of themselves, of their crumbling individualism, of their exaltation" and are suffering from a "European malaise."[3] Ling comes away from his trip to Europe deploring "the history of the psychological life of Europeans, of the new Europe, [as] a record of the invasion of the mind by emotions which are made chaotic by their conflicting intensities" (98) but concedes that "the West now takes an interest in Buddhism" (58). In China, A.D. learns to respect "the aristocracy of culture and the search for wisdom and beauty" inherent in ancient Confucianism (103), even as that tradition is vanishing. "Those of us who are worthy of China's past are disappearing one by one," he is told by a wise elder (103). Young Asians have been driven by the uncertainties of the modern world back to ancient beliefs, but they have been alienated from the universal rhythms inherent in those beliefs by the seduction of Western superficialities.

The appeal of socialism in its communist form and of myth as an element of Nazi culture did not suddenly cease but, indeed, grew rampant during the 1920s and 1930s. This growth was accompanied by an efflorescence of po-etry and fiction: hymns to socialism and to the *Volk*, odes to Stalin and to Hitler, factory novels in the Soviet Union and historical novels locating the sources of Nazi myth and doctrines in the past. Yet it is safe to say that the most memorable literary works produced by the political domination of communism and the cultural obsession with myth were works of oppo-sition: Arthur Koestler's *Darkness at Noon*, say, or the novels of Thomas Mann, in which, as he wrote to Karl Kerényi, he sought to "wrest mythol-ogy from the hands" of the Nazi obscurantists. In his so-called "mountain novel" *Die Verzauberung* (1953; The bewitchment), begun in the late 1930s, Hermann Broch portrayed, and analyzed with the tools of mass psychology, the myth-driven society of an Alpine village which comes under the spell of a Hitler-like stranger from outside. In her novel *The Wreath of Angels* (*Der Kranz der Engel*, 1946) Gertrud von le Fort traced with subtle psychological insight the seduction of a young aesthetic élitist and poet by the doctrines of National Socialism.

For those who had no desire for utopias or the East, who were not con-soled by communism or fascism, other avenues of escape offered themselves. In a 1928 address celebrating the institution of the humanistic gymnasium, Hugo von Hofmannsthal acknowledged the "sudden Orientalism" that had flamed up in opposition to the dehumanization of New Europe—but an Ori-entalism "without compelling powers." In its place he proposes "the spirit of antiquity, such a grand NUMEN that no single temple, though many are dedicated to it, can embrace it." This spirit underlies our very thinking and has shaped the European intellect. As the basis of the church, it is essen-tial to Christianity as a world religion; but it also created the language of our politics. It is "the mythos of our European being, the creation of our spiritual world (without which the religious world cannot exist), the posit-ing of cosmos against chaos."[4] Hofmannsthal's view was shared by many Europeans, and notably by those who belonged to what he defined as the "Conservative Revolution," a resynthesizing of the great bonds that resist chaos and provide the basis of every spiritual-intellectual space.[5]

This turn to the classics makes eminent sense if we consider that Euro-pean civilization was founded on the twin bases of Greco-Roman antiquity (e.g., Roman law) and Christianity. If people lost faith in one of the two foundations, then it was reasonable to look to the other for a revitalization of meaning. We know from the prefaces of works from Livy's *Ab urbe condita* to Ronald Syme's *Roman Revolution* (1939) that historians themselves have often turned to the past explicitly as an escape from the present or as a means of explaining it. Such a turn showed up specifically in the selection of classical writers whose works were suddenly rediscovered and whose lives often provided patterns of meaning for their modern admirers. The Roman poet Ovid, for instance, exerted a magical allure for a generation that had learned through the war about exile and the transitoriness of being and the need for constant transformation and metamorphosis.[6] In addition to James Joyce's *A Portrait of the Artist as a Young Man* (1916), whose title page displays an Ovidian motto and whose hero bears the Ovidian name Stephen Dedalus, the immediate postwar years produced Émile Ripert's charming biographical study, *Ovide: Poète de l'amour, des dieux et de l'exil* (1921); T. S. Eliot's *The Waste Land* (1922), which cites Ovid in its notes and revolves around the Ovidian figure Tiresias; Rilke's *Sonnets to Orpheus* (1923), which were inspired when the poet reread a translation of the *Metamorphoses* he had received from his lover; and Osip Mandelstam's volume *Tristia* (1922), which borrowed its title from Ovid's poems of exile. The mood changed around 1930, when the bimillennial of Virgil's birth was celebrated all over Europe and cultural conservatism was radically politicized.[7] Suddenly the lability of metamorphosis gave way to the bucolic (and often escapist) charm of Virgil's *Eclogues*, which underwent various translations in France, culminating in Paul Valéry's handsome *Bucoliques* (1944). Particularly the fourth eclogue, reputed for centuries to foretell the birth of Jesus, attracted such millennialists as Theodor Haecker, whose *Virgil: Father of the West* (*Vergil: Vater des Abendlands*, 1931) influenced T. S. Eliot in his Christianizing view of the Roman classic. It was Virgil of the *Georgics* who appealed to the agriphilic English, such as Vita Sackville-West, whose *The Land* (1927) displays remarkable parallels to Virgil's work, or Cecil Day Lewis, who produced a splendid translation of *The Georgics* (1940). Fairness and objectivity require mention of the fact that Virgil was also coopted by both the Italian Fascists and the Nazis for the imperial agenda that he was felt to advocate in the *Aeneid*.

Another option for those who resisted the lure of such mass movements as fascism, communism, and Nazism was the often elitist group of the likeminded. We have already seen evidence of such cliques in the circle that Stefan George gathered around his charismatic persona, in the coterie surrounding Frau Eva in Hesse's *Demian*, in Keyserling's "School of Wisdom"

in Darmstadt, or in the "élite intellectuelle" of René Guénon. Such societies provided a sense of belonging that offset the alienation from which
the modern individual often suffers and that nourished the shared cultural
values which often ran counter to those of the public at large. These groups
often revolved around internationally oriented journals through which they
sought to disseminate their views: Stefan George's *Blätter für die Kunst; La
Nouvelle Revue Français*, founded in 1909 by André Gide as a vehicle for
post-Symbolist writing; *Vivos Voco*, which Hesse cofounded in 1919 to summon the youth of Germany to a new liberalism and internationalism; *The
Criterion*, founded by T. S. Eliot in 1922 and in which he published an essay
by Hesse on modern German poetry; *Corona*, founded in 1930 as the journal of the cultural Conservative Revolution, which included translations
of classical works as well as such contemporaries as Paul Valéry, Benedetto
Croce, and W. B. Yeats; or the Catholic cultural journal *Hochland*. (The high-
land regions of Switzerland, south Germany, and Alpine France were traditionally regarded as culturally conservative and antimodern by the intellectuals of Paris, Berlin, and northern Europe.) Other platforms were provided
by such locales as the Goetheanum, an international cultural center that
Rudolf Steiner founded in Switzerland as the home of his Anthroposoph-
ical Society, or the Eranos Foundation in Ascona, Switzerland, which was
established in 1933 to explore the ideas on religion and myth evoked by C.
G. Jung. One might recall, finally, the classically oriented chapters of the
pre-Nazi German youth movement, which arose in the humanistic gymna-
siums and often organized trips to Greece in search of the antiquity praised
by Hölderlin, Nietzsche, and Stefan George.[8]

⌒∽⌒

A fascinating byway is evident in the turn to mysticism, which constituted
an element in Hesse's *Demian* and became a powerful factor in Döblin's
November 1918. This tendency was paralleled among many Jewish writers
by the rediscovery of Hasidism. An analogous obsession, especially with
Eastern mysticism, became notably conspicuous in England and the United
States. The early spokesman of the New Vedanta in England was Gerald
Heard (1889–1971), a philosopher of history and historian of consciousness,
who moved intellectually beyond philosophy and science to Vedanta, a spec-
ulative philosophy based on the Vedas. Heard wrote many works, such as
The Social Substance of Religion (1931), in which he argued that nothing
but religion could cure the chaos of the world.[9] Heard, whose Vedic-oriented
spirituality soon caught the attention of Aldous Huxley, appears to lie

behind the figure of Dr. James Miller, the mystical pacifist who converts
Anthony Beavis in Huxley's novel *Eyeless in Gaza* (1936) from his sneering
skepticism to pacifist activism.

The novel, which covers the first third of the twentieth century—from
1902, when the ten-year-old Anthony goes to his mother's funeral, to the
immediate present of 1935—portrays a world in turmoil, from the disintegration of bourgeois Victorianism to the rise of communism and fascism.
Anthony passes through the usual stages of development: the son of a godless father, he grows up self-centered and wholly negative, a cynical witness
of the confused relationships and betrayals among people with no sustaining
faith. At Oxford he flirts, albeit listlessly, with Fabian socialism and through
his friends witnesses aestheticism, communism, and the other fashions of
the day. Acquaintances returning from India offer the opportunity to ridicule
the currently chic Orientalism: in his imagination Anthony "did a slight
Joseph Conrad in the East Indies, a slight Loti even, in spite of the chro-
molithograph style."[10] His own sociological research affords him a similar
escape from reality. For Anthony and his circle "Faith's just organized and directed stupidity" (225). Indeed, they pride themselves on their trivialization
of every belief. "Art, religion, heroism, love—we've left our visiting-card on
all of them" (311). As a budding sociologist, Anthony believes in the facts
and understands "the fundamental metaphysical theory of mysticism" (89),
but it is only when he goes to Mexico in the winter of 1933–34 and meets
the physician-anthropologist James Miller that he first encounters living
mysticism. Huxley reports that Anthony achieves a kind of mystical faith;
but like most other writers he is unable to provide a persuasive account of
that faith or the process of its acquisition.

> And now at last it was clear, now by some kind of immediate experience
> he knew that the point was in the paradox, in the fact that unity was the
> beginning and unity the end, and that in the meantime the condition of
> life and all existence was separation, which was equivalent to evil. (470)

On his return to England, Anthony goes to work for Miller's pacifist organization, but Huxley leaves the ending open.

> The mind abhors a vacuum. Negative pacifism and scepticism about
> existing institutions are just holes in the mind, emptinesses waiting to
> be filled. Fascism or communism have sufficient positive content to act
> as fillers. Someone with the talents of Hitler may suddenly appear. The
> negative voice will be pumped full in a twinkling. These disillusioned

sceptics will be transformed overnight into drilled fanatics of nationalism, class war or whatever it may be. Question: have we time to fill the
vacuum with positive pacifism? Or, having the time, have we the ability?
(399)

In 1937 Huxley accompanied Heard to California, where Heard founded Tre-
buco College, an institution dedicated to the study of comparative religion.
In 1940 Huxley himself began writing for the journal *Vedanta and the West*
and was soon recognized along with Heard and Christopher Isherwood as
one of the leading "California gurus."

It is no doubt the case that this group provided the general, if not the specific, model for Larry Darrell in W. Somerset Maugham's *The Razor's Edge*
(1944), which Maugham wrote while living in Beverly Hills where with
ironic detachment he could observe the activities of the Vedanta Society in
Hollywood. Maugham's novel, like Huxley's, is a mixture of autobiography
and fiction, and the author himself appears in the central role of narrator.
But Maugham writes as a detached outsider and not, like Huxley, as a convert to mysticism.[11] Maugham had been interested for many years in Indian
philosophy, which is discussed in such earlier novels as *The Painted Veil*
(1925) and *The Narrow Corner* (1932), as well as the role of the "good man"
in modern society, a theme familiar from the many Christian socialist novels in which Jesus, or a Jesus-figure, is brought back to life in the world of
the late nineteenth century. This interest was intensified by a trip to India
that he made in 1938.

The Razor's Edge provides a vivid portrait of life in Europe and the United
States between the two world wars. In this novel Maugham is dealing for
the first time with a cast of non-English characters: mostly Americans, both
at home in Chicago and as expatriates in France. If we disregard the other
characters—and notably the fascinating figure of the cultivated and lovable
snob Elliott Templeton—the narrator's eye is focused principally on Larry
Darrell, who moves in and out of the story, refusing to be bound by the social
or ethical standards of his group. A Chicagoan like the others, he volunteers
at age seventeen for the Canadian Air Force and sees service in World War
I, where the death in battle of his closest friend changes his life. "Whatever
it was that happened to Larry filled him with a sense of the transiency of
life and an anguish to be sure that there was a compensation for the sin and
sorrow of the world."[12] Rather than settling down to marriage and a job at

home, he goes off to Europe in search of God. In Paris he studies ancient languages for two years and reads the Flemish mystic Ruysbroek. Then he works in a Belgian coal mine, where a former Polish officer introduces him to the mystical thought of Jacob Boehme and Meister Eckhart. His journeys lead him up the Rhine, where he works on a farm in Germany, then studies at Bonn University, and finally spends time in an Alsatian monastery before making his way to Spain and eventually to India. There he lives and meditates for five years in an ashram near Travancore in the presence of a venerated yogi. Eventually returning to Europe, he renounces his inheritance and goes back to the United States to drive across the country as a truck driver and then to earn his living in New York as a taxi driver.

Although there is much talk of mysticism, Maugham succeeds no more than does Huxley in rendering the experience of mysticism. Larry speaks of his "illumination" in a single passage and stresses his "overwhelming sense of its reality."

> "After all it was an experience of the same order as the mystics have had all over the world through all the centuries. Brahmins in India, Sufis in Persia, Catholics in Spain, Protestants in New England; and so far as they've been able to describe what defies description they've described it in similar terms. It's impossible to deny the fact of its occurrence; the only difficulty is to explain it. If I was for a moment one with the Absolute or if it was an inrush from the subconscious or an affinity with the universal spirit which is latent in all of us, I wouldn't know." (259)

꩜

The novels of Huxley and Maugham reflect a pronounced obsession with religious mysticism in the 1920s and 1930s. But when Weber, Valéry, and others observed a turn to spirituality in response to the shattering disorder of the war, what they had in mind was not primarily the continuity of older surrogates or the temporary emergence of new ones—antiquity, like-minded groups, sympathetic journals, Vedantic mysticism—but a genuine revival of the religious spirituality that was lost by many at the end of the nineteenth century.

Conversions

One of the conspicuous phenomena of the years surrounding World War I in Europe was the number of conversion experiences among writers and intellectuals from all religious denominations. This phenomenon, which was under way by the turn of the century and no doubt prompted the two chapters on conversion in William James's *The Varieties of Religious Experience* (1902), was intensified dramatically by the spiritual confusions of the 1920s. One of the most noted was T. S. Eliot's conversion to the Anglican Church in 1927. In Germany, their resistance to National Socialism pushed many writers to a renewal of their Protestant faith. The poet and translator Rudolf Alexander Schröder was ordained in the Bekennende Kirche (Confessing Church), which was founded in 1934 by the opposition pastor Martin Niemöller. The onetime theologian and journalist Jochen Klepper, who with his Jewish wife and stepdaughter committed suicide in 1942, kept from 1932 until his death a series of profoundly moving religious diaries about life under the Nazis, which were later published to acclaim under the title *Unter dem Schatten Deiner Flügel* (1956; Under the shadow of your wings). In other writers the renewal of faith showed up in a turn to religious subjects in their fiction: e.g., Ina Seidel's *Lennacker* (1938), which embeds a history of the Lutheran Church, or Ernst Wiechert's *Jerominkinder* (1938), which recounts a pious family's resistance to the Nazis.

Among many Jewish intellectuals—notably the philosopher Martin Buber, the novelist and Kafka biographer Max Brod, the philosopher and adult educator Franz Rosenzweig, and the scholar Gershom Scholem—World War I brought about a turn to an enlightened Judaism blending Hasidism with Zionism and often followed by emigration to Palestine, which now began to be viewed once again as the cultural and spiritual center of Judaism. During these same years the poet Else Lasker-Schüler, secularized granddaughter of a chief rabbi, who had long employed Hebrew themes in her work, emigrated to Palestine for political reasons. The future Nobel Prize-winner Nelly Sachs, who fled to Sweden, and Paul Celan, who survived the war in a Rumanian labor camp, became obsessed by the Nazi persecution of the Jews and the horrors of the concentration camps. But in none of these cases was (re-)conversion to orthodox synagogue Judaism a factor.

The new spirit was especially pronounced in Roman Catholicism. A wave of spectacular conversions had already swept across France during the fin de siècle *renouveau catholique,* when Paul Claudel, Charles Péguy, Jacques Maritain, Jacques Rivière, and others (notably Julien Green in 1916) turned to the church. Julien Benda (1867–1956), a slightly older contemporary of Martin du Gard and Hesse, states frankly in his autobiography that he grew up in a wholly secularized Jewish family, "in total liberation [*un affranchissement total*], as far as religion is concerned"[13] and learning only to respect all truly sincere religious convictions. Benda's single religious

experience appears to have been a teenage impulse to convert to Catholicism, to which he was attracted by his infatuation with the writings of
Lamartine and other French Romantics, and from which he was dissuaded
by a wise priest (80). During the 1920s, and often in specific reaction to
the depradations of the war, the surge reached England, carrying with it
Ronald Knox (1917), G. K. Chesterton (1922), Graham Greene (1925), Alfred Noyes (1926), and Evelyn Waugh (1930) among others. In Germany the
same tide bore Theodor Haecker (1921), Gertrud von le Fort (1926), Werner
Bergengruen (1936), Alfred Döblin (1940)—along with his fictional figures
Friedrich Becker and Rosa Luxemburg in *November 1918*—and Franz Wer-
fel, who like Simone Weil in France was strongly drawn to Catholicism
without taking the final step to conversion before his death in 1945. Elsewhere one might cite, for instance, the Norwegian Nobel Prize-winning
novelist Sigrid Undset (1924) or Giovanni Papini, author of the enormously
popular *Story of Christ* (*Storia di Cristo,* 1921). As one student of the genre
has observed: "The Catholic novel flowers only in desecrated soil. Like the
counter-Reformation, it is reactionary: a frightened look at the morbid anarchy of modern life, then a bitter denunciation of the degenerate kingdom of
this world."[14] While the reasons vary from country to country and from individual to individual, several of the writers documented their conversions
fictionally as well as autobiographically.

∽

Gertrud von le Fort (1876–1971) was the daughter of a titled Prussian officer
whose ancestors had come to Germany from Savoy in the seventeenth century as persecuted Protestants.[15] During her childhood the family followed
her father's military assignments from town to town, and her education was
accordingly irregular. Her only systematic schooling appears to have taken
place during the years (1890–97) the family spent in Hildesheim (Lower
Saxony). In her twenties le Fort lived at home and, following her father's
death in 1902, with her mother and sister on a family estate at Boek on
Lake Müritz in Mecklenburg as she was publishing her early poems and
stories. In 1908, at the urging of a local gymnasium teacher, she went to
Heidelberg and enrolled in the university as an auditor. Even though she
did not have the preparation necessary for regular enrollment, le Fort later
claimed that "Heidelberg represented the most important and decisive stage
of my life"[16]—a stage depicted memorably in her novel *Der Kranz der Engel*
(1946; The wreath of angels). In the course of the next six years she studied
with several prominent professors, including Carl Neumann, Karl Jaspers,

Rudolf Bultmann, and Friedrich Gundolf (in whose lectures on literature she encountered Stefan George). The major influences on her thinking were the church historian Hans von Schubert, whose lectures explored the complex relationship between religion and secular power; and especially Ernst Troeltsch, the theologian and philosopher of religion, whose courses she attended every semester and with whom she soon became closely acquainted. After Troeltsch's death she edited and published her notes of his 1911–12 lectures on religious doctrine (*Glaubenslehre*, 1925).

When World War I broke out, le Fort and her sister—despite their outspoken opposition to the war—volunteered and served for a time with the Red Cross. During the war years, while living with her mother at Boek, she continued to attend Troeltsch's lectures on the philosophy of religion at the University of Berlin, where he had moved. Then within a few days the war ended, her mother died, her brother was outlawed for opposing the new socialist government, and the government expropriated the family estates in Mecklenburg. "Along with [her mother's] life, the life of an entire epoch was extinguished."[17] Le Fort's response to this sense of utter dislocation was her conversion to Catholicism.

Le Fort grew up in a religious home. Her father, though a Kantian in his ethics and deist in his beliefs and without any religious faith, had a profound respect for the forms of religion and regularly attended church services with his family. "The religious soul of our house was my mother"—a woman whose piety was totally without sanctimoniousness, le Fort later recalled.[18] She regularly read the Bible, the *Imitatio Christi* of Thomas à Kempis, and the *Liederschatz*, a collection of evangelical church hymns. From an early age—the family's residence in the Rhineland town of Coblenz from 1884 to 1888—le Fort and her siblings also experienced Catholicism, and her father insisted that his Protestant children kneel in respect when the Corpus Christi procession bearing the Blessed Sacrament passed by.[19] Le Fort recounts how the children followed a Capuchin monk down the street, who presented them with small pictures of saints. Later, during a 1904 stay in Rome with her mother, le Fort even had an audience with Pope Pius X. After these impressions of childhood and youth the years in Heidelberg represented a further step toward a more ecumenical sense of religion. "It required the entire theological and historical vision of my Heidelberg teachers to make possible the way toward which I was striving in my inwardness, which from childhood on was focused on the unity of the church." Her subsequent conversion, she continues, meant "less a rejection of the Protestant faith than a unification of the separated denominations."[20] In particular, Troeltsch's lectures on doctrine (*Glaubenslehre*) dealt with "the terrible struggle for Christian truth. Belief in it was extensively undermined already at that time, but in its ultimate substance it was again and again affirmed and saved by Ernst Troeltsch."[21]

The final step—the move from the Protestantism of her childhood, by way of the broadened conception of faith learned in Heidelberg, to Catholicism—took place when her ties to the past had been shattered by the war, by the death of her parents, and by the loss of the family estates. In a moving seventieth-birthday tribute to Carl Muth (1867–1944), founder and editor of the influential Catholic cultural journal *Hochland,* le Fort recalls the time soon after the war when "a collapse of the spiritual and religious possessions of our people—no: of the entire world—threatened to follow the collapse of German power."[22] Sitting on her suitcase in the corridor of a crowded train, she was reading a journal that she had bought at the station, "attracted by the title, which seemed to point the way out of a chaotic present." It turned out to be a joyous and momentous experience.

> With this journal I found myself truly in a world that believed neither in the "Decline of the West" nor in the decline of our people but in its resurrection and renewal—I found myself in a Christian world. I found myself—naturally it very soon became clear to me—in the spiritual realm of a Catholic journal, but simultaneously in my own most personal home: not simply because in it non-Catholic spiritual possessions were viewed and evaluated in a broad vista, but rather because the entire attitude of this journal appeared at the same time to include my most precious possessions, the inheritance of my pious Protestant family home. Yes, precisely this impression of inclusiveness—I recall it exactly—was the essence of this unforgettable encounter. For the first time I experienced with full consciousness that despite all the painful tensions and splits within Christianity there was the common possession of a Christian culture. I experienced the spiritual outlook of a Catholic journal as a universal Christian attitude of spirit and love. I experienced the embracing maternal gesture of Catholicism. I experienced the essence of what is truly Catholic altogether. (78)

She goes on to explain the appeal of an ecumenical Catholic culture as she encountered it in *Hochland* and among Catholic intellectuals. The convert is not a person who emphasizes denominational separation but one who has overcome it: "his most essential experience is not that of a different faith to which he 'goes over' but the experience of the unity of faith that sweeps over him" (79).

In the early 1920s, in Baierbrunn outside Munich where she formed a friendship with the recently converted cultural critic Theodor Haecker, le Fort took instruction for conversion, a project that was not undermined by the paradox that the priest who instructed her left the church.[23] On the advice of a Jesuit mentor she went to Rome to continue her preparations and in March 1926 was formally received into the Catholic Church in Maria dell' Anima.

∽

The immediate literary result of her conversion was le Fort's first novel, *The Veil of Veronika (Das Schweißtuch der Veronika,* 1928), which amounts to a fictionalized account of her conversion in the form of a spiritual bildungsroman.[24] The novel is set in Rome and takes place in the year immediately preceding the outbreak of World War I. But it is a strange Rome without Italians and lacking any hint of contemporary historical events.[25] The action involves only six figures. Veronika, who is now approaching her sixteenth year, was sent, some years earlier following the death of her mother, to stay in Rome with her maternal grandmother (who is never named) and her aunt Edelgart; they are cared for by their French tutor and housekeeper Jeanette. During the winter and spring an old friend of the grandmother, known as Frau Wolke (because of the cloud of powder and perfume that surrounds her), comes for a stay with her twenty-year-old son, the poet Enzio. Grandmother was once deeply in love with Enzio's father, whom she renounced for the sake of his mother; she regards herself therefore as in no small measure responsible for his birth and almost as a surrogate mother. Aunt Edelgart, for her part, was once the beloved of Veronika's father; when her religious faith turned out to be more compelling than her love for him, he left her and married her sister; but because he never truly loved the sister (Veronika's mother) and neglected her, she died of a violent postpartum depression and insisted that Veronika be sent for upbringing to her sister, who at least initially regards her niece virtually as a daughter. But the novel is not really about plot; it is an almost wholly internalized work, dealing with the complex inner lives of the principal figures and notably their competition for Veronika's soul.

The city of Rome, which here receives one of its most memorable fictional depictions, constitutes the mirror in which the beliefs of the various characters are reflected. For the grandmother—a nonreligious worldly woman of great sophistication who likes to refer to herself as a pagan and is the onetime friend of Ferdinand Gregorovius, the great art historian and

historian of medieval Rome—it is ancient and notably Augustan Rome
around which her life revolves. Her rooms in her palazzo, a former Do-
minican monastery, look out over the Pantheon, and all her excursions lead
to monuments of classical antiquity. Enzio, whose poetry is eloquently described in terms that remind us of such German Expressionists as Georg
Heym or the early Gottfried Benn, prefers the Rome of decline and fall; everywhere he looks he sees the corruption of society mirrored in the ruins
and the stenches, like the city in Thomas Mann's *Death in Venice.* (In the
sequel he becomes a dedicated Nazi.)

> He loved [Rome] more heatedly and rapturously than all of us. For he did
> not love it as my grandmother loved it, transfigured and stripped of its
> weightiness, as the wonderful symbol of earthly grandeur and eternity, as
> the concentration of humanity and the enhancer of one's own person, but
> precisely as he had always seen it with all its abysses and riddles, with all
> its conquests of itself; he loved it with that wonderful, unsuffering love
> which—I felt it well—is reserved solely for the poet among all beings of
> this earth. (136; 213)[26]

This is the city to which Enzio dedicates the *Roman Odes* that subsequently
establish his reputation as a poet. Veronika, finally, comes to recognize and
privilege *Roma aeterna* as the seat of Catholicism with its churches and
priests and religious art.

Veronika's father, a scholar from a Protestant background who had long
since freed himself from any churchly bonds, respected his dying wife's wish
with the explicit stipulation that his daughter be raised entirely outside the
religious world of her aunt. Accordingly Veronika alone in the entire family
is not baptized and is hence, in her grandmother's fond words, "a little heathen" (119; 187). When we first meet her she fully shares her grandmother's
enthusiasm for pagan Rome. Edelgart, who regularly attends masses at the
neighboring Santa Maria sopra Minerva, is a practicing Catholic in all but
a final conversion, to which for two decades she has never been able fully
to surrender. Her mother scoffs that she is nothing but one of the "private
Catholics of mood" (*Stimmungs- und Privatkatholiken*, 24; 37–38). Her
friend Jeanette, a Catholic of uncomplicated faith, follows the advice of
wise priests who warn her that conversions should never be forced; but she
regrets that Veronika must be raised entirely outside Christianity.

Things go along smoothly for years until the freethinking Enzio, who
nurtures a quiet hostility toward Christianity and the church, is dropped
into the midst of this strained relationship. Veronika's attraction to him

soon leads her to appropriate his more decadent, even Dionysian view of Rome, as represented by its backstreets and the Colosseum as opposed to the Forum and Pantheon. When Aunt Edelgart tries to interfere with Veronika's infatuation with the handsome young poet, her niece erupts in an adolescent outburst:

> "You will never convert me to your faith. Yes, I hate, I detest your faith! And no matter how much you pray for me, I still mean always to be- lieve only what grandmother and Enzio believe! And those two are not responsible for that, but you alone. You are guilty and nobody else if I do not become a Christian." (77; 120)

Veronika quickly recovers from her anger, and during the Holy Week which soon follows she has her first religious experience. Accompanying her grandmother and Enzio to attend a Tenebrae service in Saint Peter's— purely as spectators, of course—Veronika, crouching beside the statue of Saint Veronica, finds herself inexplicably moved by the ceremony and falls spontaneously to her knees when the choir reaches the words *Jerusalem, Jerusalem, convertere ad Dominum Deum tuum* ("Jerusalem, turn back to your Lord God," 114; 178). Her grandmother, chagrined at this unseemly display of religious emotion, orders Veronika to stand up; but from this mo- ment forward a new sense of faith stirs and grows in the girl's consciousness. She is shocked and disappointed when Edelgart, having finally determined to take the ultimate step, at the last moment locks herself in her room and, refusing her conversion, suffers an attack of hysteria that requires the care of a psychiatrist. "My soul in its first gentle turn to God was still much too young, much too vulnerable and above all much too greatly dependent upon its own experience to fail to feel here initially something like a great betrayal" (123; 193). Edelgart's refusal leads to discussions about religion and theology among the visitors to her grandmother's German-Roman sa- lon, discussions to which Veronika lends an eager and thoughtful ear. In the meantime, her father has died on a scientific expedition to the tropics. In his last letter he confesses to the grandmother that his hostility to religion was motivated largely by his resentment at Edelgart's rejection; and he removes his stipulation that his daughter receive no religious instruction. In view of Edelgart's labile emotional state, he assigns as a new guardian his best friend, a professor in Heidelberg.

Over the summer the grandmother is weakened by various blows: no- tably Enzio's rejection of her and his turn in illness to his own mother; a violent dispute with Enzio's mother over their respective roles in the love of

Enzio's father; and her growing disappointment with Veronika's turn to the church. In August, following Enzio's departure, Veronika accompanies her now ailing grandmother on an expedition to the Appian Way, from which the elderly humanist loves to view Rome and the Campagna. But the heat and the strain prove to be too much for the old woman, who collapses and soon thereafter, sitting in her room in sight of the Pantheon, dies. In her sadness and in memory of her grandmother Veronika visits the Forum. There, wandering into the church of Santa Maria Antiqua, she experiences an epiphany before the crucifix, which appears to send its call into her very soul.

> When I left Santa Maria Antiqua the world was transformed just as on that unforgettable morning after the night in Saint Peter's. No longer a lonely and uncertain I, but that Eternal Love filled my soul and gave it a boundless certainty. I went though the roaring and rushing of the Forum and yet I was walking through a new Rome: I was walking through that Rome of grace which is built mysteriously, like the God-filled soul in the universe, into the Rome of the world and its splendor. (189; 295–96)

Jeanette sends her for counsel to Pater Angelo, whom she requests to instruct her in the teachings of the church. When he asks what she desires from the church, she replies, without realizing that she is using the words of the baptismal ritual, "faith" (191; 299). Soon she is able to be baptized and to receive communion; but Pater Angelo and the psychiatrist warn her not to inform her aunt immediately. Edelgart is furious when she learns that her niece has successfully undergone the conversion that she herself failed to complete. She attacks Veronika with the crucifix hanging above her bed (and which formerly hung over Edelgart's bed), but is herself injured in the struggle. On her deathbed she calls for a priest, makes a confession of her ambivalent role vis-à-vis her sister, her former fiancé, and her niece, is reconciled with Veronika, and is received into the church before her death. As the novel ends, Veronika prepares to travel north to take up residence with her new guardian.

For all its fascination as a document, *The Veil of Veronika* has conspicuous weaknesses as a novel. A sixteen-year-old girl offers an unlikely vehicle for thoughts and feelings that motivated the fifty-year-old and highly educated Gertrud von le Fort in her own conversion. In the first-person narration the author is clearly projecting ideas and observations of her maturity onto the teenager. The intimately private experience of conversion cannot be expressed in words or communicated. At the crucial moment, therefore, Veronika writes:

> I do not want to reveal the mysteries of God with my soul, but just as grace even in the sacrament offers itself in a concealed form, so I will embrace what happened to me with that silence which is the most profound speech of love and also of blissfulness and also of gratitude. (196; 307)

In addition, despite the grandmother's paganism, Edelgart's religious hysteria, and Enzio's Dionysian proto-Nazism, the utterly ahistorical atmosphere of the novel inadequately represents the spiritual floundering of the postwar period that edged le Fort toward her own conversion. (In the sequel Enzio repeatedly teases Veronika by calling her a "prewar phenomenon.") Moreover, despite its vivid evocations of the Rome of antiquity, of decline, and of religious faith, the structure of the novel is stiltedly constructed around its symbolic figures. Because the action is almost wholly interiorized, its appeal is largely spiritual. But precisely for this reason the novel has established itself as one of the standard and enduringly popular works of German Catholic literature.[27] It stands as a remarkable monument of the return to religious faith in response to the disorder of the world around the time of World War I.

Evelyn Waugh's *Brideshead Revisited* (1945), which enjoyed an enormous popular success upon first publication and again thirty years later as a PBS television series, has been called "the most important conversion novel of modern England."[28] It is the first-person account, according to its subtitle, of "the sacred and profane memories of Captain Charles Ryder." These memories, written down in 1942 by the thirty-nine-year-old Ryder, are precipitated by happenstance: his army company has been transferred for training purposes to a place that he soon recognizes as Brideshead, the estate of the Flyte family, to which he enjoyed ambivalently close ties for some twenty years. During his first semester at Oxford in the early 1920s, Ryder met the "magically beautiful" but emotionally unstable Sebastian Flyte, the younger son of the family. In the first of the novel's two books—entitled "Et in Arcadia Ego" (I too [am, was] in Arcadia) and with all the ambiguity implicit in the inscription in Poussin's painting *Arcadian Shepherds*—Charles is introduced

to Brideshead and to Sebastian's family: his mother, Teresa Lady March-
main, his older brother "Bridey," and his sisters Julia and Cordelia. Lord
Marchmain, he learns, left his family during World War I and moved to
Venice with his Italian mistress Cara.[29]

Charles, the only son of a widowed and self-centered independent scholar, seems to have found a second family at Brideshead. Though himself an
agnostic, as an Oxford aesthete and promising artist he is greatly attracted
by the lifestyle of the old and titled Anglo-Catholic family. He becomes
an interested observer of and participant in their destinies and, during the
holidays that he spends at Brideshead, decorates one of the rooms with landscape panels. Lord Marchmain's originally Catholic family, it emerges, had
become Anglican during the Reformation; but when he married his devoutly
Catholic wife, he reconverted, at least superficially, and added to the manor
a handsome chapel specifically for her, even though Brideshead was not an
old-established center of Catholicism. But her religiosity eventually out-
weighed her love and drove her husband into the arms of the mistress with
whom he has been living happily since the war. Meanwhile Teresa sought
comfort more and more in the warm embrace of the church—especially in
"the poetry, the Alice-in-Wonderland side, of religion" (127)—and acquired
the reputation locally as a saint.

> Religion predominated in the house; not only in its practices—the daily
> mass and rosary, morning and evening in the chapel—but in all its inter-
> course. "We must make a Catholic of Charles," Lady Marchmain said,
> and we had many little talks together during my visits when she deli-
> cately steered the subject into a holy quarter. (126)

Their devout son Bridey, whose narrow-minded obtuseness sometimes
masks a kind of *sancta simplicitas*, nearly became a Jesuit but, because
he was the eldest, was dissuaded from that goal and, following three years at
Oxford, is now trying to decide on a career. Sebastian, too, though he is much
more relaxed in his religion and claims that he doesn't really like Catholics,
regularly attends mass. The lovely Julia, a "half-heathen" (89) like Sebastian, is a freethinker, but their younger sister Cordelia remains fervently
devout and hopes to become a nun. When Charles first meets the family
and says that they are "just like other people" (89), Sebastian exclaims:

> "My dear Charles, that's exactly what they're not—particularly in this
> country, where they're so few.[30] It's not just that they're a clique—as a
> matter of fact, they're at least four cliques all blackguarding each other

half the time—but they've got an entirely different outlook on life; everything they think important is different from other people. They try and hide it as much as they can, but it comes out all the time." (89)

The war and its aftermath have created the unstable conditions under which the various destinies play themselves out in Europe of the 1920s and 1930s. Marchmain, as we noted, left his family. The peculiarities of Charles's father, who "has not been really in touch with things—lives in his own world" (41), also date from the war years, when his wife was killed in an air raid. When the story begins in 1923, for Charles's scout at Oxford "as for thousands of others, things could never be the same as they had been in 1914" (22). Passing references to communists, Fascists, and Nazis hint at the political turmoil of the era. And the various escape mechanisms that we have observed also play a role: the frantic aestheticism of Charles, Sebastian, and their Oxford friends; the trip to the Near East on which Lady Marchmain sends Sebastian with his tutor to remove him from what she regards as Charles's bad influence; the trip to Latin America that Charles, as a successful painter, undertakes years later in an effort to find inspiration and to revitalize his work.

The novel involves intriguing plot elements and social satire, narrated with Waugh's customary ease and elegance: the course of Charles's professional career as a master of architectural paintings; Sebastian's flight to North Africa, where he maintains a homosexual relationship with a boorish young German who has deserted from the Foreign Legion; Cordelia's departure from her novitiate and service with the ambulance corps in the Spanish Civil War; Julia's and Charles's unhappy marriages from which they escape, years later, into a happy but brief affair; Bridey's failed plans—to go into the army, into Parliament, into the army—his duties as heir to Brideshead, and his late miserable marriage. But essentially the novel is a story of the conversions related in part 2, which bears the subtitle "A Twitch upon the Thread"—an allusion to the fishing metaphor used by G. K. Chesterton in his Father Brown stories to suggest that any sinner who has seen the grace of God can still be saved.

Close to the end of the novel we learn that Sebastian, in North Africa, has gone back to the church, which he had never left as definitively as Julia had. There he leads a saintlike existence as a beloved lay brother in a monastery, guiding tourists and slipping occasionally back into alcoholism. The central conversion, strikingly reminiscent of father and son in *Jean Barois*, is Lord Marchmain's deathbed return to Catholicism, which Waugh called the whole point of the novel and which is based upon a scene he personally witnessed.[31] Marchmain converted originally only to please his wife, telling her, "You have brought back my family to the faith of their ancestors" (220). Following their separation—as a devout Catholic she refuses him a divorce—he again turned away from the church and became a scoffer. Shortly before his death he decides to return from Italy to Brideshead to die. When Bridey insists on introducing a priest into his room, Marchmain throws him out, telling him: "Father Mackay, I am afraid you have been brought here under a misapprehension. I am not *in extremis,* and I have not been a practising member of your Church for twenty-five years" (327). Several weeks later, while Bridey and Cordelia are away, Lord Marchmain's condition suddenly becomes worse, and Julia, whose thoughts have been changing in the course of the summer, sends for the priest again over the opposition of Cara and Charles, who tell her that "[w]e mustn't take advantage of him, now he's weak, to comfort our own consciences" (336). When Lord Marchmain falls unconscious, Father Mackay goes in to pronounce the last rites, absolving him of his sins and making the sign of the cross. In this emotionally charged moment even Charles falls to his knees—like Veronika in the Vatican—hoping for "a sign, if only of courtesy, if only for the sake of the woman I loved, who knelt in front of me, praying, I knew, for a sign" (338). At that moment Lord Marchmain moves his hand to his head and makes the sign of the cross. "I've known it happen that way again and again," the priest tells Charles afterward. "The devil resists to the last moment and then the Grace of God is too much for him. You're not a Catholic, I think, Mr. Ryder, but at least you'll be glad for the ladies to have the comfort of it" (339).

As a result of this seeming miracle, Julia decides that she cannot marry Charles even though their divorces have both come through.

> I've always been bad. Probably I shall be bad again, punished again. But the worse I am, the more I need God. I can't shut myself out from His mercy. This is what it would mean; starting a life with you, without Him.... I saw to-day there was one thing unforgivable ... the bad thing I was on the point of doing, that I'm not quite bad enough to do; to set up a rival good to God's ... it may be a private bargain between me and God, that if I give up this one thing I want so much, however bad I am, He won't quite despair of me in the end. (340)

As the novel ends, in the summer of 1939, all four Flyte children—Lady Marchmain died shortly before her husband—have returned to the bosom of the church, and Charles is left as the guardian of their memory. When he returns to Brideshead during the war—he entered the army four years earlier, he tells us, as his "last love" (5)—he learns that Bridey is in Palestine with his yeomen guard and that Cordelia and Julia are serving there too in some saintlike capacity.

Charles himself for long had no religion. "I was taken to church weekly as a child, and at school attended chapel daily, but, as though in compensation, from the time I went to my public school was excused church in the holidays" (85). He grows up regarding the narrative of Christianity as a myth and its ethical teaching as of dubious value. Although he resists the label of atheism, he calls himself an agnostic (91) and has fled into aestheticism in an effort to keep life at a distance, to "see everything secondhand" (291), as Julia tells him angrily. His career decision to paint buildings rather than portraits exemplifies his detachment from humanity. For years he finds the Catholicism of his Brideshead friends incomprehensible. He tells Bridey that "if I ever felt for a moment like becoming a Catholic, I should only have to talk to you for five minutes to be cured. You manage to reduce what seem quite sensible propositions to stark nonsense" (164). When he falls to his knees at Lord Marchmain's deathbed, it is only for Julia's sake. Yet he has learned a great deal in the course of the years. When she finally rejects him, he tells her: "I hope your heart may break; but I do understand" (341).

Various hints in the novel imply that Ryder has subsequently converted as well—a conversion that Waugh made explicit in his 1960 revision of the novel.[32] In the prologue, when his junior officer Hooper is describing the new headquarters, he tells Ryder that "there's a sort of R.C. church attached," saying it's "more in your line than mine" (16–17). And when Ryder visits the chapel in the epilogue, he finds the lamp burning before the altar and says a prayer, "an ancient, newly learned form of words" (350).[33]

Ryder has come to appreciate the cultural significance of Catholicism. He speaks of his junior officer, in his shallowness and ignorance of history, as "a symbol of Young England" (9). Later, when he reads the letters of Lady Marchmain's three brothers, all of whom died in World War I, he reflects: "These men must die to make a world for Hooper; they were the aborigines, vermin by right of law, to be shot off at leisure, so that things might be safe for the travelling salesman, with his polygonal pince-nez, his fat wet hand-shake, his grinning dentures" (139). And on the last page, as he leaves the chapel, he thinks again of the ancient Marchmain family, who built their house generation after generation "until, in sudden frost, came the age of Hooper; the place was desolate and the work all brought to nothing.... Vanity of vanities, all is vanity" (351). Yet the small red flame of the altar lamp still burns. "It could not have been lit but for the builders and the tragedians, and there I found it this morning, burning anew among the old stones" (351). It is this thought that enables Ryder's account, after all the personal tragedies and sadness, to end on a positive note. In his movement from art to faith, as Waugh's biographer has shrewdly observed, Charles Ryder precisely inverts the process of secularization that Joyce depicted thirty years earlier in his *Portrait of the Artist as a Young Man.*[34]

⟿

If we now pause to recapitulate, many parallels to *The Veil of Veronika* seem obvious. Both novels are first-person narratives by figures who relate their "sacred and profane memories": Veronika and Charles Ryder. In both novels a place—Rome and Brideshead—provides the focal point and central symbol (even though Waugh's novel has many scenes set in Oxford, Venice, London, Paris, and Morocco). Both novels revolve around families caught up in complicated relationships of religious faith, extending from the paganism of Veronika's grandmother and Lord Marchmain to the religious fanaticism of Edelgart and Lady Marchmain, each of whom has driven off a fiancé/husband through her excessive spirituality.[35] Both works move steadily toward and culminate in acts of conversion beginning with the deathbed conversions of Edelgart and Lord Marchmain. But the greater parallel shows up in the spiritual development from "half-heathen" to religiosity in Veronika and Julia. The late conversions of both Veronika and Ryder are anticipated by scenes in which they spontaneously fall to their knees in prayer. In both plots the fragile family balance is upset by the intrusion of a nonbelieving outsider in the persons of Enzio and Charles Ryder, which leads to their love affairs with Veronika and Julia.

Despite these striking parallels, the similarities can hardly be attributed to literary influence. They are due, rather, to the nature of the two novels as conversion narratives by writers seeking to find fictional equivalents for their own conversions. Their weaknesses result from the authors' inability to provide adequate fictional motivation, especially in the cases of Veronika and Julia, for that intensely private experience. The differences are no doubt due to the fact that Waugh (1903–66) was already fifteen years past his conversion and the author of several earlier novels when he wrote *Brideshead Revisited*, while le Fort was a recent convert writing her first novel.

Waugh discussed his conversion in the essay "Converted to Rome: Why It Has Happened to Me," which he wrote and published just three weeks after he was received into the Roman Catholic Church on 29 September 1930. He begins by discrediting three errors adduced popularly to explain why the Catholic Church was recruiting so many intelligent men and women in contemporary England: "the Jesuits have got hold of him"; "he is captivated by the ritual"; and "he wants to have his mind made up for him." At the present moment in European history Waugh sees the essential issue as being not between Catholicism and Protestantism but "between Christianity and Chaos"—that is, the now almost routine turn to faith as a response to disorder. It is in this context that Waugh claims that "Christianity is essential to civilization"—a view also widely proclaimed by such contemporaries as Gertrud von le Fort, Theodor Haecker, Hillaire Belloc, and T. S. Eliot.[36] But Waugh goes on to argue that "Christianity exists in its most complete and vital form in the Roman Catholic Church." First, Catholicism has a coherent and consistent teaching. Second, the church has a competent organization and discipline. Finally, Catholicism is by its nature universal and thus represents Christianity in its unity and totality.[37]

Waugh's progress toward conversion, as he describes it in his autobiography, is typical in its stages.[38] His father was a practicing Anglican who enjoyed churchgoing without any "genuine intellectual conviction about any element of his creed" (68). As a boy Waugh went through a religious phase, attracted at age eleven by the services of Anglo-Catholicism and learning how to serve at the altar. "I rejoiced in my nearness to the sacred symbols and in the bright early-morning stillness and in a sense of intimacy with what was being enacted" (93). He even expressed the intention of becoming a parson—a "phase of churchiness" to which his mother, the stepdaughter of a clergyman, was distinctly unsympathetic. When he went off to Lancing College in 1917 he was still, "if not genuinely devout, a particularly church-loving boy" with aspirations of becoming a parson. But by his last year, on 18 June 1921, he could write in his diary: "In the last few weeks I have ceased to be a Christian. I have realized that for the last two terms at least I have been an atheist in all except the courage to admit it myself" (141). Losing all taste for matters ecclesiastical, he was now "eager to dispute the intellectual foundations of Christianity" (142) and, in the school debating societies, discussed such issues as the immortality of the soul, divine omniscience, and the relevance of institutional religion.

This insouciance continued during his career at Oxford, which he spent surrounded by a brilliant circle of friends dedicated to aesthetics and joie de vivre, though many of them were devout Anglicans and Catholics; indeed, one of his closest friends, Alastair Graham, converted to Catholicism in his last year there. Waugh, known to his friends as a promising artist rather than as a writer, left Oxford in 1924 with an undistinguished Third in his examinations. The next four years, which his Oxford friend Harold Acton labeled Waugh's "Dostoievski period,"[39] constituted a period of frustrated love affairs, drinking, and depression as Waugh moved purposelessly from art school to teaching and occasional journalism. But it was also during this period that he edged gradually toward his career as a writer, with an essay on the Pre-Raphaelites (1926), the biography *Rossetti* (1928), the satirical novel *Decline and Fall* (1928), which brought him his early literary recognition, and the novel *Vile Bodies* (1930), which harvested fame and the wealth that enabled him to support himself as a writer. In 1928–29 Waugh went through a brief and unhappy marriage, which ended in a divorce precipitated by his wife's adultery.

These experiences no doubt contributed to his conversion, which took place in 1930. Waugh kept no diary during the period of his unhappy marriage and leading up to his conversion. Indeed, believing that the spiritual phenomenon was not explicable in psychological terms, Waugh was as noncommunicative about his own conversion as he was about the motivations in *Brideshead Revisited* or, later, in the biography of his friend, *Ronald Knox* (1958).[40] But his notations from the summer of 1930 record frequent lunches and meetings with Father Martin D'Arcy SJ, whose "fine, slippery mind" he admired[41] and who received him into the Catholic Church on 29 September of that year. Father D'Arcy later wrote that "talking with him was an interesting discussion based primarily on reason. I have never myself met a convert who so strongly based his assent on truth. It was a special pleasure to make contact with so able a brain."[42]

As Waugh's career flourished, as he settled down into a second and happy marriage, and as his sense of religion matured, his faith grew beyond the rational appeal of Catholicism to embrace its meaning in history and for the spiritual life of the individual. It was this Catholicism representing Christianity in its entirety and as the vehicle of personal grace that he sought to depict in *Brideshead Revisited*, which, as it neared completion, he regarded as "the first of my novels rather than the last."[43] As he explained in *Life* magazine in an open letter to American readers, the book seeks to portray the whole human mind and soul, and that means above all to show "man in his relation to God."[44]

Congruities

If this were a Hegelian bildungsroman of the spirit, we would now be in a position to recapitulate a steady process of development moving from the loss of faith in the late nineteenth century, through the successive stages of aestheticism, flight, socialism, myth, and utopia in the early twentieth century, and on to a (re)conversion to faith in the period *entre deux guer-res*. But the psychology of the individual is not so straightforward as the phenomenology of spirit.

The single common denominator among the roughly thirty writers considered here is their loss of faith in the religion (Christianity in almost every case) to which they were born. In the earlier works, autobiographical and fictional alike, loss of faith constituted the main theme. In later works the sensation of spiritual emptiness is simply the initially posited factor that motivates the search for new modes of faith and that justifies the religious structure inevitably sought in the surrogate.

From that point on, however, vast differences are evident among the writers treated, no one of whom passes through all five stages of the Hegelian process. A few writers, to be sure, explore more than one stage. Hermann Hesse enjoyed a period of early aestheticism, an aestheticism whose products were too juvenile to bear comparison with those of George, Valéry, and Joyce. From there he moved on to India, both in travel journals and in an enormously popular novel; he flirted with myth in *Demian* and ended with a grand utopian vision in *The Glass Bead Game*. Stefan George moved easily from art for art's sake to the spiritual community of his circle, where he mythified his beloved Maximin. But most writers were content to experience a single surrogate, and few of them succumbed to any return to faith of the sort undergone by the mystics and converts of the 1920s and 1930s. In sum, the readings betray an aggregate of individual cases rather than any overriding pattern among the many writers and thinkers considered in the foregoing chapters. Whereas believers—and of course there were many—continue to be sustained by their faith, spirits that have lost that faith are unable to survive in the "disenchanted" world, and so they look elsewhere. But that "elsewhere" is typically an individual quest, undertaken alone.

In the prewar works it was primarily a disgust with contemporary European society and its values that motivated the turn to art or the flight to India. But after 1914 the loss of faith and cultural malaise were intensified to an almost unbearable pitch by the ravages of World War I and its consequences. It was no longer simply dissatisfaction with a disenchanted world. That world itself, along with its social structures and cultural values, had been radically transformed. Accordingly the individual sought comfort in the group, whether socialist or fascist or elitist or utopian, because otherwise the sense of meaninglessness and powerlessness was overwhelming.

Yet in the final analysis all the surrogates turned out to be inadequate. George went beyond art into the group, just as Valéry moved beyond it into public life. (Only Joyce was able to maintain his aesthetic posture, possibly because he remained in exile.) The travelers to India returned to Europe, having failed to find what they sought and retaining nothing but memories of fleeting epiphanies on mountaintops. The enthusiastic socialists saw their ideals degenerate into the cruel bureaucracies of communism, just as the mythophiles deplored the distortion of their visions in the service of Nazism and Fascism. Others turned their backs on their utopias, realizing that their lives must be lived in the present world of reality.

When even the surrogates had been proved illusory, a few individuals turned back to the consolation of religious faith, whether in the form of mysticism or through conversion. Most, however, resolved to live out their lives without faith and without surrogates. It was at this point in Western cultural and intellectual history that existentialism appeared on the scene with its message that, in an absurd and meaningless world, one can only strive to endure with a certain degree of dignity and authenticity. But that is another story.

The story we have been telling is worth our attention precisely because today's secularized society, especially in Europe but also among many root- less Americans, finds itself in a situation remarkably similar to that of almost a century ago, even if our surrogates display a conspicuous tendency toward the trivial. In place of an élitist art for art's sake we have the virtual reality of computer games, "reality" shows, and participatory forms of art in which we are encouraged to lose ourselves. The trip to India, formerly available to a select few, has grown to encompass holiday flights and cruises to every part of the world, to which we are enticed by travel clubs, alumni groups, and ads promising escape from the demands of our daily lives. The dreams of socialism have given way to the cushions of government enti- tlements and retirement plans. Television and the movies provide us with our myths. Las Vegas, retirement communities on golf courses, and gated residential enclaves offer a little corner of utopia in our own world. And quickie versions of religion in the form of New Age fads promise an easy reentry into faith, should we wish it. When contemporary celebrities with great fanfare turn from their "art" to one of the fashionable new "faiths," they are reenacting an unwitting parody of the very process we have been describing—the first time as tragedy, as Marx quipped, and the second time as farce. The desires of our modern society have combined with the mar- vels of technology to breed many mechanisms of escape, but the surrogates are original only in form, not in substance. Yet beyond those twenty-first- century modes of faith awaits, inevitably and inescapably, the problematic reality of a world still disenchanted and of lives still unfulfilled.

NOTES

CHAPTER ONE

1. Theodore Ziolkowski, *The Mirror of Justice: Literary Reflections of Legal Crises* (Princeton: Princeton University Press, 1997).

2. Arnaldo Momigliano, "Religion in Athens, Rome, and Jerusalem in the First Century B.C.," in his *Pagans, Jews, and Christians* (Middletown: Wesleyan University Press, 1987), 74–91, here 76–78; and Carl Koch, "Roman State Religion in the Mirror of Augustan and Late Republican Apologetics," in *Roman Religion*, ed. Clifford Ando (Edinburgh: Edinburgh University Press, 2003), 296–329, here 300.

3. I take the terms from Clifford Ando's introduction to *Roman Religion*, 11–13.

4. Arnaldo Momigliano, "Roman Religion: The Imperial Period," in *Pagans, Jews, and Christians*, 178–201.

5. See Bart D. Ehrman, *Lost Christianities: The Battles for Scripture and the Faiths We Never Knew* (New York: Oxford University Press, 2003).

6. G. W. Bowersock, *Fiction as History: Nero to Julian* (Berkeley: University of California Press, 1994), esp. 99–119 ("Resurrection") and 121–43 ("Polytheism and Scripture"); and Momigliano, *Pagans, Jew, and Christians*, 142–58.

7. Theodore Ziolkowski, *Hesitant Heroes: Private Inhibition, Cultural Crisis* (Ithaca: Cornell University Press, 2004).

8. See also Michael Burleigh, *Earthly Powers: Religion and Politics in Europe from the Enlightenment to the Great War* (London: HarperCollins, 2005); and Thomas Nipperdey, *Deutsche Geschichte 1866–1918* (Munich: Beck, 1990), 507–28 ("Die Unkirchlichen und die Religion"}.

9. Nikki R. Keddie, "Secularism and Its Discontents," *Daedalus* (Summer 2003): 14–30, here 14–15.

10. Siegfried Kracauer, "Die Wartenden," *Frankfurter Zeitung* (12 March 1922), rpt. in *Das Ornament der Masse. Essays* (Frankfurt am Main: Suhrkamp, 1977), 106–19, here 107.

11. Martin E. Marty, "Our Religio-secular World," *Daedalus* (Summer 2003): 42–48.

12. René Guénon, *La Crise du monde moderne* (1927; Paris: Gallimard, 1946), 126–34. On Guénon, Traditionalism from the 1920s to the present, and its political

spinoffs, see Mark Sedgwick, *Against the Modern World: Traditionalism and the Secret Intellectual History of the Twentieth Century* (New York: Oxford University Press, 2004).

13. See the cover story in the Christmas issue of *Time*, 22 December 2003. In her confessional study of "the secret Gospel of Thomas," *Beyond Belief* (New York: Random House, 2003), Elaine Pagels repeatedly—notably at the beginning of each chapter—returns to the interaction of her personal experience and her scholarship.

14. George Gallup Jr. and Timothy Jones, *The Next American Spirituality: Finding God in the Twenty-first Century* (Colorado Springs: Cook Communications, 2000), 178.

15. Niall Ferguson, "Why America Outpaces Europe (Clue: The God Factor)," *New York Times*, section 4 ("Week in Review"), 8 June 2003, 3.

16. Lizette Alvarez, "Fury, God and the Pastor's Disbelief," *New York Times*, 8 July 2003, A4.

17. Kenneth L. Woodward, "An Oxymoron: Europe without Christianity," *New York Times*, 14 June 2003, A15.

18. Joseph Weiler, as quoted in *Die Zeit*, 17 April 2004, 3.

19. Barbara Gunnell, "Religion: Why Do We Still Give a Damn?" *New Statesman*, 3 May 2004, 18–19.

20. Nicholas D. Kristof, "Believe It, or Not," *New York Times*, 15 August 2003, A29.

21. Jan Ross, "Mehr Gott wagen," *Die Zeit*, 28 May 2003, 1.

22. "Heimkehr in ein unchristliches Land," *Spiegel*, 15 August 2005.

23. Max Weber, introduction to "Die Wirtschaftsethik der Weltreligionen," in *Gesammelte Aufsätze zu Religionssoziologie*, 2 vols. (Tübingen: Mohr, 1947), 1: 237–75, here 253. The essay has been translated under the title "The Social Psychology of the World Religions," in Max Weber, *Essays in Sociology*, trans. Hans H. Gerth and C. Wright Mills (New York: Oxford University Press, 1958), 267–301.

24. "Burnt Norton," in T. S. Eliot, *The Complete Poems and Plays, 1909–1950* (New York: Harcourt, 1958), 118. Eliot had coined his phrase earlier in *Murder in the Cathedral* (1935), ibid., 209.

CHAPTER TWO

1. Edmund Blunden, introduction to James Thomson, *The City of Dreadful Night and Other Poems* (London: Methuen, 1932), 7, 14.

2. See the characterizations by contemporaries in William David Schaefer, *James Thomson (B.V.): Beyond "The City"* (Berkeley: University of California Press, 1965), 1–6.

3. Ibid., 37–81.

4. Ernst Haeckel, *The Riddle of the Universe at the Close of the Nineteenth Century* (1899), trans. Joseph McCabe (New York: Harper, 1901), 308.

5. Charles Coulston Gillispie, *Genesis and Geology: A Study in the Relations of Scientific Thought, Natural Theology, and Social Opinion in Great Britain, 1790–1850* (Cambridge: Harvard University Press, 1951).

6. Andrew Dickson White, *A History of the Warfare of Science with Theology in Christendom*, 2 vols. (New York: Appleton, 1896), 2: 168–208.

7. This fascinating story has been written many times. See the summary and bibliography in Theodore Ziolkowski, *Fictional Transfigurations of Jesus* (Princeton: Princeton University Press, 1972), 30–41.

8. See James Wood, "The Broken Estate: The Legacy of Ernest Renan and Matthew Arnold," in *The Broken Estate: Essays on Literature and Belief* (New York: Random House, 1999), 242–63, here 242–47. Wood's discussion is weakened by his neglect of the German Higher Criticism, upon which both Renan and Arnold based their views.

9. Arthur Schopenhauer, *Sämmtliche Werke*, ed. Julius Frauenstadt, new ed., 6 vols. (Leipzig: Brockhaus, 1922), 6: 347–421, here 370, 420.

10. James George Frazer, *The Golden Bough: A Study of Magic and Religion*, 12 vols. (New York: Macmillan, 1935), 1: xxvi.

11. William James, *The Varieties of Religious Experience: A Study in Human Nature* (1902; rpt. New York: New American Library, 1958), 24, 381.

12. Max Weber, *The Protestant Ethic and the Spirit of Capitalism*, trans. Talcott Parsons, rev. introduction by Randall Collins (Los Angeles: Roxbury, 1998), 182.

13. See White, *History of the Warfare of Science with Theology*.

14. *Kilvert's Diary: Selections from the Diary of the Rev. Francis Kilvert*, ed. William Plomer (London: Penguin, 1977).

15. William James, "The Will to Believe," in *The Will to Believe and Other Essays in Popular Philosophy* (1897; rpt. New York: Dover, 1956), 1–31, here 5–6.

16. Albert Schweitzer, *The Quest of the Historical Jesus: A Critical Study of Its Progress from Reimarus to Wrede*, trans. W. Montgomery (1910; rpt. New York: Macmillan, 1968), 401.

17. Lance St John Butler, *Victorian Doubt: Literary and Cultural Discourses* (New York: Harvester Wheatsheaf, 1990), 9. Curiously, Barbara W. Tuchman, in her "portrait of the world before the war, 1890–1914," *The Proud Tower* (1966; New York: Ballantine Books, 1996), makes no mention of the religious controversies that dominated public discourse in all major nations.

18. Susan Budd, *Varieties of Unbelief: Atheists and Agnostics in English Society, 1850–1960* (London: Heinemann, 1977), 104–23.

19. Wolfgang Braungart, *Ästhetischer Katholizismus: Stefan Georges Rituale der Literatur* (Tübingen: Niemeyer, 1997), 54–61.

20. See Martin Swales, *The German Bildungsroman from Wieland to Hesse* (Princeton: Princeton University Press, 1978); and Michael Minden, *The German Bildungsroman: Incest and Inheritance* (Cambridge: Cambridge University Press, 1997). Jerome Hamilton Buckley, *Season of Youth: The Bildungsroman from Dickens to Golding* (Cambridge: Harvard University Press, 1974), 119, singles out Samuel Butler's *The Way of All Flesh* as an exception for the role that evangelical religion plays in it.

21. J. Hillis Miller, *The Disappearance of God: Five Nineteenth-Century Writers* (Cambridge: Harvard University Press/Belknap, 1963), 12–13.

22. Herman Melville, *Moby Dick; or, The Whale* (New York: Modern Library, 1950), 56.

23. Gustave Flaubert, *Madame Bovary*, trans. and ed. Paul de Man (New York: Norton, 1965), 28.

24. T. R. Wright, "*Middlemarch* as a Religious Novel, or Life without God," in *Images of Belief in Literature*, ed. David Jasper (New York: St. Martin's, 1984), 138–52. "Nowhere in George Eliot's work is the absence of God so noticeable as in *Middlemarch*" (139).

25. U. C. Knoepflmacher, *Religious Humanism and the Victorian Novel: George Eliot, Walter Pater, and Samuel Butler* (Princeton: Princeton University Press, 1965), 115. See also Butler, *Victorian Doubt*, 12–13.

26. I cite the Constance Garnett translation as revised by the editors: Leo Tolstoy, *Anna Karenina*, ed. and intro. by Leonard J. Kent and Nina Berberova (New York: Modern Library, 1933).

27. Ibid., editors' introduction, xxiv.

28. Theodor Fontane, *Ausgewählte Werke*, introduction by Thomas Mann, 5 vols. (Leipzig: Reclam, [1928]), 5: 124.

29. See Ziolkowski, *Fictional Transfigurations*, 55–97. Here I disagree with Butler, *Victorian Doubt*, 89–90, who reads these works as novels of doubt.

30. Robert Minder, "Das Bild des Pfarrhauses in der deutschen Literatur von Jean Paul bis Gottfried Benn," in *Kultur und Literatur in Deutschland und Frankreich* (Frankfurt am Main: Insel, 1962), 44–72.

31. Quoted in ibid., 71.

32. Friedrich Nietzsche, *Werke in drei Bänden*, ed. Karl Schlechta, 3 vols. (Munich: Hanser, 1954–56), 2: 205 (section 343). Nietzsche makes the same statement elsewhere in the book (notably sections 105 and 125).

33. Friedrich Nietzsche, *Gesammelte Werke*, 23 vols. (Munich: Musarion, 1920–29), 11: 78.

34. Ibid., 14: 79.

35. Tolstoy, *A Confession, The Gospel in Brief, and What I Believe*, trans. Aylmer Maude (London: Oxford University Press, 1951), 5. *A Confession*, though circulated in Russia in 1882, was first printed in Geneva in 1888.

36. Edmund Gosse, *Father and Son: A Study of Two Temperaments* (New York: Scribner's, 1907), 297.

37. Philip Henry Gosse, *Omphalos: An Attempt to Untie the Geological Knot* (1857; rpt. Woodbridge, Conn.: Ox Bow Press, 1998), chap. 10. According to what Gosse calls his theory of "prochronism," when God summoned his idea of the world into existence, "at the selected stage it appears, exactly as it would have appeared at that moment of its history, if all the preceding eras of its existence had been real" (351).

38. Edmund Gosse to Sydney Holland, 15 January 1908, in Evan Charteris, *The Life and Letters of Sir Edmund Gosse* (New York: Harper, 1931), 308.

39. Robert Graves, *Goodbye to All That* (1929), new rev. ed. (London: Cassell, 1957), 11.

40. Budd, *Varieties of Unbelief*, 104–7.

CHAPTER THREE

1. Jerome Hamilton Buckley, *Season of Youth: The Bildungsroman from Dickens to Golding* (Cambridge: Harvard University Press, 1974), 123.

2. Samuel Butler, *The Way of All Flesh* (New York: Dutton, 1911), 19–20 (chap. 5). For the convenience of readers using other editions I cite both page and chapter.

3. U. C. Knoepflmacher, *Religious Humanism and the Victorian Novel: George Eliot, Walter Pater, and Samuel Butler* (Princeton: Princeton University Press, 1965), 257–95, provides an excellent analysis of the novel according to Butler's evolutionary ideas.

4. Knoepflmacher, ibid., 271, argues persuasively that Theobald and Christina represent an ironic and parodic analogy to Casaubon and Dorothea in *Middlemarch*.

5. Buckley, *Season of Youth*, 119.

6. Knoepflmacher, *Religious Humanism*, 279, identifies three stages in Ernest's "reconversion to his 'true self'": Battersby/Roughborough, Cambridge/London, and afterward.

7. Roger Martin du Gard, "Consultation littéraire," *Nouvelle Revue Française*, December 1958, 1117–33, here 1128 (24 Aug.1918). This series of letters, which the author wrote to his friend Pierre Margaritis in 1918, has recently been included in Martin du Gard's *Correspondance générale*, ed. Maurice Rieuneau, 8 vols. (Paris: Gallimard, 1980–), 2: 877–964.

8. Victor Brombert, *The Intellectual Hero: Studies in the French Novel, 1880–1955* (Philadelphia: Lippincott, 1961), 96.

9. Martin du Gard, "Consultation littéraire," 1129 (1 Sept. 1918).

10. I cite the sometimes rather free translation by Stuart Gilbert, *Jean Barois* (New York: Viking, 1949) but revise it against the text in the two-volume Pléiade edition: Roger Martin du Gard, *Oeuvres complètes*, with a preface by Albert Camus (Paris: Gallimard, 1955), 1: 205–559.

11. Nietzsche does not figure prominently in the critical studies of Martin du Gard; but statements of this sort invariably recall the author of *Beyond Good and Evil*, whom the author was reading in 1910 and lists among the philosophers to whom he felt the greatest affinity. See his *Journal*, ed. Claude Sicard, 13 vols. (Paris: Gallimard, 1992), 1: 297. Nietzsche enjoyed "une vogue incontestable" in France in the early 1900s outside the confines of university philosophy, and all his important works had been translated. See Luis Pinto, *Les Neveux de Zarathoustra: la réception de Nietzsche en France* (Paris: Seuil, 1995), 25–78, here 25.

12. Martin du Gard, "Consultation Littéraire," 1123 (23 Jan.), 1126 (6 Feb.).

13. Henri Peyre, *The Contemporary French Novel* (New York: Oxford University Press, 1955), 44. See also Brombert, *Intellectual Hero*, 94–118, esp. 105–11; David L. Schalk, *Roger Martin du Gard: The Novelist and History* (Ithaca: Cornell University Press, 1967), 18–54, esp. 26–27; and Catherine Savage, *Roger Martin du Gard* (New York: Twayne, 1968), 41–64, esp. 52–58.

14. Martin du Gard, "Consultation littéraire," 1119 (18 Jan. 1918).

15. E.g., Peyre, *Contemporary French Novel*, 43.

16. See Réjean Robidoux, *Roger Martin du Gard et la religion* (Clamecy: Aubier, 1964), esp. 25–79. The chapter on Martin du Gard in Charles Moeller, *Littérature du XXe siècle et christianisme*, 5 vols. (Paris: Casterman, 1956–93), 2: 165–216, is vitiated by the author's narrowly orthodox view that Catholic education ("la formation chrétienne") around 1880 was "false"—that "all the aspects of faith cited in *Jean Barois*" are false (215) and that therefore Martin du Gard was, so to speak, whipping dead dogs. "Faith is truth and not simply blind belief [*fidéisme*]. If it is reasonable, the

opposition on which Martin du Gard based his novel falls apart; *Jean Barois* now has nothing but the value of a historical document, moreover a simplistic and partial one, regarding a past epoch, that of the 1880s" (216).

17. Camus, "Roger Martin du Gard," in Martin du Gard, *Oeuvres complètes*, 1: xix. Camus's essay was reprinted in *Nouvelle Revue Française*, October 1955, 641–71.

18. In a letter of 30 July 1916; Martin du Gard, *Correspondence générale*, 2: 150.

19. See Robidoux, *Roger Martin du Gard et la religion*, 25–79, for the most thorough biographical presentation of his religious development. The picture can now be filled in more reliably on the basis of the published correspondence.

20. Martin du Gard, "In Memoriam" (1916), in *Oeuvres complètes*, 1: 561–76.

21. Martin du Gard, "Consultation littéraire," 1134 (14 Sept. 1918).

22. I take the phrase from Robidoux, *Roger Martin du Gard et la religion*, 26.

23. Martin du Gard to Pierre Quentin-Bauchart, 21 August 1901, *Correspondence générale*, 1: 64.

24. Ibid., 1: 62–63.

25. Ibid., 1: 64.

26. Martin du Gard to Marcel Hébert, 8 August 1901, *Correspondence générale*, 1: 55.

27. Martin du Gard to Pierre Quentin-Bauchart, 21 August 1901, *Correspondence générale*, 1: 65.

28. Martin du Gard, *Oeuvres complètes*, 2: 597 (*Summer 1914*, 592). The other two were the Dreyfus Affair and World War I.

29. Martin du Gard, *Correspondence générale*, 1: 59–60.

30. Robidoux, *Roger Martin du Gard et la religion*, 381, concludes his thoughtful and sympathetic study with the observation that Martin du Gard's attitude can best be characterized as "tranquil agnosticism," being not a strident denial but a calm acceptance of the impossibility of knowing.

31. Camus, "Roger Martin du Gard," xviii. "Le stoïcien Luce représente probablement l'idéal de Martin du Gard." See also Brombert, *Intellectual Hero*, 113.

32. *Jean Barois*, Gilbert's translation, 357. Martin du Gard uses the more polite term *mirage* (1: 551) rather than "mumbo-jumbo."

33. Martin du Gard, "Consultation littéraire," 1128 (24 Aug. 1918).

34. Martin du Gard to Félix Le Dantec, 26 November 1913, *Correspondence générale*, 1: 338.

35. Philippe van Tieghem, "*Jean Barois* et nous," *Nouvelle Revue Française*, December 1958, 1064–67.

36. The best accounts of Hesse's childhood are to be found in his various autobiographical writings. See the selection of the most important ones in Hermann Hesse, *Autobiographical Writings*, ed. Theodore Ziolkowski, trans. Denver Lindley (New York: Farrar, Straus and Giroux, 1971).

37. Quoted here from *My Belief: Essays on Life and Art*, ed. Theodore Ziolkowski, trans. Denver Lindley (New York: Farrar, Straus and Giroux, 1975), 177.

38. Since my focus in this book is on Sinclair's spiritual development, I will not deal here with all the factors that make a convincing case for Demian as a postfiguration of Christ. See Theodore Ziolkowski, *Fictional Transfigurations of Jesus* (Princeton: Princeton University Press, 1972), 151–61.

39. The infatuation of this generation with older women—"the mature woman, the maternal woman who is older than we but decides to share our youth," as it is put by a figure in Heimito von Doderer's novel *Die Dämonen*, 2 vols. (Munich: Biederstein, 1956), 1: 255–56—deserves a separate investigation. Cf. Octavian and the Marschallin in Hofmannsthal/Strauss, *Der Rosenkavalier.*

40. Cited in my own translation from the text in vol. 3 of Hesse's *Gesammelte Schriften*, 7 vols. (Frankfurt am Main: Suhrkamp, 1957), 114.

41. Gerschom Scholem, *Walter Benjamin*, Leo Baeck Memorial Lecture, 8 (New York: Leo Baeck Institute, 1965), 16.

42. From "Epilogue," in Roger Martin du Gard, *Summer 1914*, trans. Stuart Gilbert (New York: Viking, 1941), 979–80. For a discussion of this novel, see chap. 4 below.

43. Theodore Ziolkowski, *The Novels of Hermann Hesse: A Study in Theme and Structure* (Princeton: Princeton University Press, 1965), 34–51, traces three stages in the development of Hesse's chiliastic vision.

44. Hermann Hesse/Romain Rolland, *D'une rive à l'autre: Correspondence et fragments du journal*, ed. Pierre Grappur (Paris: Albin Michel, 1972), 46.

45. From the essay "Besuch aus Indien" (1922), *Gesammelte Schriften*, 3: 857.

46. From the essay "O Freunde, nicht diese Töne!" (1914), in *If the War Goes On . . . Reflections on War and Politics*, trans. Ralph Manheim (New York: Farrar, Straus and Giroux, 1971), 13.

47. Hesse, *My Belief*, 7–85, here 71. This paradigm shift is paralleled in such fields as history of religion, anthropology, sociology, and psychology by the shift of interest from deities to rituals—that is, to the social aspects of religion. See Albert Henrichs, "Götterdämmerung und Götterglanz: Griechischer Polytheismus seit 1872," in *Urgeschichten der Menschheit: Die Antike im 20. Jahrhundert*, ed. Bernd Seidensticker and Martin Voehler (Stuttgart: Metzler, 2001), 1–19.

48. Ralph Waldo Emerson, *Lectures and Biographical Sketches, Complete Works*, Centenary ed. (Boston: Houghton Mifflin, 1903–4), 10: 181–214, here 211.

49. Huston Smith, *Condemned to Meaning*, John Dewey Society Lectureship Series, 7 (New York: Harper & Row, 1965), 90.

50. Karl Jaspers, *Myth and Christianity: An Inquiry into the Possibility of Religion without Myth* (New York: Noonday, 1958), 5.

CHAPTER FOUR

1. G. W. F. Hegel, *Phänomenologie des Geistes*, ed. Johannes Hofmeister (Hamburg: Meiner, 1952), 521.

2. Theodore Ziolkowski, *German Romanticism and Its Institutions* (Princeton: Princeton University Press, 1990), 329–37. See also Jacques Barzun, *The Use and Abuse of Art*, Bollingen Series, 35, A. W. Mellon Lectures in the Fine Arts, 22 (Princeton: Princeton University Press, 1973), 24–46 ("The Rise of Art as Religion"), who does not distinguish between art as an expression of religion and art as a surrogate for religion.

3. In the essay "The Work of Art in the Age of Mechanical Reproduction," *Illuminations*, ed. Hannah Arendt (New York: Wolff/Harcourt, 1968), 219–53, here 226.

4. Wolfgang Braungart, *Ästhetischer Katholizismus. Stefan Georges Rituale der Literatur* (Tübingen: Niemeyer, 1997), 3–34; and Justus H. Ulbricht, "Der 'neue Mensch' auf der Suche nach 'neuer Religiosität,'" *Der Deutschunterricht* 50 (1998): 38–48.

5. Hermann Bahr, "Die Moderne," *Moderne Dichtung* 1 (1890): 13–15, rpt. in Hermann Bahr, *Zur Überwindung des Naturalismus. Theoretische Schriften 1887–1904*, ed. Gotthart Wunberg (Stuttgart: Kohlhammer, 1968), 35–38, here 35.

6. Edith Landmann, *Gespräche mit Stefan George* (Düsseldorf: Küpper/Bondi, 1963), 78.

7. For the varied responses to George and his work, see *Stefan George, 1868–1968. Der Dichter und sein Kreis*, catalogue of the Marbach exhibition (Munich, 1968). The most exhaustive accumulation of biographical evidence is available in the chronology *Stefan George/Leben und Werk. Eine Zeittafel*, ed. H.–J. Seekamp, R. C. Ockenden, M. Keilson (Amsterdam: Castrum Peregrini, 1972). For a narrative account in English, see Robert E. Norton, *Secret Germany: Stefan George and His Circle* (Ithaca: Cornell University Press, 2002).

8. From the volume *Tage und Taten* (1903); I quote George's works from the two–volume edition of *Werke* (Munich: Bondi, 1958), here 1: 479–81.

9. I take most of the factual details regarding individual poems from Ernst Morwitz, *Kommentar zu dem Werk Stefan Georges* (Munich: Küpper/Bondi, 1960), here 40. On the interpretation of individual poems, see also Claude David, *Stefan George: son oeuvre poétique*, Bibliothèque de la Société des Etudes Germaniques, 9 (Lyon, 1952).

10. E. R. Curtius, "Stefan George in Conversation," in his *Essays on European Literature*, trans. Michael Kowal (Princeton: Princeton University Press, 1973), 107–28, here 128.

11. Hansjürgen Linke, *Das Kultische in der Dichtung Stefan Georges und seiner Schule*, 2 vols. (Munich: Küpper/Bondi, 1960); and Braungart, *Ästhetischer Katholizismus*, 176–204.

12. Georg Fuchs, *Sturm und Drang in München um die Jahrhundertwende* (Munich: Callwey, 1936), 123–31.

13. On the photographs, see Braungart, *Ästhetischer Katholizismus*, 118–45.

14. From the volume *Die Fibel* (1990), *Werke* 2: 465–518. Here I disagree with what Friedrich Wolters, *Stefan George und die Blätter für die Kunst. Deutsche Geistesgeschichte seit 1890* (Berlin: Bondi, 1930), 14, seems to mean when he says: "Vom christlichen Glauben tönt kaum noch ein Anklang hinein." On the one hand, he has lost his faith; but, on the other, there are many resonances of regret.

15. See notably Braungart, *Ästhetischer Katholizismus*; but also Hermann Drahn, *Das Werk Stefan Georges, seine Religiosität und sein Ethos* (Leipzig: Hirt, 1925), esp. 67–102.

16. As a student at Duke University in the early 1950s, I sometimes encountered Ernst Morwitz at the nearby University of North Carolina, one of George's most loyal disciples and the translator of his poetry into English. Morwitz drifted around the Chapel Hill campus in a long black cloak reminiscent of George's and gave readings, or chantings, of George's poetry in the solemn, rhythmic manner reputed to be that of the Master himself.

17. Braungart, *Ästhetischer Katholizismus*, 162–67.

18. See Ulrich K. Goldsmith, *Stefan George: A Study of His Early Work* (Boulder: University of Colorado Press, 1959).

19. E. K. Bennett, *Stefan George* (New Haven: Yale University Press, 1954), 40–41.

20. Albert Soergel and Curt Hohoff, *Dichtung und Dichter der Zeit*, 2nd ed., 2 vols. (1911; Düsseldorf: Bagel, 1961), 1: 408.

21. Braungart, *Ästhetischer Katholizismus*, 224–31, here 224.

22. Wolters, *Stefan George und die Blätter für die Kunst*, 16.

23. *Blätter für die Kunst 1892–1919* (rpt. Düsseldorf: Küpper/Bondi, 1968), 1: 1.

24. Stefan George, "Über Dichtung," in *Werke*, 1: 530.

25. Fuchs, *Sturm und Drang in München*, 86.

26. On George's sense of mission, see Hans Reiss, *The Writer's Task from Nietzsche to Brecht* (Totowa, NJ: Rowman and Littlefield, 1978), 28–46.

27. George's angel is wholly different from the angel that Rilke encountered ten years later at Duino Castle, a timeless being from a higher level of reality for whom the poet in his *Duino Elegies* must interiorize the things of human life and experience. See Theodore Ziolkowski, *The Classical German Elegy, 1795–1950* (Princeton: Princeton University Press, 1980), 241–45.

28. Stefan George, "Vorrede zu Maximin," *Werke*, 1:522–23, published originally in *Maximin: Ein Gedenkbuch* (1906).

29. Braungart, *Ästhetischer Katholizismus*, 242.

30. For the (highly biased) view of a disciple, see Wolters, *Stefan George und die Blätter für die Kunst*. For a more detached appraisal, see Norton, *Secret Germany*.

31. "Und er kann töten, ohne zu berühren," in the poem "Der Prophet" (1891), which describes a frightening encounter with George; Hugo von Hofmannsthal, *Gedichte und lyrische Dramen*, ed. Herbert Steiner (Vienna: Fischer, 1952), 502.

32. Ernst Osterkamp, *"Ihr wisst nicht wer ich bin." Stefan Georges poetische Rollenspiele*, Carl Friedrich von Siemens Stiftung: Themen, vol. 74 (Munich, 2002), 37.

33. In the preface to the *Gesamtausgabe* of 1927–1934, *Werke*, 1: 347.

34. Hans Blumenberg, *Schiffbruch mit Zuschauer: Paradigma einer Daseinsmetapher* (Frankfurt am Main: Suhrkamp, 1979), 83.

35. Quoted in "Introduction biographique," in Paul Valéry, *Oeuvres*, ed. Jean Hytier, 2 vols. (Paris: Gallimard, 1957–60), 1: 52.

36. Paul Valéry, *Lettres à quelques-uns* (Paris: Gallimard, 1952), 104.

37. Quoted in notes regarding *La Jeune Parque*; *Oeuvres*, 2: 1615.

38. For biographical details I follow principally the "Introduction biographique" in Valéry, *Oeuvres*, 1: 11–72.

39. Personal notes quoted in "Introduction biographique," in Valéry, *Oeuvres*, 1: 20.

40. Denis Bertholet, *Paul Valéry, 1871–1945* (Paris: Plon, 1995), 73–89.

41. Valéry to Pierre Louÿs, 22 June 1890, *Lettres à quelques-uns*, 13.

42. Valéry to Pierre Louÿs, 14 September 1890, ibid., 21.

43. Valéry to Pierre Louÿs, 21 December 1890, ibid., 41.

44. "Au Sujet d'Euréka," in Valéry, *Oeuvres*, 1: 854–67, here 855. I quote the translation by Malcolm Cowley and James R. Lawler: Paul Valéry, *Leonardo, Poe, Mallarmé*, Bollingen Series, XLV/8 (Princeton: Princeton University Press, 1972), 161.

45. Valéry, *Leonardo, Poe, Mallarmé*, 66; "Note et Digression" (1919), in Valéry, *Oeuvres*, 1: 1199–1233, here 1201.

46. Valéry, *Oeuvres*, 1: 1155; *Leonardo, Poe, Mallarmé*, 5.

47. Valéry, "Monsieur Teste en Images," in *Album de Monsieur Teste, avec gravures de l'auteur* (Paris: Charpentier, 1945). I quote from the translation by Jackson Mathews, *Monsieur Teste*, Bollingen Series XLV/6 (Princeton: Princeton University Press, 1973), 158.

48. Paul Valéry, *Cahiers*, ed. Judith Robinson, 2 vols. (Paris: Gallimard, 1974), 2: 1099, 1102.

49. Valéry, "Au sujet du *Cimetière Marin*," in *Oeuvres*, 1: 1497.

50. Valéry, "Avant-propos à la connaissance de la déesse," in *Oeuvres*, 1: 1273.

51. Valéry, "Cantiques spirituelles" (1941), in *Oeuvres*, 1: 445–73, here 457.

52. Valéry, "Discours sur l'esthétique" (1937), in *Oeuvres*, 1: 1294–1314, here 1300.

53. Valéry, *Oeuvres*, 1: 1314–40, here 1327.

54. Valéry, "Au sujet du *Cimetière marin*," in *Oeuvres*, 1: 1502.

55. Valéry, "Propos sur la poésie" (1927), in *Oeuvres*, 1: 136–78, here 1363.

56. Valéry, *Oeuvres*, 1: 1412–15.

57. Valéry to Albert Mockel; *Lettres à quelques-uns*, 123.

58. Valéry, "La Crise de l'esprit," in *Oeuvres*, 1: 988–1014, here 988–89. The article was commissioned by the English weekly *The Athenaeum* and first appeared there in English as two "Letters from France" (11 April and 2 May 1919). I translate here from the French original.

59. I am consciously ignoring the entire complex question of the poem's genesis, as first explored by L.-J. Austin, "Paul Valéry compose *Le Cimetière Marin*," *Mercure de France*, nos. 1076 and 1077 (1 April and 1 May 1953): 577–608, 47–72. I see no need, for the purposes of this chapter, to comment further on the metrics and strophic form of the poem, which have occupied specialists in French literature. The key document for both issues is Valéry's own essay "Au sujet du *Cimetière marin*," in *Oeuvres*, 1: 1496–1507.

60. Valéry, *Oeuvres*, 1: 147–51.

61. Reproduced in Claude Launay, *Paul Valéry* (Paris: La Manufacture, 1990), following page 160.

62. Here I follow the analytical consensus represented by Bernard Weinberg, "An Interpretation of Valéry's *Le Cimetière Marin*," *Romanic Review* 38 (1947): 133–58; Francis Scarfe, *The Art of Paul Valéry: A Study in Dramatic Monologue* (London: Heinemann, 1954), 251–59; James R. Lawler, *Form and Meaning in Valéry's Le Cimetière Marin* (Carlton: Melbourne University Press, 1959); and Walter Putnam, *Paul Valéry Revisited* (New York: Twayne, 1995), 68–77. In contrast, Alain in his commented edition of Valéry's *Charmes*, 2nd ed. (Paris: Gallimard, 1952), 230, acknowledges "une sorte de première partie" in the first eight strophes, but indicates no further divisions in the last sixteen; and Gustave Cohen, *Essai d'Explication du Cimetière Marin* (Paris: Gallimard, 1933), sees a division into four acts of six strophes each.

63. Valéry contended that the poem was only accidentally fixed in the form as we know it—that it is "the result of the division of an interior process by a fortuitous

event" ("Au sujet du *Cimetière Marin*," in *Oeuvres*, 1: 1496–1507; here 1500). He reports that his friend Jacques Rivière, visiting him one afternoon in 1920, found him engaged with his work-in-progress and contemplating the suppression, the substitution, the variation of its parts. Rivière prevailed on him to give up his poem, and it was published that year at the random stage of composition that it had reached. Indeed, the randomness is demonstrated by the fact that, for its inclusion two years later in the volume *Charmes*, Valéry rearranged several of the first nine strophes of the poem.

64. Valéry, *Oeuvres*, 2: 673.

65. I take the details of Joyce's life from Richard Ellmann, *James Joyce* (New York: Oxford, 1959), esp. chaps. 3–6.

66. Ibid., 27.

67. Harry Levin, *James Joyce: A Critical Introduction* (1941; Norfolk, Conn.: New Directions, 1960), 45.

68. "Epiphany" is the most familiar example. See Theodore Ziolkowski, "James Joyces Epiphanie und die Überwindung der empirischen Welt in der modernen deutschen Prosa," *Deutsche Vierteljahrsschrift* 35 (1961): 595–616, for a comparative perspective.

69. Ellmann, *James Joyce*, 68.

70. Joyce's *Portrait* has often been compared to other English novels; see Jerome H. Buckley, *Season of Youth: The Bildungsroman from Dickens to Golding* (Cambridge: Harvard University Press, 1974), 225–47. But the comparison to similar contemporary works in France and Germany exposes generational similarities lacking in the diachronic English surveys.

71. Quoted here and elsewhere according to James Joyce, *A Portrait of the Artist as a Young Man*, ed. R. B Kershner (Boston: Bedford/St. Martin's, 1993), 215.

72. That Stephen, on his return to Dublin in *Ulysses*, turns out to be Icarus rather than Daedalus, the son rather than the father, is beside the point here. See Joseph C. Heininger, "Stephen Dedalus in Paris: Tracing the Fall of Icarus in *Ulysses*," *James Joyce Quarterly* 23 (1986): 435–46.

73. Some readers—for instance, Buckley, *Season of Youth*, 238—have found the sermon on hell unnecessarily long-winded. But the weight of the sermon is required to offset the "sin" of the preceding chapter and to justify Stephen's temporary reconversion.

74. The ending has been much debated: does Joyce mean for Stephen to escape like Daedalus or, ironically, to fall like Icarus? As I read the novel and have argued here, its entire trajectory suggests the identification with Daedalus and the successful escape from Ireland to a life of art.

75. See George's poem "Ikarus" (1886–87; from *Die Fibel*); *Werke* 2: 486.

CHAPTER FIVE

1. Kate Teltscher, "India/Calcutta: City of Palaces and Dreadful Night," in *The Cambridge Companion to Travel Writing*, ed. Peter Hulme and Tim Young (Cambridge: Cambridge University Press, 2002), 191–206, which is limited almost wholly to English accounts.

2. Christiane C. Günther, *Aufbruch nach Asien. Kulturelle Fremde in der deutschen Literatur um 1900* (Munich: Judicium, 1988), 46.

3. See A. Leslie Willson, *A Mythical Image: The Ideal of India in German Romanticism* (Durham: Duke University Press, 1964). See also Vidhagiri Ganeshan, *Das Indienbild deutscher Dichter um 1900* (Bonn: Bouvier, 1975), 39–56; Günther, *Aufbruch nach Asien*, 46–52; Gerhard Koch's afterword to *Indien: Wunder und Wirklichkeit in deutschen Erzählungen des 20. Jahrhunderts*, ed. Gerhard Koch (Frankfurt am Main: Insel, 1986), 399–430; and Kamakshi P. Murti, *India: The Seductive "Other" of German Orientalism* (Westport: Greenwood, 2001), which features an aggressively postcolonial and feminist standpoint. I have not seen Marc Cluet, ed., *Le Fascination de l'Inde en Allemagne, 1800–1930* (Rennes: Presses Universitaires, 2004).

4. Novalis, *Schriften*, ed. Paul Kluckhohn and Richard Samuel, 4 vols. (Stuttgart: Kohlhammer, 1960–75), 1: 79.

5. Ibid., 3: 520.

6. Karl S. Guthke, "Benares am Rhein–Rom am Ganges. Orient und Okzident im Denken A. W. Schlegels," in his *Das Abenteuer der Literatur. Studien zum literarischen Leben der deutschsprachigen Länder von der Aufklärung bis zum Exil* (Bern: Francke, 1981), 242–58.

7. Helmuth von Glasenapp, *Das Indienbild deutscher Denker* (Stuttgart: Koehler, 1960), 68–101.

8. A.-H. Anquetil-Duperron, *Oupnek'hat, id est, secretum tegendum, opus ipsa in India rarissimum, continens antiquam et arcanam, seu theologicam et philosophicam doctrinam e quattuor sacris Indorum libris* (1801–2).

9. Arthur Schopenhauer, "Einiges zum Sanskritlitteratur," *Parerga und Paralipomena*, *Sämmtliche Werke*, ed. Julius Frauenstädt, 2nd ed., 6 vols. (Leipzig: Brockhaus, 1922), 6: 427 (bk. 2, sections 184–91, here section 185).

10. Written in Dresden in 1816 and published posthumously; quoted in editor's introduction to *Sämmtliche Werke*, 1: 153–54. See also Rüdiger Safranski, *Schopenhauer und die wilden Jahre der Philosophie. Eine Biographie* (1987; rpt. Reinbek bei Hamburg: Rowohlt, 1996), 301–5.

11. Ibid., 2: 493.

12. Ibid., 6: 425–31.

13. Ibid., 2: 9.

14. Glasenapp, *Indienbild deutscher Denker*, 39–60.

15. Ibid., 102–9, 123–26.

16. Ibid., 186–202.

17. H. P. Blavatsky, *Isis Unveiled* (1877), rev. ed., 2 vols. (Wheaton: Theosophical Publishing House, 1972), vi.

18. Bhupal Singh, *A Survey of Anglo-Indian Fiction* (1934; rpt. London: Curzon, 1975).

19. Edward W. Said, *Orientalism* (New York: Pantheon, 1978), focuses almost entirely on Anglo-French orientalism and makes no reference to any of the German pilgrimagers—nor, surprisingly, to Annie Besant, Madame Blavatsky, and the Theosophical Society. The same restriction impairs Murti, *India: The Seductive "Other,"* who applies Said's controversial theory to German literature.

20. E. R. Curtius, "Stefan George in Conversation," in his *Essays on European Literature*, trans. Michael Kowal (Princeton: Princeton University Press, 1973), 107–28, here 126.

21. On Loti's life see Michael G. Lerner, *Pierre Loti* (New York: Twayne, 1974); and Christian Genet and Daniel Hervé, *Pierre Loti l'enchanteur* (Gémozac: La Caillerie, 1988).

22. Pierre Loti, *L'Inde (sans les Anglais)*, 52nd ed. (Paris: Calmann-Lévy, [1911]). I quote in my own translation from this edition, which is identical in text and pagination with the first edition of 1903.

23. Raphael Barquissau, *L'Asie française et ses écrivains (Indochine-Inde)* (Paris: Jean Vigneau, 1947), includes only a brief appendix on India (207–19); his bibliography cites over 130 novels, 60 volumes of poetry, and 90 travel books on Indochina, but none on India. On the French quest for alternative thought patterns in exoticism and Surrealism, see also Michael Rössner, *Auf der Suche nach dem verlorenen Paradies: Zum mythischen Bewußtsein in der Literatur des 20. Jahrhunderts* (Frankfurt am Main: Athenäum, 1988), 100–154.

24. It is amusing, but also significant, that the English and American translations by R. Sherard (1906) and A. F. Inman (1913) omit the parenthesized subtitle.

25. Several photographs from Loti's trip are reprinted in Genet and Hervé, *Pierre Loti l'enchanteur*, 307–12.

26. See Marie-Jeanne Hublard, *L'Attitude religieuse de Pierre Loti* (Fribourg: St. Paul, 1945), 87–119; and Keith G. Millward, *L'Oeuvre de Pierre Loti et l'esprit "fin de siècle"* (Paris: Nizet, 1955), 295–316.

27. Loti to Juliette Adam, 5 April 1882, *Lettres à Madame Adam* (Paris: Plon, 1924).

28. Millward, *L'Oeuvre de Pierre Loti*, 171–217.

29. Since Loti gives no names but only titles and positions, it is not always certain whom he has met. In this case, however, he specifically mentions "le chef de la Société théosophique" (352); and Olcott was president from 1891 until 1907.

30. Annie Besant, who founded the Central Hindu College at Benares, is by exception named–not in the text but in a footnote (410). Besant is mistakenly identified by Genet and Hervé, *Pierre Loti l'enchanteur*, 307 n. 4, as a Frenchwoman.

31. C. B. Schomaker, "Waldemar Bonsels und sein Werk," *Monatshefte für Deutschen Unterricht* 28 (1936): 337–48.

32. Waldemar Bonsels, *Indienfahrt*, ed. W. Leopold (New York: Crofts, 1932).

33. Waldemar Bonsels, *Indienfahrt* (Frankfurt am Main: Rütten & Loening, 1922), 170.

34. Such early appraisals as Schomaker, "Waldemar Bonsels und sein Werk," or C. R. Goedsche, "Bonsels' *Indienfahrt*: A Travel Book as a Work of Art," *Monatshefte für Deutschen Unterricht* 27 (1935): 81–87, accepted the work at face value as a genuine account, as, for the most part, does Ganeshan, *Indienbild deutscher Dichter*, 138–61.

35. See Kamal Karnick, "Wahrheit und Dichtung in Bonsels' *Indienfahrt*" and especially Lini Hübsch-Pfleger, "Briefe und Dokumente zur *Indienfahrt*," in *Indien als Faszination. Stimmen zur "Indienfahrt" von Waldemar Bonsels*, Ambacher

Schriften 6, ed. Rose-Marie Bonsels (Wiesbaden: Harrassowitz, 1990), 13–93 and 94–119.

36. Waldemar Bonsels, *Mein Austritt aus der Baseler Missions-Industrie und seine Gründe* (Munich-Schwabing, 1904); rpt. Ambacher Schriften 2 (1987). See Hübsch-Pfleger, "Briefe und Dokumente," 110–11.

37. Albrecht Oepke, *Moderne Indienfahrer und Weltreligionen* (Leipzig: Doerfling & Francke, 1921); see Karnick, "Wahrheit und Dichtung," 21.

38. Ganeshan, *Indienbild deutscher Dichter*, 157.

39. This parallel has not been noted in the secondary studies, which tend to remain narrowly within the German canon.

40. Albert Soergel and Curt Hohoff, *Dichtung und Dichter der Zeit*, 2 vols. (Düsseldorf: Bagel, 1961), 524–39; H. G. Wendt, *Max Dauthendey: Poet-Philosopher* (New York: Columbia University Press, 1936); Ganeshan, *Indienbild deutscher Dichter*, 57–137; and Gabriele Geibig, *Der Würzburger Dichter Max Dauthendey (1867–1918). Sein Nachlaß als Spiegel von Leben und Werk*, Schriften des Stadtarchivs Würzburg 9 (Würzburg: Schöningh, 1992), esp. 9–71 ("Biographie").

41. Like Edmund Gosse, Dauthendey provided a sensitive portrait of the relationship with his father in *Der Geist meines Vaters. Aufzeichnungen aus einem begrabenen Jahrhundert* (Munich: Langen, 1912).

42. Ibid., 318.

43. Ibid., 365.

44. Max Dauthendey, *Gedankengut aus meinen Wanderjahren*, 2 vols. (Munich: Langen, 1913), 2: 34.

45. Wendt, *Max Dauthendey: Poet-Philosopher*, 117–23.

46. Dauthendey, *Geist meines Vaters*, 7.

47. Ibid., 309, 368–69.

48. Dauthendey, *Gedankengut*, 1: 185–86.

49. Ibid., 2: 342.

50. Ibid., 2: 257.

51. Dauthendey, "Cook-Passagier um die Erde" (1907), first published in Geibig, *Der Würzburger Dichter*, 100–120.

52. Quoted by Ganeshan, *Indienbild deutscher Dichter*, 79.

53. Dauthendey, *Gedankengut*, 2: 256.

54. Ibid., 2: 255.

55. Max Dauthendey, *Die geflügelte Erde. Ein Lied der Liebe und der Wunder um sieben Meere* (Munich: Langen, 1910), 40–170, 205–35.

56. Donald Prater and Volker Michels, eds., *Stefan Zweig. Leben und Werk im Bild*, (Frankfurt am Main: Insel, 1981), 84–85, contains photographs from Zweig's Indian sojourn. See also Ganeshan, *Indienbild deutscher Dichter*, 291–307.

57. Stefan Zweig, *Die Welt von Gestern. Erinnerungen eines Europäers* (1942), 34th ed. (Frankfurt am Main: Fischer, 2003), 208–18, here 212–13.

58. Stefan Zweig, "Benares: die Stadt der tausend Tempel," in his *Begegnungen mit Menschen, Büchern, Städten* (Berlin: Fischer, 1955), 254–61, here 255.

59. Curtius, "Stefan George in Conversation," 126.

60. Melchior Lechter, *Tagebuch der indischen Reise. Als Manuskript gedruckt* (Berlin: Einhorn-Presse, 1912). I have used the copy numbered 186 in the Rare Book Collection of Princeton University's Firestone Library.

61. Hesse to Romain Rolland, 6 April 1923, Hermann Hesse/Romain Rolland, *D'une rive à l'autre. Correspondance, fragments du Journal et textes diverses*, ed. Pierre Grappin (Paris: Albin Michel, 1972), 102.

62. Adrian Hsia, *Hermann Hesse und China. Darstellung, Materialien und Interpretation* (Frankfurt am Main: Suhrkamp, 1974), 29–47 ("Indien"); and Vridhagiri Ganeshan, *Das Indienerlebnis Hermann Hesses* (Bonn: Bouvier/Grundmann, 1974), 19–42.

63. In the essay "Mein Glaube" (1931), *Gesammelte Schriften*, 7 vols. (Frankfurt am Main: Suhrkamp, 1957), 7: 371; henceforth *GS*

64. Hesse, "Besuch aus Indien" (1922), *GS* 3: 856–61, here 857.

65. Hesse, "Erinnerung an Indien. Zu den Bildern des Malers Hans Sturzenegger, 1916," *GS* 3: 851.

66. Hesse, *Aus Indien, GS* 3: 813.

67. *GS* 5: 564.

68. Hesse to Ludwig Thoma, 6 Jan. 1912, *Gesammelte Briefe*, ed. Ursula and Volker Michels, 4 vols. (Frankfurt am Main: Suhrkamp, 1973–86), 1: 204.

69. Hesse, "Aus einem Tagebuch des Jahres 1920," *Corona* 3 (1932): 201–2.

70. Hermann Hesse, "Keyserlings Reisetagebuch," in *Gesammelte Werke in zwölf Bänden*, ed. Volker Michels (Frankfurt am Main: Suhrkamp, 1970), 12: 466–69.

71. Rolland's journal for September 1920, Hesse/Rolland, *D'une rive à l'autre*, 69.

72. I cite the text according to Graf Hermann Keyserling, *Das Reisetagebuch eines Philosophen*, 5th ed., 2 vols. (Darmstadt: Otto Reichl, 1921). The entire first volume is devoted to India; vol. 2 records the remaining journey through Indochina, China, Japan, Honolulu, and the United States. The pagination runs consecutively through both volumes. On Keyserling and India, see Ganeshan, *Indienbild deutscher Dichter*, 234–84; and Glasenapp, *Indienbild deutscher Denker*, 135–39.

73. Henry Miller, "The Philosopher Who Philosophizes," in *The Wisdom of the Heart* (Norfolk: New Directions, 1941), 71–77, here 73.

74. G. Lowes Dickinson, *Appearances* (Garden City: Doubleday, 1915).

75. Singh, *Survey of Anglo-Indian Fiction.*

76. E. M. Forster, *The Hill of Devi and Other Indian Writings* (London: Edward Arnold, 1983), 289–99, here 296.

77. Others were in his posthumously edited Indian journals; both are reprinted in the new edition of *The Hill of Devi*, 5–16, 117–228. See also Adwaita P. Ganguly, *India: Mystic, Complex and Real. A Detailed Study of E. M. Forster's* A Passage to India: *His Treatment of India's Landscape, History, Social Anthropology, Religion, Philosophy, Music and Art* (Delhi: Motilal Banarsidass, 1990).

78. Ganguly, *India*, 22–23.

79. Singh, *Survey of Anglo-Indian Fiction*, 2.

80. Dickinson had a similar reaction to the "frivolling" of "women too empty-headed and men too tired" for anything else (*Appearances*, 15).

81. E. M. Forster, *Two Cheers for Democracy* (New York: Harcourt, 1951), 67.

82. Ibid., 108.

83. Dickinson, *Appearances*, 5.

84. E. M. Forster, *A Passage to India* (New York: Harvest/HBJ, 1984), 105.

85. Forster, "India Again" (1946), in *Two Cheers for Democracy*, 321.

86. Ganguly, *India*, 29–30, 308.

87. Walt Whitman, *Leaves of Grass. Inclusive Edition*, ed. Emory Holloway (Garden City: Doubleday, 1954), 343.

CHAPTER SIX

1. Thomas Mann, *Gesammelte Werke in zwölf Bänden* (Frankfurt am Main: Fischer, 1960), 12: 490–536, here 491.

2. Helmuth von Glasenapp, *Das Indienbild deutscher Dichter* (Stuttgart: Koehler, 1960), 173, discussing the Marxist rejection of Indian thought.

3. Richard Crossman, introduction to *The God That Failed*, ed. Crossman (1949; rpt. Chicago: Regnery Gateway, 1983), 6.

4. Ibid., 169.

5. Ibid., 15.

6. Hubertus Prinz zu Löwenstein, *Abenteurer der Freiheit. Ein Lebensbericht* (Frankfurt am Main: Ullstein, 1983), 164.

7. Czeslaw Milosz, *The Captive Mind*, trans. Jane Zielonko (New York: Knopf, 1953).

8. Whittaker Chambers, *Witness* (New York: Random House, 1952), 8.

9. Roger Martin du Gard, *Summer 1914*, trans. Stuart Gilbert (New York: Viking, 1941), 78; 2: 86. The second number refers to volume and page of the Pléiade edition of his *Oeuvres complètes* (Paris: Gallimard, 1955), against which I check and occasionally alter Gilbert's often free translation.

10. In addition to personal experience—he spent the months immediately prior to the war in Paris and was mobilized on 3 August 1914—and printed sources, the author consulted experts on the period and even attended meetings of young socialist workers as he was writing. See David L. Schalk, *Roger Martin du Gard: The Novelist and History* (Ithaca: Cornell University Press, 1967), 104–6. For a readable account of prewar socialism (the Second International), its dissensions, and its ultimate usurpation by various nationalisms, see Barbara W. Tuchman, *The Proud Tower: A Portrait of the World before the War, 1890–1914* (1966; rpt. New York: Ballantine, 1996), 407–62.

11. Per Hallström, in his presentation speech for Martin du Gard's Nobel Prize in 1937, misses the point when he suggests that "the description of these agitators is one of the least successful passages in the book; the overall impression, whether intended or not, is that these men are not worthy of their mission." That is precisely the author's point. See *Nobel Lectures. Literature, 1901–1967* (Amsterdam: Elsevier, 2003); at www.nobel.se/literature/laureate/1937/press.html.

12. Stuart Gilbert's translation of the first six volumes of the *roman-fleuve* appeared, without the volume titles, under the collective heading *The Thibaults* (New York: Viking, 1946).

13. Martin du Gard, *Oeuvres complètes*, 2: 759–1011.

14. Roger Martin du Gard, "Banquet Speech" (10 Dec. 1937), in *Nobel Lectures. Literature 1901–1967*.

15. A representative selection of key passages from all three works is conveniently available in Irving Howe, ed., *Essential Works of Socialism*, (New York: Holt, Rinehart and Winston, 1970).

16. First published in its entirety in Alfred Döblin, *Jagende Rosse, der Schwarze Vorhang und andere frühe Erzählwerke*, ed. Anthony W. Riley (Olten: Walter, 1981), 7–25.

17. Alfred Döblin, "Revolutionstage im Elsaß" (1919), in *Schriften zur Politik und Gesellschaft* (Olten: Walter, 1972), 63.

18. Döblin, "Die Vertreibung der Gespenster" (1919), in *Schriften zur Politik und Gesellschaft*, 71–82.

19. Döblin, "Erster Rückblick" (1928), in *Die Vertreibung der Gespenster. Autobiographische Schriften, Betrachtungen zur Zeit, Aufsätze zu Kunst und Literatur*, ed. Manfred Beyer (Berlin: Rütten & Loening, 1968), 6–76, here 29–30.

20. See, for instance, Döblin, "Die deutsche Utopie von 1933 und die Literatur," in *Schriften zu Ästhetik, Poetik und Literatur*, ed. Erich Kleinschmidt (Olten: Walter, 1989), 367–408, here 396.

21. Considerable analysis has been devoted to Döblin's political ideals, which remained reasonably constant even as he shifted his allegiances with respect to the parties that could best realize those ideals. A concise summary is provided by David Dollenmayer, "Der Wandel in Döblins Auffassung von der deutschen Revolution," in *Internationale Alfred Döblin-Kolloquien. Basel 1980/New York 1981/Freiburg i.Br. 1983*, ed. Werner Stauffacher, *Jahrbuch für Internationale Germanistik*, Series A, Congress Reports 14 (Bern: Peter Lang, 1986), 56–63.

22. See Theodore Ziolkowski, *Dimensions of the Modern Novel: German Texts and European Contexts* (Princeton: Princeton University Press, 1969), 99–137.

23. Döblin, "Katastrophe in der Linkskurve" (1930), in *Schriften zur Politik und Gesellschaft*, 247–53.

24. Alfred Döblin, *Wissen und Verändern! Offene Briefe an einen jungen Menschen* (Berlin: Fischer, 1931), 36.

25. Heidi Thomann Tewarson, "Alfred Döblins Geschichtskonzeption in 'November 1918. Eine deutsche Revolution,'" in *Internationale Alfred Döblin-Kolloquien*, 64–75.

26. References to, and quotations from, this material are conveniently available in the notes to the four-volume edition of *November 1918. Eine deutsche Revolution. Erzählwerk in drei Teilen*, ed. Werner Stauffacher (Munich: Deutscher Taschenbuch Verlag, 1955), which I cite in the following discussion.

27. Döblin, "Epilog," in *Die Vertreibung der Gespenster*, 130–47, here 142.

28. This was first studied in detail and using the manuscripts by Manfred Auer, *Das Exil vor der Vertreibung: Motivkontinuität und Quellenproblematik im späten Werk Alfred Döblins* (Bonn: Bouvier, 1977), 56–102.

29. The two-volume English translation by John Woods, *November 1918: A German Revolution* (New York: Fromm International, 1983), omits the first volume, combines the second and third under the title *A People Betrayed*, and omits one entire set of episodes.

30. Hans Mayer, "Eine deutsche Revolution. Also keine," *Der Spiegel* 33 (1978): 124ff.

31. Winfried G. Sebald, "Alfred Döblin oder die politische Unzuverlässigkeit des bürgerlichen Literaten," in *Internationale Alfred Döblin-Kolloquien*, 133–39, here 133, 137.

32. For a review of critical opinion see Wulf Koepke, *The Critical Reception of Alfred Döblin's Major Novels* (Rochester: Camden House, 2003), 178–203.

33. The figure of the itinerant evangelist pursuing an *imitatio Christi* was popular in German literature of the period around World War I: e.g., Gerhart Hauptmann's *The Fool in Christ Emanuel Quint* (*Der Narr in Christo Emanuel Quint*, 1910) and the three tales constituting Hermann Hesse's *Knulp* (1915). See Theodore Ziolkowski, *Fictional Transfigurations of Jesus* (Princeton: Princeton University Press, 1972), esp. chaps. 3 ("The Christian Socialist Jesus") and 4 ("The Christomaniacs").

34. On the first volume as a parody of the revolution see David B. Dollenmayer, *The Berlin Novels of Alfred Döblin* (Berkeley: University of California Press, 1988), 152.

35. Ibid., 127.

36. For a sensible discussion of the issue and the controversy see Anthony W. Riley, "The Aftermath of the First World War: Christianity and Revolution in Alfred Döblin's *November 1918*," in *The First World War in German Narrative Prose*, Essays in Honour of George Wallis Field, ed. Charles N. Genno and Heinz Wetzel (Toronto: University of Toronto Press, 1980), 93–117.

37. Dollenmayer, *Berlin Novels*, 159–65.

38. Ignazio Silone, in Crossman, *God That Failed*, 100.

39. On Silone's identification of church and Party see the splendid chapter in R. W. B. Lewis, *The Picaresque Saint: Representative Figures in Contemporary Fiction* (Philadelphia: Lippincott/Keystone, 1961), 109–78, esp. 113–21.

40. Silone's novel was first published in 1936 in German and English translations; the Italian text appeared in Switzerland in 1937. I refer throughout to the revised edition of 1955 which Silone, to distinguish it from the original *Pane e vino* of 1936–37, called *Vino e pane* (Milan: Mondadori, 1955). Both versions have been separately translated into English under the title *Bread and Wine*: the first by Gwenda David and Eric Mosbacher (London: Methuen, 1936); the revised edition by Harvey Fergusson II (New York: Atheneum, 1962). I cite Fergusson's translation according to the Signet Classic reprint.

41. Ziolkowski, *Fictional Transfigurations of Jesus*. There (194–206) I analyze those aspects in detail and, in the chapter entitled "Comrade Jesus" (182–224), adduce other examples of the same phenomenon. In fact, as we have seen, a certain *imitatio Christi* dominates the last period of Becker's life and the last pages of *November 1918*; but the Jesus analogy plays only a peripheral role in Döblin's novel.

42. Ignazio Silone, *A Handful of Blackberries*, trans. Darina Silone (New York: Harper, 1953), 226–27.

43. Raymond Aron, "L'Avenir des religions séculières," in *Une histoire du vingtième siècle*, ed. Christian Bachelier (Paris: Plon, 1996), 153–73.

44. T. S. Eliot, *Idea of a Christian Society* (New York: Harcourt, 1940), 64.

CHAPTER SEVEN

1. Carol Geldermann, *Henry Ford: The Wayward Capitalist* (New York: Dial, 1981), 151–92, here 177.

2. Ernst Breisach, *Historiography: Ancient, Medieval, and Modern* (Chicago: University of Chicago Press, 1983), 261–67.

3. G. P. Gooch, *History and Historians of the Nineteenth Century* (1913; rpt. Boston: Beacon Press, 1959).

4. Theodore Ziolkowski, *Clio the Romantic Muse: Historicizing the Faculties in Germany* (Ithaca: Cornell University Press, 2004).

5. Friedrich Nietzsche, "Vom Nutzen und Nachteil der Historie für das Leben," in *Werke in drei Bänden*, ed. Karl Schlechta, 3 vols. (Munich: Hanser, 1954–56), 1: 237.

6. Hermann Hesse, "Weltgeschichte," in *Politik des Gewissens. Die politischen Schriften*, ed. Volker Michels, 2 vols. (Frankfurt am Main: Suhrkamp, 1977–81), 1: 276–80, here 276–77.

7. Alfred Döblin, "Glossen, Fragmente," *Neue Rundschau* 1 (1920), rpt. in *Schriften zur Politik und Gesellschaft* (Olten: Walter, 1972), 126–38, here 127–28.

8. Paul Valéry, "De l'histoire," in *Oeuvres*, ed. Jean Hytier, 2 vols. (Paris: Gallimard, 1957–60), 935–37.

9. Nietzsche, *Werke in drei Bänden*, 1: 223.

10. See in this connection Walter Kaufmann, *Nietzsche: Philosopher, Psychologist, Antichrist*, 4th ed. (Princeton: Princeton University Press, 1974), 12–15, 142.

11. From the preface to the fourth edition of 1927; rpt. Theodor Lessing, *Geschichte als Sinngebung des Sinnlosen* (Hamburg: Rütten & Loening, 1962), 11.

12. Carl Schmitt, *Political Theology: Four Chapters on the Concept of Sovereignty*, trans. George Schwab (Cambridge: MIT Press, 1985), 36.

13. Oswald Spengler, *Der Untergang des Abendlandes: Umrisse einer Morphologie der Weltgeschichte* (Munich: Beck, 1963), 512.

14. Theodore Ziolkowski, *Fictional Transfigurations of Jesus* (Princeton: Princeton University Press, 1972), 142–49 ("The Mythic Jesus").

15. Eliot's essay first appeared in *Dial*; rpt. in *Forms of Modern Fiction* (1948), ed. William Van O'Connor (Bloomington: University of Indiana–Midland, 1959), 120–24, here 123.

16. See, for instance, W. B. Stanford, *The Ulysses Theme: A Study in the Adaptation of a Traditional Hero* (Oxford: Blackwell, 1954); André Dabezies, *Visages de Faust au XXe siècle: Littérature, Idéologie, et Mythes* (Paris: Presses universitaires de France, 1967); and the following works by Theodore Ziolkowski: *Fictional Transfigurations of Jesus; Virgil and the Moderns* (Princeton: Princeton University Press, 1993); *The Sin of Knowledge* (Princeton: Princeton University Press, 2000); and *Ovid and the Moderns* (Ithaca: Cornell University Press, 2005).

17. Emilio Gentile, *Il culto del littorio. La sacralizzazione della politica nell'Italia fascista* (Rome: Laterza, 1993); trans. Keith Botsford, *The Sacralization of Politics in Fascist Italy* (Cambridge: Harvard University Press, 1996). In this book, as well as several others, Gentile has persuasively identified the theological thought patterns underlying Italian Fascism: the "rites" of the "holy militia" (*santa milizia*) and of the revolution, the "revealed" religion of politics, the political theology of the new state and its "true paradise," the meaning of faith and its "temples," the liturgy of the "harmonious collective," and so forth. But in Italian Fascism, Gentile identifies myth essentially and narrowly with the persona and cult of Mussolini, and not as the free-floating power motivating National Socialism in Germany.

18. Erich Unger, *Wirklichkeit, Mythos, Erkenntnis* (Munich: Oldenbourg, 1930), 3. Some of the material in the next four sections—translated, expanded, and revised

to suit the theme of this book—is based on my essay "Der Hunger nach dem Mythos: Zur seelischen Gastronomie der Deutschen in den Zwanziger Jahren," in *Die sogenannten Zwanziger Jahre*, First Wisconsin Workshop, ed. Reinhold Grimm and Jost Hermand (Bad Homburg: Gehlen, 1970), 169–201.

19. Alfred Baeumler, *Alfred Rosenberg und der Mythus des 20. Jahrhunderts* (Munich: Hoheneichen, 1943).

20. Harry Levin, "Some Meanings of Myth," in *Myth and Mythmaking*, ed. Henry A. Murray (New York: Braziller, 1960), 103–14.

21. In his introduction to Thomas Mann/Karl Kerényi, *Gespräch in Briefen* (Zurich: Rhein, 1960), 20.

22. Henry Hatfield, "The Myth of Nazism," in Murray, *Myth and Mythmaking*, 199–220; Jean F. Neurohr, *Der Mythos vom Dritten Reich. Zur Geistesgeschichte des Nationalsozialismus* (Stuttgart: Cotta, 1957).

23. Max Müller, *Contributions to the Science of Mythology*, 2 vols. (London: Longmans, 1897), 1: 68; Paul Valéry, "Petite lettre sur les mythes" (1928), in *Oeuvres*, 1: 961–67: "*Mythe* est le nom de tout ce qui n'existe et ne subsiste qu'ayant la parole pour cause" (1: 963–64). Valéry represents an exception to Levin's generalization about French mythoclastic skepticism; for Valéry goes on to say that "les mythes sont les âmes de nos actions et de nos amours. Nous ne pouvons agir qu'en nous mouvant vers un fantôme. Nous ne pouvons aimer que ce que nous créons" (1 : 967).

24. Kurt Hoffmann, ed., *Die Wirklichkeit des Mythos. Zehn Vorträge* (Munich: Knaur, 1965)

25. Benjamin Hederich, *Gründliches mythologisches Lexikon* (1724), quoted from the photomechanical reproduction of the 1770 edition (Darmstadt: Wissenschaftliche Buchgesellschaft, 1967), xi.

26. On the history of myth scholarship see Fritz Strich, *Die Mythologie in der deutschen Literatur von Klopstock bis Wagner* (Halle: Niemeyer, 1910); Walter F. Otto, "Der Durchbruch zum antiken Mythos im XIX. Jahrhundert," in *Die Gestalt und das Sein. Gesammelte Abhandlungen über den Mythos und seine Bedeutung für die Menschheit* (Düsseldorf: Diederich, 1955), 211–25; Klaus Ziegler, "Mythos und Dichtung," in *Reallexikon der deutschen Literaturgeschichte*, 2nd ed., 4 vols. (Berlin, 1962–63), 2: 569–84; Richard M. Dorson, "Theories of Myth and the Folklorist," in Murray, *Myth and Mythmaking*, 76–89; and Ute Heidmann Vischer in the new edition of the *Reallexikon*, 3 vols. (Berlin: De Gruyter, 2000), 2: 664–68. Kurt Hübner, *Die Wahrheit des Mythos* (Munich: Beck, 1985), 48–90, offers a systematic survey of myth interpretations (allegorical, ritualistic-sociological, psychological, transcendental, structuralistic, symbolic, and others) but in no historical sequence.

27. Glenn W. Most, "From Logos to Mythos," in *From Myth to Reason? Studies in the Development of Greek Thought*, ed. Richard Buxton (Oxford: Oxford University Press, 1999), 25–47, points out that the great late eighteenth-century classicist Christian Gottlob Heyne was one of the first writers to use the Latinized Greek vocable *mythus* to designate the prelogical thinking of the Greeks. But since Heyne's writings were almost wholly in Latin, they had no immediate effect on vernacular usage.

28. Friedrich Schlegel, *Literary Notebooks, 1797–1801*, ed. Hans Eichner (Toronto: University of Toronto Press, 1957), 252. Schlegel usually writes the word in Greek, presumably because the form "Mythos" still had no validity in German.

29. D. F. Strauss, *Das Leben Jesu*, 3rd ed. (Leipzig: Brockhaus, 1874), 159 (in the section "The Concept of Mythus").

30. Wilhelm Traugott Krug, *Allgemeines Handwörterbuch der philosophischen Wissenschaften* (Leipzig: Brockhaus, 1927), where both forms occur: "Mythe" and "Mythos."

31. Thomas Mann, *Gesammelte Werke in zwölf Bänden* (Frankfurt am Main: Fischer, 1960), 9: 507–8.

32. See John J. White, *Mythology in the Modern Novel: A Study of Prefigurative Techniques* (Princeton: Princeton University Press, 1971).

33. Modern investigations that claim to find "myth" in writers of the nineteenth century to whom the concept was not yet known say more about the mythophilia of the twentieth century than about the actual development of the concept. See Gerhard Schmidt-Henkel, *Mythos und Dichtung. Zur Begriffs- und Stilgeschichte der deutschen Literatur im neunzehnten und zwanzigsten Jahrhundert* (Bad Homburg: Gehlen, 1967), who analyzes the "individual-mythic images" in various German writers. Levin, "Some Meanings of Myth," proposes the term "pseudo-myths" for such private myths. For the Romantic background see George S. Williamson, *The Longing for Myth in Germany: Religion and Aesthetic Culture from Romanticism to Nietzsche* (Chicago: University of Chicago Press, 2004).

34. Richard Wagner, *Mitteilung an meine Freunde*, in *Sämtliche Schriften und Dichtungen*, 6th ed., 16 vols. (Leipzig: Breitkopf & Härtel, 1912–14), 4: 311–12. On Wagner see Williamson, *Longing for Myth*, 180–210.

35. The differentiation that emerges from the writings of Wagner and Nietzsche differs from the definition that André Jolles proposes in his *Einfache Formen*, 2nd ed. (Darmstadt: Wissenschaftliche Buchgesellschaft, 1958), 100: "Myth is the simple form that results from our intellectual preoccupations; in contrast, the form in which it manifests itself to us each time is *Mythus* or *a Mythus*." Jolles's differentiation may be regarded as useful for the purposes of his investigation, but it has no etymological justification.

36. Wagner, *Oper und Dramen*, in *Sämtliche Schriften*, 4: 39.

37. Schelling, *Philosophie der Mythologie* (Darmstadt: Wissenschaftliche Buchgesellschaft, 1966), 2: 140, claims expressly that "mythology arose under circumstances that admit no comparison with those of the present consciousness and which one can comprehend only to the extent that one dares to go beyond them."

38. Nietzsche, "Richard Wagner in Bayreuth," in *Werke in drei Bänden*, 1: 413.

39. Nietzsche, *Geburt der Tragödie*, *Werke in drei Bänden*, 1: 125.

40. Ibid., 1: 63.

41. Wagner, *Oper und Drama*, in *Sämtliche Schriften*, 4: 41.

42. Nietzsche, *Geburt der Tragödie*, 1: 125.

43. Williamson, *Longing for Myth*, 211–33.

44. Wagner, *Oper und Dramen*, in *Sämtliche Schriften*, 4: 34, 39.

45. Nietzsche, *Geburt der Tragödie*, 1: 125.

46. Already here one detects the beginnings of the "friend-enemy scheme" of Nazi literary scholarship, to which Karl Otto Conrady refers: "Deutsche Literaturwissenschaft und Drittes Reich," in *Germanistik: Eine deutsche Wissenschaft* (Frankfurt am Main: Suhrkamp, 1967), 94.

47. Dieter Borchmeyer, "Mythos," in *Moderne Literatur in Grundbegriffen*, ed. Dieter Borchmeyer and Viktor Žmegač, 2nd ed. (Tübingen: Niemeyer, 1994), 292–308, here 292.

48. Fifteen years later, in response to World War I and the incipient mythomania in Germany, Hesse drastically altered his views. When the narrator of the novel *Demian* (1919) has listened to a friend reviewing all that he knows about ancient mystery cults and esoteric forms of religion, he realizes that the theologian is destined to remain mired in the past that obsesses him, while he, Sinclair, feels called to look into the future. "All of this seemed to me to be more curious and interesting than important for life. It sounded like erudition, like a weary search among the shards of former worlds. And suddenly I felt a repugnance against this whole way, against this cult of mythologies, against this mosaiclike play with traditional forms of belief." *Gesammelte Schriften*, 7 vols. (Frankfurt am Main: Suhrkamp, 1957), 3: 217.

49. Peter Lutz Lehmann, *Meditationen um Stefan George* (Düsseldorf: Küpper, 1965), 31–82: "Neue Mythologie."

50. Ernst Bertram, *Nietzsche. Versuch einer Mythologie*, 7th ed. (Berlin: Bondi, 1929), 11–15.

51. Spengler, *Untergang des Abendlandes*, 512–13.

52. Albrecht Schaeffer, *Elli oder Sieben Treppen. Beschreibung eines weiblichen Lebens* (Leipzig: Insel, 1919), 15.

53. Hugo von Hofmannsthal, "Die Ägyptische Helena," in *Prosa*, 4 vols. (Frankfurt am Main: Fischer, 1955), 4: 459–60.

54. Hofmannsthal, "Vermächtnis der Antike," *Prosa*, 4: 313–16.

55. Peter Gay, *Weimar Culture: The Outsider as Insider* (New York: Harper & Row, 1968); see also John R. Harrison, *The Reactionaries: A Study of the Anti-Democratic Intelligentsia* (London: Gollanz, 1966).

56. Ludwig Klages, *Der Geist als Widersacher der Seele*, 4th ed. (Munich: Barth, 1960), 850–51.

57. Arthur Liebert, *Mythus und Kultur* (Berlin: Pan, 1925), 64.

58. Rudolf Kayser, *Die Zeit ohne Mythos* (Berlin: Schmiede, 1923), 13, 101.

59. Walther Rehm, *Griechentum und Goethezeit. Geschichte eines Glaubens* (1936; 2nd ed. Leipzig: Dieterich, 1938), 20.

60. E. M. Butler, *The Tyranny of Greece over Germany* (1935; rpt. Boston: Beacon, 1958), 336.

61. Gerbrand Dekker, *Die Rückwendung zum Mythos. Schellings letzte Wandlung* (Munich: Oldenbourg, 1930), 217.

62. This entire development is no doubt related to the rediscovery of the archaic in classical antiquity, which reached its height in the 1920s. See Glenn W. Most, "Die Entdeckung der Archaik: Von Ägina nach Naumburg," in *Urgeschichten der Moderne: die Antike im 20. Jahrhundert*, ed. Bernd Seidensticker and Martin Vöhler (Stuttgart: Metzler, 2001), 20–39, here 36.

63. Kayser, *Zeit ohne Mythos*, 105.

64. Dekker, *Rückwendung zum Mythos*, 209, 217, 196. Dekker is alluding to the powerful Renaissance satire against obscurantists, the *Epistolae obscurorum virorum* (1515–17), known in German as *Dunkelmännerbriefe*.

65. Ernst Cassirer, *Philosophie der symbolischen Formen. Zweiter Teil: Das mythische Denken*, ed. Claus Rosenkranz, vol. 12 of *Gesammelte Werke*, ed. Birgit Recki, 25 vols. (Hamburg: Felix Meiner, 2002), xiv.

66. Kayser, *Zeit ohne Mythos*, 22.

67. Alfred Rosenberg, *Der Mythus des 20. Jahrhunderts. Eine Wertung der seelischgeistigen Gestaltenkämpfe unserer Zeit*, 25th–26th ed. (Munich: Hoheneichen, 1934), 1–2. The English translation by Vivian Bird—*The Myth of the Twentieth Century* (Torrance, CA: Noonday, 1982)—is rather free and occasionally inaccurate; it contains a useful preface and introduction to Rosenberg and his role in National Socialism.

68. Oddly, Hübner, *Die Wahrheit des Mythos*, does not consider Rosenberg and National Socialist myth in his chapter on myth in politics (349–65).

69. The defamation of reason became a common theme in Nazi literature. See the documentation in Ernst Loewy, *Literatur unterm Hakenkreuz. Das Dritte Reich und seine Dichtung. Eine Dokumentation* (Frankfurt am Main: Europäische Verlagsanstalt, 1966), 51–62.

70. Goethe's *Faust*, pt. 1, l.1740.

71. Novalis, *Geistliche Lieder* no. 7, in *Schriften: Die Werke Friedrich von Hardenbergs*, ed. Paul Kluckhohn and Richard Samuel, 2nd ed., 4 vols. (Darmstadt: Wissenschaftliche Buchgesellschaft, 1960), 1: 167.

72. Julius Langbehn, *Rembrandt als Erzieher: Von einem Deutschen*, ed. Gerhard Krüger (Berlin: Theodor Fritsch, 1944), 214–15 ("Macht des Blutes"). Langbehn's book, which had enjoyed forty-six printings by 1903, remained popular throughout the Nazi period.

73. Stefan George, "Vorspiel VIII," in *Der Teppich des Lebens* (1899).

74. Friedrich Georg Jünger, *Aufmarsch des Nationalismus*, ed. Ernst Jünger (Berlin: Vormarsch-Verlag, 1926), 21; quoted in Loewy, *Literatur unterm Hakenkreuz*, 86.

75. Friedrich Hussong in a special issue of *Literarische Welt* (1932); quoted by Schmidt-Henkel, *Mythos und Dichtung*, 265–66.

76. Jünger, *Aufmarsch des Nationalismus*, 21; quoted in Loewy, *Literatur unterm Hakenkreuz*, 86.

77. Hans Friedrich Blunck, *Mahnsprüche* (Jena: Diederichs, 1940), 59; quoted in Loewy, *Literatur unterm Hakenkreuz*, 66. Loewy's documentation contains several other examples of the Nazi blood fetish.

78. Kayser, *Zeit ohne Mythos*, 106.

79. Dekker, *Rückwendung zum Mythos*, 217.

80. Alfred Döblin, "Kritik der Zeit" (1949), in *Schriften zur Politik*, 458–63, here 463.

81. Baeumler, *Alfred Rosenberg und der Mythus des 20. Jahrhunderts*, 68.

82. Thomas Mann to Karl Kerényi, 27 January 1934, *Gesammelte Werke*, 11: 629–30.

83. Mann appropriates the argument and the term (*Dunkelmänner*) that Gerbrand Dekker used in *Rückwendung zum Mythos*.

84. Mann, "Joseph und seine Brüder. Ein Vortrag" (1942), *Gesammelte Werke*, 11: 654–69, here 665–66.

85. In a short note, "Mythos und Dichtung bei Thomas Mann," in Hermann Broch, *Kommentierte Werkausgabe,* ed. Paul Michael Lützeler (Frankfurt am Main: Suhrkamp, 1975), 9/1: 30–31.

86. Broch, "Geist und Zeitgeist, " in *Kommentierte Werkausgabe*, 9/2: 177–201, here 196–97.

87. Broch, *Hofmannsthal und seine Zeit*, in *Kommentierte Werkausgabe*, 9/1: 111–284, here 134.

88. Broch, "Die mythische Erbschaft der Dichtung," in *Kommentierte Werkausgabe*, 9/2: 202–11.

89. Broch, "Mythos und Altersstil," in *Kommentierte Werkausgabe*, 9/2: 212–33, here 217.

90. Gottfried Benn, "Der neue Staat und die Intellektuellen" (1933), in *Gesammelte Werke in vier Bänden*, ed. Dieter Wellershoff (Wiesbaden: Limes, 1959–61), 1: 440–49, here 440.

91. Benn, "Dorische Welt. Eine Untersuchung über die Beziehung von Kunst und Macht" (1934), *Gesammelte Werke*, 1: 262–94, here 290, 278.

92. Benn, "Pallas" (written 1943; published 1949), in *Gesammelte Werke*, 1: 362–70, here 367.

93. Benn, "Verlorenes Ich" (1943) in *Gesammelte Werke*, 3: 215–16.

94. Ernst Cassirer *The Myth of the State* (New Haven: Yale University Press, 1966), 282.

95. Kurt Anglet, *Messianität und Geschichte. Walter Benjamins Konstruktion der historischen Dialektik und deren Aufhebung ins Eschatologische durch Erik Peterson* (Berlin: Akademie, 1995), 25–50.

96. Walter Benjamin, *Das Passagen-werk (N7a, 7),* in *Gesammelte Schriften*, 7 vols. (Frankfurt am Main: Suhrkamp, 1972–89), 5: 588.

97. Broch, *Hofmannsthal und seine Zeit*, in *Gesammelte Werke*, 6: 65.

98. For further examples see Hans Schumacher, "Mythisierende Tendenzen in der Literatur, 1918–1933," in *Die deutsche Literatur in der Weimarer Republik*, ed. Wolfgang Rothe (Stuttgart: Reclam, 1974), 281–303; and Thomas Koebner, "'Isis, Demeter—das waren Zeiten!' Mythen Rekonstruktion und Mythenskepsis in der Literatur der dreissiger und vierziger Jahre. Ein Versuch," in *Schreiben im Exil. zur Ästhetik der deutschen Exilliteratur 1933–1945*, ed. Alexander Stephan and Hans Wagener (Bonn: Bouvier, 1985), 71–94. Alfred Döblin presents a more complicated case. Although in his works he used many analogies from the Bible, classical mythology, and modern figures who have achieved "mythic" status, he sought to interpret those myths from a Christian point of view. See Helmuth Kiesel, *Literarische Trauerarbeit. Das Exil- und Spätwerk Alfred Döblins* (Tübingen: Niemeyer, 1986), 301–11.

99. Gerhart Hauptmann, "Einsichten und Ausblicke," in *Das gesammelte Werk*, 17 vols. (Berlin: Fischer, 1942), 17: 413.

100. Erich Voegelin, *Political Religions*, trans. T. J. DiNapoli and E. S. Easterly III, Toronto Studies in Theology 23 (Lewiston: Edwin Mellen, 1986).

101. Max Horkheimer and Theodor W. Adorno, *Dialektik der Aufklärung. Philosophische Fragmente* (1947; rpt. Frankfurt am Main: Fischer, 1988).

102. It would be worth another investigation to determine the role of myth in the ideology of the neo-Nazi movements that have resurged in Germany in recent decades.

103. Karl Jaspers and Rudolf Bultmann, *Die Frage der Entmythologisierung* (Munich: Piper, 1954); I quote from the English translation, *Myth and Christianity: An Inquiry into the Possibility of Religion without Myth* (New York: Noonday, 1958).

104. Hans Blumenberg, *Arbeit am Mythos* (Frankfurt am Main: Suhrkamp, 1979), 685.

105. Emil Angehrn, *Die Überwindung des Chaos. Zur Philosophie des Mythos* (Frankfurt am Main: Suhrkamp, 1996).

106. Leszek Kolakowski, *The Presence of Myth*, trans. Adam Czerniawski (Chicago: University of Chicago Press, 1989), vii.

107. Günter Grass, *örtlich betäubt, Werke in 10 Bänden*, ed. Volker Neuhaus (Darmstadt: Luchterhand, 1987), 4: 151.

108. See the useful international anthology *Texte zur modernen Mythentheorie*, ed. Wilfried Barner, Anke Detken, and Jörg Wesche (Stuttgart: Reclam, 2003).

109. Mircea Eliade, *Le Mythe de l'éternel retour* (Paris: Gallimard, 1949) and *Mythes, rêves et mystères* (Paris: Gallimard, 1957); Claude Lévi-Strauss, "The Structural Study of Myth," in *Myth:. A Symposium, Journal of American Folklore* 78 (1955): 428–44; and Roland Barthes, *Mythologies* (Paris: Seuil, 1957).

110. Jean-Pierre Sironneau, ed., *Le retour du mythe* (Grenoble: Presses universitaires de Grenoble, 1980).

111. Jean-Jacques Wunenburger, "Mytho-phorie. Formes et transformations du myth," *Religiologiques* 10 (1994): 49–70; rpt. in Barner, Detken, and Wesche, *Texte zur modernen Mythentheorie*, 287–300.

112. Joseph Campbell, *The Mythic Dimension: Selected Essays, 1959–1987*, ed. Antony Van Couvering (San Francisco: Harper, 1997).

113. Joseph Campbell, with Bill Moyers, *The Power of Myth* (New York: Doubleday, 1988).

114. Mary Midgley, *The Myths We Live By* (London: Routledge, 2003), 1.

115. Stephen C. Ausband, *Myth and Meaning, Myth and Order* (Macon, GA: Mercer University Press, 1983), 117.

116. Michael Hochgesang, *Mythos und Logik im 20 Jahrhundert. Eine Auseinandersetzung mit der neuen Naturwissenschaft, Literatur, Kunst und Philosophie* (Munich: Beck, 1962), 88. See in this connection Erich Kahler, "Das Fortleben des Mythos" (1945), in *Die Verantwortung des Geistes* (Frankfurt am Main: Fischer, 1952). Kahler is concerned not with the concept of myth per se but with the process of mythicization that he sees as evident in every area of modern life—in Germany as well as abroad.

CHAPTER EIGHT

1. On the early "ethico-religious utopians," beginning with the prophets and the Judeo-Christian apocalypticists and extending to Augustine and Savonarola, see Joyce Oramel Hertzler, *The History of Utopian Thought* (New York: Macmillan, 1923), 7–98.

2. Glenn Negley and J. Max Patrick, *The Quest for Utopia* (New York: Schuman, 1952), 3–5. The two traditions—utopia and uchronia—are a commonplace in utopia scholarship. See Frank E. Manuel and Fritzie P. Manuel, *Utopian Thought in the*

Western World (Cambridge: Harvard University Press, 1979), 16–17; and the first part of Hertzler's *History of Utopian Thought.*

3. Vlesvolod Slessarev, *Prester John: The Letter and the Legend* (Minneapolis: University of Minnesota Press, 1959).

4. Manuel and Manuel, *Utopian Thought*, 309–31, here 325.

5. For other examples and illustrations see Alberto Manguel and Gianni Guadalupi, *The Dictionary of Imaginary Places* (1980; New York: Harvest/HJB, 1987).

6. Theodore Ziolkowski, *Clio the Romantic Muse: Historicizing the Faculties in Germany* (Ithaca: Cornell University Press, 2004).

7. For other examples of utopian socialism see Hertzler, *History of Utopian Thought*, 181–224.

8. Wells freely acknowledged that the dialogue form was based on Plato's *Republic*, along with the order of the Samurai, the superior beings who like Plato's Guardians are responsible for the welfare of the state. See H. G. Wells, *Experiment in Autobiography* (New York: Macmillan, 1934), 562–63.

9. H. G. Wells, *A Modern Utopia*, introduction by Mark R. Hillegas (Lincoln: University of Nebraska Press, 1967), 11.

10. This is another principle of utopian thought; see Hertzler, *History of Utopian Thought*, 259–60.

11. Marcuse's thesis appeared fresh and original to the students only because they had read no history. Hertzler, in the concluding chapter of his *History of Utopian Thought*, had already extensively discussed "the passing of Utopias," which he attributed—anticipating Marcuse by more than forty years—to the possibility of their realization through modern science and technology. On Marcuse's role in the history of utopian thought, see Manuel and Manuel, *Utopian Thought*, 794–800.

12. Herbert Marcuse, "The End of Utopia," in *Five Lectures: Psychoanalysis, Politics, and Utopia*, trans. Jeremy J. Shapiro and Shierry M. Weber (Boston: Beacon, 1970), 62–82, here 62. Marcuse's rather confused argumentation is possible only because he defines "utopia" in an idiosyncratic manner, as "projects for social change that are considered impossible" because they "contradict real laws of nature" (63) and not, as normally understood, as political structures not yet realized but fully capable of realization.

13. On post-'68 utopian initiatives see Manuel and Manuel, *Utopian Thought*, 801–14, here 809.

14. Wilhelm Voßkamp, ed., *Utopieforschung. Interdisziplinäre Studien zur neuzeitlichen Utopie*, 3 vols. (Stuttgart: Metzler, 1982; paperback rpt. Frankfurt am Main: Suhrkamp, 1985).

15. Ernst Bloch, *The Spirit of Utopia*, trans. Anthony Nassar (Stanford: Stanford University Press, 2000), 279.

16. On Bloch's utopian vision, see Gert Ueding, "Ernst Blochs Philosophie der Utopie," in Voßkamp, *Utopieforschung*, 1: 293–303.

17. Hans Freyer, "Das Problem der Utopie," *Deutsche Rundschau* 183 (1920): 321–45.

18. Edgar Salin, *Platon und die griechische Utopie* (Munich: Duncker & Humblot, 1921), vii.

19. Lewis Mumford, *The Story of Utopias*, introduction by Hendrik Willem Van Loon (New York: Boni and Liveright, 1922), 11.

20. Hertzler, *History of Utopian Thought*, 1.

21. Alfred Doren, "Wunschräume und Wunschzeiten," in *Vorträge der Bibliothek Warburg 1924/1925*, ed. Fritz Saxl (Berlin: Teubner, 1927), 158–205.

22. Paul Tillich, *Politische Bedeutung der Utopie im Leben der Völker* (Berlin: Weiss, 1951); rpt. in Tillich's *Writings in Social Philosophy and Ethics*, ed. Erdmann Sturm, vol. 3 of *Main Works/Hauptwerke*, ed. Carl Heinz Ratschow (Berlin: De Gruyter/Evangelisches Verlagswerk, 1998), 531–82, here 575.

23. Karl Mannheim, *Ideology and Utopia*, trans. Louis Wirth and Edward Shils and with a preface by Louis Wirth (New York: Harcourt, 1953), 49–50.

24. Richard Gerber, *Utopian Fantasy: A Study of English Utopian Fiction since the End of the Nineteenth Century* (London: Routledge, 1955), 146–48, cites some forty titles published from 1914 to 1924; and Hans-Jürgen Krysmanski, *Die utopische Methode. Eine literatur- und wissenssoziologische Untersuchung deutscher utopischer Romane des 20. Jahrhunderts* (Cologne: Westdeutscher Verlag, 1963), 27, 150–52, lists about a dozen from the years around World War I. I do not have similar figures for other literatures; but see Hans Günther, "Aspekte und Probleme der neueren Utopiediskussion in der Slawistik," in Voßkamp, *Utopieforschung*, 1: 221–32.

25. The post-1918 utopian fictions, while discussed in literary criticism, have been largely ignored by scholars of social utopias. Hertzler's *History of Utopian Thought* ends with Bellamy, Wells, and the prewar "pseudo-utopias." The Manuels, in *Utopian Thought*, are generally unimpressed by fictional utopias, making only passing reference to such writers as Wells and Zamiatin. Negley and Patrick, *Quest for Utopia*, cite a dozen titles of postwar (1918–1924) works in their "Selected List of Utopian Works 1850–1950" (19–20) but discuss and quote none of them in the body of their annotated anthology. Ernst Bloch, in *Freiheit und Ordnung: Abriß der Sozial-Utopien* (New York: Aurora, 1946), 181, is downright contemptuous of post-Marxian utopias, which he terms collectively "dilettantism," dismissing in two sentences Wells's *Men Like Gods* (a "future-idyll") and Aldous Huxley's *Brave New World* ("fascist").

26. George Orwell, "Wells, Hitler, and the World State," in *Critical Essays* (New York: Macmillan, 1946), 83–88, here 87; also in *Collected Essays, Journalism, and Letters*, ed. Sophia Orwell and Ian Angus, 4 vols. (New York: Harcourt, 1968), 2: 139–45.

27. See Brian Murray, *H. G. Wells* (New York: Continuum, 1990), 146–58.

28. H. G. Wells, *Experiment in Autobiography: Discoveries and Conclusions of a Very Ordinary Brain (since 1866)* (New York: Macmillan, 1934), 86.

29. Rebecca West, in her review of Wells's *Marriage*, *Freewoman* (19 Sept. 1912), rpt. in *H. G. Wells: The Critical Heritage*, ed. Patrick Parrinder (London: Routledge, 1972), 203–8, here 207. It was this review, as intelligent as it was critical, that led to the friendship between Wells and West.

30. H. G. Wells, *The Outline of History: Being a Plain History of Life and Mankind*, new edition (New York: Macmillan, 1930), 123.

31. H. G. Wells, *God the Invisible King* (New York: Macmillan, 1917), ix.

32. Howard Fink, "The Shadow of *Men Like Gods*: Orwell's *Coming Up for Air* as Parody," in *H. G. Wells and Modern Science Fiction*, ed. Darko Suvin with Robert

M. Philmus (Lewisburg: Bucknell University Press, 1977), 144–58. Orwell's view prevailed for several decades; see typically Richard Hauer Costa, *H. G. Wells* (New York: Twayne, 1967): "Wells, in what is virtually his last utopian satire, is at the same point he had been in his first one a quarter-century before" (125); Mark R. Hillegas in his introduction to H. G. Wells, *A Modern Utopia* (Lincoln: University of Nebraska Press, 1967), calls it "Wells's second most important utopia" (xvii); or Murray, *H. G. Wells*, who calls the novel "a kind of extended comic strip, a political cartoon" (67). In recent criticism, however, the parodic character of the novel as well as its literary merits has come increasingly to be acknowledged; see J. R. Hammond, *H. G. Wells and the Modern Novel* (London: Macmillan, 1988), 126–43, who contrasts the novel in detail with Wells's earlier utopian fictions.

33. J. R. Hammond, *An H. G. Wells Companion: A Guide to the Novels, Romances and Short Stories* (London: Macmillan, 1979), 113: "It is as if Wells is acknowledging the impossibility of achieving such a world within a measurable time span and so postulates a different dimension of both time and space."

34. Hammond, *H. G. Wells and the Modern Novel*, 141.

35. It is not represented, for instance, in Parrinder's *Critical Heritage*.

36. H. G. Wells, *Men Like Gods* (New York: Macmillan, 1923), 302–3.

37. Hammond, *H. G. Wells and the Modern Novel*, 128, suggests plausibly that the jolt Mr. Barnstaple experiences symbolizes the impact of the war on Wells's outlook.

38. The novel is in certain respects a roman à clef, involving the statesman Arthur Balfour (Cecil Burleigh) and the editor-translator Edward Marsh (Freddy Mush). Other figures are familiar types: a Hollywood mogul, a wealthy lord, a French publicist, a self-centered actress, a lovely socialite, and their chauffeurs.

39. Hammond, *H. G. Wells and the Modern Novel*, 135. Hammond analyzes the artistry of the novel, and notably its imagery and structural parody of familiar utopian forms, in persuasive detail.

40. Hammond, *H. G. Wells Companion*, 114.

41. Yevgeny Zamiatin, "The Goal," in *A Soviet Heretic: Essays by Yevgeny Zamyatin*, trans. Mirra Ginsburg (Chicago: University of Chicago Pres, 1970), 127.

42. Zamiatin, "H. G. Wells," in *Soviet Heretic*, 259–90, here 265.

43. Zamiatin, "Maxim Gorky," in *Soviet Heretic*, 246–58, here 250.

44. Zamiatin, "Tomorrow," in *Soviet Heretic*, 51–52, here 52.

45. For biographical information I have relied principally on D. J. Richards, *Zamyatin: A Soviet Heretic* (New York: Hillary House, 1962); Alex M. Shane, *The Life and Works of Evgenij Zamjatin* (Berkeley: University of California Press, 1968); and Shane's more recent essay "Yevgeny Ivanovich Zamyatin," in *European Writers. The Twentieth Century*, ed. George Stade, vol. 10 (New York: Scribner, 1990), 1181–1203.

46. Zamiatin, "Autobiography, 1929," in *Soviet Heretic*, 7–14, here 8–9.

47. Zamiatin, "Chekhov," in *Soviet Heretic*, 224–30, here 225.

48. Zamiatin, "H. G. Wells," in *Soviet Heretic*, 261, 276.

49. Zamiatin, "Autobiography, 1929," 10.

50. Richards, *Zamyatin*, 8; and Shane, *Life and Works*, 9.

51. Shane, *Life and Works*, 12.

52. Zamiatin, "Autobiography, 1922," *Soviet Heretic*, 3–4.

53. Ibid., 4.

54. Zamiatin, "Autobiography, 1929," 13.

55. "L. Andreev," quoted by Shane, *Life and Works*, 19.

56. Unpublished lecture, quoted by Shane, *Life and Works*, 22.

57. Zamiatin, "On Literature, Revolution, Entropy, and Other Matters," in *Soviet Heretic*, 107–12, here 107–8.

58. Zamiatin, "Scythians?" in *Soviet Heretic*, 21–33, here 21.

59. Zamiatin, "Tomorrow," in *Soviet Heretic*, 51–52.

60. Zamiatin, "Paradise," in *Soviet Heretic*, 59–67.

61. Zamiatin, "I Am Afraid," in *Soviet Heretic*, 53–58, here 58.

62. Although Huxley categorically denied any influence by Zamiatin's novel, the parallels between the two works are too conspicuous to be overlooked. Orwell, in contrast, gratefully acknowledged his indebtedness to his Russian predecessor. See Robert Russell, *Zamiatin's We*, Bristol Classical Press/Critical Studies in Russian Literature (London: Duckworth, 2000), 11–14; and Richards, *Zamyatin*, 65–68. On the influence of other utopias see Russell, 29–30.

63. Shane, *Life and Works*, 246–48, contains a bibliography of his various editions. See also Patrick Parrinder, "Imagining the Future: Wells and Zamyatin," in Suvin, *H. G. Wells and Modern Science Fiction*, 126–43.

64. Zamiatin, "H. G. Wells," in *Soviet Heretic*, 285.

65. Yevgeny Zamyatin, *We*, trans. Mirra Ginsburg (New York: Viking, 1972), 83. On *We* see especially Gary Kern, ed., *Zamyatin's We: A Collection of Critical Essays* (Ann Arbor: Ardis, 1988); and Russell, *Zamiatin's We*, which includes a review of the criticism as well as a detailed running commentary on the text. Because the novel was long forbidden in the Soviet Union, most of the criticism has been Western, and notably Anglo-Saxon.

66. Russell, *Zamiatin's We*, 19–20.

67. Ibid., 39–40.

68. Kern, *Zamyatin's We*, 20; see also Richards, *Zamyatin*, 68.

69. Kern, *Zamyatin's We*, 24–25.

70. See Richard A. Gregg, "Two Adams and Eve in a Crystal Palace: Dostoevsky, the Bible and *We*," *Slavic Review* 4 (1965): 680–87; rpt. in Kern, *Zamyatin's We*, 61–70.

71. On Symbolism, see Zamiatin's 1918 essay "Contemporary Russian Literature," in *Soviet Heretic*, 34–50, esp. 38–40.

72. Richards, *Zamyatin*, 105.

73. See Russell, *Zamiatin's We*, 1–5.

74. Kern's introduction to *Zamyatin's We*, 9.

75. C. F. W. Behl, *Zwiesprache mit Gerhart Hauptmann. Tagebuchblätter* (Munich: Kurt Desch, 1948), 205 (12 March 1944).

76. Krysmanski, *Die utopische Methode*, 41, claims that Hauptmann was "miles away from the type of a 'utopist.'" Other commentators object that his works are not utopian because they allegedly lack a political dimension. For a review of the research see Philip A. Mellen, *Gerhart Hauptmann and Utopia*, Stuttgarter Arbeiten zur Germanistik 17 (Stuttgart: Akademischer Verlag Hans-Dieter Heinz, 1976), 3–13.

77. Gerhart Hauptmann, "Die abgekürzte Chronik meines Lebens," *Sämtliche Werke*, Centenar-Ausgabe, ed. Hans-Egon Haas, 11 vols. (Frankfurt am Main: Propyläen, 1962–74), 11: 461–79, here 475–76.

78. On Hauptmann's life see Eberhard Hilscher, *Gerhart Hauptmann* (Berlin: Verlag der Nation, 1969); and Wolfgang Leppmann, *Gerhart Hauptmann: Leben, Werk und Zeit* (Bern: Scherz, 1986).

79. *Buch der Leidenschaft* (1930); rpt. in Gerhart Hauptmann, *Die großen Beichten* (Berlin: Propyläen, 1966), 772 (26 Feb. 1895).

80. Felix A. Voigt, "Die Insel der Seligen. Ein Beitrag zur Deutung der Weltanschauung Gerhart Hauptmanns," *Germanisch-Romanische Monatsschrift* 22 (1934): 276–90, here 280. Voigt also notes that Hauptmann studied Plato (in Schleiermacher's translation) in 1894, that his own copies of Plato were dog-eared from use (in 1934), and that he kept up with the major works of modern Plato research (notably Wilamowitz-Moellendorf).

81. Mellen, *Gerhart Hauptmann and Utopia*, 105. Mellen's useful study takes its criteria from Tillich's *Politische Bedeutung der Utopie im Leben der Völker*.

82. Hauptmann, *Das Abenteuer meiner Jugend* (1937), in *Die großen Beichten*, 300.

83. On Hauptmann's interest in "Christomaniacs" and the psychiatric interpretation of religion see Theodore Ziolkowski, *Fictional Transfigurations of Jesus* (Princeton: Princeton University Press, 1972), 98–141, esp. 105–21.

84. Letter quoted by Hilscher, *Gerhart Hauptmann*, 332.

85. Hauptmann, "Abgekürzte Chronik," 476.

86. On Hauptmann's shifting views regarding the war, see Hans von Brescius, *Gerhart Hauptmann. Zeitgeschehen und Bewusstsein in unbekannten Selbstzeugnissen. Eine politisch-biographische Studie* (Bonn: Bouvier, 1976), 67–94; and Peter Sprengel, *Gerhart Hauptmann. Epoche—Werk—Wirkung* (Munich: Beck, 1984), 222–29.

87. Quoted by Hilscher, *Gerhart Hauptmann*, 314.

88. First printed in Hauptmann's *Sämtliche Werke*, 10: 365.

89. Quoted from the archives by Brescius, *Gerhart Hauptmann*, 87.

90. Quoted from the archives by Brescius, *Gerhart Hauptmann*, 91.

91. Quoted from the archive by Brescius, *Gerhart Hauptmann*, 96.

92. See Horst Brunner, *Die poetische Insel. Inseln und Inselvorstellungen in der deutschen Literatur* (Stuttgart: Metzler, 1967).

93. Behl, *Zwiesprache*, 84 (23 January 1942).

94. Mellen, *Gerhart Hauptmann and Utopia*, 39–40: "In short, *Die Insel* deals with a utopian plan for a civilization, constructed by women under the auspices of a religion which is ostensibly founded upon the powers of the Great Mother."

95. The date is not specified, but the women speculate that their ship was perhaps destroyed by a drifting mine from the Russo-Japanese war (1904–5).

96. Roy C. Cowen, *Hauptmann-Kommentar zum nichtdramatischen Werk* (Munich: Winckler, 1981), 117.

97. I quote the text from *Die großen Romane* (Berlin: Propyläen, 1968), 413–634, here 505.

98. This idea had received much publicity thanks to Max Nordau's sensationalizing book *The Conventional Lies of Our Civilization* (*Die konventionellen Lügen der Kulturmenschheit*, 1883).

99. Karl S. Guthke, *Gerhart Hauptmann: Weltbild im Werk*, 2nd ed. (Munich: Francke, 1980), 152–57, accurately terms the novel a "Roman des mythischen Existierens."

100. Behl, *Zwiesprache*, 111.

101. Hauptmann, "Paralipomenon II," in *Sämtliche Werke*, 11: 357–71. The dating of the epilogue is inconsistent with that of the main text, which suggests that the action covers a twenty-year period from about 1905 to 1924. According to the epilogue Phaon first goes back to Europe to claim his inheritance, then studies at German universities and lives in various European cities—London, Berlin, Paris, Rome—before returning with Diodata to an elegant but isolated existence on their Polynesian island where the narrator meets them shortly before the outbreak of World War I (when Phaon is in his sixties) and first sees the manuscript of Phaon's report. This set of circumstances would push the original shipwreck back into the 1860s, a date inconsistent with many details in the text.

102. See the discussion in *Kindlers Neues Literatur-Lexikon*, vol. 7, p. 397. Mellen, *Gerhart Hauptmann and Utopia*, 63, is more accurate when he terms the novel a "social utopia." For a review of other criticism, see Cowen, *Hauptmann-Kommentar*, 117–20.

103. Mellen, *Gerhart Hauptmann and Utopia*, 39–65, provides a careful and thorough discussion of the novel's thematic implications.

104. For a comparison of the two works and an analysis of their surprising parallels, see Hilscher, *Gerhart Hauptmann*, 387–90. In particular, the ironic tone, the delight in myth, and the discussions of timely issues in a location set off from the everyday world link the two contemporary novels.

105. Parrinder, "Imagining the Future," 140, contrasts two models of science fiction: "the Wellsian model—the humanist-narrative fable in which a man whom one accepts as representative of human culture confronts the biologically and anthropologically unknown"; and that of Zamiatin, which "aims to create the experience and language of an alien culture directly."

CHAPTER NINE

1. Max Weber, "Wissenschaft als Beruf," in *Schriften zur Wissenschaftslehre*, ed. Michael Sukale (Stuttgart: Reclam, 1991), 237–73, here 255. English under the title "Science as Vocation," in Max Weber, *Essays in Sociology*, trans. Hans H. Gerth and C. Wright Mills (New York: Oxford University Press, 1958), 129–56.

2. Theodore Ziolkowski, *The Novels of Hermann Hesse: A Study in Theme and Structure* (Princeton: Princeton University Press, 1965), 283–338.

3. André Malraux, *The Temptation of the West*, trans. Robert Hollander (New York: Random House/Vintage, 1961), 76–77.

4. Hugo von Hofmannsthal, "Vermächtnis der Antike," in *Die Berührung der Sphären* (Berlin: Fischer, 1931), 255–59, here 257–58.

5. Hugo von Hofmannsthal, "Das Schrifttum als geistiger Raum der Nation," in *Berührung der Sphären*, 422–42, here 441–42.

6. Theodore Ziolkowski, *Ovid and the Moderns* (Ithaca: Cornell University Press, 2005).

7. Theodore Ziolkowski, *Virgil and the Moderns* (Princeton: Princeton University Press, 1993); and Armin Kohler, *Die konservative Revolution in Deutschland, 1918–1932: Ein Handbuch*, 2nd ed. (Darmstadt: Wissenschaftliche Buchgesellschaft, 1972).

8. Hubert Cancik, "Jugendbewegung und klassische Antike (1901–1933)," in *Urgeschichten der Moderne: Die Antike im 20. Jahrhundert*, ed. Bernd Seidensticker and Martin Vöhler (Stuttgart: Metzler, 2001), 114–35. That the turn to the *Jugendbund* was often associated with a rejection of the church is made explicit in cases cited by Cancik, 130.

9. Robert Lorin Calder, *W. Somerset Maugham and the Quest for Freedom* (London: Heinemann, 1972), 224–53, here 239.

10. Aldous Huxley, *Eyeless in Gaza* (New York: Harper, 1936), 347.

11. Calder, *W. Somerset Maugham and the Quest for Freedom*, 250.

12. W. Somerset Maugham, *The Razor's Edge* (New York: Pocket Books, 1946), 83 (chap. 2, pt. vii).

13. Julien Benda, *La Jeunesse d'un clerc* (Paris: Gallimard, 1968), 30.

14. Albert Sonnenfeld, *Crossroads: Essays on the Catholic Novelists* (York, SC: French Literature Publications Company, 1982), 1. The notion is widespread in criticism of Catholic literature. See, for instance, Donat O'Donnell (pseud. for Conor Cruise O'Brien), *Maria Cross: Imaginative Patterns in a Group of Modern Catholic Writers* (New York: Oxford University Press, 1952), esp. 229–39; or Theodore P. Fraser, *The Modern Catholic Novel in Europe* (New York: Twayne, 1994), xvi–xviii.

15. Gisbert Kranz, ed., *Gertrud von Le Fort: Leben und Werk in Daten, Bildern und Zeugnissen* (Frankfurt am Main: Insel, 1976); Nicholas J. Meyerhofer, *Gertrud von le Fort*, Köpfe des 20. Jahrhunderts 119 (Berlin: Morgenbuch, 1993); and especially le Fort's own autobiographical sketches: *Aufzeichnungen und Erinnerungen* (Zürich: Benziger, 1951) and *Hälfte des Lebens: Erinnerungen* (Munich: Ehrenwirth, 1965).

16. Le Fort, *Hälfte des Lebens*, 83.

17. Le Fort, "Mein Elternhaus," in *Aufzeichnungen*, 11–25, here 25.

18. Ibid., 23.

19. Le Fort, *Hälfte des Lebens*, 23. The slender volume contains warmly drawn portraits of all the places where the family in its peregrinations resided.

20. Ibid., 84.

21. Ibid., 87.

22. Le Fort, "Zum 70. Geburtstag von Karl Muth," in *Aufzeichnungen*, 77–81, here 77.

23. Meyerhofer, *Gertrud von le Fort*, 38.

24. When the novel was later published together with its sequel, *Der Kranz der Engel* (1946; The wreath of angels), it was renamed *Der römische Brunnen* (The Roman fountain) and the entire two-part work was then called *Das Schweißtuch der Veronika*. The titles symbolize the antagonism between Italy and Germany, between Rome and Heidelberg (the setting of the second novel), because the "wreath of angels" refers to a well-known decoration on the castle at Heidelberg. See vol. 1 of Gertrud von le Fort, *Erzählende Schriften*, 3 vols. (Munich: Ehrenwirth, 1956).

25. The time is never specified within the novel; it emerges only from the opening pages of the sequel, which begins shortly after the war. For a full and thoughtful discussion of the novel see Ita O'Boyle, *Gertrud von le Fort: An Introduction to the Prose Work* (New York: Fordham University Press, 1964), 3–23.

26. The first number refers to the pagination in the edition of the Fischer Bücherei (Frankfurt am Main, 1959); and the second to that in vol. 1 of *Erzählende Schriften*.

27. See Robert Faesi, "Gertrud von le Fort," in *Christliche Dichter der Gegenwart*, ed. Hermann Friedmann and Otto Mann (Heidelberg: Rothe, 1955), 267–83; and Fraser, *Modern Catholic Novel*, 126–39. O'Donnell, *Maria Cross*, restricts itself to French and English-Irish writers, ignoring the German dimension. On her continuing popularity among readers in many countries as well as scholars, see Meyerhofer, *Gertrud von le Fort*, 96–98.

28. Karlheinz Deschner, "Evelyn Waugh," in Friedmann and Mann, *Christliche Dichter der Gegenwart*, 224–37, here 233.

29. Evelyn Waugh, *Brideshead Revisited: The Sacred and Profane Memories of Captain Charles Ryder* (Boston: Little, Brown, 1946). In the manuscript and the 1960 revision (Penguin) the novel is divided into three parts. See Douglas Lane Patey, *The Life of Evelyn Waugh: A Critical Biography* (Oxford: Blackwell, 1998), 390.

30. Fraser, *Modern Catholic Novel*, 67, makes precisely this point. "The Catholic novel in England is a product of a radically different background and set of circumstances from those that had existed in France. . . . Catholics in England comprised only about 10 percent of the population during the nineteenth century, with most of this number being from poor Irish stock. Less than 3 percent of English Catholics were of the noble families. . . . Unlike French Catholics who, regardless of their political affiliation, shared a common Catholic heritage, English Catholics were isolated and alienated from their own society." He might also have added Germany where the Catholic population is roughly one-third of the nation and enjoys state recognition and support.

31. Waugh to Ronald Knox, 14 May 1945: "It was, of course, all about the death bed. I was present at almost exactly that scene"; in *The Letters of Evelyn Waugh*, ed. Mark Amory (New Haven: Ticknor and Fields, 1980), 206. Waugh is referring to the death of his Oxford friend Hubert Duggan.

32. Patey, *Life*, 391.

33. For a full and thoughtful discussion of Ryder's conversion see Patey, *Life*, 224–33.

34. Ibid., 235.

35. In the sequel Veronika actually sacrifices what Enzio calls here "demonism of piousness" (*Dämonie der Frömmigkeit*) and cuts herself off from the church and the Eucharist in order to marry him in the hope of saving him; Enzio eventually acknowledges her faith and is redeemed. Le Fort, *Erzählende Schriften*, 1: 622.

36. In *Der Kranz der Engel* le Fort repeatedly emphasizes this notion: "Western culture will live exactly as long as Western religion. It is not the former that sustains the latter, but vice versa"; *Erzählende Schriften*, 1: 595.

37. Evelyn Waugh, *The Essays, Articles, and Reviews*, ed. Donat Gallagher (London: Methuen, 1983), 103–5, here 103.

38. Evelyn Waugh, *A Little Learning: The First Volume of an Autobiography* (London: Methuen, 1964), based on the author's early diaries and going to about 1925. Unfortunately Waugh never wrote the succeeding part of his autobiography. The most reliable and objective source is Patey's *Life*.

39. Patey, *Life*, 16.

40. Ibid., 343. Patey (35–43) offers the most thorough and sensitive analysis of Waugh's conversion.

41. *The Diaries of Evelyn Waugh*, ed. Michael Davie (London: Weidenfeld and Nicolson, 1976), 320 (8 July 1930).

42. Quoted by Patey, *Life*, 37.

43. Waugh, *Diaries*, 566 (21 May 1944).

44. Waugh, "Fan-Fare," in *Essays*, 300–304, here 302.

INDEX